Inside Game/Outside Game

A CENTURY FOUNDATION BOOK

INSIDE GAME OUTSIDE GAME

Winning Strategies for Saving Urban America

DAVID RUSK

BROOKINGS INSTITUTION PRESS
Washington, D.C.

Library of Congress Cataloging-in-Publication Data
Rusk, David
    Inside game/outside game: winning strategies for saving urban America
/ by David Rusk.
    p. cm.
Includes bibliographical references and index.
ISBN 0-8157-7650-0 (cloth : alk. paper)
ISBN 0-8157-7651-9 (pbk : alk. paper)
1. Urban policy—United States. 2. Metropolitan areas—United
States. 3. Metropolitan government—United States. 4. Land
use—United States—Planning. 5. Urban poor—Housing—United
States. 6. Revenue sharing—United States. I. Title.
HT123.R843 1998
307.76'0973—ddc21   98-25430
                                                              CIP

First softcover printing August 2001

Digital printing

The paper used in this publication meets minimum requirements of the American National Standard for Information Sciences—Permanence of Paper for Printed Library Materials: ANSI Z39.48-1984.

Typeset in Minion

Composition by Cynthia Stock
Silver Spring, Maryland

To
Dean and Virginia Rusk
Carlos and Delcia Bence
Irving and Adele Moskovitz

Foreword

FOR A TIME in the 1960s to 1970s, urban problems occupied center stage in American public policy debates, remaining an important part of politics well into the succeeding decade. Republican President Nixon, for example, felt the need for a prominent urban strategist—Daniel Patrick Moynihan, a Democrat at that—on his personal staff. Gradually, however, the plight of the cities, like many other pressing matters, was pushed aside, first by the central drama of the Vietnam War and subsequently by the Watergate scandal and, still later, the oil crisis.

Urban problems finally lost what little remained of their glamour during the 1980s. Today, in fact, the Clinton White House boasts no similar special competence in this area at all. The dominant topic of political conversation since the early 1980s has been the question of how to get government out of the way of the quest for personal wealth. Unfortunately, this change in subject was not the result of resolving urban issues. In fact, throughout this period the segregation by race and income in most of the older and some of the not so old core cities and bordering suburbs has been increasing. Persistent division by race and income underlies the recent subtle, but unmistakable, reemergence of the exploitation of racial tensions to influence political outcomes.

More recently, these trends have taken a new form. Perhaps as a logical consequence of modern economic dislocations and increasingly expensive and abrasive politics, the basic functions of government, more and more, have taken on a two-tier character. What sort of government you get depends not only on where you live but on what you can afford. There is a new sharpening of the disparity between the services, often privatized, available to the well-off and those provided by government for average-income and poor citizens. The consequences of this development are magnified by the steepening of inequality in income and wealth over the past twenty-five years. In the present climate, the bold and expensive urban initiatives that might directly address these developments are, in effect, political nonstarters.

On the other hand, not all of the changes in America have been negative, either for city dwellers in general or for the ethnic and racial minorities who comprise the bulk of the urban poor in particular. African Americans, especially, have made great strides. The Census Bureau reports, for example, that the share of black households earning more than $35,000 a year (inflation-adjusted) increased from 24.9 percent in 1970 to 32 percent in 1995. And the surge in Hispanic populations is changing the calculus of politics in some of the nation's largest states. An optimist might say that the apparently intractable nature of urban problems is a passing phase—that the economic, social, and political conditions necessary for a rekindling of the spirit of constructive change in our cities are already discernable.

In the pages that follow, David Rusk, former mayor of Albuquerque and currently a nationally recognized consultant to numerous American cities, is at once realistic about the current situation in many cities and remarkably positive about the potential for future improvement. The key to his optimism is his belief that a cluster of specific and practical public policy changes could reverse recent trends and spark an urban renaissance. The core of his prescriptions involves three strategies: regional land use planning, regional fair-share affordable housing, and regional revenue sharing. Most important is mandatory mixed-income housing policy for all new residential construction. He makes a compelling case for each, explaining the dramatic changes that implementation could bring.

Rusk is no Pollyanna, and his ideas will not appeal to everyone. Even a critic, however, would be hard put to argue that he fails to come to grips with the scale of the problem and the constraints on potential solutions. If Rusk is right when he says that no typical cocktail of government programs will make enough of a difference, then his approach may serve as the foundation for a new set of priorities for those who, over the next generation, will engage in the immense task of revitalizing the urban cores of metropolitan areas.

Finally, Rusk knows that any discussion of public policy in urban areas would be incomplete without an interpretation of the complex interaction of racial attitudes and politics. His personal view in this area is, again, that of an optimist: one who stresses the significance of the progress made on these matters, even while acknowledging that we have miles to go.

Rusk's book continues a long history of concern with urban problems at The Century Foundation, ranging from the work of a group of task forces in the 1970s and 1980s (*CDCs: New Hope for the Inner City, A Nice Place to Live, New York World City, Living Cities*) to August Heckscher's *Open Spaces: The Life of American Cities* to the more recent *Breaking Away: The Future of Cities*, edited by Julia Vitullo-Martin.

On behalf of the Trustees of The Century Foundation, I thank David Rusk for this, his latest contribution to our thinking about one of the great unfinished issues of the twentieth century.

Richard C. Leone, President
The Century Foundation
November 1998

Acknowledgments

For the information and insights in this book, I am indebted to the hundreds of individuals and organizations that, as clients and colleagues, have invited me into their communities over the past six years.

This book was written with the encouragement and generous support of The Century Foundation. Greg Anrig first proposed this project, which subsequently received the enthusiastic support of Richard Leone and the foundation's board of trustees. Sarah Ritchie ably shepherded the project along, and Beverly Goldberg guided me through the process of securing a publisher.

With its long history of publishing influential works, I am fortunate that the Brookings Institution Press accepted this project. This has given me the opportunity to work with Nancy Davidson, who has shown both patience and persistence in dealing with a manuscript that has always been a work in progress. She was ably assisted by Venka Macintyre, whose stylistic judgment greatly improved the clarity of my writing; Carlotta Ribar, who proofread the pages; and Julia Petrakis, who prepared the index.

I have benefited from the comments of many colleagues who have reviewed my work at various stages. These have included Carl Abbott, Thomas Bier, Michael Burton, Jack L. Dustin, Linda Gum, Mossik Hacobian, John Klofas, Myron Orfield, Charles Palms, john powell, Henry Richmond, Paul Scully, Joyce Segal, Ralph Sell, Ethan Seltzer, Bernard Tetreault, Richard Tustian, Donald Vermillion, and Marc Weiss. My brother, Richard Rusk, a gifted writer, also read several chapters and provided valued suggestions. I am, of course, solely responsible for all judgments and statements of fact.

In addition to all the hosts of my field work, I am indebted to the research staff of the Census Bureau library, in particular Douglas Carroll, Paul Neuhaus, Justin Murray, and William Turner, for their assistance.

I also thank my children, Gregory, Patrick, and Monica, their spouses, Becky Brown and Mark Maghini, and my grandchildren, Daniel and Dylan, for their forbearance, since book writing is always a family undertaking.

Finally, my most valued collaborator has been Delcia, my wife and partner. We have visited many communities together, sharing impressions and ideas. She has entered tens of thusands of data items in spreadsheets and has relieved me of all of the administrative detail of our small but busy enterprise. She is always my most insightful reviewer and loving critic.

Contents

TABLES

FIGURES

1

Journeying through Urban America

"WHERE YOU STAND depends on where you sit." The old adage certainly applies to my perspective on urban America. For the twenty years before researching and writing my first book, *Cities without Suburbs*, I sat in Albuquerque, New Mexico, four of those years in the mayor's chair (1977–81). Having lived previously in the San Francisco Bay area, outside New York City, and in Washington, D.C., I found Albuquerque a very different setting indeed.

Despite several decades of dramatic regional growth, even today Albuquerque remains an almost metropolitan city. Between 1940 and 1990, the population of Bernalillo County, Albuquerque's home county, grew almost sevenfold, from 69,391 to 480,577. Through aggressive annexation of land and subsequent development, Albuquerque expanded its boundaries as well: from just 3 square miles in 1940 to 132 square miles by 1990, while its population ballooned from 35,449 to 384,736.[1] The city captured 86 percent of the region's population growth and almost 90 percent of the new tax base.

Such expansion had big advantages. Tapping most of the region's tax base, the city government was able to keep tax rates relatively low and apply

1. By 1996 Albuquerque's municipal area had expanded further to 150 square miles, and its population was 419,681, making it the country's thirty-sixth largest city.

1

them uniformly. (Businesses paid the same property tax rates, for instance, as homeowners.) The city's biggest source of revenue was its share of the state-collected gross receipts tax applied to the sale of all goods and services; the overall tax rate was 5.75 percent (of which the city government received 1.75 percent). Used primarily for construction bonds, the city's property tax was about 11–12 mills (about one-third of 1 percent of market value). Periodically, the city government might go through a local budget crunch, but, compared with the fiscal crises many other cities faced, Albuquerque's problems were minor. Having near-metropolitan jurisdiction, the city government could balance its needs and revenues at moderate tax rates.

Being an almost metropolitan city brought nonfiscal benefits as well. Albuquerque society was much more open than in other communities I had lived in. There were still economic disparities. "Anglos" averaged higher incomes and lower poverty rates than Hispanics, blacks, or Indians.[2] Albuquerque had its richer neighborhoods and its poorer neighborhoods. But, overall, Anglos, Hispanics, blacks, the wealthy, middle class, and poor mixed together much more than in many other places.[3]

Though New Mexico remained one of the nation's poorer states, steady economic growth was certainly one cause of this greater melding. Another factor was undoubtedly the community's relative newness. Founded in 1706, Albuquerque grew primarily after World War II, a period in which racially restrictive housing covenants were declared unconstitutional and civil rights legislation began reshaping the behavior of people and institutions (even if hearts and minds were slower to change).

Albuquerque's greater social wholeness was also helped by the relative unity of its major public institutions. The city served 80 percent of the region's population, for there were only two other small municipalities in the area.[4]

2. In Southwestern parlance, all non-Hispanic whites are "Anglos," whether their names are Jones, Schmidt, Puccini, Pulaski, or Goldstein.

3. Later research confirmed my impressions. Among the country's 117 largest metropolitan areas in 1990, Albuquerque had the third most integrated neighborhoods and third most integrated public schools for the region's small African American population (2.7 percent). For its much larger Hispanic population (37 percent) it ranked somewhat lower on the scale—twenty-fourth for neighborhoods (out of seventy-eight metro areas) and fifty-third for schools (out of 107 metro areas). Black and Hispanic median family incomes were both 63 percent of Anglo median family income, both percentages above national averages. In terms of segregation of the poor, Albuquerque ranked twenty-ninth of the eighty-six largest metro areas.

4. These were the village of Los Ranchos de Albuquerque (5,075 residents) in the North Valley and the tiny mountain village of Tijeras (340 residents). Two self-governing Indian pueblos, Isleta and Sandia, were such different worlds that, as mayor, I saw them as merely blank spaces on the Bernalillo County map.

County government looked after the 18 percent of the region's residents who lived in unincorporated areas. More remarkable, the region had a single, unified public school system, the Albuquerque Public Schools, which even jumped county boundaries to serve urbanizing portions of an adjacent county.

From time to time some citizens might complain about the city government's or the school district's "bigness," but, supported by broad tax bases, both the city and the school district generally served all neighborhoods and schools well.[5] The city and county adopted a common comprehensive land use plan. City zoning encouraged relatively small subdivisions with varied housing types. By design, public housing complexes were small and scattered into many areas of the city. Although the public schools never had a court-ordered busing plan, the school board tweaked boundaries periodically to reduce social and economic disparities.

During my two decades in New Mexico, Albuquerque was certainly not exempt from the ills of American society. But racial and ethnic disparities were less prevalent and more muted than in other metro areas. Albuquerque was simply a more relaxed, more open, more integrated community, and the better for that.

The Theory of Relative Elasticity

In 1991 my wife, Delcia, and I returned to Washington, D.C., where we had lived before moving to Albuquerque. Upon turning my attention to urban trends across the nation, I was immediately struck by the contrast between Albuquerque and many other cities, Washington included. Albuquerque stood out for its sound economic, social, and fiscal health. Were there others like it?

With a personal computer and spreadsheet, I began to build a database from census reports: first for the 50 largest metro areas, then for the 100 largest, finally for all 320 metro areas in the country. I published articles

5. With almost 80,000 students, Albuquerque Public Schools was the nation's twenty-fourth largest school district in 1990. Indeed, Albuquerque Public Schools tapped the broadest possible tax base: the entire state of New Mexico. The state government funds 94 percent of the annual operating budgets of the eighty-eight local school districts through a statewide school equalization funding formula. The other 6 percent are federal funds. Like city governments, New Mexico school districts turn to property tax only for capital projects (construction and major renovation of school buildings).

about my findings in the *New York Times* and the *New Democrat* magazine of the centrist Democratic Leadership Council. These led to an invitation to spend the summer of 1992 as a guest scholar on urban affairs at the Woodrow Wilson International Center for Scholars in Washington, D.C. The center's press made a commitment to publish my research.

By summer's end I had written the first draft of a book. I had categorized all metro areas by the population trends in their central cities: "long-time losers," "past-their-peakers," "old suburban boomers," "new suburban boomers," and "cities without suburbs" (a phrase I had coined for the *New Democrat* article). Cities without suburbs, like Albuquerque, had expanded rapidly. Their regions contained many suburban-type subdivisions, but most were found within the city limits. Cities without suburbs dominated their metropolitan regions.

But this typology was unsatisfactory. It merely indicated where all central cities fell on a demographic scale by the 1990s. The classifications did not suggest why the cities had come to be where they were.

During my research I had tracked the geographic and population expansion of all metro areas from 1950 to 1990. I had measured each city's territorial expansion. The almost universal drop in city population densities decade by decade had intrigued me. Late one October night, having finished a major revision of my draft, I was pondering the matter. Suddenly, the thought struck me. "Initial density times rate of boundary expansion equals *elasticity*."[6] My inspiration hardly matched Einstein's "$E = mc^2$" in cosmic significance, but I was excited enough about my own Theory of Relative Elasticity to spend the next thirty-six hours without sleep, pushing around data on spreadsheets.

What emerged was a new way to describe something that had been happening to America's 522 central cities for the past four decades.[7] Postwar development had been horizontal, not vertical. America's urban areas were growing outward (becoming less densely populated), not upward (becoming more densely populated). Cities that had expanded their boundaries through annexation, as had Albuquerque and Charlotte, or through city-county consolidation, as in the case of Nashville-Davidson County and Indianapolis-Marion County, were *elastic* cities.[8] Elastic cities defended them-

6. Subsequent analysis showed that it was more accurate to place three times greater weight on a city's rate of boundary expansion than on its initial population density. This revision was incorporated into the second edition of *Cities without Suburbs*.

7. For more detailed discussion of urban elasticity, see Rusk (1995).

8. A few cities, Los Angeles being one, had begun the postwar period having already annexed

selves against suburban sprawl by capturing a substantial share of new development.

By contrast, many other cities entered the postwar era already densely populated and unable to expand their boundaries at all. New York, Detroit, Cleveland, Baltimore, and Washington would fall into this category.[9] These inelastic cities could not defend themselves against suburban sprawl. They not only did not capture their share of new growth; they *contributed* to suburban expansion. Inelastic cities steadily lost middle-class households, retail stores, offices, and factories to their new suburbs. Despite the revival of many downtown business districts in the 1980s and 1990s, more and more city neighborhoods became warehouses for the region's poor, particularly blacks and Hispanics. With shrinking tax bases and burgeoning service needs, many inelastic city governments slid into fiscal crisis.

Elasticity's consequences for cities were clear. What fascinated me was that the social and economic profile of entire metro areas could be characterized to a large extent by the relative elasticity of their central cities. Schools and neighborhoods in "inelastic" metro areas, for example, were more racially segregated than they were in "elastic" metro areas. Inelastic metro areas were more economically segregated as well, as shown in table 1-1 (the higher the segregation index rating, the greater the degree of segregation of poor households from the rest of the nonpoor).

Over several decades, elastic regions also had higher rates of job creation and income growth than inelastic regions.[10] Income disparities between city and suburban residents were less pronounced. Particularly after adjusting for relative costs of living, many elastic regions had higher real incomes.

Would many of the same explanations I offered for Albuquerque's greater social and economic mobility apply to whole categories of cities and metro areas, classified by elasticity? Is there a regional bias in the data? Yes. Most elastic regions are found in the South and West. Does more vigorous eco-

---

vast areas that were still largely undeveloped. With relatively low initial density, they had room internally to accommodate more growth and were also classified as elastic cities.

9. In the 1950 census 28 central cities had population densities of more than 10,000 persons per square mile. New York City topped the list with 25,046 residents per square mile (Manhattan's population density was 69,017 per square mile). Some 100 central cities would be unable to expand their existing municipal boundaries at all (that is, they were *zero-elastic* cities).

10. A heated academic debate surrounds the issue of the economic interdependence of cities and suburbs. As a practical matter, I have found that when a chamber of commerce must produce an alibi for the sad state of the central city, the whole region is in trouble.

Table 1-1. *Segregation of Poor Households in 117 Major U.S. Metro Areas, by Census Tract, 1990*

Elasticity category	Number of metro areas	Segregation index[a]
Zero	23	47
Low	22	43
Medium	24	40
High	23	39
Hyper	25	34

a. This table employs a common "dissimilarity index" that measures the relative evenness or unevenness of the distribution of a target population across census tracts, schools, and the like. A score of 100 would indicate total segregation (that is, all poor households, and only poor households, live in certain neighborhoods and all nonpoor live everywhere else).

nomic growth facilitate social mobility? Certainly. Social change comes easier in good economic times, and the Sun Belt has outperformed the Rust Belt in recent decades. Have the crises faced by America's old-line manufacturers affected local economic growth differentially? Of course. In the early 1970s, if a region's economy was heavily dependent on "smokestack" industries, it was headed for hard times, regardless of the central city's elasticity. Are elastic regions generally younger, growing up in an era of civil rights laws? Yes.

Metropolitan regions are complex systems influenced by many factors, and I have never meant to suggest that elasticity explains all metropolitan trends. However, a city's past elasticity—its ability to defend its market share of sprawling new development—is an excellent barometer of its current social, economic, and fiscal health.

Big Boxes versus Little Boxes

The way local governance is organized regionally is an important factor shaping regional social, economic, and fiscal patterns. The more fragmented local governance, the more fragmented regional society by race, ethnic group, and income class. I have seen these patterns over and over again, not only in census data but also in visiting scores of metropolitan areas themselves. In regions with "big-box" governments, different racial, ethnic, and income groups tend to mix together more readily than in regions with multiple "little-box" governments.

School integration is a straightforward example of this phenomenon. In 1990 about one-quarter of all school-age children in both metro Charlotte and metro Cleveland were African American. With its countywide school systems, including the unified Charlotte-Mecklenburg County district, metro Charlotte had only nine school districts. For almost a quarter-century Carolina school districts have operated under federal court-ordered desegregation plans. Metro Charlotte's school segregation index measured a low 33, and a 22 within the Charlotte-Mecklenburg unified system.[11]

By contrast, metro Cleveland had fifty-six separate school systems, including thirty-two in Cuyahoga County. Federal desegregation orders covered only the Cleveland Public Schools.[12] By 1990 the city school system enrolled less than 30 percent of the region's public school students and was two-thirds black, whereas most suburban systems were overwhelmingly white. Metro Cleveland's school segregation index measured a high 79, the nation's seventh worst.[13]

In a less obvious way, the same kinds of factors help produce more racially and economically mixed societies in regions with large, constantly expanding central cities. Public housing is often more scattered across a broader range of neighborhoods within elastic cities than within the combination of inelastic cities and their independent suburbs. City neighborhoods tend to feature a greater mixture of owner-occupied and rental housing than suburban neighborhoods. Many black families may be readier to move into largely white neighborhoods within the city itself than into almost totally

11. The segregation index used here, as in table 1-1, is a "dissimilarity index" that, in this case, measures the relative unevenness of the distribution of black students among the region's public high schools. A score of 100 would equal total apartheid; a score of 0, in metro Charlotte or metro Cleveland's case, would mean that one-quarter of the population in every public high school in the metropolitan area is African American. A 22 means that only 22 percent of the African American high school students in the Charlotte-Mecklenburg system would have to shift schools in the "right" proportions for every high school's enrollment to mirror the districtwide minority enrollment.

12. Under the U.S. Supreme Court's 1974 decision in *Milliken* v. *Bradley,* suburban school districts do not have to participate in desegregation plans with central-city systems.

13. Moreover, the Charlotte region's more integrated public schools retained a higher proportion of school-age children (93 percent) than did the Cleveland region's public schools (81 percent). Undoubtedly, the greater availability of Catholic education in the urban North contributed to the lower share of school-age children in the Cleveland region's public school systems. However, relatively few white parents appeared to be fleeing the Charlotte area's more integrated systems. Some 91 percent of white school-age children attended metro Charlotte's public schools (84 percent within Charlotte-Mecklenburg) compared with only 76 percent in metro Cleveland's fifty-six school districts. (Only 56 percent of Cleveland's white school-age children attended the Cleveland public schools.)

white-dominated suburbs. If necessary, they can still find black champions down at city hall.

What happens *inside* large, expanding, elastic cities, however, is probably less important than what does *not* happen *outside* in many suburbs surrounding inelastic cities. Again, metro Cleveland has 89 municipalities and 42 townships, including 60 local governments in Cuyahoga County alone. There is always another level of local government below county government. Suburban cities, villages, and townships cover every square foot of the four-county region, and all 131 exercise their own independent planning and zoning powers. A few communities, such as Shaker Heights and Cleveland Heights, have welcomed racial integration in recent decades. The unspoken mission of most little city councils, little township boards, and little school boards, however, is "to keep our city/our town/our schools just the way they are for people just like *us*" (whoever "us" happens to be). This tacit agenda is often enforced through fierce resistance to multifamily housing (not to speak of the public firestorm that greets any proposed suburban public housing project). Suburbs invented and perfected the practice of "exclusionary zoning."

By contrast, Charlotte's seven-county region, with almost two-thirds of metro Cleveland's total population, counts only fifty local governments, and dominant Mecklenburg County encompasses only the city of Charlotte and six suburban municipalities. By 1990 more than half of Mecklenburg County's 527 square miles was still unincorporated and under the county government's authority. Even now, a countywide joint planning commission and single planning staff serve all eight jurisdictions. Any new development will ultimately be incorporated into one of the seven existing municipalities. Charlotte and its six suburban neighbors have executed formal agreements specifying zones of future annexation for each. The Charlotte area is not beset by the intense turf protection that afflicts the Cleveland area.

Elasticity: An Elusive Tool

As mentioned earlier, most elastic cities are found in the South and West and most inelastic cities in the Northeast and Middle West. In writing my first book, I realized that elasticity analysis might therefore create the false impression that it is just a way of describing contrasts between the Sun and Rust belts. My initial analysis was based on trends in all 320 metro areas. To communicate the central themes more effectively, however, I paired specific communities that many readers could relate to. To minimize the Sun Belt–Rust Belt dichotomy, in *Cities without Suburbs* I intentionally contrasted elastic and inelastic cities and their metro areas within the same section of the country or even within the same state. Rather than comparing high-elastic Charlotte with zero-elastic Cleveland, for example, I looked at Cleveland alongside high-elastic Columbus, Ohio's capital city. Matching regions by population size and racial composition, I paired high-elastic Indianapolis with low-elastic Milwaukee; hyperelastic Nashville with low-elastic Louisville; hyperelastic Raleigh with low-elastic Richmond, two southern state capitals; and high-elastic Madison with zero-elastic Harrisburg, two northern state capitals. In every instance, the anticipated demographic, economic, and social contrasts appeared as expected.

The primary policy recommendation of *Cities without Suburbs* was that cities should try to maintain or reacquire elasticity: they should secure or defend workable annexation laws, promote city-county consolidations, and support unifying school districts. They should create, in effect, quasi-metropolitan, more unified, big-box governance structures that could help diminish the racial and economic segregation that has created an underclass in many of America's major urban areas.

At the same time, I already understood how difficult it is to change formal government structures. In the past half-century, voters around the country have turned down five times as many proposed city-county consolidations as they have approved. If anything, *Cities without Suburbs* was meant to be just a wake-up call. To say to much of the Northeast and Middle West, whose experiences dominate the perceptions of federal urban policymakers: "Hey, we do things differently in the other half of the country and it works better." And to say to the South and West: "Watch out. Hold on to the good policies you've got. Don't follow the rest of the country down the failed path of growth-constrained cities."

"Where you stand depends on where you sit." Since *Cities without Suburbs* first appeared in April 1993, I have hardly sat down anywhere. I have made over 300 trips to more than ninety metro areas as a speaker and consultant on urban affairs. I have completed a dozen statewide studies and analyzed fifty-eight metro areas in depth.

Two-thirds of my work has been in the Northeast and the Middle West, where local governance is much more highly fragmented than in the South and West. In some northern regions, the policy prescriptions set out in *Cities without Suburbs* regarding a city's elasticity are still relevant. In most of the northern tier of states, they are not. Local government boundaries are cast in concrete from Maine through Pennsylvania. In the Middle West, annexation is still a possibility for some cities (Columbus and Springfield, Ohio, for example). Sometimes formal governmental consolidation can occur in extraordinary circumstances. In 1969, then-mayor Richard Lugar maneuvered the consolidation of Indianapolis and Marion County through Indiana's Republican-controlled political system. In Michigan, the Kellogg Corporation hammered local voters into merging Battle Creek City and suburban Battle Creek Township in 1982. Both mergers stimulated an almost Sun Belt–like dynamism in the expanded Indianapolis and Battle Creek. Where annexation or consolidation is still feasible, my advice is "Do it."

Acting as One

But from the outset I have had to answer this question: if a highly fragmented region cannot, in effect, *become one* governmentally, can the many individual governments be brought to *act as one?* What are the most critical issues on which they must collaborate? What are the qualities of highly elastic cities that might be duplicated without formally changing local government structure? In other words, what policies might serve as substitutes for elasticity?[14]

The central issue facing most cities is the concentration of poverty, particularly the existence of high-poverty ghettos and barrios. In highly fragmented regions, high concentrations of poverty also produce wide fiscal disparities among different jurisdictions. In more unified regions, consolidated city-county governments or constantly expanding central cities serve as quasi-regional revenue-sharing mechanisms. Elastic city governments convert taxes from wealthier neighborhoods into services for poorer neighborhoods. Fiscally, highly fragmented regions could "act as one" if they adopted regional revenue or tax base sharing.

Second, moving people is far more important than moving money. In America's metropolitan areas three out of four poor whites live in middle-class, often suburban neighborhoods; most poor whites are part (albeit a marginal part) of mainstream society. By contrast, one out of two poor Hispanics and three out of four poor blacks live in poor inner-city neighborhoods. All cities have their poorer neighborhoods, but elastic cities tend to show less severe concentrations of minority poor; a somewhat higher percentage of poor minority households are mainstreamed in middle-class

---

14. John Blair of Wright State University has referred to such policies as "elasticity mimics."

neighborhoods. To "act as one," regional housing policies could require a fair share of low- and moderate-income housing in all suburban jurisdictions in order to help disperse high concentrations of poor households from central cities.

A third critical issue has emerged in my own thinking since I first wrote *Cities without Suburbs:* the need to control suburban sprawl. My policy perspective in *Cities without Suburbs* was "Sprawl happens; capture it." A central theme of this book is "It is better to control sprawl than just capture it."

I am indebted to many people for educating me about sprawl's consequences, but above all to Henry Richmond, a long-time leader of Oregon's growth management movement. Sprawl has most often been criticized for ravaging the natural landscape, but its impact on the human landscape has been even more deplorable. In the prewar era, city neighborhoods typically developed piecemeal at different periods of time.[15] Older cities featured different styles and types of housing and were much more diverse communities economically. By contrast, postwar suburban subdivisions were almost always built all at once, tended to offer only one type of housing in limited styles, and targeted a relatively narrow income range.

Most metropolitan areas are now slowly becoming less segregated by race but steadily more segregated by income. Elastic cities may sprawl across the landscape, but they tend to have higher densities than the uncoordinated developments mushrooming in the multiple little cities and townships around inelastic cities. Most elastic cities have substantial power to control regional development more tightly (though they rarely use such power fully). Limiting sprawl through regional land use planning would also help metropolitan areas "act as one."

Playing the Outside Game

This book's primary concern is the plight of central cities in the Northeast and Middle West. Most cannot annex and most cannot consolidate. How can they be helped? My answer is a three-pronged agenda:

—To help control sprawl, require regional land use planning.

—To help dissolve concentrations of poverty, ensure that all suburbs have their fair share of low- and moderate-income housing.

—To help reduce fiscal disparities, implement regional revenue sharing.

---

15. I am old enough that "prewar" and "postwar" refer to World War II.

These are the key policies that form the "outside game." Part 2 of this book details the best practices I have seen for each of these regional strategies.

Chapter 8 discusses the history and impact of Oregon's statewide land use law in the Portland area. After two decades of implementing an antisprawl "urban growth boundary," the Portland area is clearly marching to a different drummer than most of urban America—and reaping enormous benefits from a booming economy and high quality of urban life.

Chapter 9 examines the nation's best and oldest mixed-income housing laws in Montgomery County, Maryland. For twenty-five years a county ordinance has mandated that all new subdivisions and apartment developments—many in the county's wealthiest neighborhoods—provide for a minimum of 15 percent low- and moderate-income housing.

Chapter 10 explores the Dayton area's ED/GE plan, the nation's most significant voluntary, multijurisdictional revenue-sharing program. It is both a remarkable success story and a reminder of the limits of voluntary cooperation among fiercely independent local governments. The state-mandated tax base–sharing program in the Minneapolis-St. Paul area, for example, has more than 100 times the fiscal impact of the Dayton area's voluntary system.

Chapter 11 points out who realistically must put such regional programs into effect—state legislatures—and how to build majority legislative coalitions. Minnesota shows how: ally central cities and older, now declining suburbs.

Part 3 examines other tools and organizing strategies for regionalism. Chapter 12 details the struggles in Washington, D.C., to end the federal public housing program's impact as the greatest instrument of economic segregation in American life. Chapter 13 provides case studies of key members of regional reform movements—coalitions of inner-city and suburban churches, business organizations, universities, grass-roots citizens' groups—and ends with assessments of the role of philanthropic foundations and city mayors.

Finally, chapter 14 sums up my thoughts on what it will take to break out of the grip of our growing divisions and become the America we say we want to be.

Grading the Inside Game

But first, in part 1, we need to explore further how many of our cities got into their present sad state and the attempts to counter urban neighborhood decline over the past three decades. For three decades the federal government has targeted poor areas with a succession of antipoverty initiatives—community action programs, model cities programs, community development block grants, urban development action grants, empowerment community and enterprise zone funds and tax credits—all variations on what I call the "inside game." Chapters 2 and 3 analyze the impact of thirty-four widely lauded "community development corporations." These are private, nonprofit, community-based organizations engaged in housing development, commercial redevelopment, and local social service programs. Chapter 4 highlights the twin factors—sprawl and race—shaping metropolitan development patterns. Chapter 5 elaborates on "the Sprawl Machine," chapter 6 on "the Poverty Machine," and chapter 7 on "the Deficit Machine."

In part 1, based on hard, cold facts on income and population, I conclude that playing only the "inside game" is a losing strategy for even the most exemplary players. For both poverty-impacted cities and poverty-impacted neighborhoods, even the strongest inside game must be matched by a strong "outside game"—the regional strategies outlined in part 2.

In a sense this book traces a personal journey. In 1963, fresh out of the University of California at Berkeley, I began my professional career as a civil rights and antipoverty organizer with the Washington Urban League. With the advent of the federal war on poverty, our local Urban League took responsibility for spurring community action in one of Washington's poorest black ghettos. Neighborhood residents themselves were the primary organizers, but in the 1960s I spent many nights and weekends in meetings of block clubs, neighborhood improvement clubs, a self-help organization for ex-convicts, and other community action groups.

Moving on to New Mexico, in the early 1970s I was active in Albuquerque's Model Cities program as director of the city-county comprehensive manpower program. Later, in 1974, I was a citizen member of the Citizens Advisory Group shaping Albuquerque's initial allocation of community development block grant (CDBG) funds.[16] As mayor of Albuquerque, I oversaw CDBG expenditures and secured the first "pocket of poverty" grant from the Carter administration's urban development action grant (UDAG) program in 1979.

Since returning to Washington in 1991, I have revisited the scene of my 1960s antipoverty work. Part of the old neighborhood has literally disap-

---

16. The community development block grant program was the Nixon administration's largely cosmetic repackaging of the model cities program.

peared in the wake of "progress." A bare parking lot, hugging a wide trench for an aborted interstate freeway, has replaced my old office building. The tenements of DeFrees Street have vanished under the new Astroturf athletic field of Gonzaga High School. Row houses on lower New Jersey Avenue were bulldozed to make way for two new hotels and several office buildings. Parts of upper New Jersey Avenue and adjacent streets have a gap-toothed look: rubble-strewn, weed-covered empty lots and boarded-up, sometimes partly burned, abandoned buildings alternate with aging, but still-occupied row houses. Elsewhere there are newer, modest, garden-style apartments and townhouses, clearly an improvement over past conditions.

Thirty-three years ago the Urban League helped local residents set up a tent city on several vacant acres of land on New York Avenue and North Capitol Street. The tent city, proclaimed "the nation's first Demonstration City," stood in protest of bureaucratic foot-dragging on a long-promised public housing project.[17] Today that project, a combination high-rise for senior citizens and family townhouses, is undergoing total renovation after more than two decades of hard use. Some of the residents displaced by new hotels, office buildings, and the high school ball field still live there. It is hard to see, however, that life is significantly better in a neighborhood that so many, including many residents themselves, tried to improve over three decades.

A word of explanation for the very personal tone of this book. *Cities without Suburbs* and *Baltimore Unbound*, my second book, were both written for what several years ago were fashionably called "policy wonks." Those earlier books featured tables and tables of statistics. Of the 140-plus pages of *Cities without Suburbs*, only 5 or 6 contained personal references.

There will be plenty of data in this book as well. Over the past six years many listeners at the hundreds of speeches I have given have said that, though I am a good enough speaker, it is the data I present that make such a compelling case. I am not going to abandon my most persuasive sales technique.

But successful political reform movements are not about data. They are about real people in real situations: inspired legislators, courageous city and county officials, determined citizen activists. I hope that the success stories told here will inspire some readers to step forward in their own communities. There is nothing so special about a Portland, a Montgomery County (Maryland or Ohio), or a Minnesota that their successes cannot be repeated elsewhere.

17. Within a week, the Johnson White House had renamed the just authorized demonstration cities program the model cities program.

I also appear personally at many points in these pages. I am not trying to insert myself Forrest Gump–like into the middle of significant events. In fact, I had nothing to do with creating the policies and programs I most admire.

Over the past six years, however, I have been at least periodically on the scene in many communities in which regional reform movements are gathering momentum. Often I have been the "national expert" brought in to help local sponsors attract added attention to their reform agenda. Any major success requires local leaders to do all the heavy lifting, and they, not I, will deserve most of the credit.

It has long been a saying in my family that "there is a tremendous difference between the world of opinion and the world of decision." As a former federal official, city department head, state legislator, and mayor, I have been part of the world of decision. As an author, speaker, and consultant, I am now clearly part of the world of opinion. Many of the judgments I make and policies I recommend are easy for me to discuss but very difficult for elected officials to embrace.

I recognize that. Everything recommended in these pages, however, has been adopted by some group of city or county officials or state legislators. They have stepped up to make the tough decisions. Their states and communities are much better places for their vision, tenacity, and courage.

PART ONE

The Inside Game

PART 1 OPENS with a visit to the Bedford Stuyvesant Restoration Corporation. Founded in 1967 primarily by New York Senator Bobby Kennedy, "Restoration" is the grandfather of all nonprofit community development corporations (CDCs), which now number more than 2,000 nationwide. In the early 1990s CDCs became popular organizations to support in business, foundation, and government circles. Any pretense of devoting serious federal money to fighting inner-city poverty had vanished during the Reagan-Bush years. Nor would the Great Society be revived with the return of a Democrat to the White House in 1993.[1] In his 1996 State of the Union speech, President Bill Clinton would proclaim that "the era of Big Government is over."

CDCs, embodying all the characteristics emphasized in the political buzzwords of the day, seemed the logical choice to fill the vacuum. They are "private sector" entities (though most rely heavily on government grants). Technically nonprofit organizations, CDCs seem to operate "like a business," at least more than government agencies do. CDCs deal primarily in "hard services" rather than "soft services." Almost all are bricks-and-mortar operations. CDCs build or renovate low- and moderate-income housing. They struggle to revive neighborhood shopping centers. Though some CDCs run extensive recreation and social service programs as well, one can visit a new CDC-built housing development, shop at a CDC-

---

1. In actuality, the high-water mark of federal urban aid occurred during the Nixon years, especially with the creation of general revenue sharing.

revived supermarket, or (more rarely) walk through a new, CDC-recruited factory, warehouse, or telemarketing center in an inner-city neighborhood.

"Self-help," "citizen participation," "empowerment" are constantly invoked. Each new generation of aspiring inner-city activists, I have observed, assumes that the decay and decline around them reflect, in part, the fact that *they* have not been involved. Empower the new generation, and we will lead the neighborhood to the Promised Land. Generation after generation, "empowerment" is always a surefire rallying cry.

To the world beyond ghettos and barrios, part of the CDC movement's bedrock appeal is no doubt its commitment to solving inner-city poverty *in place*. To improve the lives of inner-city residents, most CDC advocates believe, new opportunities for low-income residents have to be created in inner-city neighborhoods, although more progressive CDCs may seek to attract some middle-income households from the outside, dabbling in the import market. CDCs rarely design programs for the export market, that is, to help neighborhood residents move out.

As chapters 2 and 3 show, these tactics are producing discouraging results: even the nation's best CDCs, despite some block-by-block victories, are losing the war against poverty itself. In effect, CDCs are expected to help a crowd of poor people run up a down escalator, an escalator that is engineered to come down faster and faster than most poor people can run up.

In these pages I do not mean to criticize CDCs themselves. Those that I have visited or worked with have had many able and extraordinarily committed staff and volunteers (both residents of the target neighborhoods themselves as well as recruits from the larger business, professional, and governmental community). In fact, given the adverse conditions they face, most CDCs are engaged in a truly heroic struggle.

My exasperation stems from the way in which the CDC paradigm allows powerful institutions to shirk once again their responsibility to confront racial and economic segregation. It is easier to pair corporate money and volunteers with inner-city schools than to allow inner-city students to attend the schools that corporate executives' own children attend. It is easier to give foundation grants for affordable housing projects in inner-city neighborhoods than to demand a "fair share" of low- and moderate-income housing in neighborhoods where many foundation executives dwell. It is easier for a governor, senator, or president to thump the drum of inner-city revitalization: "Let's solve (and keep) the problems *in there*" rather than admit that part of the solution must be found *out here,* where the bulk of the voters now live. Easier? Not easier at all, if the goal is to achieve substantial progress. It is "easier" only in that this path is more socially and politically comfortable.

A small case in point: in 1992 Senator Bill Bradley (D-N.J.) made headlines with a remarkable speech (at least, for the 1990s) on the U.S. Senate floor. It was reprinted many times and widely distributed as a pamphlet titled "Race and the American City."[2] "Slavery was our original sin, just as race remains our unresolved dilemma," the senator said. "The future of American cities is inextricably bound to the issue of race and ethnicity." He then gave a blunt, unflinching, eloquent analysis of American cities, decrying the fact that they "are poorer, sicker, less educated, and more violent than at any time in my lifetime." Bradley predicted that "the future of urban America will take one of three paths: abandonment, encirclement, or conversion."

—*Abandonment* means that "like the small town whose industry leaves, the city will wither and disappear. . . . The self-destruction has reached a point of no return and [cities] will crumble from within."

—*Encirclement* means "that people in cities will live in enclaves. The racial and ethnic walls will go higher. The class lines will be manned by ever increasing security forces and communal life will disappear."

—*Conversion* means "winning over all segments of urban life to a new politics of change, empowerment, and common effort. It is as different from the politics of dependency as it is from the politics of greed."

"When politicians don't talk about the reality that everyone knows exists, they cannot lead us out of our current crisis," the senator warned. "Institutions are no better than the people that run them."

Senator Bradley talked the talk, but his legislative proposals several months later hardly laid a hand on the "current crisis." His multipoint program, as I recall, was a watery gruel of more federal assistance for neighborhood-level, miniproject activities. Once again, a national leader was treating symptoms rather than systemic causes.

Among all states, New Jersey has the ninth most racially segregated metro areas and the seventh most racially segregated schools, but there were no proposals to combat what the senator targeted as "racism . . . alive and well." Among all states, New Jersey's central cities have the second largest gap between city and suburban incomes, the third lowest average

2. Quotations are taken from the reprint by the Massachusetts Mutual Life Insurance Company distributed by Senator Bradley's office.

incomes, and the fifth worst poverty burden, but there was no effort to amend federal tax policies that continue to favor suburban homeowners over city apartment dwellers. During the 1980s new development in New Jersey consumed land at almost twice the rate of population growth, yet there were no proposals to curb the massive federal subsidies for sprawl-inducing highways and sewage lines.

Knowing how the Congress actually works, my guess is that Senator Bradley's proposals were a hastily approved pastiche of ideas that caught the attention of some junior aide or of the senator himself during tours of New Jersey's distressed cities. But all in all, in a state where voters are 70 percent white and 85 percent suburban, the senator's package was a politically comfortable set of proposals. As part 1 shows, sprawl and race—the two factors underlying the senator's description of America's cities as "poorer, sicker, less educated, and more violent" than at any time in his life—have become deeply institutionalized.

2

Bedford Stuyvesant:
Beginnings

"AREN'T THE offices of Bedford Stuyvesant Restoration Corporation located near here?"

The desk sergeant at New York City's Seventy-Ninth Precinct looked up at me.

"The 1300 block of Fulton Street," he replied. "We'll have a squad car take you there."

"No thanks. I can walk. It must be only four or five blocks away." A little startled by his suggestion, I did not want to be any trouble to my impromptu hosts. As a middle-aged white man in a business suit with a briefcase in one of Brooklyn's toughest black ghettos, I would probably have accepted his offer if it had been eleven o'clock at night. The time, however, was eleven on a beautiful, sunny May morning.

Located catty-corner to Von King Park, the one-story, 1960s-style precinct house was not at all like the gritty, cacophonous New York police stations portrayed on TV cop shows such as *Hill Street Blues* or *NYPD Blue*. In fact, it looked like a typical police substation in Albuquerque. The tree-shaded streets were lined with elegant old brownstones and bland, mid-rise apartment buildings. In the morning sunlight the scene looked benign enough.

"Wait for a squad car," the sergeant firmly insisted. "You don't know the neighborhood."

I waited for the squad car.

I had come to Bedford Stuyvesant on the spur of the moment. That afternoon I was to address the 1995 national conference of the Council on Foundations, meeting nine miles away in Manhattan's New York Hilton. The topic of the three-day conference was foundation support for private anti-poverty programs in the nation's inner cities. The conference organizers had scheduled field trips to the South Bronx and Brownsville. These were the sites of the latest showcase programs by widely praised community development corporations such as Banana Kelly Neighborhood Improvement Association and the East Brooklyn Congregations.

The neighborhood tours were sure to be spiritually uplifting and professionally reassuring for the many foundation participants. They would be shown examples of renovated, not-for-profit, low-income housing projects and trim high-rises for senior citizens. They would visit colorful, lively day care centers and job training programs with encouraging initial placement results. A highlight of the tour would be Charlotte Street, a suburban-style neighborhood of new, single-family townhouses with neat, postage-stamp front yards where, just a few years before, the ruins of abandoned tenements smoldered in the midst of Fort Apache, The Bronx.

Having been a civil rights and antipoverty worker in the 1960s, however, I had more institutional memory than many of the younger foundation officials I would be addressing. There are *always* exemplary new programs to see. But do this year's success stories translate into long-term progress for many inner-city neighborhoods?

So, without any advance planning, after getting off the shuttle from Washington, D.C., I opened the Brooklyn volume of the New York City phone book and located what looked like a police station serving the Bedford Stuyvesant area. After verifying that fact with a brief phone call, I took the long cab ride from La Guardia to the Seventy-Ninth Precinct.

From Bedford Corners to Bed-Stuy

While waiting to talk with the precinct's community relations officer (who was off at a neighborhood meeting), I brushed up on Bedford Stuyvesant's history from a four-page mimeographed brochure the desk sergeant handed me. The community began as Bedford Corners, a Dutch farming community in the 1600s. By the mid-nineteenth century Bedford Corners had become a suburban locale of large houses and great lawns for white middle- and upper-income families. The opening of the Brooklyn Bridge in 1883 and the coming of elevated railroads shortly thereafter intensified development. Dozens of blocks of impressive brownstone, graystone, and gray brick homes in the Romanesque Revival style were built in Bedford and neighboring Stuyvesant.

The new republic's first census in 1790 had recorded a population of 204 for Bedford Corners, one-third of whom were identified as black slaves. With the free black communities of nearby Weeksville and Carrsville, these formed the core of the area's black population. In the 1920s this core began expanding rapidly as tens of thousands of black migrants moved into the area. Many came from deteriorating Manhattan neighborhoods (soon to be connected to Brooklyn by the A-train, immortalized by Duke Ellington). Legions more arrived from Deep South cotton states during the Great Migration.

The racial turnover was swift and often bitter. In fact, the handout noted, "the *Brooklyn Eagle* first coined the term Bedford Stuyvesant in its reports of whites and Blacks stockpiling arms to be used against each other." The handout continued:

> Not unlike Harlem, considered the center of Black activity for decades, Bedford Stuyvesant was a Mecca with flaws. Limited employment gains made during the labor shortage of World War I were erased by the Depression. Single-family homes were subdivided into single-room dwellings to accommodate the influx of newcomers. High interest mortgage rates encouraged neglect by absentee landlords. Real estate associations promoted racially exclusionary zoning. Police protection dwindled as did sanitation service when the white population fled. Prohibitive prices and ethnic and class discrimination, coupled with a deterioration of city services, gave rise to Bedford Stuyvesant's reputation as a large American ghetto.

By the 1950s, most white residents had fled to new subdivisions in Queens and Long Island. With almost 400,000 black residents, "Bed-Stuy" had become the nation's second largest black community, surpassed only by Chicago's South Side.

Having finished the pamphlet, I learned what I could from the police station's walls. There were graphs showing the crimes reported over the previous three months.[1] Not knowing the precinct's current population, I could not calculate a rough crime rate. Coming from the mayhem of Washington,

---

1. For January–March 1995, Precinct Seventy-Nine recorded 11 murders, 454 robberies, 325 burglaries, 132 grand larcenies, 26 rapes, 220 felony assaults, 139 grand larceny auto, and 322 other felonies. I later calculated, in roughest terms, that Bed-Stuy's murder rate was about half of Washington, D.C.'s rate.

D.C., where I now lived, the eleven homicides recorded for the three months struck me as relatively low. (With just under 600,000 residents, the nation's capital would record 469 murders that year.) A map of the precinct charted where crimes had occurred by "community policing district," the 1990s revival of the 1890s police beat. On the walls were the name, rank, and photograph of each officer assigned to the precinct. The command reflected the New York Police Department's citywide demographics (overwhelmingly white and male) rather than Bedford Stuyvesant's demographics (86 percent black, 55 percent female).

The community relations officer returned from the neighborhood meeting. His responses to my unscheduled interview were polite, professional, and unmemorable. It was after the interview that I had asked about the location of the Bedford Stuyvesant Restoration Corporation.

Once in the squad car, I suggested that I was in no hurry and would be happy to see some of the neighborhood as we cruised. We drove back and forth along one-way streets, weaving steadily closer to Fulton Street. It was a quiet morning, no calls on the radio, nothing happening on the sidewalks. I asked about crime levels in the precinct. "Better than some, worse than others" was the noncommittal reply. If the officers could wish for one thing for the neighborhood, what would it be? "Get rid of the drugs. Without drugs, 90 percent of the problems would go away," the older officer responded.

Restoration: Vanguard of Hopes and Dreams

Restoration Plaza could not be missed. A converted, abandoned milk bottling factory, now doubled in size, it was easily the largest building complex for blocks. It surrounded a courtyard where various neighborhood retail businesses were located: a Baskin-Robbins, a Lerner Shops, Chemical Bank, Citibank, Consolidated Edison, Brooklyn Union Gas. I walked through the lobby, past the Billie Holiday Theater, and was directed to the sixth-floor offices of "Mr. Palms."

White, mustached, late-sixties, Charley Palms was the organization's vice president. Hired in October 1967, he was almost an original staff member and was specially recognized in Restoration's twenty-fifth anniversary booklet.[2] Our chat about Restoration's history and accomplishments reaffirmed the reasons why I had made the pilgrimage to Bedford Stuyvesant.

2. Facts and quotations about Restoration's history and achievements are taken from *Bedford Stuyvesant Restoration Corporation 1967–92: 25 Years of Making a Difference* and other agency handouts.

Bedford Stuyvesant Restoration Corporation is the progenitor of about 2,000 community development corporations serving many of the nation's poorest urban ghettos and barrios. Restoration was the first, intended as the model for all that were to come. Its pedigree could not have been more high-powered. The organization was conceived in 1966 in the wake of Senator Robert F. Kennedy's highly publicized walk through Bed-Stuy. New York's junior senator was naturally eager to help one of the poorest districts in his state. He was also rankled by Lyndon Johnson's putting the LBJ brand on what Bobby Kennedy viewed as a piece of his assassinated brother's legacy. During Bobby Kennedy's years as John F. Kennedy's attorney general, many antipoverty program concepts, including "community action," had been incubated in the President's Committee on Juvenile Delinquency, housed in the Department of Justice. Renamed and expanded manyfold, the war on poverty was now the keystone of President Johnson's Great Society.

Responding to neighborhood appeals, Kennedy decided to initiate a new poverty-fighting vehicle, a community-based, private, not-for-profit "community development corporation." "The program for the development of Bedford Stuyvesant will combine the best of community action with the best of the private enterprise system," Kennedy told a neighborhood gathering in December 1966. "Neither by itself is enough, but in their combination lies our hope for the future."

As political godfathers for the new organization, Kennedy recruited New York's charismatic mayor, John Lindsay, and New York's senior U.S. senator, Jacob Javits. Business muscle could not have been stronger: IBM chairman Thomas B. Watson Jr., Citibank chairman Walter Wriston, CBS chairman William Paley, former secretary of the treasury Douglas Dillon, and a half dozen other blue-chip corporate and foundation leaders.

Kennedy and Javits joined forces to amend the federal Economic Opportunity Act to launch a "special impact program." The Kennedy-Javits amendment mandated federal funding for the infant community development corporation. Kennedy announced a seven-point action plan that, he hoped, would serve as a national model for inner-city revival. The plan called for the formation of two key organizations:

—Bedford Stuyvesant Renewal and Rehabilitation Corporation (forerunner of the Bedford Stuyvesant Restoration Corporation). Directed by a board of distinguished community representatives, the group would spearhead the neighborhood's economic, social, and physical development by sponsoring housing construction and rehabilitation, cultural and recreational facilities, job training programs, industrial and small business development, and programs to improve public schools.

—Its big business partner, the Bedford Stuyvesant Development and Services Corporation (D & S), would "involve and draw on the talents, energies, and knowledge of some of the foremost members of the American business community."

Other steps included recruiting a professional staff, enlisting the support of city and state governments, securing major federal grants from the Department of Housing and Urban Development and the Labor Department as the core financial support, and acquiring additional private foundation funding. New York's Pratt Institute and internationally renowned architect I. M. Pei would develop a series of plans for the area's physical redesign.

On the eve of the program's inauguration, Kennedy summed up the task ahead and the stakes involved:

> This is a unique effort—the only one of its kind and scope in the country. We have to show that it can be done. . . . We are striking out in new directions, on new courses, sometimes without a map or compass to guide us. We are going to try, as few have tried before, not just to have programs like others have, but to create new kinds of systems for education and health and employment and housing. We here are going to see, in fact, whether the city and its people, with the cooperation of governments and private business and foundations, can meet the challenges of urban life in the last third of the Twentieth Century.
>
> And it is Bedford Stuyvesant that is the vanguard—Bedford Stuyvesant that can take the lead. If we here can meet and master our problems; if this community can become an avenue of opportunity and a place of pleasure and excitement for its people, then others will take heart, and men all over the United States will remember your contribution with the deepest of gratitude. . . . But if this community fails, then others will falter, and a noble dream of equality and dignity in our cities will be sorely tried.[3]

Touring Bed-Stuy: A Different Burger King

Now, that last third of the twentieth century was almost over. Had Bedford Stuyvesant succeeded or failed? To pursue the answer, my wife, Delcia, and I returned several months later for a follow-up visit. Arriving early for our

---

3. *Bedford Stuyvesant Restoration Corporation 1967–92.*

appointment, we decided to have a cup of coffee at the Burger King across the street from Restoration's offices. A Burger King was a good sign. Taken for granted by millions of suburbanites, a new Burger King, Pizza Hut, or McDonald's franchise is tangible evidence of economic progress in scores of dusty southwestern crossroad towns, and in big-city ghettos as well. (A McDonald's was just down Fulton Street.)

This was almost a standard Burger King: same menu, same prices, scrubbed, cheery, and well lit. It was more interesting than most Burger Kings. In a glassed-in eating area toward the back, what may have been "the oldest, established, permanent, floating *chess* game in New York" was in progress. Shouting good-natured taunts and slapping their timers with a flourish, two black men were playing the kind of speed chess depicted in the film *Searching for Bobby Fischer.* Vanquishing a younger opponent, the champion—wiry, gap-toothed, of indeterminate middle age—and his new challenger greeted each other with well-honed trash talk worthy of two NBA point guards. Neither of the players was visibly a customer of Burger King, but the staff seemed to welcome the chess tournament as a local variation from the standard Burger King formula.

In two other ways, however, this was not a typical suburban Burger King. Heading for the rest rooms, we found the rest room doors could be opened only by special tokens (free but dispensed judiciously by the counter personnel). In addition, customers and staff had to slide tokens, cups of coffee, hamburgers and fries, or handfuls of bills and change through narrow openings cut through the inch-thick, ceiling-high, bulletproof Plexiglas shields that spanned the entire counter area.

Leaving the Burger King, over the next several hours we took a windshield tour of the neighborhood. Our host again was Charley Palms, joined by Lester Matthews, a courtly black man who had been a lifelong neighborhood leader and now was, like Charley, a Restoration staff member.

Pathmark Supermarket

Driving out of Restoration's underground garage, both men pointed out the Pathmark supermarket taking up one whole end of Restoration Plaza. Except for the large Pathmark sign, the supermarket was easy to miss. The blank, fortress-like brick walls gave no hint of the nature or volume of the business inside.

The Pathmark was one of Restoration's proudest victories. Opened in 1979, the 30,000-square-foot store was the first new supermarket to be built in Bedford Stuyvesant in nearly thirty years. At a cost of $2.5 million, the project was a joint venture; two-thirds was owned by Restoration and one-third by Supermarkets General of New Jersey, owner of the Pathmark chain.

Chalking up annual sales of over $25 million, Restoration Supermarkets Corporation is listed annually among the top fifty black-owned companies in the United States each year by *Black Enterprise* magazine. Of more importance, an evaluation study found that Pathmark shoppers pay more than 30 percent less than they would at the few, small-volume corner grocery stores scattered throughout the neighborhood.

Housing Renovation

Better housing was always one of Restoration's priorities. To demonstrate quick, tangible community impact, its first program in 1967 was a crash effort to renovate the faces of 394 brownstones covering 11 blocks of Bedford Stuyvesant; in the process, Restoration trained seventy-two unemployed neighborhood residents to do the work. Over a period of almost three decades the pilot effort expanded, giving facelifts to the exteriors of 4,200 homes covering 150 blocks. During the same period Restoration built or renovated 2,225 housing units. Some new projects fit right into the neighborhood's historic fabric. Fulton North blended forty apartment units onto second and third floors over street-level retail shops in the classic New York tradition. Other housing developments sought to transform the area. The 267 units in Restore Village were spread among four new, four- to eight-story brick buildings grouped around an interior park and playground in an I. M. Pei–designed "superblock."

To promote homeownership, in April 1968 Restoration persuaded a consortium of eighty New York banks, insurance companies, and savings and loan associations, led by Citibank, to commit approximately $65 million in Federal Housing Administration (FHA) insured loans to a new home mortgage pool for Bedford Stuyvesant residents.[4] About 1,500 homeowners received mortgages or major renovation loans from the pool, which became a for-profit, wholly owned subsidiary called Restoration Funding Corporation. (By 1994 Restoration Funding was no longer active.) In 1986–88 alone, Restoration took over, renovated, and resold more than $3 million of predominantly one- to six-unit brownstone or brick townhouses. Some hous-

4. This was nine years before the federal Community Reinvestment Act of 1977 made such lending practices mandatory for all federally regulated mortgage lenders.

ing improvements were less visible from the street. From 1980 onward, under a state contract, Restoration "weatherized" more than 5,800 apartments for low-income and elderly residents.

To our practiced eyes, which had seen poor neighborhoods in almost fifty metro areas, the physical proof of Restoration's housing programs was evident during our windshield tour. There were still a few tough-looking blocks of deteriorated tenements, and most streets did not have the spruced-up look of wealthier neighborhoods. But nowhere did we see the unmistakable signs of wholesale urban abandonment found in Detroit or Saint Louis: weedy lots strewn with bricks, concrete blocks, broken glass, crumpled beer cans, rusting auto hulks, evicted sofas and rotting mattresses interspersed among the tottering, broken-sash structures still standing.

Brownstones

What left a lasting impression of Bedford Stuyvesant were the magnificent Victorian brownstone and graystone townhouses that still lined so many blocks. It was these very brownstones, filled with hard-working black owners, "committed to raising their families and building their neighborhood," that had initially captured Bobby Kennedy's attention.

With a veteran real estate agent's curiosity, Delcia asked about estimated sales prices. A four-story brownstone in good condition? Probably $80,000 to $90,000, Lester estimated. An equal architectural gem but in visible need of major renovation? Perhaps $40,000 to $50,000. (In Manhattan's East Sixties, now-scarce brownstone mansions sold for up to one hundred times as much.)

Frankly, we were amazed. Just a scant ten minutes by the A-train from lower Manhattan and almost abutting downtown Brooklyn, where new office towers housed Wall Street's back office operations, were undoubtedly the best housing values in metropolitan New York. "Location, location, location" is the real estate industry's mantra. The brownstones of Bed-Stuy actually have perfect "location," but, like so much in American life, the realtor's adage is just code. "Location, location, location" really means "neighborhood, neighborhood, neighborhood." The difference between the $5,000,000 brownstone of the East Sixties and the $50,000 brownstone of Bedford Stuyvesant was not the physical geography of their location but the human geography of their surroundings. It was a sad truth we had seen affirmed in scores of cities.

"With this supply of wonderful houses," Delcia said to Charley and Lester, "Bedford Stuyvesant always has the potential to make a strong comeback."

"We know," Lester replied. "In fact, Rod [Roderick Mitchell, Restoration's current president] has ended our low-income housing programs. He feels we have too much low-income housing already and would like to emphasize new affordable housing for working people."

"I think he's right on the mark," I responded.

IBM Plant

Our tour was approaching another Restoration icon, a modern, two-story factory occupying an entire city block on the corner of Nostrand and DeKalb.

"Is this where the IBM plant was located?"

"Still is," Charley replied.

"I thought IBM recently closed it down?"

"They did," Charley explained, "but the plant was sold to IBM's former employees. It still operates as a supplier to IBM and others under contract."

"Is it doing OK?"

"As far as I know."

I hoped so. The IBM plant had been Restoration's biggest economic development coup. In 1968 Restoration and D & S, its big business-dominated twin, persuaded IBM to take a long-term lease on an old, eight-story brick warehouse at the corner of Gates and Nostrand and convert it into a computer component factory. (It was not a hard sell since IBM's chairman and chief executive officer, Thomas B. Watson Jr., was a founding director of D & S.)

Initially employing 120 local residents, the facility soon grew to 400 employees. Needing a new facility, in 1975 IBM built a new $10.2 million factory just several blocks up Nostrand Avenue on a site previously reserved for a new school. Bedford Stuyvesant, local representatives stated, ranked among IBM's top ten plants in efficiency and productivity, a claim shrouded in some doubt when the operation failed to survive IBM's cost-cutting corporate downsizing in 1993. However, sold to its employees and renamed Advanced Technological Solutions, a year later the plant was the biggest minority employee–owned manufacturing company in the United States.

As the former IBM plant faded in our rearview mirror, I wanted to draw out Lester more.

The Crack Cocaine Plague

"What are some of the changes you've seen over these years?"

"For one thing, as we're driving around today, we haven't seen anybody 'nodding,'" he replied, describing a familiar phenomenon of heroin addiction. "When Restoration started, even early in the morning, you'd see all sorts of men and women nodding out on the streets. We pretty well got rid of that."

"When did crack hit the neighborhood?" (Almost any knowledgeable inner-city activist, as Lester Matthews certainly was, can name the year, often the month, when crack cocaine moved into the neighborhood.)

Lester flinched, almost as if he had been jabbed in the solar plexus. "Let's see," he said finally. "That must have been the early summer of 1986. I remember that I'd be driving around, and I suddenly began noticing all these young men congregated on different street corners . . . same corners every day. I thought maybe something good was happening, until I found out what was going on."

"I have the impression that real progress was being made until crack hit."

Lester nodded in agreement. "That's true, that's true," he said wistfully, almost to himself.

Islands of Progress

As our tour was coming to a close, we set out to locate two census tracts where the poverty level had dropped significantly in the past two decades. In tract 277 the poverty rate had fallen from 36 percent to 27 percent; in adjacent tract 279, from 42 percent to 26 percent. Something dramatic had to have happened.

As indeed it had. We found several blocks lined with dozens of new, brick-faced, two-story townhouses, all obviously the work of the same builder. They lacked the style and craftsmanship of the brownstones of a century before, but the new townhouses undoubtedly had the modern kitchens, bathrooms, and family rooms that many middle-class households demand today.

Saying good-bye to our hosts back at Restoration's offices, Delcia and I walked back down Fulton Street toward the subway station at the intersection with Nostrand Avenue. Fulton was alive as crowds of people brushed by sidewalk vendors. We almost had to step out into the street to pass the busiest corners. The sidewalk vendors actually upgraded the appearance of Fulton Street. Obscured by the vendors' overhanging umbrellas and awnings, more and more storefronts were shuttered and padlocked as we moved farther away from Restoration Plaza.

Our windshield tour had given us only a surface impression of Restoration's work in Bedford Stuyvesant. We had not visited the Family Health Center, serving 55,000 outpatients annually. We had not been among the 40,000 people who attend performances at the Billie Holiday Theater every year. We were not among the 20,000 residents whom Restoration had placed in temporary and permanent jobs over the quarter-century. In many ways it was hard not to be impressed with Restoration's achievements.

But was the Bedford Stuyvesant community better off than it had been before Bobby Kennedy's walk in 1966? For that answer we turned to cold, hard census statistics.

Tale of the Tracts: Vanishing Populations

Boxing fans look to the "Tale of the Tape" to handicap a boxing match. So-cial analysts and economists must look to the Tale of the Tracts to judge how well the battle against neighborhood decline is going. Beginning with the 1970 census, the U.S. Bureau of the Census has published detailed income data, census tract by census tract, for each of the country's metro areas. This allows independent researchers to study neighborhood trends readily, with-out the assistance of big mainframe computer centers found only at univer-sities, government agencies, and major think tanks. Taking the list of eighty-five census tracts Charley Palms supplied, I was able to construct my own profile of Bedford Stuyvesant from 1970 to 1990, a period covering the bulk of Restoration's twenty-eight years of activity.

During that period Bedford Stuyvesant lost 100,000 residents. The fig-ure dropped from 375,761 residents recorded in 1970 to only 275,457 in 1990, which amounted to a 27 percent decline. Of course, having a smaller population is not automatically a negative development, particularly in com-munities suffering from overcrowded housing. With a general trend toward smaller household size, even among poor households, most neighborhoods must increase the total number of households just to maintain a constant population level. However, Bedford Stuyvesant lost households as well. Their number dropped from 114,887 households in 1970 to 94,879 in 1990 (a 17 percent decrease). Because the figures reflected occupied housing units, the number of households was not as subject to the Census Bureau's notorious undercounting of poor urban residents. In effect, the neighborhood was slowly depopulating.

Bedford Stuyvesant was also becoming blacker and browner. The propor-tion of African American residents rose from 81 percent in 1970 to 82 per-cent in 1990. By 1990, most of the non-black residents were Hispanic (14 percent). In fact, a majority of residents were Hispanic in almost 10 percent of Bedford Stuyvesant's census tracts, forming a barrio within a ghetto.

The area's "Anglo" population (that is, non-Hispanic whites, to use the southwestern term) had shrunk to 9,020. Most were clustered in blocks along Washington Avenue and Eastern Parkway, the western and southern edges of Bedford Stuyvesant. Since several census tracts span Bedford Stuyvesant's traditional boundaries, a block-level analysis would probably show that many of these Anglo households actually lived just outside Bedford Stuyvesant itself.

Rising Poverty

What about reducing poverty, Restoration's reason for being? In 1970 an estimated 21,352 families in the area were under the poverty threshold. Twenty years later that figure was unchanged: 21,233 families. With a smaller population base, the poverty rate among families had increased from 23.7 percent to 34.4 percent. If all persons in poverty are measured (including unrelated individuals who were not family members), the total number of poor persons had declined from 103,402 in 1970 to 93,557 in 1990. Again, measured against a smaller population base, the poverty rate for individuals had increased from 27.5 percent to 34.0 percent.

What would be the effect of the "census undercount" on these figures? Census enumerators do not miss many doctors, lawyers, business executives, factory workers, secretaries, and civil servants. They miss street people. To the extent that a more accurate count could be made in Bedford Stuyvesant, it would probably reveal even higher poverty rates.

The overall figures also masked changes at the tract level. Tracts with 20 percent to 40 percent of the residents below the poverty level are typically designated "poverty neighborhoods." In "high-poverty neighborhoods," the poverty level ranges from 40 to 60 percent. Those with more than 60 percent poverty are "hyperpoverty neighborhoods."

Of eighty-five census tracts in 1970, Bedford Stuyvesant recorded sixty-four poverty neighborhoods and seven high-poverty neighborhoods. In only fourteen census tracts was the poverty level below 20 percent. The lowest poverty rate (13.7 percent) was found in a tract spanning Washington Avenue, Bed-Stuy's western boundary.

By 1990, however, the number of high-poverty neighborhoods (40 to 60 percent poor) had increased from seven to thirty-seven, because many neighborhoods had become much poorer. Meanwhile, the number of relatively more affluent neighborhoods had shrunk from fourteen to only three, leaving the remaining forty-five tracts with poverty neighborhood status.

Overall, poverty rates increased significantly in sixty-four tracts, were stable in seventeen tracts, and decreased significantly in only four tracts (including tracts 277 and 279 just discussed). In only tract 197 (again on the area's western boundary) had economic conditions improved to the point where that neighborhood escaped poverty classification.[5]

In short, during two decades in which the poverty level in the Greater New York region dropped from 14 percent to 12 percent, poverty in Bedford Stuyvesant increased from 27.5 percent to 34.0 percent, and only one out of seventy-one poverty neighborhoods rose out of poverty status.

Shrinking Markets

Looking at another set of statistics, I found a partial explanation for the juxtaposition of a successful Pathmark supermarket and the many shuttered storefronts along Fulton Street. Bedford Stuyvesant's total neighborhood buying power was $811 million in 1970. By 1990 neighborhood buying power had risen to a nominal $2.4 billion. Yet, adjusted for twenty years of inflation, neighborhood buying power had actually decreased 12 percent.

In effect, Bedford Stuyvesant offered a big enough market for a Pathmark, a Baskin-Robbins, a Burger King, or a McDonald's, all of which have established products and formulas for selling them successfully. But marginal mom-and-pop stores faced the reality of fewer customers with fewer dollars to spend. After two decades of effort, as measured by poverty levels and neighborhood buying power, Bedford Stuyvesant was poorer than when Restoration began. Had Restoration failed?

Developing Minority Leadership

Restoration has had many individual success stories. One of the high-profile success stories was that of Franklin Thomas, Restoration's first president. He joined Restoration with impeccable credentials. Born in Bedford

---

5. I was puzzled, however, about why poverty levels never rose above 60 percent in Bedford Stuyvesant. During our tour we had seen many large public housing complexes. Across urban America, a large public housing complex is almost invariably the core of a high-poverty or hyperpoverty neighborhood. Several months later I found out that New York City's housing policies differ from the federal standard. Whereas federal policies give priority to the poorest of the poor, New York City allocates about one-third of every project to the elderly (of whatever income level), one-third to working-class households, and only a third of the units to welfare recipients and other desperately poor households. Although all residents of city housing complexes have no more than modest incomes, the city's policy promotes some degree of social and economic diversity.

Stuyvesant, Thomas was a basketball star at Columbia University, where he also received a law degree. Deputy police commissioner of the city of New York at age thirty-one, he authored the civilian review board plan. An original board member, he became Restoration's president when political infighting within the new organization led to its reorganization in May 1967. Assembling a top-level staff, he helped write the application that resulted in a $7 million first-year grant from the U.S. Department of Labor, with the required local match coming from the Ford Foundation. After a decade leading Restoration, he left to head the Ford Foundation itself, becoming the first African American chief executive of a major national foundation.

Many other Bedford Stuyvesant residents were also propelled into broader community leadership roles after serving on Restoration's board, committees, and task forces. Staff jobs were key rungs on the ladder to professional careers for many young African American college graduates. Scores of other community residents found their first clerical or paraprofessional jobs with Restoration.

These comments are not offered (nor should they be read) from a cynical point of view. One of the success stories of community-based, antipoverty programs has been leadership development. Antipoverty jobs have opened doors to opportunity for a whole generation of African American and Hispanic mayors, city council members, state legislators, members of Congress, public administrators, corporate executives, and other professionals.

Grading Restoration's Twenty-Five Years

In evaluating Restoration's success or failure, one must also consider the fate of Bed-Stuy's 100,000 "missing" residents. Some of the population decline was just the effect of an aging community. However, over the two decades tens of thousands of residents also left Bedford Stuyvesant. Many would have been helped by Restoration's job training and placement programs. Others would have used steady wages at the IBM plant or other local businesses created by Restoration to move out.

"Where have most people moved to?" I had asked Lester. He had thought for a minute. "Queens. Long Island."

In short, today's black emigrants from Bedford-Stuyvesant move out in the same general direction as white Bedford Stuyvesant residents a generation before. (Often black emigrants move into the same set of suburban communities that are now rapidly resegregating. Long Island's suburbs are as racially segregated as New York City itself.)

What would have happened without Restoration's efforts? Would Bed-Stuy be even poorer, more disorganized, more crime-ridden? Common sense suggests the answer would be "probably." Since it began, Restoration's slogan has been "making a difference." I believe that Restoration has made a difference for the good, including beyond its neighborhood boundaries.

Several months after our second visit, Charley Palms made the latter point in a letter to me. "The back offices of Chase Manhattan, Morgan Stanley, Goldman Sachs, Bear Stearns, Charles Schwab, and other businesses have moved in from lower Manhattan and currently occupy the newly developed One Pierrepoint Plaza and MetroTech in downtown Brooklyn," Charley wrote. "They employ more than 12,000 people. It is projected that by the year 2000, MetroTech Center, combined with other new developments in downtown Brooklyn, will have more than 30,000 new jobs."

"Many of us believe," Charley concluded, "that if Restoration had not maintained stability in central Brooklyn, the redevelopment of downtown Brooklyn would never have happened—a view corroborated in a conversation I had with a Vice President at Chase Manhattan two years ago."[6]

Charley makes a fair point. I will concede that, to some degree, Restoration's efforts contributed to the revival of downtown Brooklyn. Nevertheless, the hard fact remains: the Bedford Stuyvesant community is poorer today than when Restoration began. And, with a rising concentration of poverty, falling relative incomes, and slowly declining real buying power, Bedford Stuyvesant's capacity to be, in Bobby Kennedy's words, an "avenue of opportunity" (much less to be a "place of pleasure and excitement") grows less and less with each passing decade.

If Bedford Stuyvesant Restoration Corporation, the vanguard, is failing as a neighborhood antipoverty program, are other community development corporations that followed faltering as well? Or was Restoration's failure really an exception to a general pattern of success?

6. Letter to the author, March 27, 1996.

3

Walnut Hills, Jamaica Plain, and Other Neighborhoods

THE OHIO RIVER lay at my feet. From my vantage point on top of Cincinnati's Walnut Hills, I could see a handful of sailboats and powerboats dotting the river, blue and shimmering under a crisp October sky. An occasional barge or river freighter bulled its way along. Two large boat marinas hugged the opposite shore of Kentucky's Kenton County. All in all, it was a beautiful view. Our ancestors knew where to build cities.

"Cincinnati discouraged building any private marinas on the north side of the river," commented Ed Burdell, who, with his partner Bill Woods, was my guide. "All the marina development—and much of the high-end housing associated with boat owners—is now happening over on the Kentucky side."

"We do have one boat tied up on the north side," Bill said, pointing to a large, enclosed barge down on the river off to our left. "That's the only floating high school classroom in the country . . . specializes in teaching nautical sciences. The Cincinnati Public Schools are very proud of it."

To my right, Cincinnati's downtown, one of the country's more vigorous and interesting central business districts, was screened from direct view by the bulge of Mount Adams. At the foot of Walnut Hills a narrow ribbon of concrete—the Columbia Parkway—wound its way. Set far back from the riverbank, a few grim, rusting industrial hulks and warehouses still marked the area. Otherwise, the Ohio River's floodplain had been largely left as natural areas or grassy playing fields. Abandoned riverfront and lakefront industrial districts, now available for recycling into high-end condominiums and townhouses, are one of the great, underexploited assets of many of America's aging industrial cities. Successful urbanites will pay big money for a glimpse of moving water.

That idea was obviously not original with me. To my left, on East Walnut Hills, three large condominiums—the Edgecliff, the Ingleside, River Terrace—shot into the air. Condo owners probably paid quite a premium to have a balcony looking out over the Ohio rather than backward into the city. In the Walnut Hills neighborhood itself, once fine Victorian mansions had shed more recent lives as partitioned rooming houses and were made whole again, sparkling under new paint and trim applied by their young urban professional owners. What was happening in Walnut Hills? In a word, regentrification.

Walnut Hills: Regentrification and Decline

I had come to Cincinnati to address a seminar of business and civic leaders. My side trip to Walnut Hills was prompted by intense curiosity. Out of thirty-four of the country's best community development corporations, the Walnut Hills Redevelopment Foundation target area was one of only four in which average household income had risen as a percentage of average household income in the whole metropolitan area. And Walnut Hills's progress was a minuscule advance, at best. In 1980 the income of the average Walnut Hills household was 43 percent of the metro Cincinnati average; by 1990 the ratio had nudged upward to 44 percent.

I was standing in the middle of the sole reason for the Walnut Hills neighborhood's economic resurgence. Census tract 19 is the only tract of the five in the Walnut Hills Redevelopment Foundation's target area that has riverfront views. The other four are away from the river, stretching back into one of Cincinnati's poorest black ghettoes.

Parts of the area had long been African American, Ed and Bill explained. The big houses were built beginning in 1895, when Walnut Hills was opened up as a streetcar suburb for Cincinnati's wealthier families. Behind us, across what was once Lincoln Avenue, shotgun homes had been built for the mansion owners' black servants.[1]

In the decades after World War II, the wealthy families moved away to new suburban havens, and the mansions went into a long decline. The 1980 census had outlined tract 19's dismal numbers. Totaling 838 households (three-quarters black, one-quarter white), tract 19 was a high-poverty neighborhood. Some 43 percent of families and individuals were poor. In fact, tract 19 had the highest poverty rate of the five tracts. Its average household income, at $9,251, was only 44 percent of the Greater Cincinnati average.

By contrast, the 1990 census reflected a rapid regentrification. The number of total households had increased to 929 (a growth rate approaching 10 percent). Single-person households—young lawyers, architects, stockbrokers, and other professionals—accounted for almost all of the increase. There was a net increase of only fifteen family households in tract 19 during the decade.

Also, the net increase was entirely white. During the decade, tract 19's black population dropped from 1,400 in 1980 to 1,035 in 1990, but its white population climbed from 468 to 750. (Although the net increase was white, some black middle-class professionals had undoubtedly moved into tract 19 as well.) Its poverty rates had been halved, to 21 percent of family households and 25 percent of all residents. Most impressively, tract 19's average annual household income had risen from 44 percent to 74 percent of the Greater Cincinnati average.

Without the stimulus of river view location, however, the other four census tracts of the Walnut Hills Redevelopment Foundation's target area had not only shown no signs of regentrification, but they had followed the familiar pattern of deepening poverty and racial segregation. The four "inland" tracts combined dropped from 3,673 households in 1980 to 3,300 in 1990 (a 10 percent decrease). Already hypersegregated by 1980, the four tracts saw the percentage of black residents inch upward, from 94 percent to 95 percent. Both the absolute numbers of poor families and poor persons and rates of poverty increased. The family poverty rate jumped from 33 percent to 40 percent, and poverty among all individuals climbed from less than 39

---

1. After 1968 Lincoln Avenue was renamed Martin Luther King Jr. Drive. It was another bittersweet example of how, as a gesture to black communities, the name of the great champion of an integrated society had been so often attached to streets, schools, and parks in the heart of many of America's most segregated black neighborhoods.

percent to almost 46 percent. Nominal buying power among residents of the four inland tracts increased from $32.6 million in 1980 to $44.5 million in 1990, but, adjusted for inflation, real buying power declined by 20 percent.

However, back in tract 19, with its middle-class resurgence, nominal buying power grew from $7.8 million in 1980 to $26.3 million in 1990. Adjusted for inflation, the real buying power of tract 19 residents almost doubled (registering a 97 percent growth rate) in just ten years. Tract 19's surging prosperity more than offset the steady decline of its four neighboring tracts, producing the small increase in overall buying power (1 percent) that had drawn me to visit the area. Except for the regentrification of tract 19, the Walnut Hills Redevelopment Foundation's target zone would have been yet another example of unrelieved economic decline.

Boston's Urban Edge Housing Corporation

A second CDC-served neighborhood in my national survey that had experienced relative improvement in average household income was in the Boston area.[2] Since 1974 the Urban Edge Housing Corporation has served parts of Boston's Roxbury and Jamaica Plain neighborhoods. Overall, the buying power of these areas increased 17 percent between 1970 and 1990, and average household income rose from 73 percent of the Boston area average in 1980 to 76 percent in 1990. However, like Walnut Hills, these two communities did not experience uniform improvement during these two very different decades.

The Target Area

Urban Edge's primary service area covers a cluster of three census tracts in Roxbury and two in Jamaica Plain that I will call the "target area." In the 1970 census the target area had almost 20,000 residents: more than 40 percent were African American and about one-quarter Hispanic. It was one of the poorest sections of Boston; 22 percent of all families and 25 percent of all individuals fell below the poverty line (this was three times the Boston region's poverty rates). Average household income was only 61 percent of the regional average.

2. The other CDCs whose target areas gained ground economically were San Francisco's Mission Housing Corporation and Phoenix's Chicanos por La Causa.

The 1970s brought further economic decline. The target area's overall population dropped by 10 percent, while poverty rates escalated to 33 percent for families and individuals, and average household income declined to 57 percent of the regional average.

During the 1980s, however, the "Massachusetts Miracle" took hold. The Boston region boomed with new high-tech firms springing up all along Route 128. Relatively few target-area residents may have gone to work for Wang or Digital Electronics Corporation, but the benefits of the economic boom clearly trickled down to the neighborhood. The target area's population became stabilized; only 24 household units were lost (compared with more than 200 during the previous decade). Poverty rates inched back downward for families (28 percent) and individuals (30 percent), though average household incomes slipped further, to 55 percent of the regional average.

Meanwhile, the target area had become more racially isolated. The 1990 census showed that the African American population had increased to 50 percent, and most of the remaining population was Hispanic (41 percent), largely first- and second-generation Puerto Rican immigrants.

Jamaica Plain

Beyond Urban Edge's target area, the rest of the Jamaica Plain neighborhoods (which I will call "Jamaica Plain") presented an entirely different face. Jamaica Plain was neither predominantly minority nor poor. In 1970 these four census tracts were almost 90 percent non-Hispanic whites. African Americans constituted just 2 percent of the residents, and Hispanics totaled about 10 percent. Individual poverty rates in the four census tracts ranged from 8 percent to 14 percent, with the overall level at 12 percent. Average household income was a relatively healthy 84 percent of the Boston area average.

For Jamaica Plain, the 1970s were stressful as well. The community shrank by about 350 households. The number of poor residents rose by one-fifth, and, with middle-class households leaving, the individual poverty rate in Jamaica Plain as a whole pushed up to 17 percent. Average household income dipped to 71 percent of the regional average.

The economic boom of the 1980s again made Jamaica Plain a hot residential area. Almost 500 households were added back to the community, some of them minority households. As a result, Jamaica Plain became one of Boston's more racially diverse neighborhoods. Its black population rose to 12 percent and its Hispanic population to 23 percent. The poverty rate dropped back to 12 percent, and household income rebounded to 78 percent of the regional average. Most remarkably, Jamaica Plain's overall buying power increased 56 percent during the 1980s (compared with a 24 percent decline during the previous decade). Combined with a lesser resurgence in the target area's buying power, the overall neighborhood buying power in Urban Edge's service area increased 17 percent during the two decades. It was this statistic that had drawn my attention to Roxbury-Jamaica Plain originally.

Which would be the pattern of the 1990s—the decline of the 1970s or the resurgence of the 1980s? With the bloom off the Massachusetts Miracle, was Urban Edge's target area sinking deeper into ghetto poverty in the 1990s? Was Jamaica Plain continuing to prosper as a racially diverse but stable community, or was it losing ground again? What had been the contribution of Urban Edge Housing Corporation? Its housing programs accounted for only about 5 percent of all housing units but a larger percentage of the new housing created. Had Urban Edge made a crucial difference?

Touring Roxbury and Jamaica Plain

To try to answer these questions, I visited Urban Edge in June 1996 to meet with Mossik Hacobian, its veteran executive director, and to take a tour of the neighborhood. Urban Edge's headquarters filled four apartments converted to offices in a forty-unit, low-income apartment complex located on what is euphemistically called Egleston Square. The "square" was simply the intersection of two major streets—Columbus Avenue and Washington Street—without any park, plaza, or other monumental space, which, anywhere but Boston, would be required to justify the designation *square*. As I climbed out of my cab in front of the Urban Edge offices, I saw a half dozen men wearing bright blue shirts with "Urban Edge Property Management" stitched over the chest. They were busy sweeping around the housing complex and around Cleaves Court, another Urban Edge–managed property across the street.

Using a slide presentation, Mossik outlined the history of Urban Edge. It had begun as a fair housing brokerage business. Urban Edge's original offices had been located on Centre Street deep in Jamaica Plain. "But we realized that the 'urban edge'—the boundary between the haves and the have-nots—was moving east toward Roxbury," Mossik explained. "Columbus Avenue was the boundary between black Roxbury and the Latino section of Jamaica Plain. There might as well have been a Berlin Wall running right down the middle of Columbus Avenue. Urban Edge consciously placed our new offices on the African American side of the avenue to break through that boundary."

Over the years Urban Edge had grown into a major operation. With an annual budget of $3.8 million and a staff of sixty, Urban Edge is now one of the five largest employers in the target area. It has developed 670 units of affordable housing, which it continues to manage through an affiliated property management company. In September 1995 it was awarded a contract by the Boston Housing Authority to manage Walnut Park tower, a 168-unit high-rise apartment for senior citizens located a block from Urban Edge's headquarters. In the last half-dozen years, Urban Edge has expanded its role beyond housing development and management to provide a wide range of social services for its tenants, including youth programs and antigang activities.

A focal point of Urban Edge's recent activity has been the development of Egleston Center, a small, 7,000-square-foot neighborhood shopping center on the corner of Columbus Avenue and Washington Street. It features a McDonald's and a branch of Fleet Bank. Three blocks away the bank had earlier opened a temporary facility in a trailer in order to build up its clientele. The new Fleet Bank is the first bank branch ever on Egleston Square. "Fleet Bank isn't coming as an act of charity," Mossik commented. "It saw a market opportunity."

"Market opportunity" certainly characterizes Urban Edge's latest plans. "We feel that we have largely succeeded in the Egleston Square area," Mossik continued. "We're shifting our focus northward a half-mile up Columbus Avenue to the Jackson Square area. Egleston Square is one important meeting ground between Boston's Roxbury and Jamaica Plain neighborhoods. Jackson Square is another important geographic connector between these two communities. With 10,000 people living near Jackson Square, 8,000 rail commuters passing through the MTA station, and 70,000 cars driving through the intersection, Jackson Square also represents a tremendous commercial opportunity."

"I'd like to see it very much," I said. "I also very much want to visit census tract 812 in Roxbury. During the 1970s and 1980s that tract experienced an enormous drop in the number of poor families. I'm curious to find out what happened. It's almost as if a major public housing project shut down."

Mossik and his colleague, Fiona O'Connor, my tour guide, checked a map. "Bromley-Heath . . . the largest public housing project in Massachusetts . . . it's located right there," they confirmed. "In the mid-1980s the Boston Housing Authority began a major renovation of Bromley-Heath. Whole buildings have been vacated for long periods of time. The Census Bureau must have counted the project midway through that process."

Jamaica Plain: Where the Mixes Match

For the next two hours we crisscrossed much of Roxbury and Jamaica Plain. Several highlights of the tour stood out.

—Saint John Street in the heart of Jamaica Plain. It was an excellent example of an urban neighborhood of an earlier age: a dense collection of varied buildings with wood-frame, single-family homes and duplexes mixed in with small apartment buildings. Mature broad-leafed trees hung over the narrow, one-way street, reduced to barely one lane by the parked cars on either side, which further shielded the sidewalks from the flow of traffic. Ivy, honeysuckle, and other flowering plants climbed the sides of many of the buildings. Within Jamaica Plain, Saint John Street was not atypical, and it was easy to understand why the neighborhood had undergone such a strong revival. "Everybody lives on this street," Fiona said, "from Ph.D.'s to car mechanics, of every racial and ethnic background. Over the last fifteen or so years Jamaica Plain has become very proud and very protective of its diversity. The slogan of our Jamaica Plain Business Association is 'Jamaica Plain— Where the Mixes Match.' "

—The subtle transitions along Centre Street. Centre Street began among vacant lots and low-slung auto shops near Jackson Square in Roxbury, moved through a zone of bodegas and tiendas catering to the Hispanic population, and metamorphosed into a trendy, upscale collection of boutiques, coffee shops, and restaurants in the heart of regentrified Jamaica Plain. Outside a newly opened sushi bar, we saw a film production crew setting up on the corner of Hyde Square. "What are you filming?" I yelled out as we slowed. "A commercial for the Boston Tourism Bureau," a crew member replied. Jamaica Plain had arrived.

—Stoney Brook Co-operative, a new cluster of gray-and-white, affordable townhouses developed by Urban Edge near a long, linear park created by relocation of the Metropolitan Transit Authority's Orange Line. The townhouses were very attractive, and, though new, matched the style of the neighborhood. What I most remember was how the tenants were selected. "There were over 500 qualified applicants for just fifty units," Fiona explained, "but because this would be a co-op project, and our goal was to create a real community, Urban Edge added a special screening criterion. Specifically, we were looking for a demonstrated history of community involvement, the ability to join together for common goals. Past membership in a PTA, being a church leader, an active member of a political ward organization. As a result Stoney Brook is filled with real community activists. Later this year the co-op's board will take over all ownership and management responsibilities from Urban Edge. More important, all these live wires have had a tremendous impact on the surrounding neighborhood. They've energized a whole range of community organizations."

—The Bromley-Heath public housing complex, a jumble of massive, four- and six-story, brown concrete boxes covering about a dozen square blocks. Major renovations were still under way, as construction crews could be seen working around several vacant buildings. Undoubtedly, when Bromley-Heath was first built in the 1950s, it was considered the last word in safe, sanitary, decent housing for low-income families. By comparison with almost every neighborhood surrounding it, however, Bromley-Heath looked sterile and massively institutional.

Bromley-Heath was the first tenant-managed public housing project, constantly touted as a national model. Shortly after my visit I wrote "perhaps tenant management has made a difference, but I doubt that the social environment faced by hundreds of children growing up in Bromley-Heath is better than in scores of massive public housing projects around the country." Sadly, in October 1998, after thirty-eight residents were arrested as drug traffickers, amid charges of widespread mismanagement, the Boston Housing Authority took back control of Bromley-Heath.

Guaranteeing Permanent Diversity?

Back at Urban Edge's offices, I congratulated Mossik for his organization's visible success. We chatted about the delicate balancing act the CDC faced on the "urban edge," that boundary between the haves and the have-nots. One of Mossik's comments, in particular, struck me. "Fifteen years ago we realized that if we could create strong, stable, multifamily developments for low-income families, that would change everything. The neighborhoods would no longer be in the hands of speculators."

What was Mossik really saying? I wondered. Community development corporations are typically characterized as antipoverty programs. Would Jamaica Plain, if not Roxbury itself, have regentrified even more uniformly without Urban Edge's involvement? Were market forces in Jamaica Plain so strong that, without Urban Edge, the neighborhood would have become wall-to-wall yuppie, with poor Hispanics and African Americans being steadily pushed out into some other forgotten corner of the Boston area? In that case, Urban Edge had performed a different—but invaluable—role: guaranteeing that there would always be a place in the Jamaica Plain community for low- and moderate-income households. Urban Edge's housing programs had been a mechanism for creating the very diversity of income classes (with the resultant racial and ethnic diversity) that Jamaica Plain's middle-class activists might exalt, but that market mechanisms are incapable of keeping in place.

"You know," I concluded, "Urban Edge's greatest contribution may turn out to be showing how a stable, truly diverse community can really be established and maintained for the long run. That would be a great lesson for America."

The CDC Movement

Since the birth of the Bedford Stuyvesant Restoration Corporation in 1967, the number of community development corporations has grown dramatically. In the wake of the Kennedy and Javits initiative, perhaps one hundred CDCs had been organized by 1970 under the provisions of the amended federal Economic Opportunity Act. By the early 1990s the National Council for Community Economic Development, the CDCs' national trade association, estimated that as many as 2,000 CDCs had been organized in urban and rural areas around the country. The greatest concentrations are found in inner-city neighborhoods in the Northeast and industrial Middle West.

The most extensive study of community development corporations was completed in 1992 by the Community Development Research Center, an arm of the New School for Social Research in New York City. Through a combination of data collection and field visits, the Community Development Research Center reviewed a sample of 130 established CDCs in twenty-nine cities.

Averaging twelve years in existence, the sampled CDCs were "larger, more complex, and more accomplished" than the average CDC. Just over one-quarter (27 percent) were founded before 1973. As the Research Center noted, "These groups were born of the activist spirit of the '60s—product of the War on Poverty and the Civil Rights Movement, and reactions to the negative effects of the federal urban renewal program." About twice as many groups (53 percent) were founded between 1973 and 1980, while the final one-fifth were established during the Reagan years (1981–88), "a period in which federal funding for CDCs and their programs fell dramatically. Reliance on state and local government, the establishment of public/private partnerships to support local development, and regional and national nonprofit organizations helped these CDCs meet 'the bottom line.'"

Most CDCs are small. In the sample of 130, the typical CDC has an annual operating budget of $700,000 and employs a full-time paid staff of seven: five professionals and two clerical support staff. ("Even these figures overstate CDCs' financial strength," the study noted, "since sampled CDCs have budgets about four times larger than the typical CDC nationally.")

Housing Programs

Low-income housing development is the principal activity of most CDCs. Eighty-seven percent of the sample CDCs are engaged in housing, with most of these (86 percent) assuming the role of developer or co-developer. Most CDCs are involved in both rehabilitating existing housing (87 percent) and building new units (67 percent). In recent years the typical CDC's output has been twenty-one new or rehabilitated housing units a year. (That level of production actually compares favorably with that of private homebuilders. Three-quarters of for-profit developers build fewer than twenty-five units a year.) Over the course of its twelve-year existence, the typical CDC has built or rehabilitated 150 units, of which it still actively manages about 75 low-income rental properties. Other common housing activities include counseling first-time homebuyers, sponsoring paint-up and clean-up campaigns, and operating home-repair and weatherization programs.

Commercial Development

Two-thirds of the CDCs sampled develop commercial real estate as well, most taking on the same roles as catalyst, developer, and manager that they carry out in housing development. CDCs are more likely to develop retail, office, and mixed-use properties than industrial sites. With their housing emphasis, CDCs are naturally drawn to renovating or building local shopping districts that serve neighborhood residents. The typical CDC studied has produced 33,000 square feet of retail and office space, about the size of a small department store in a community shopping center. CDCs active in commercial development commonly organize promotional campaigns for neighborhood shopping districts, work to upgrade streetscapes and security, and administer loan funds to commercial tenants for property improvements.

Slightly more than half of the CDCs sampled (57 percent) also are engaged in developing business enterprises. Most offer technical assistance and counseling to local firms. Many also provide management training and administer Small Business Administration loans. However, only one out of five CDCs currently owns or operates a business. Forty percent of CDCs that have ever been venture capital investors and more than 25 percent that have ever been active business owners have withdrawn as business owners because of the considerable financial risks and staff time and energy consumed. Though a few firms owned by older CDCs have become major businesses, two-thirds of CDC-owned businesses report annual gross sales of less than $1 million, and most management training programs have trained fewer than one hundred people. In short, as housing developers, as commercial developers, as business promoters, the typical CDC is a small business serving small businesses.

Grading Exemplary CDCs

A substantial body of literature has grown up around the community development movement, analyzing and promoting it. Most studies focus on process and projects. Only a few have assessed the impact of CDC activity on economic conditions in their target neighborhoods. It was that information gap that I set out to help fill.

For guidance I turned to two outstanding national support organizations at the core of the community development movement, mentioned earlier in the chapter: the National Council for Community Economic Development and the Community Development Research Council. I asked each organization to recommend a list of the nation's outstanding urban CDCs. My only stipulation was that each CDC had to have been established before 1980, so that I could track social and economic changes over at least a decade in its target neighborhood, through the 1980 and 1990 censuses.

From their recommendations emerged a list of thirty-four "exemplary" CDCs. The organizations ranged from Newark's New Community Corporation (1,200 employees; $200 million annual budget) to Omaha Economic Development Corporation (4 employees; $170,000 annual budget).

Through the national groups' own reports or direct contacts with the CDCs, Delcia and I verified when each began operations and the identification of the census tracts that most closely define their target neighborhoods.

Then we began to crunch the numbers, dividing the CDCs into two groups. Those founded by 1970 were evaluated over the twenty-year span between the 1970 and 1990 censuses; those founded between 1971 and 1979 were evaluated over a ten-year span between the 1980 and 1990 censuses.

Between 1980 and 1990, poverty rates in the twenty-three newer CDC target areas increased from 23 percent to 26 percent for families and from 25 percent to 29 percent for individuals (see figure 3-1). By contrast, rates for the metropolitan areas in which the CDCs were located remained stable over the same period, hovering around 8 percent for families and 10 percent for individuals.

Over the twenty-year period from 1970 to 1990, the family poverty rate in neighborhoods served by older CDCs increased from 19 percent to 28 percent, and the rate for individuals jumped from 23 percent to 30 percent. Over the same period the metrowide family and individual poverty rates were stable at 7 and 9 percent, respectively.

A second measure of neighborhood economic trends is the ratio of average household income in CDC target areas to average household income metrowide. For the ten-year group, average household income in target areas declined from 64 percent to 58 percent of average household income metrowide; for the twenty-year group, the figure dropped from 61 percent to 53 percent (see figure 3-2).

Neighborhood buying power also showed significant trends. For the ten-year group, CDC neighborhood buying power was flat (showing no growth), while metrowide buying power increased 22 percent. For the twenty-year group, CDC neighborhood buying power plummeted 18 percent, while metro-area buying power averaged a 64 percent increase.

Chapter 2 posed the question: is the steady economic decline experienced by Bedford Stuyvesant "an exception to a general pattern of success" among CDCs in general? The sad answer is "not at all." Bedford Stuyvesant's record was about the average experience over the two decades; in fact, Bed-Stuy's decline in neighborhood buying power (12 percent) was considerably less than the decline in neighborhoods served by older CDCs as a group (22 percent). In short, in cities across the country, the thirty-four target areas served by the most successful CDCs as a group still became poorer, fell farther behind regional income levels, and lost real buying power.

A brief summary, of course, blurs substantial variations among the different communities. From a detailed analysis of the thirty-four CDCs, it is evident that a handful of target areas have experienced some economic improvement. (See appendix tables A-1, A-2, and A-3.)

Figure 3-1. *Family and Individual Poverty Rates in Thirty-Four Communities Served by Exemplary CDCs, 1970–90*

Percent

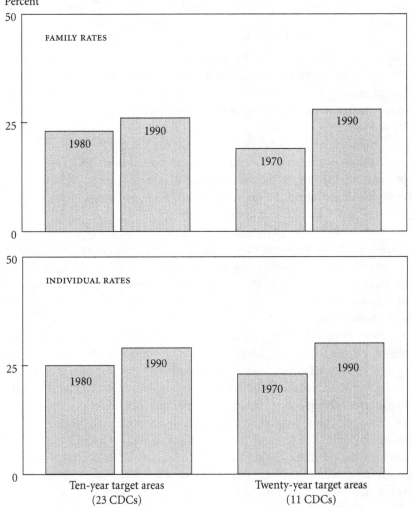

Ten-year target areas (23 CDCs)

Twenty-year target areas (11 CDCs)

—Family poverty rates, individual poverty rates, or both, stabilized or declined slightly in only seven target areas (Boston's Urban Edge Housing Corporation, the area of the South Bronx served by MBD Community Housing Corporation, San Francisco's Mission Housing Development Corporation and Chinese Community Housing Corporation target areas, Washington, D.C.'s Marshall Heights CDC, Newark's New Community Cor-

Figure 3-2. *Income Levels in Thirty-Four Communities Served by Exemplary CDCs, 1970–90*[a]

Percent

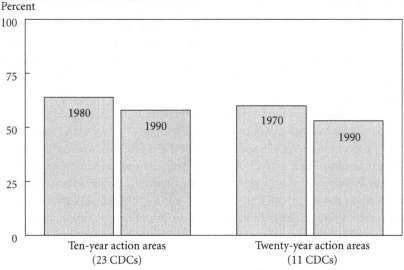

a. Ratio of average household income in CDC to average household income in metro area.

poration, and La Casa de Don Pedro). As the earlier discussion of the experiences of Walnut Hills and Urban Edge shows, an improvement in a target area's overall statistics can almost always be attributed to the impact of some highly localized development. Family poverty rates in the Marshall Heights neighborhood, for example, declined slightly because two large public housing projects were all but abandoned.

—Average household incomes rose slightly as a percentage of regional average household income in only four target areas (Urban Edge, Mission Housing, Walnut Hills, and Phoenix's Chicanos por La Causa). All other target areas lost ground in comparison with the rest of their metropolitan areas.

—Virtually every target neighborhood registered a decline in overall population and, more significantly, in total households. Only target areas served by East Boston and Urban Edge, Cleveland's Miles Ahead, San Francisco's Chinese Community Housing Corporation, and the South Bronx's MBD and Banana Kelly added households.

—Higher poverty rates and declining numbers of households translate into declining neighborhood buying power. In twenty-three of thirty-four target areas, real neighborhood buying power dropped. Efforts to stimulate local retail businesses typically faced a neighborhood market with fewer—and poorer—potential customers. Real neighborhood buying power plummeted by one-third to one-half in areas served by Chicago's Bickerdike Redevelopment Corporation and Bethel Housing, Inc., the Community Development Corporation of Kansas City, Newark's New Community Corporation, New York's West Harlem Community Organization, and Phoenix's Chicanos por La Causa.

By contrast, regional buying power increased in all seventeen metro areas covered, ranging from almost negligible 2 percent growth in Lima, Ohio, and 4 percent in metro Cleveland, to 54 and 85 percent in Greater Los Angeles and the San Francisco-Oakland Bay Area, respectively, to 199 percent in metro Phoenix. Almost invariably, growth in real neighborhood buying power was associated with in-migration of new households, whether new households were primarily yuppies (as in East Boston, Urban Edge, and Walnut Hills), Hispanics (as in Los Angeles's Vermont-Slausson and the South Bronx), or Asians (as in San Francisco's target neighborhoods).

—Fifteen of the thirty-four target neighborhoods had predominantly African American populations (40 percent or more). Ten of the fifteen lost between 6 and 45 percent of their households and had rising poverty rates. Of the five target areas with stable or slightly rising numbers of households, New York City's Jamaica area, for example, is a quasi-suburban community that would not qualify as a high-poverty area; the poverty rate rose from only 12 percent in 1970 to 14 percent in 1990, and average household income has been stable at 85–90 percent of the regional average. A tremendous influx of Hispanics and Asians, replacing white out-migration, has also brought great economic and social vitality to the Jamaica area. Cleveland's Miles Ahead neighborhood is a long-established, stable, middle-class black community in which poverty rates have also been relatively low (13–16 percent).

South Bronx Miracle: A Pyrrhic Victory

The South Bronx deserves special attention. It is the poster child of the community development movement, and deservedly so. Neighborhood-based groups such as Banana Kelly and MBD Community Housing Corporation hung on through neighborhood conditions rivaling the devastation experienced by European cities during World War II and fought for reinvestment to rebuild their communities. With substantial assistance facilitated by the Local Initiatives Support Corporation (LISC), which helped mobilize a massive injection of private mortgage financing, and a revival of services from the city of New York, areas of the South Bronx have been reborn as livable communities for moderate- and middle-income households.[3] Fifteen years ago, smoldering, abandoned tenements and rubble-filled vacant lots dominated the cityscape. As they whizzed past on their way to midtown's Grand Central Station, suburban rail commuters shuddered at the hellish scenes until they, too, became so inured to the destruction that they stopped even glancing up from their morning *New York Times* or *Daily News.*

Today, Fort Apache, The Bronx, has disappeared beneath the trim front yards and modest, new single-family row houses of Charlotte Street, an almost suburban-style subdivision recreated in the heart of the city. It is a remarkable achievement. The statistics in appendix table A-1 covering Banana Kelly and MBD's impact pick up the story at rock bottom (around 1980). Table 3-1 provides a slightly longer view of what has happened in the South Bronx. Between 1970 and 1980 (shortly after both CDCs began their activities) the MBD neighborhoods had lost 71 percent of their households. Banana Kelly's target area was almost abandoned.

The impact of the two CDCs' housing programs is reflected in part in the household growth in the MBD area and Banana Kelly during the 1980s. Since many of the organizations' new housing construction and rehabilitation projects did not open until the 1990s, the census for the year 2000 will undoubtedly record further revival. It is, as I stated earlier, an impressive record for the coalition of neighborhood-based organizations, major mortgage finance institutions, and city government.

Yet what is the long-term prognosis? Even if one acknowledges the South Bronx's mini-renaissance, these two target areas had higher poverty rates in 1990 than in 1970, lower household incomes in relation to regional averages, and far fewer resident households. Overall, real neighborhood buying power had dropped by two-thirds.

---

3. Founded in 1979 by the Ford Foundation (shortly after Franklin Thomas left Bedford Stuyvesant Restoration Corporation to head up the foundation), LISC is the nation's largest provider of financing and technical support for CDCs that are "transforming distressed neighborhoods into healthy communities." Since its creation, LISC has raised more than $3.1 billion from 1,900 individuals and corporate and foundation donors. LISC's loans, grants, and equity investments, leveraging another $3.8 billion in mortgage loans, helped 1,500 CDCs build or rehab over 80,000 homes and create 10.3 million feet of commercial and industrial space.

Table 3-1. *Population and Economic Trends in the South Bronx, 1970–90*
Percent unless otherwise noted

| | Target area | |
| | MBD Community Housing | Banana Kelly Community |
Trend	Corporation	Association
Family poverty rate		
1970	37	34
1980	45	49
1990	43	51
Individual poverty rate		
1970	41	38
1980	47	46
1990	45	53
Local income/regional average		
1970	49	51
1980	43	46
1990	41	37
Total number of households		
1970	20,330	24,783
1980	5,850	9,897
1990	6,279	11,689
Change in total households		
1970–80	−71	−60
1980–90	7	18
1970–90	−69	−53
Change in neighborhood buying power		
1970–80	−78	−69
1980–90	37	28
1970–90	−69	−60

In effect, what happened in the South Bronx was urban renewal by abandonment and arson. The neighborhood organizations have seized victory from the ashes, but it is a Pyrrhic victory for the city. Many more such victories and the city of New York, like the "victorious" Greek King Pyrrhus, will be completely undone.

Do CDCs Make a Difference?

Would target neighborhoods have declined faster without the efforts of the thirty-four CDCs? Did the CDCs "make a difference"? In my review of the census data, I did not try to answer these questions. "What if?" is a question that history can never answer, and complex social issues do not readily lend themselves to controlled laboratory experiments.

One study has compared four CDC-served neighborhoods and four similar ("control") neighborhoods not served by CDCs in Philadelphia and Pittsburgh between 1970 and 1980 (or between 1970 and 1990 in terms of noneconomic data).[4] All eight neighborhoods lost between 20 percent and 51 percent of their population over the 1970–90 period; population loss was reflected in a drop in housing units, which ranged from 4 percent to 37 percent. During the 1980s real median incomes declined between 16 percent and 46 percent in all eight neighborhoods. In six of the eight, poverty rates increased during the decade. In Pittsburgh's Lincoln-Lemington and Hazelwood areas (both *non*-CDC neighborhoods), poverty rates edged downward from 26.7 percent to 24.0 percent and 25.6 percent to 21.3 percent, respectively, even though unemployment increased from 5 to 27 percentage points in all eight neighborhoods, including these latter two.

Between 1970 and 1990 married-couple families as a percentage of all households declined precipitously from 44–77 percent in 1970 to 13–56 percent in 1990. Conversely, the percentage of female-headed households ballooned everywhere, from 19–51 percent in 1970 to 32–72 percent two decades later. By 1990 the North Central neighborhood of Philadelphia (called "the grimmest ghetto in all of America" by one expert) had almost five times as many female-headed households (72 percent) as married-couple households (13 percent).

In head-to-head matchups there was little to choose between the CDC target areas and the control neighborhoods. The four sets of neighborhoods performed about equally in terms of population loss, loss of housing units, increased housing vacancies, and increased unemployment rates. Control neighborhoods actually fared slightly better than CDC neighborhoods, with a smaller increase in poverty rates, smaller losses of married-couple families and smaller increases in female-headed households, and less decline in median income.

4. All statistics and quotations regarding the Philadelphia-Pittsburgh study are drawn from McDevitt (1992).

The only statistic in which CDC neighborhoods outperformed control neighborhoods was in achieving modest increases in owner-occupied housing. At the low percentage changes observed, the increases may well reflect some direct impact of CDC homeownership programs. However, in the north central Philadelphia neighborhood served by National Temple Non-Profit Development Corporation, after homeownership increased marginally from 13.1 percent to 19.7 percent during the 1980s, it dropped again to 14.7 percent by 1990. Improving percentages of homeowners in ghetto communities may be as much a reflection of wholesale abandonment of rental housing by landlords as an increase in actual homeowners.

"What would the National Temple neighborhood be like without the CDC?" the study asked. "In a neighborhood as desolate as National Temple [the CDC area] or North Central [the control area], CDCs may not make the physical impact in new businesses and housing that is possible in other [less impoverished] neighborhoods. However, neighborhood-based agencies [such as the National Temple CDC] which also provide social services can make a great deal of difference in the 'quality of life' for local residents, reducing a desperate life to one at least able to meet some basic needs."

Commenting on a Pittsburgh-area matchup, the study observed that "Homewood has seriously deteriorated over the last 20 years. The impact of the Homewood-Brushton Revitalization and Development Corporation has yet to be demonstrated in the neighborhood demographics. . . . Yet, looking into the future, the CDC is creating a perception of progress and the perception may carry the neighborhood into the future. Lincoln-Lemington [the control neighborhood] lacks such an effort, and its business district is boarded up. Without such intervention, what will the impression of Lincoln-Lemington be in the future?"

Summing up the overall study, the report concluded: "These are neighborhoods where life is becoming more difficult for the residents and those who can flee are doing so. Clearly community development corporations have not been able to stem the massive market and demographic forces at work. . . . Perhaps the fairest way to assess CDC contributions is to look at specific programs over time with reference to what the CDC has done and what the need is in the neighborhood."

Clearly, in trying to assess the neighborhood-wide impact of CDCs, there is a problem of scale. Against the "massive market and demographic forces" are arrayed CDCs that I have characterized as small businesses. How valid is it to evaluate the effectiveness of relatively small neighborhood organizations against the much larger panorama of the neighborhoods they target with their housing, commercial development, and social service programs?

Newark's New Community Corporation

Inadequate scale, however, hardly describes Newark's New Community Corporation. Commonly regarded as the nation's most successful CDC, New Community Corporation dominates life in Newark's Central Ward. It was founded in 1968 in the wake of Newark's bloody, destructive riot the previous summer. Led since its inception by Monsignor William J. Linder, the CDC still works closely with Saint Rose of Lima parish. New Community has built or renovated 2,706 units of rental housing, about half for senior citizens. Almost 60 percent of all units are covered by federal rent subsidies. Three-quarters of all housing in the Central Ward is owned and managed by New Community.

With its staff of more than 1,200 persons, New Community provides extensive social programs for its tenants and other Newark residents. Seven Babyland Nurseries provide day care for 700 children. A new Pathmark supermarket and shopping center attract 50,000 shoppers a week. New Community operates a nursing home, an elementary school, medical offices, a job placement center, a restaurant, a wellness center, and a newspaper. As journalist Nicholas Lemann has remarked, "In the neighborhood where New Community operates, there is almost no private-sector economic activity. New Community, an imaginative and energetic harvester of grants, loans, subsidies and tax abatements from government, foundations and business, owns outright almost everything there."[5]

The Tale of the Tracts traces an intriguing picture of the Central Ward's recent history. Already in steady decline, by the 1970 census New Community's target area still had almost 23,000 residents (88 percent black). Exactly one-third of all residents (33.3 percent) fell below the poverty line, and average household income was only 44 percent of the average income for the whole Newark region.

By the 1990 census the area's population had been halved to less than 11,000. The number of total households had dropped from 6,199 to 3,613. In part, New Community's housing programs had come to dominate the

5. Nicholas Lemann, "The Myth of Community Development," *New York Times Magazine*, January 9, 1994, p. 27.

Central Ward because the community had shrunk to meet the CDC almost halfway. Almost everyone who had the power of choice had chosen to move, except for those housed in New Community's housing developments.

Almost everyone, but not all. In 1988 New Jersey's largest private homebuilder began developing market-rate townhouses in census tract 64, the first such housing built in the Central Ward in two decades. By 1994, more than 600 units were occupied, and the Society Hill project will have 1,100 townhouses when completely redeveloped. Located near Newark's central business district and New Jersey's University College of Medicine and Dentistry, the townhouses have found a strong market among largely black, professional households.

In 1970, census tract 64 was the Central Ward's poorest area. Almost 45 percent of its 824 households were poor; the average household income was only 34 percent of the metropolitan average. Over the next two decades tract 64's previous population virtually vanished. By the 1990 census the 824 households had dropped to 297, but most were newcomers, residents of the new Society Hill townhouses. The number of poor families had dropped from 216 to 16; the number of poor residents, from 1,313 to 88. The 1990 poverty rate was 14.2 percent (only 11.4 percent among families). Average household income had shot up to 68 percent of the regional average, and 135 percent of the citywide average itself. In short, Society Hill was being transformed into one of Newark's more prestigious neighborhoods.

Throughout the rest of the New Community target area, however, poverty levels had remained high (32 percent), and average household incomes continued to slide to 37 percent of the regional average. Despite the 64 percent reduction in total households, because of the much greater affluence of newcomers to Society Hill, tract 64's real buying power declined only 15 percent. By contrast, the rest of the New Community neighborhood lost 39 percent of its buying power.

Society Hill "is a vote of confidence in New Community's ability to stabilize the area," Lemann decided. "The neighborhood feels organized and safe," in part, a result of the 120 unarmed security officers who patrol New Community's housing developments. And perhaps the Society Hill townhouses, occupied by middle-class residents very different from New Community's core constituency, are the greatest testimonial to New Community's impact. It may not be necessary to destroy a neighborhood in order to save it, the basic vision of federal urban renewal programs of the 1950s and 1960s. But New Community, like Walnut Hills and Jamaica Plain, demonstrates the hard reality of inner-city poverty. Poor, minority neighborhoods escape poverty only when new, middle-class households move in. Regentrification has been the only escape route for poverty neighborhoods.

Up the Down Escalator

To an audience of foundation executives on the afternoon of my first visit to Bedford Stuyvesant, I reached for a metaphor to describe the tragic dilemma of community-based, antipoverty programs in a place such as Bedford Stuyvesant. "It is like helping a crowd of people run up a down escalator. No matter how fast they run, the escalator comes back down at them faster and faster. Some individuals can run so hard—some programs will function so well—that they succeed in getting to the top of the down escalator. But then they jump off. *They move.* All the others are carried back down to the bottom, and the climb out of poverty becomes steeper and steeper for those that try later."

"Most foundations support programs to help people run up the down escalator," I told the audience. "The real challenge is to rewire the direction of the escalator so that it is moving with, not against, ghetto residents. That escalator has to carry ghetto residents upward, and generally outward as well. The true 'empowerment zone' is the whole regional economy and the whole regional society."

Old Data or Current Trends?

That speech to the Council on Foundations was in May 1995. My visits to Bed-Stuy, Walnut Hills, Urban Edge, and others occurred in 1995 and 1996. The data I have presented end with the 1990 census. (Income and poverty data actually are reported for 1989.) In late 1997 *Time* magazine's lead article, "City Boosters," proclaimed that "a new breed of activist mayors is making City Hall a hothouse for innovation." Among the mayors cited were Cleveland's Michael White, Philadelphia's Ed Rendell, Chicago's Richard Daley, and Milwaukee's John Norquist. The first three cities were all placed among my cities "past the point of no return" in *Cities without Suburbs* (Milwaukee just barely missed the list). For such cities—and the thirty-four CDCs just analyzed—am I guilty of relying on old 1990 census data that no longer reflect the realities of the late 1990s?

As I continue to present my trend analyses in different communities, I face the constant challenge of updating census data. The census itself releases periodic raw population updates for states, counties, and the largest cities. Income data at the city and neighborhood level are either nonexistent (Census Bureau) or highly unreliable (some commercial consulting services).[6]

For political jurisdictions, I have found two useful and reliable sources of annual data: annual property valuation records and reports on home sales from local boards of realtors. For the 1990s the general picture these records show is that the sustained economic boom has helped cities, but the gaps between cities (and some older suburbs) and their surrounding, more prosperous suburbs continue to grow.

In 1990, for example, Baltimore accounted for 31 percent of its metro area's population but only 20 percent of the gross assessed valuation of all commercial, industrial, and residential property. By 1995 Baltimore had lost another 50,000 residents and dropped to 28 percent of the region's population and only 15 percent of the property tax base. The spectacular revival of Baltimore's Inner Harbor–Downtown area, fueled by substantial public (and therefore tax-exempt) investments like Camden Yards, Ravens Stadium, the National Aquarium, a mammoth convention center expansion, and the University of Maryland's Medical School, was not sufficient to offset the lost value hemorrhaging out of commercial, industrial, and residential property elsewhere in the city. Similarly, while between 1990 and 1995 Detroit slipped from having 24 percent to 22 percent of its region's population, the city's share of the region's state-equalized valuation of all property declined further, from 7.4 percent to 6.1 percent.

The regional housing market did testify to Detroit Mayor Dennis Archer's hard, courageous efforts to revive Detroit: in 1996 home sale prices in the city increased faster than the rate of inflation for the first time in twenty-five years. Indeed, the city's rate of increase was the best in the region that year. Detroit's recent performance, however, has been the exception. As housing markets revived around the country in the 1990s, the improvement in city home prices typically lagged suburban housing markets.

To update neighborhood-level economic trends between decennial census reports, however, one can turn to local school records. Throughout the nation, every public elementary and secondary school and most parochial and private schools receive federal aid to provide children from low-income

6. The Internal Revenue Service does release fascinating, annual county-by-county summaries of median household incomes based on tax returns.

households with free or reduced-price school lunches. Although the income eligibility standards are higher than the poverty level, school lunch figures, particularly for elementary schools, serve as a rough indicator of neighborhood income trends.[7]

Studies that I have done in a dozen regions (Baltimore, Buffalo, Dayton, and others) show that the percentages of low-income children have increased in central-city school systems even as regional unemployment rates have plummeted. This suggests that, in the midst of regional prosperity, many low-income neighborhoods targeted by CDCs are continuing to decline.

Median home sale prices in Chicago's West Garfield Park, the target area of Bethel Housing, Inc., doubled from 1990 to 1995—an eye-catching success story. Yet during the same period the percentage of children receiving free or reduced-price lunches in the neighborhood's five elementary schools climbed from 95 percent in 1990–91 to 99 percent in 1996–97.

Matching local public schools with CDC target areas is tricky. Boundaries generally do not coincide, and enrollment patterns can be affected by citywide busing programs. In many northern cities, in particular, parochial schools provide a low-cost alternative for many inner-city families. In some communities charter schools are also beginning to offer alternatives to the local public schools.

Undoubtedly, many housing programs are having a positive impact. Over fifteen years (1982–97) the New York City Housing Partnership Homeownership Program had built or begun construction on over 13,500 housing units in the city's five boroughs.[8] (I passed one of its construction sites during my tour of Bedford-Stuyvesant.) New owners are primarily working-class families, often new immigrants grasping the first rung on the ladder of homeownership.

However, I have encountered only one instance where a housing revitalization program has probably helped reduce the percentage of low-income children in local public schools: Battle Creek, Michigan's Neighborhoods, Inc. In all others that I have tracked, regentrification has not begun to improve the school environment of the neighborhood's remaining low-income children.

7. High school students are well known for avoiding even applying for free lunch support, no matter how stressed financially.
8. Orlebeke (1997, p. 212).

A definitive evaluation must await the Tale of the Tracts, Census 2000-style. Until then, the evidence of my experience is that, even in the midst of what is now a seven-year economic expansion, prosperity has not reached into the heart of many of America's poorest ghettos and barrios. The down escalator just goes faster and faster. The good guys are not winning with just an inside game.

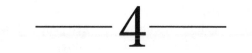

Pilot Small's Airport and the RKO Keith's Balcony: Sprawl and Race

WHAT IS THIS "down escalator"? How does it work? Any American—black *or* white—who has grown up in or around an American city can answer these questions by just thinking about his or her own personal experiences. My own answers begin with "Pilot Small's airport." For a half dozen years immediately after the end of World War II, my family lived in Alexandria, Virginia, in a new, sprawling, garden apartment development called Parkfairfax. Constructed in 1944–45, Parkfairfax was created to house the postwar crush of young government and military families, busily launching the baby boom.

As a child, I would leaf through a popular series of children's books: *Farmer Small, Sailor Small, Fireman Small,* and so on. My favorite was *Pilot Small.* On those Sundays when my father could rip himself away from General George C. Marshall's State Department, he would often bundle the family into our GI-style 1946 Ford and drive out to "Pilot Small's airport." It was somewhere off in the country, what seemed like half an hour's drive away. We would watch Piper Cubs, Cessnas, and (a real thrill) an occasional bi-plane land and take off from the little "general aviation" airport (as I learned to designate such a facility three decades later as mayor of Albuquerque).

When I was a little older, my parents would let me take the bus to downtown Washington by myself, where I would go to RKO Keith's or the Warner

Theater to see *Task Force,* or *Thunderbolt,* or *The Sands of Iwo Jima.* I scarcely noticed that, on the trip into Washington, colored people always had to ride in the back of the bus. As I watched my war movies, I occasionally cast a jealous glance back up into that mysterious balcony where colored people had to sit: a great place to watch a movie, I thought, but where white kids like me rarely ventured.

One-quarter of the 1.2 million residents of metropolitan Washington were "non-white," in the terminology of the 1950 census, but (except for Margaret, our once-a-week cleaning lady) I rarely came in contact with any colored people. None lived in Parkfairfax. There were none at my legally segregated Charles Barrett Elementary School. There were few colored customers in neighborhood stores we frequented, and no colored employees behind the counters. Whether in Virginia or in the District of Columbia, I was rarely in a colored neighborhood, except when my father and I would go to Griffith Stadium to watch the Washington Senators play. (Griffith Stadium was located on Georgia Avenue near the intersection with Florida Avenue, a neighborhood that, over the previous four decades, had become the heart of "the other Washington.")

During the 1960s, after a dozen years away in New York and California, I lived again in the Washington area, this time in the District of Columbia itself. For five years I was a civil rights staffer with the Washington Urban League, working with antipoverty programs in Negro neighborhoods, before moving on to a job with the Labor Department's Manpower Administration.

Now, in the 1990s, I again live in the Washington area after twenty years in Albuquerque, New Mexico. I have revisited the sites of many childhood memories, seen now with a keener professional eye.

I automatically assumed that Pilot Small's airport had vanished, but vague childhood memories left me with no idea where it had been located. A check with local planning departments turned up a small pamphlet, "Ghost Airports of Fairfax County." Pilot Small's Airport must have been the Washington and Virginia Airport, located just three to four miles from Parkfairfax near Bailey's Crossroads and built in 1947. At its peak, 135 Piper Cubs, Cessnas, and PT-19s were tied down at the little airport with its two graveled runways.

Pilot Small's airport had, indeed, vanished. In 1970 the property was sold to a developer, who built Skyline Center, a hundred-acre complex of stores, offices, apartments, and townhouses. Some 38,000 people now live on the site of my Pilot Small's airport and in the surrounding Bailey's Crossroads area (equal to one-third of Fairfax County's entire population in 1950).

In fact, Skyline Center is practically the geographic center of a vast metropolitan region embracing 4.5 million people spread across the federal district, five Maryland counties, a dozen Virginia counties, and three counties in West Virginia. Metropolitan Washington today stretches roughly 80 miles north-south from Frederick, Maryland, to Fredericksburg, Virginia, and 110 miles east-west from Saint Mary's City, Maryland, to Martinsburg, West Virginia.

RKO Keith's, the Warner Theater, and every other movie palace in downtown Washington have also disappeared. (In fact, not a single movie theater is still open in any predominantly black area of the nation's capital.) Griffith Stadium also has long since crumbled under the wrecker's ball, making way for Howard University Hospital. The Washington Senators are gone, too, not once but twice. In 1961 the Griffith clan moved the original fifty-eight-year franchise north to Minneapolis–Saint Paul to become the Minnesota Twins. (The Griffiths were rumored to be looking for a whiter community in which to do business.) Then, in 1971, the David Rusk family and the born-again Washington Senators, an expansion franchise, both went west, the Rusks to New Mexico, the Senators to Dallas-Fort Worth to become the Texas Rangers.

Parkfairfax, though, remains a vale of memories. Completely built out at its inception and always well maintained, Parkfairfax looks exactly the same today, over 200 eight-unit, two-story, red brick or white brick buildings, just as I remember them. There are a few small changes. The bus stops have "Metro" signs rather than "WM&VA" signs. The trees and bushes have forty-five years' more growth on them. In 1978–79 Parkfairfax converted to condominiums; all 1,684 remodeled units are now owner-occupied. Whether occupants are renters or homeowners, of course, would not be visible to the eye, but another change is. A modest level of diversity has come to Parkfairfax. Parkfairfax is no longer all white, but 3.7 percent African American, 3.3 percent Hispanic, and 2.7 percent Asian.

African Americans are hardly invisible in today's Washington area. There are black anchormen and anchorwomen on all the local newscasts. Three of the nine members of the Alexandria City Council are black, as were two members of the seven-member Alexandria school board.[1] The federal government has three black cabinet secretaries, forty members of the Black

1. In 1997, after Virginia switched from appointed to elected school boards, the Alexandria school board suddenly found itself without a single black member for a district in which 40 percent of the pupils were African American.

Congressional Caucus, and 79,000 black employees at all levels in the national capital area.

Clearly, blacks and whites have traveled some distance toward Martin Luther King's dream. However, the hard truths of the Bedford Stuyvesants, Roxburys, and Central Wards, or, in the Washington area, the Anacostia or the Shaw neighborhoods, testify that our nation still has a long path to travel.

My emblematic Pilot Small's airport and the RKO Keith's balcony—sprawl and race—are the twin forces that have dominated urban America since World War II. Urban sprawl and racial segregation feed upon and reinforce each other. The greater the sprawl, the more far-flung the dispersion of middle-class households. The greater the dispersion of middle-class households, the greater the abandonment of older neighborhoods in central cities and older suburbs. The greater the abandonment of older neighborhoods, the greater the concentration of poor minorities in those areas. The greater the concentration of poor minorities, the greater the increase in crime and violence, drug and alcohol addiction, family disintegration, unemployment and welfare dependency, school failure, and neighborhood deterioration. The greater the social meltdown of the "inner city" (which now connotes a set of social conditions more than location), the greater the incentives for those remaining residents who can choose where to live—middle-class households—to join the suburban diaspora.

And so, the cycle of peripheral growth and core abandonment accelerates in many metropolitan areas across the country. Under the impact of regional development patterns, Pilot Small's airport vanished, but, ephemerally integrated, RKO Keith's vanished as well.

Sprawl, Metropolitan Style

It is hard to exaggerate the sprawling geographical expansion of urban America and its impact on both land and people. In 1950 (when I was still looking wide-eyed at Pilot Small's airport), the national census identified 168 metropolitan areas. These I will call "old metro areas." Some 84 million people, or 56 percent of the nation's population, lived in these old metro areas. Typically, they contained one large "central city" and its surrounding county. Of the 168 such areas, 115 covered only one county. Larger, more complex metro areas usually included several counties. In all, the 168 old metro areas contained 304 counties, covering almost 208,000 square miles.

At the middle of the twentieth century, the central cities of these areas dominated the urban landscape and housed much of its population, to an extent largely forgotten now, on the threshold of the twenty-first century. The 193 old central cities contained almost 60 percent of their regional populations; their suburbs were home to only 40 percent.[2] Under the city's dominance, a sense of unity spread over the surrounding region. Most area children attended the city school system. Most area residents used city parks and libraries. Most area workers rode city buses, streetcars, and subways to blue- and white-collar jobs within the city, or, occasionally, to nearby factories just outside the city limits. Most of the region's voters cast their ballots for the same set of local offices. Although there were often fierce rivalries among ethnic and racial groups, common city-based public institutions were unifying forces (except in the legally segregated South, with its sets of parallel institutions).

By 1990 the demographic proportions were reversed. The original 168 old metro areas had sprawled to embrace 345,000 square miles in 536 counties. Some 159 million people, or 66 percent of the nation's population, lived in these old metro areas. However, their central cities had shrunk in relative importance, now housing only one-third of their metropolitan populations; two-thirds now lived in their suburbs.

As the population of the central cities declined, local governance became increasingly balkanized. Just four decades earlier, 60 percent of the nation's metropolitan residents had been governed by 193 city councils and commissions and by 193 mayors or city managers. By 1990, almost 70 percent of the population of the same 168 regions fell under the governance of approximately 9,600 suburban cities, towns, villages, townships, and counties.

Urban growth, of course, has not been limited to long-established urban centers. Another 152 urban areas have grown to a scale to achieve metropolitan status, containing another 34 million persons in 1990. Some of the "young" metro areas are far-flung outliers of great metropolitan centers such as New York, Chicago, or Los Angeles. But most young metro areas have developed as independent urban centers in their own right. Many are located in southern and western states, a result of the long-term population shift to the Sunbelt. Many are also blessed with favorable annexation laws, such that their central cities have been able to capture much of their regional growth within their expanded borders. By 1990 these cities contained 21 million people, or 62 percent of their metropolitan populations, and covered 240,000 square miles in 211 counties.

---

2. Some metro areas, like Albany-Schenectady-Troy, New York, had several central cities.

Thus, after four decades of urban sprawl, metropolitan America (including old and new metro areas) had grown from an area of 208,000 square miles housing 84 million people to an area of 585,000 square miles housing 193 million people. Almost three-quarters of all Americans live in the nation's 320 metro areas. The total population in these areas has increased 128 percent, but the land area accommodating that population has increased by 181 percent. The density of population of these metropolitan areas has fallen from 407 persons per square mile in 1950 to 330 persons per square mile in 1990. By this measure, the postwar development of America's urban areas has been consuming land about 50 percent faster than the growth in population.

Exploding Urbanized Areas

Calibrating the phenomenon of urban sprawl according to the county-by-county expansion of metropolitan areas, however, understates the voracious consumption of land in the postwar period. On the basis of commuting patterns to major job markets, the Census Bureau defines metro areas as groups of entire counties. Yet, on first being added to a metro area, only a small portion of a county may be urbanized. County-based tabulation of the growth of metro areas may add either too much land or too little.

As an example of understated urban growth, from 1950 through 1990 the census defined the Albuquerque metro area as 1,163-square-mile Bernalillo County. By this measure, in the above discussion, the Albuquerque metro area does not register as having grown at all in land area: in 1950 the metro area was Bernalillo County; in 1990 it was the same, geographically unaltered, Bernalillo County.[3]

In reality, from 1960 to 1990 what the census also defined as Albuquerque's "urbanized population" grew from 241,216 to 487,120, and the amount of "urbanized land" from 78 square miles to 226 square miles. While its urbanized population doubled, Albuquerque's urbanized land area almost tripled.

What picture emerges from calculating the growth of America's "urbanized areas" (as contrasted with the growth of county-defined metropolitan areas)? The 1950 census also reported that 69 million people resided in 157 urbanized areas covering almost 13,000 square miles. By 1990 the population of these same 157 areas had grown to more than 130 million people occupying almost 46,000 square miles. While the urbanized population grew

3. In 1992, having assessed the results of the 1990 census, the federal government added two more counties to the Albuquerque metro area.

88 percent, urbanized land expanded 255 percent (which amounts to three times the rate of population growth). By 1990 the average resident of these 157 communities was consuming 90 percent more land area than just forty years before.

I have analyzed data on urban sprawl for all 396 urbanized areas designated in the 1990 census; continuous data are available for only 157 for the four decades discussed above. However, as a speaker and consultant, I have worked in depth in fifty-eight metro areas. On my initial visit I have always taken an auto tour of the region, trying to see examples of new and old neighborhoods, ranging from the best to the worst. (I pay less attention to new commercial areas. After the first dozen tours, I realized that all suburban strip commercial centers and shopping malls look alike.)

Appendix table A-4 presents sprawl data for these fifty-eight regions. Overall, from 1950 to 1990 urbanized land expanded 305 percent while urbanized population grew only 80 percent—an almost 4-to-1 ratio. During the 1980s new suburban growth occurred at an average of about 1,500–2,000 persons per square mile. The density of new development in the 1980s was about one-fourth of the density of population of central cities in 1950 in these fifty-eight metro areas.[4]

No Room at the Inn

This pattern of sprawling growth embodies a vision of metropolitan development dominated by universal ownership of a single-family home in a small, self-governing community distant from the workplace; universal car ownership; and a workplace in a low-rise, parklike setting with immediately adjacent parking.[5]

It is a vision that, in many respects, has been substantially achieved. Since mid-century, home ownership has risen from 40 percent to 65 percent, one of the world's highest rates of homeownership. While the nation's population has increased by only 75 percent since 1950, motor vehicles have increased by 300 percent—and vehicle miles traveled by over 200 percent.[6]

---

4. Appendix table A-4 shows that several urbanized areas experienced new growth at *negative* densities (for example, Buffalo, Detroit, Peoria, and Pittsburgh). Clearly, that is impossible. What the data reflect is that these suburban areas are experiencing overall population loss as older suburbs are now beginning to lose population just as their central cities have for decades. Without doing tract-by-tract analysis, it is not possible to factor out suburban population losses to calculate actual density of new development.

5. See Downs (1994).

6. Bureau of the Census (1975; 1997, table 1010).

By 1990, the average American household owned 1.77 cars, trucks, minivans, or recreational vehicles that were driven over 15,000 miles annually. Over 91 percent of all workers (nine out of ten driving alone) logged one-third of those total annual miles commuting to their jobs, 55 percent of which were now located in suburbs outside central cities.[7]

Critics of this vision object to its wastefulness, citing the high costs of the infrastructure needed to serve low-density development; the loss of precious farmland, greenbelt, and recreational areas; the increased air and groundwater pollution; the growing dependence on oil (particularly foreign oil); and other environmentally based concerns. In the 1990s these issues have fueled the "sustainable communities" movement.

To return to the metaphorical down escalator, this vision of metropolitan development makes no room for low-income households. Although postwar housing construction moved from a retail to wholesale scale, factory-produced, prefabricated homes never succeeded (despite some initial enthusiasm by both private investors and the federal government). Instead, factory-type assembly-line techniques moved outdoors to the building site. Postwar builders such as William Levitt learned to develop giant subdivisions, moving specialized work crews from site to site.

In the early postwar years, homebuilders targeted the moderate-income market, seeking to meet the pent-up demand for new homes by returning veterans and blue-collar workers. In more recent decades, however, homebuilders have increasingly concentrated on a more upscale market, aimed at higher-income households (in fact, the higher the better). Though several builders may be involved in developing a typical subdivision, offering a number of housing styles, all build for a relatively narrow band of the income scale. New subdivisions designed for a wide range of household incomes are uncommon. New subdivisions are rare indeed that purposefully mix middle-income households and low-income households (even if the latter are supported by generous government subsidies).

If not in new suburbs, then, where are low-income families to be housed? According to Oliver Byrum, former planning director for Minneapolis,

> After enough observation and thought, the obvious finally becomes obvious. Low-income people and poverty conditions are concentrated in inner city areas because that is where we want them to be. It is, in fact, our national belief, translated into metropolitan housing policy, that this is where

---

7. Bureau of the Census (1997, table 1015).

they are supposed to be. Additionally, they are to have as little presence as possible elsewhere in the metropolitan area.

It is only a slight overstatement to suggest that an unspoken agreement has been struck between the city and suburbs. Suburban communities don't want poor people, and in some ways the central cities need the needy. The poor don't fit the image of the suburban good life with its neighborhoods, schools, parks, shopping centers and jobs. The cities need them to occupy housing and neighborhoods that the more affluent market has rejected, as statistics to make the case for special funding consideration from higher levels of government, as voters, as clients for the public and nonprofit social service and housing bureaucracy and system. Cities need their housing assistance as a source of financing, and as occupants for redevelopment areas.

Summing up, Byrum continues,

Cheap shelter is to be mostly created by the devaluation of inner city neighborhoods.... Revitalization [of inner-city neighborhoods] is in direct conflict with our national housing policy of devitalization as a means of providing low-income shelter.[8]

Concentrated Poverty: A Racial Phenomenon

Not *all* low-income households are concentrated in poverty-stricken inner-city neighborhoods, however. The country's 320 metropolitan areas in 1990 contained 10.8 million poor whites, 6.9 million poor blacks, and 4.8 million poor Hispanics, almost as many poor whites as poor blacks and Hispanics combined. In a typical metro area, however, three out of four poor whites lived in middle-class, mostly suburban neighborhoods. By contrast, three out of four poor blacks and one out of two poor Hispanics lived in inner-city "poverty neighborhoods" where at least 20 percent of the residents were poor.

Using the 1990 census, I calculated the relative concentration of poor persons by racial and ethnic group for fifty-eight metro areas where I have spoken and consulted. At that time, only 26 percent of poor whites lived in poverty neighborhoods, whereas 54 percent of poor Hispanics and 75 percent of poor blacks did so (see appendix table A-5).

The concentration by race and ethnicity was even more dramatic in high-poverty neighborhoods, where 40 percent or more of the residents were

8. See Byrum (1992, pp. 12–13).

poor: only 5 percent of all poor whites lived in high-poverty neighborhoods, in contrast to 18 percent of poor Hispanics and 32 percent of poor blacks. In effect, only one of out every twenty poor whites lived in a high-poverty neighborhood, the grim circumstance faced by one out of every three poor blacks.

Living in poverty is tough enough for any household, regardless of race. For the great majority of poor whites, however, poverty is an individual household condition. Most poor whites are not surrounded by other poor people. For most poor blacks, and, to a lesser degree, for poor Hispanics, poverty is a communal crisis, as well as an individual hardship.

Segregated housing markets have created this disproportionate concentration of poor blacks and poor Hispanics. There has certainly been progress in breaching the walls of residential apartheid. Progress can be measured first in changes in social attitudes. A poll taken in 1942 found that only 36 percent of whites felt that it would make no difference to them "if a Negro with the same income and education as theirs moved into their block."[9] By 1972 that percentage had risen to 85 percent.[10]

Slow Racial Desegregation

Slow progress can also be measured in actual results. The dissimilarity index first mentioned in chapter 1 can be used to determine how evenly or unevenly a minority group is distributed, for instance, across neighborhoods or classrooms. A score of 0 indicates an absolutely mathematically even distribution, or complete integration; a score of 100 indicates an absolutely uneven distribution, or complete segregation.

For example, if the population of a metro area is 25 percent black, then a dissimilarity index of 0 would mean that blacks make up 25 percent of the population (neither more nor less) in every neighborhood in the metro area. A dissimilarity index of 100 would mean that all blacks, and only blacks, live in certain neighborhoods, and all whites, and only whites, live everywhere else. A dissimilarity index of 65 would mean that 65 percent of all blacks would have to move to other neighborhoods (in the mathematically appropriate proportions) for all neighborhoods to be 25 percent black.

Table 4-1 traces the movement toward greater residential integration in thirty-two of the country's largest metropolitan areas between 1970 and 1990.

9. Thernstrom and Thernstrom (1997, p. 141).
10. Thernstrom and Thernstrom (1997, p. 221).

Table 4-1. *Black Residential Segregation in Thirty-Two Major Metro Areas, 1970–90*

Dissimilarity index (100 = total segregation)

Metro area	1970	1980	1990	1970–90
Northern				
Boston	81	78	68	−13
Buffalo	87	79	82	−5
Chicago	92	88	86	−6
Cincinnati	77	72	76	−1
Cleveland	91	88	85	−6
Columbus	82	71	67	−15
Detroit	88	87	88	0
Gary-Hammond-East Chicago	91	91	90	−1
Indianapolis	82	76	74	−8
Kansas City	87	79	73	−14
Los Angeles-Long Beach	91	81	73	−18
Milwaukee	91	84	83	−8
New York	81	82	82	1
Newark	81	82	82	1
Philadelphia	80	79	77	−3
Pittsburgh	75	73	71	−4
St. Louis	85	81	77	−8
San Francisco-Oakland	80	72	66	−14
Average	85	80	78	−7
Southern				
Atlanta	82	79	68	−14
Baltimore	82	75	71	−11
Charlotte	67	61	53	−14
Dallas-Ft. Worth	87	77	63	−24
Greensboro-Winston-Salem	65	56	61	−4
Houston	78	70	67	−11
Memphis	76	72	69	−7
Miami	85	78	70	−15
New Orleans	73	68	69	−4
Norfolk-Virginia Beach- Newport News	76	63	50	−26
Oklahoma City	90	71	60	−30
San Antonio	77	63	54	−23
Tampa-St. Petersburg	80	73	69	−11
Washington	81	70	66	−15
Average	79	71	64	−15

Sources: Douglas S. Massey and Nancy A. Denton. *American Apartheid: Segregation and the Making of the Underclass* (Harvard University Press, 1993), p. 64; Roderick J. Harrison and Daniel H. Weinberg, "Racial and Ethnic Segregation in 1990," U.S. Bureau of the Census, April 1992; and author's calculations based on census data.

At the outset, segregation levels were very high in both northern metro areas and southern metro areas. Over the next two decades, southern communities progressed at almost twice the rate of northern areas. The largest improvement was recorded in San Antonio, Dallas-Fort Worth, Norfolk-Virginia Beach-Newport News, and Oklahoma City. In other metro areas, such as Detroit, New York, and Newark, progress was nonexistent. By 1990, however, of the thirty-two metro areas listed, only Norfolk-Virginia Beach, Charlotte, and San Antonio had moved from being highly segregated into a status of more "moderate" segregation. Despite some progress, all other twenty-nine metro housing markets were still highly segregated.

Atlanta: Desegregation . . . and Resegregation

How would this statistical index translate into a more practical description of racial residential patterns? In the Atlanta metro area, for example, the African American percentage has held constant at about 27 percent for several decades. Metro Atlanta's dissimilarity index dropped from 82 in 1970 to 68 in 1990, a substantial improvement over twenty years. During these two decades, much of Atlanta's large black middle class moved out of the city into the suburbs, primarily into southern Fulton, DeKalb, and Clayton counties. For the most part, however, new black suburbanites were not moving into new subdivisions but into hand-me-down, older suburban neighborhoods. These older neighborhoods were either rapidly being vacated by former white residents or, at least, were no longer considered choice neighborhoods for middle-class whites moving into the Atlanta area.

In the metro area's ten core counties, the 1980 census showed only twenty-four census tracts with reasonably proportionate racial balance. (As a rule of thumb, I would define racial balance as being within ten percentage points of the regional racial percentages, that is, 17–37 percent black and 63–83 percent white in the Atlanta region). By the 1990 census, the proportion of black residents had increased substantially in twenty-one of the twenty-four tracts. In the space of ten years, eight tracts had gone from racial balance to 60–87 percent black. Steady resegregation accompanied black suburbanization almost everywhere in the Atlanta area.

Atlanta's dissimilarity index score of 68 still left most blacks and most whites living in substantially segregated communities in 1990, but the most extreme apartheid was reduced over the two decades. In 1970, 59 percent of the area's blacks lived in forty-one census tracts that were 90 percent or more black; one-quarter of all blacks lived in eighteen tracts that were totally seg-regated (that is, 99 percent black). On the other side of the color line, in 1970 more than 81 percent of all whites lived in 143 tracts that were 90 percent or more white, and 49 percent—almost half of all whites—lived in totally segregated tracts (that is, 99 percent white).

By 1990, however, only 6 percent of all whites and 10 percent of all blacks lived in totally segregated tracts. The hard edges of total apartheid had been rounded off. However, almost two-thirds of whites still lived in 90 percent or more white tracts, and more than one-third of all blacks still lived in 90 percent or more black tracts.

The Atlanta area offers a test of the proposition that rising economic prosperity will reduce the concentration of poverty. It would be hard to con-ceive of a more vibrant regional economy than that experienced by the At-lanta area in recent decades. From 1970 to 1990 real per capita income in metro Atlanta grew 49 percent, and during the 1980s alone the growth rate was 29 percent, both figures far above the national metro averages for the same periods.

In the wake of the region's strong economic growth, particularly during the 1980s, overall poverty levels dropped from 11.8 percent to 9.6 percent. Among white residents, the poverty rate fell steadily, from 7.0 percent in 1970 to 4.9 percent in 1990. The poverty rate among black residents was 28.6 percent in 1970, or four times the white poverty level. Over the twenty years, black poverty also dropped, to 22.4 percent regionwide, but was still more than four times the white poverty level.

During that same period, however, the number of poverty neighbor-hoods grew dramatically, from fifty-six to ninety-one. Most poverty neigh-borhoods were (and are) located in the city of Atlanta. Atlanta had fifty of the region's fifty-six poverty neighborhoods in 1970 and seventy-two of ninety-one in 1990. As these trends show, however, concentrations of pov-erty formed in older suburban areas as well. Six suburban poverty neigh-borhoods in 1970 grew to nineteen, with the greatest number being in the inner suburbs: DeKalb County and the Tri-Cities area of southern Fulton County.

Equally ominous is the greater intensity of poverty within many of the neighborhoods. In 1970 Atlanta had only fourteen high-poverty neighbor-hoods (40 to 60 percent poor) and five hyperpoverty neighborhoods (more than 60 percent poor). By 1990 the number of high-poverty neighborhoods had increased to twenty-one, and the number of hyperpoverty neighbor-hoods almost tripled to fourteen.

These were not neighborhoods of concentrated white poverty, but of concentrated black poverty. Of the ninety-one poverty neighborhoods in the region, only thirteen (half in the suburbs) had whites in the majority. There were probably only eight in which poverty among white residents themselves exceeded 20 percent; higher poverty levels among black residents probably pushed the other five tracts over the 20 percent threshold. There were *no* high- or hyperpoverty census tracts in which the majority of residents were white.

Although the region's black upper middle class had grown and become suburbanized, many still lived in poverty neighborhoods. Almost one out of five black households with incomes above the regional household median lived in poverty neighborhoods (down from one out of three in 1970). In the Atlanta region an upper-middle-class black household was twice as likely to live in a poverty neighborhood as a poor white household because of continued racial segregation in housing markets.

Despite the region's two decades of unparalleled prosperity, the city of Atlanta itself ended the period more burdened by concentrated poverty than it began, and some inner suburbs were becoming poverty-stricken as well.

Higher Economic Segregation

The trends in poverty neighborhoods for the fifty-eight metro areas I have studied firsthand are analyzed in appendix table A-6. There is a striking contrast between regional poverty trends and neighborhood poverty trends. Between 1970 and 1990 the overall poverty rate for the fifty-eight metro areas increased slightly from 10.7 percent to 11.7 percent. The increase for the group as a whole was due entirely to increasing poverty levels in the industrial heartland, which accounted for all of the twenty-six metro areas (except Oklahoma City) whose poverty levels increased by more than one percentage point. By contrast, over the two decades poverty levels dropped by more than one percentage point in sixteen metro areas, all located along the northeastern seaboard or in the Sun Belt.

However, the number of poverty neighborhoods increased in almost every metro area from 1970 to 1990. In the fifty-eight regions the number of poverty tracts almost doubled; within those totals, the number of high-poverty tracts (that is, with greater than 40 percent poverty rates) almost tripled.

Only in Norfolk-Virginia Beach-Newport News, which experienced the greatest reduction in its regional poverty rate, and Mobile, Alabama, did the total number of poverty neighborhoods decrease. All of the Mobile area's net decrease was accounted for by new development in Baldwin County (located across the bay from Mobile itself). In 1970 fourteen census tracts in then largely rural Baldwin County still had many poor farm families. As the Mobile area prospered, many whites sought out new homes in Baldwin County rather than in Mobile County. Over a period of two decades suburbanization dropped Baldwin County's poverty rate from 22.6 percent to 14.3 percent, and the number of poverty tracts in the county shrank from fourteen to four. Across Mobile Bay, on the other hand, the number of poverty neighborhoods in the cities of Mobile and majority-black Pritchard grew from forty to forty-seven, and all but six of the poverty neighborhoods had African American majorities.

Several other metro areas held their own. In Tallahassee, whose economic progress was spurred by the growth of the state government and Florida State University, the number of poverty tracts was stable, as was the case in Gainesville, home of the University of Florida. In metro Charlotte the number of poverty neighborhoods barely increased. In metro Richmond the number of poverty neighborhoods increased modestly. All were regions with solid economic growth and sustained progress toward greater racial integration.

But economic growth alone is not sufficient to stem the growth of poverty neighborhoods. The Grand Rapids area has had one of the country's most prosperous economies. The poverty rate has been stable (around 8 percent). Between 1973 and 1988, the Grand Rapids area experienced a 55 percent increase in jobs, a rate of increase equal to that in metro Charlotte. Most remarkably, the area had a 22 percent *increase* in manufacturing employment, although undoubtedly education and skill requirements rose for jobs in the manufacturing sector. But Grand Rapids is also a very racially segregated society (a dissimilarity index of 72). Any adverse economic adjustments affecting black workers were magnified within highly segregated black neighborhoods. Despite the region's prosperity, the number of poverty neighborhoods grew from twelve to twenty-two, and almost half of these had minority populations even though the entire region had less than a 10 percent minority population.[11]

In a study of the dynamics of high-poverty districts in 318 metro areas, Paul Jargowsky, a social scientist at the University of Texas at Dallas, found

---

11. Immigration of low-skilled Hispanics into the city of Holland in neighboring Ottawa County also helped increase the region's poverty neighborhoods.

that ghetto poverty increased significantly between 1980 and 1990.[12] The number of all blacks living in ghetto areas increased from 4.3 million in 1980 to 5.9 million in 1990. The percentage of the total black population (of all income levels) living in ghetto areas increased from 20 percent to almost 24 percent. This, however, means that more than three-quarters of the black population does not live in urban ghettos (as defined by Jargowsky). Booming postindustrial economies around Boston, New York, Philadelphia, Baltimore, Washington, and Atlanta, for example, allowed many middle-class blacks to leave what Jargowsky terms ghettos for new suburban homes (even though racial resegregation often followed).

Most ominous for many central cities, the geographic scope of urban ghettos expanded dramatically during the 1980s even as, with the flight of the black middle class to the suburbs, the population density of ghettos declined. The number of census tracts Jargowsky classifies as ghettos grew from 3,256 to 5,003—a 54 percent increase—while population density declined 11 percent in ghetto areas.

In a follow-up study, Jargowsky devised an ingenious "neighborhood sorting index" to measure the degree of economic segregation within different racial and ethnic groups. Jargowsky noted:

> Metropolitan areas usually show incredible diversity, with widely varying levels of and changes over time on most socio-demographic indicators. In contrast, the trend toward greater levels of economic segregation was remarkably widespread. In the 1980s, 108 out of the 111 metropolitan areas for which I calculate a change in Neighborhood Sorting Index had an increase in [economic segregation] among blacks. For whites, [economic segregation] increased in 253 out of 318 metropolitan areas; for Hispanics, [economic segregation] increased in 39 out of 49 metro areas.
>
> This trend is characteristic of virtually every region as well as metropolitan areas of different sizes. For whites, the increases [in economic segregation] were modest but consistent over time. For blacks and Hispanics, the increases were modest in the 1970s but much larger on average in the 1980s. The rapid increases in economic segregation, especially among blacks, have contributed to ghetto poverty. Against the backdrop of modest decreases in racial segregation in the 1980s, these trends suggest that class may come to rival race as the organizing principle of the metropolis.[13]

---

12. Jargowsky (1994). In this study Jargowsky defined a ghetto as a majority-black neighborhood with a poverty rate of 20 percent or more.

13. Jargowsky (1996).

Table 4-2. *Percentage of Racial Groups Living in High-Poverty Neighborhoods, 239 Metro Areas, 1970–90*

Percent

Racial group	1970	1980	1990
All income levels			
White	0.8	0.8	1.4
Black	14.4	15.2	17.7
Hispanic	9.6	8.6	10.5
Poor			
White	2.9	3.3	6.3
Black	26.1	28.2	33.5
Hispanic	23.6	19.2	22.1

Source: Paul A. Jargowsky, *Poverty and Place: Ghettos, Barrios, and the American City* (New York: Russell Sage, 1997), pp. 38, 41.

In 1997 Jargowsky published his most comprehensive analysis of neighborhood poverty.[14] This work focuses on what I have termed "high-poverty neighborhoods," those in which 40 percent or more of the population is poor. Such neighborhoods are clearly in extreme economic and social crisis. In my work I have emphasized the lower poverty threshold (that is, more than 20 percent) because most neighborhoods just past that poverty level (particularly minority neighborhoods) steadily deteriorate into high-poverty status within one or two decades.

In Jargowsky's terminology, high-poverty neighborhoods in which two-thirds of the residents are black are called "ghettos," those with two-thirds Hispanic residents are "barrios," and those with two-thirds white residents are "white slums." High-poverty areas with no dominant racial group are "mixed slums." Jargowsky used these definitions to categorize 2,866 high-poverty census tracts in the country's 318 metro areas. Of the total, 1,329 (or 46 percent) were black ghettos; 334 (or 12 percent) were Hispanic barrios; 387 (or 14 percent) were white slums; and the rest (816, or 28 percent) were mixed slums.

Table 4-2 again shows the disproportionate experience of concentrated poverty among the nation's different racial groups. The percentage of whites of *all* income levels living in high-poverty neighborhoods grew slightly from

14. Jargowsky (1997).

1970 to 1990, but by 1990 barely one white out of one hundred lived in a high-poverty neighborhood. By contrast, for all income levels more than one out of ten Hispanics and one out of six blacks lived in high-poverty neighborhoods. When the situation of *poor* persons is examined in each racial group, their isolation increased across all groups. Barely one out of twenty poor whites was living in a high-poverty neighborhood in 1990, compared with one out of five poor Hispanics and one out of three poor blacks.[15]

Thus poor whites rarely live in "deadly neighborhoods" (that is, high-poverty census tracts), and poor whites infrequently reside in "transitional" or "depressed" neighborhoods (that is, poverty census tracts) where neighborhood conditions and opportunities are usually steadily getting worse.

Jargowsky's findings bring us back full circle to the intersection of race and urban sprawl. Patterns of sprawling metropolitan development divide Americans more and more by income class. Every suburban enclave of privilege is balanced by an inner-city enclave of social misery.

That poor blacks have become more isolated than ever in poor inner-city neighborhoods is, in part, an ironic result of the success of the civil rights movement. The black middle class has expanded dramatically over the past generation. Between 1970 and 1990 the percentage of African Americans in executive, managerial, and professional occupations increased, the result of higher educational levels, general economic prosperity, lowered discriminatory barriers, and affirmative action. As Jargowsky's neighborhood sorting index along racial lines confirms, many black middle-class households have moved from old inner-city neighborhoods to new suburban opportunities.

I do not begrudge their decisions. Every family head must make the best decisions for the family's future, and black families have no greater responsibility to put up with rising crime, declining schools, and deteriorating neighborhoods than anyone else. But black suburbanization has contributed significantly to the greater isolation of poor African Americans.

The dynamics of poverty neighborhoods can perhaps be better understood through an analogy from nuclear physics. Every person, every family can be said to live with a certain level of stress that yields (metaphorically) a low level of radiation. Generally, that radiation is benign and easily contained within a stable community. However, many things can happen to

15. The proportions of poor of different racial groups living in high-poverty tracts in Jargowsky's study of 318 metro areas matches almost exactly the proportions in my sample of fifty-eight metro areas visited (see appendix table A-3).

increase the level of radioactivity within a family: sudden unemployment, a divorce, a severe illness, and the like. Nothing generates more stress, however, than sustained poverty.

As poverty increases, the interaction between stressed families also increases, particularly as stable, middle-class families move away. Once these "control rods" are removed and the concentration of poverty reaches a critical level, a chain reaction begins in the community: crime and delinquency rise, alcoholism and drug addiction increase, schools fall into decline, neighborhoods deteriorate, unemployment and welfare dependency increase, and social meltdown begins.

Poor blacks almost invariably live in neighborhoods that have reached these critical levels. Poor whites almost never do. There is a world of difference.

5

The Sprawl Machine

A FABLE

The Chairman looked up from the well-thumbed, back issue of *Time* magazine as his chief of staff led the procession into the conference room. This is "The American Century," *Time*'s publisher, Henry Luce, had confidently proclaimed a year before Pearl Harbor. America's massive mobilization had indeed keyed the Allied victory over the Axis powers, and, though the Americans would not know it for four anxious decades, America's economic strength and, above all, its message of freedom would ultimately smother the Soviet Union, the third of the century's great totalitarian powers. The Chairman knew that the next fifty years were already a lost cause. The task he had set his chief of staff and the strategic planning group was to determine how to so weaken America that the twenty-first century would be his century once again.

The Chairman nodded almost imperceptibly, and several chairs squeaked as the dozen committee members nervously took their assigned places. The thirteenth, the chief of staff, remained standing by the briefing board at the opposite end of the room.

"America is the most formidable instrument ever created by the Other Side," the chief of staff began. "We have concluded that America can never be defeated by an external threat. America can only be vanquished from within. We must destroy Americans' confidence in themselves."

The Chairman's eyes bored into his chief of staff, expectantly.

"The Strategic Planning Group recommends that we concentrate on eroding American civilization at its most visible points. We propose to destroy America's cities—New York, Chicago, Los Angeles, Philadelphia, Detroit—all their great urban centers. Destroy the core, and within fifty years a majority of Americans will be convinced that America is 'headed in the wrong direction,' that 'government cannot do anything right,' and that 'you cannot trust the government.' Whatever else America achieves—eradicating polio, reaching the moon, inventing the computer, winning the cold war itself—the very visible failure of its cities will erode American self-confidence."

The Chairman frowned as he remembered Sherman burning Atlanta in '64 . . . the Great Chicago Fire of '71 . . . the San Francisco earthquake of '06 . . . the Big One in Los Angeles in . . . (when will that be?). Whatever we've thrown at them, he reflected, only challenges the Americans to redoubled effort.

Another might have trembled at the slightest hint of the Chairman's displeasure, but the chief of staff had stood at the Chairman's right hand for eons and he ignored the Chairman's frown. "We propose to persuade many Americans to abandon their cities voluntarily. We have a plan to encourage them to do just that," the chief of staff continued. "Belial argued that we should exploit that common American view that cities are inherently bad places— Sodom and Gomorrah, stress Jefferson's yeoman tradition, all that— but, having actually spent time among them, Aaron urged that we play to Americans' innate optimism. Aaron," he said, calling one of the committee members up to the front.

Still wearing his hair pulled back in the old style, wearing a frayed brown frock coat, knee breeches, and white stockings, Aaron took his place at the briefing board. "We will subtly recast the American Dream. The American Dream has always been based on a naive belief in opportunity: work hard, play by the rules, and you can build a better life for your children. For millions, the start was a farm on the frontier. For millions more just coming off the boat, a factory job in the cities. And schools, always schools, whether the one-room, little red school house or PS 141."

Aaron could sense the Chairman's impatience, so he hurried on. "We shall give the American Dream a new, more material form: a house outside the city in the 'suburbs,' as we'll call them, a little private yard, a car, 'television' to isolate people in their own homes. No need to weaken America by trying to create another breakaway republic in the Mississippi Valley again. We will create a new vision of the Good Life that will lure millions of Americans into willingly dividing their nation up all by themselves."

Aaron was warming to his argument. "Everything will be organized to sell this new American Dream. Advertising, newspapers, magazines, radio, movies, this 'television' I mentioned, politicians' promises, laws, easy loans, everything. We'll make it just easy enough for certain people to achieve this new American Dream. The politicians will be convinced that every step, every policy is for the public good."

He uncovered a flip-chart headed "Operation Suburban Sprawl." A series of dates and events ran down the page. "These new suburbs will be massively subsidized, but in ways that ultimately jeopardize city life. Cheap mortgage financing for new houses, but no help for apartment renters. Tax deductions for homeowners' mortgage interest, for property taxes, for home sale profits (but only if the seller buys another, even bigger house). Billions of tax dollars to build new highways leading out of the cities into the suburbs, but a relative pittance for city subway and bus systems. We'll make it easy for business to plow over 'greenfields' for new suburban office buildings and factories. We'll make it tough to recycle 'brownfields,' old abandoned factory sites in the cities. Families, jobs, stores will be drawn out of the cities into the new suburbs. The cities will slowly be abandoned by all except the poorest. The cities will be converted into giant almshouses."

The chief of staff stepped back. "The brilliance of this plan is that just as we are succeeding in making the cities a Hell on Earth, these suburbs will become the new Purgatory. Suburban highways will become choked with traffic as driving more and more miles becomes the only way to shop or get to work. The air will fill with exhaust fumes, and runoff from new development will foul streams and lakes. Farmlands and forests will disappear under the bulldozer's blade. And we'll promote a soul-deadening sameness—residential streets that all look the same, strip shopping centers, shopping malls—two-thirds of all businesses will be the same stores from coast to coast. Variety and uniqueness will disappear."

"Why would Americans willingly let all this happen?" One of the committee members had dared to interrupt. It was more objection than question. Old Anarch had always been a skeptic.

"Americans will readily divide themselves to be conquered," the chief of staff responded. "Part of their national myth is the little community of stalwart citizens that govern themselves 'democratically,' the New England town meeting and all that. We have already laid the groundwork for fragmenting these new suburbs into many, many little governments. Each will follow its own perceived self-interest. 'One man's sprawl is another man's tax base.' It will be more effective than another Tower of Babel in dividing these Americans. And they will defend each little town and each little school district fiercely under the banner of 'local home rule.' They will forget that, to achieve great purposes, Americans have always banded together. We failed to keep those lovely Articles of Confederation in effect. We lost the War between the States. But this strategy will divide Americans more than ever. Many will truly believe Jefferson's nostrum about 'that government governs best which governs least.' They will be incapable of uniting to solve their common problems."

("Jefferson didn't even believe that himself," Aaron muttered. "He illegally bought Louisiana.")

"It all will be," the chief of staff concluded, with a deferential bow to the Chairman, "truly diabolical."

"I'm still unconvinced," Anarch interjected. "It just doesn't seem enough. It's too bloodless . . . too lacking in emotional impact. The Americans have many, many fine city neighborhoods . . . good city school systems . . . excellent streetcar systems . . . some with subway systems as well. The cities are all linked by the world's greatest network of railroads. How can we rely on the appeal of this new American Dream to pull millions of Americans away from all they already have? Is there not some factor that can drive them away as well?"

"Race." The Chairman's first word echoed throughout the room. "We have always confounded the Americans over race." With great deliberation, he ordered, "Play the race card."

Finally, the chief of staff broke the silence. "We have many acolytes to recruit. There is, for example, a promising young homebuilder on Long Island outside New York City: Levitt ... William Levitt, I believe. Great attitude. Levitt recently said, 'America can solve its housing problem or America can solve its race problem. America cannot solve both problems.' Have we your permission to proceed with Operation Suburban Sprawl?"

"Execute."

National Suburban Policy

This is, of course, just a fable. There never was a cabal (satanic or otherwise) that plotted the postwar downfall of so many American cities. But such a conspiracy would have been redundant. It would have been hard to devise consciously a more coherent set of national policies to undermine our cities than those that the federal government adopted piecemeal. Collectively, federal laws have added up to a "national *suburban* policy" that has reshaped urban America during the postwar decades. (We can safely focus our survey on federal government policies, knowing that human nature has created enough devilry at state and local levels without any master plan.)

Low-Cost Home Mortgages

The earliest installment of our national suburban policy was probably the National Housing Act of 1934, which created the Federal Housing Administration in an effort to stabilize and then to expand homeownership. The successor to the Home Ownership Loan Corporation, the FHA insured low-interest mortgage loans made by banks and savings and loan associations to middle-income households. In and of itself, such a program inherently favored newer suburbs, with their predominantly single-family homes, over older cities, with their much higher proportions of rental housing.

During its early decades, however, the FHA also promulgated rating standards that systematically discriminated against poorer urban neighborhoods, particularly those with substantial minority populations. The FHA would insure mortgages, its regulations stated, only in "racially homogeneous" neighborhoods. It even issued officials maps "redlining" certain city areas (generally minority neighborhoods), placing them off-limits for mortgage loans, whereas no such strictures applied to the emerging suburbs.[1]

The Servicemen's Readjustment Act of 1944, or the "GI Bill of Rights," was undoubtedly one of the most beneficial pieces of social legislation ever enacted in this country. Almost 8 million GIs returning from World War II, and 12 million more servicemen and -women from the cold war years were able to attend colleges, universities, and trade schools to build the skills that have been the basis of much of America's postwar prosperity. Low-cost mortgage loans from the Veterans Administration (VA) financed homeownership for 14 million veterans. Like FHA-insured mortgages, however, VA-guaranteed mortgages had the effect of accelerating the growth of new suburbs and reducing the demand for housing in older city neighborhoods.

The FHA and VA made the members of the white working class and middle class an offer they could not refuse. In 1934 the FHA began by requiring a 20 percent down payment and single-digit interest loans; by the early 1950s, the FHA required only 5 percent down. The VA went one better, requiring no down payment. As one committed city dweller described the postwar market,

> We could find nothing that could meet our needs in any [city] neighborhood we cared to live in at a [rent] we could afford. Instead, what we did find, poring over the real estate pages of the paper, was ad after ad urging us to buy a house in the suburbs. We weren't interested in living in the suburbs, and had not planned on buying a home, but the terms made us rub our eyes in disbelief. It was impossible to resist at least going out to look. Imagine, a six-room house with a yard of its own which could be 'carried'—amortization, taxes, insurance—for a monthly payment lower than the rent on our one-room apartment.[2]

1. In the 1930s, the FHA was struggling "for all the community support [it] could muster. [It] was not going to pioneer in the thicket of race relations. [The FHA was] going to follow sound business principles in order to protect the solvency of its programs. The FHA wanted its housing to be in harmonious and stable neighborhoods. The insurance manuals suggested the use of zoning ordinances and physical barriers to protect racial stability, and racially restrictive covenants were a precondition of mortgage insurance. The FHA Insurance Manual used in the thirties and forties 'read like a chapter of the Nuremberg Laws.'" Welfeld (1988).

2. Louis Schlivek, *Man in Metropolis*, quoted in Welfeld (1988).

By the early 1950s, the FHA and VA were insuring half the mortgages in America and accounted for one-third of all new housing starts. By 1996 the FHA and VA were insuring just 20 percent of the home mortgage market, but the amount of outstanding mortgage loans covered was still massive: the FHA's mortgage portfolio was $423 billion, while mortgages guaranteed by the VA topped $212 billion.

The Secondary Mortgage Market

Established by federal statute in 1938, the Federal National Mortgage Association (FNMA) did not come into its own until after World War II, when it created the secondary mortgage market. Most of the nation's largest banks, thrifts, insurance companies, and pension funds—the primary sources of mortgage money—were located in the slow-growing East. Much of the new housing demand was developing in the fast-growing South and West, where local financial institutions could not scrape together enough money to meet mortgage needs. The FNMA bridged regional imbalances between the supply and demand for mortgage money.

By 1968, the FNMA became "Fannie Mae," a quasi-private corporation, stockholder-owned and federally regulated. It was joined by "Freddie Mac" (the Federal Home Loan Mortgage Corporation, owned, in effect, by the nation's private savings and loan associations) and "Ginnie Mae," a government agency created to guarantee mortgages backing various federal housing subsidy programs. By the 1970s all three financial cousins had perfected the marketing of "mortgage-backed securities." They would package tens of thousands of FHA, VA, and conventional mortgages as collateral for bonds sold on Wall Street, raising billions of dollars more that Fannie Mae, Freddie Mac, and Ginnie Mae would loan back to frontline mortgage lenders.

The avalanche of mortgage money from the secondary mortgage market gave further impetus to suburban development. Until congressional action in the early 1990s, these government-sponsored enterprises (GSEs) were not required to direct a minimum share of funds raised for mortgages to city-based homebuyers.

The financial impact of the federally chartered mortgage pools was even greater than the FHA and VA backing of private lenders. In 1995 the total value of Fannie Mae's mortgage portfolio was $767 billion, Freddie Mac's $559 billion, Ginnie Mae's $472 billion, and that of other federal programs (primarily the Farmers Home Administration) $44 billion. That amounted to more than $1.8 trillion in the federally organized mortgage pools, the great bulk of it invested in suburban, single-family homes.

By contrast, in 1995 direct federal subsidies for low-income households totaled less than $26 billion, of which one-third was for 1.4 million units in public housing projects and two-thirds paid various forms of rent subsidies for low-income households in private apartments. Attributing an amortized value to the public housing inventory would raise the federal government's annual support of low-income rental housing to about $60 billion.

To sum up FHA, VA, and GSE intervention in the home mortgage market, the federal government provides about forty times more support for suburban-oriented, middle-income homeownership than it does for largely city-based, lower-income rental housing.

Pro-Homeowner Tax Policies

From the dawn of the federal income tax (1913), according to the Internal Revenue Service, taxpayers have been able to deduct home mortgage interest against their tax liability. The intent once again was to encourage homeownership. No such tax offsets were provided for apartment renters. For fiscal year 1999 the annual value of the mortgage interest deduction was estimated to be $54.4 billion in tax breaks for 40 million homeowners (only about one-quarter of whom itemize their deductions).[3] Treating this "tax expenditure" just as if it were a budget appropriation has turned the mortgage interest deduction into the federal government's sixth largest expenditure after social security payments, national defense, medicare, interest paid on the national debt, and medicaid assistance.

Stimulating higher homeownership through mortgage interest deductibility may even be unnecessary. Canada and Australia have achieved America's high level of homeownership without such tax subsidies. However, the home mortgage interest deduction is widely viewed as politically untouchable. Even several "flat tax" proposals discussed during the 1996 Republican presidential primary season incorporated continued deductibility of home mortgage interest.

The Internal Revenue Act Amendments of 1951 created the rollover

3. Bureau of the Census (1997, tables 521, 1204).

requirement for home sales. Ostensibly motivated by the capital gains tax problems faced by defense workers shifting from regions with high housing costs to those with low costs, Congress exempted homesellers from any capital gains tax liability if they bought a home of equal or greater price. The effect was to encourage homebuyers to step up constantly in price, and often step out of central cities and older suburbs as well.[4]

Urban Renewal

Title 1 of the Housing Act of 1949 created the federal urban renewal program. At first glance, this would seem to have been a pro-cities measure. Between 1953 and 1986, the federal government provided $13.5 billion for slum clearance and urban redevelopment. Cities used urban renewal money to redesign central business districts, build multilevel parking garages (above and below ground), and convert city streets into pedestrian malls for specialty stores to attract suburban shoppers again. Luxury hotels and apartments were built to attract rich visitors and residents alike. Efforts were made to upgrade the neighborhood environs of major medical centers, museums, concert halls, and theaters that served city residents and suburbanites.

Unfortunately, the era of urban renewal coincided with the era of international-style architecture: giant glass and steel, single-purpose boxes, sometimes perched on stilts, surrounded by concrete and marble plazas, filled with planters but no people. The varied, chaotic, busy street life that historically defined vital cities was designed out of countless urban renewal areas. Sometimes the traditional grid patterns of city streets disappeared as urban renewal areas aped suburban office campuses. In the many cities I have visited, I have found few urban renewal areas of the 1950s and 1960s to be interesting. Many of the most vital downtown areas of the 1990s are those that had the good sense or good luck to escape the federal bulldozer of the 1960s.

More ominous for the future of cities, however, was the bitter truth of the axiom that urban renewal meant "Negro removal." Needless to say, physical housing conditions in many of the black ghettos that were bulldozed were bad. In the long run, however, the replacement homes of many displaced residents were worse: massive, new high-rise public housing complexes often located in isolated sections of the city. Such massive projects as Robert Taylor Homes and Cabrini-Green in Chicago or Baltimore's Lexing-

---

4. See chapter 13 for a fuller discussion of the impact of federal capital gains tax treatment on housing markets.

ton Terrace and Lafayette Courts became black holes of high crime and poverty that expelled, rather than attracted, middle-class households within gravitational range. In many communities, the federal urban renewal program created both dull, lifeless downtown areas that failed to pull suburbanites back into the city and high-poverty, high-crime public housing complexes that pushed other households into the suburbs even faster.

Federal Transportation Policy

The National Interstate and Defense Highway System Act of 1956, espoused by President Dwight D. Eisenhower during the cold war, was ostensibly justified as a national defense measure. The national network of interstate highways would supposedly allow more effective mobilization of the nation's military resources. Ike remembered the difficulty encountered in moving military units and supplies across the country during the Great War.[5] Broad highways radiating outward also would allow quicker evacuation of America's cities under the threat of nuclear attack. Of course, new highways were two-way streets. Ribbons of concrete allowed new suburbanites to flee the residential areas of cities permanently while still commuting daily back to their city-based jobs.

In launching the most massive peacetime expenditure program ever, President Eisenhower permanently reshaped metropolitan America. From 1956 to the mid-1990s, when the 54,714-mile interstate highway system was nearing completion, the federal government spent a total of $652 billion (in 1996 dollars) on highway aid. Despite the program's original emphasis on long-distance interstate roads, over half of the funds had gone into building 22,134 miles of new highways *within* metropolitan areas. This fostered a vast decentralization of the country's urban centers. By contrast, under the Urban Mass Transit Act of 1964, federal aid to public bus and subway systems, which tend to promote greater centralization, totaled only $85 billion (in 1996 dollars). Federal transportation policy, in effect, channeled almost seven times more money into suburban sprawl than into helping maintain more compact urban centers.

"9.9 cents a gallon" is the price on an old gasoline pump, part of a Depression-era gas station preserved in the Museum of Albuquerque, "2.3 cents

5. After World War I, on General Pershing's orders, Major Eisenhower led a convoy of seventy-nine military vehicles over the partly paved Lincoln Highways from Washington, D.C., to San Francisco. The trip took fifty-six days.

federal and state taxes included." Sixty years later, in 1996, the average gallon of gas cost 128.8 cents, including a federal tax of 18.4 cents and state tax of 19.3 cents.

Faced with a short-term spike in nominal gas prices in 1996, Republican presidential candidate Bob Dole was quick to call for a repeal of the 4.3 cents per gallon that had been added as part of President Clinton's deficit reduction package three years earlier. Just weeks before, the national media had heralded the fact that, in inflation-adjusted terms, the cost of a gallon of gasoline had reached an all-time low.

Indeed, by a wide margin, Americans enjoy the cheapest gasoline in the world. Filling up the tank costs about one-third as much as it does in European countries, where gasoline sells at the equivalent of about $3–$4 a gallon. In Europe the untaxed cost of gasoline is about $1 a gallon, the same level as in the United States. The difference is almost entirely in the level of taxes paid. U.S. national policy is to promote cheap gasoline, maximize the use of private automobiles, and, in the process, subsidize the massive decentralization of urban activity across the suburban landscape. European countries keep gasoline relatively expensive, subsidize public transportation extensively, and generally encourage a more compact urban lifestyle.

Does cheap gasoline mean that Americans spend less on transportation than Europeans? Not at all. It is estimated that the average, auto-dependent American household spends almost 20 percent of its annual income on transportation compared with half that level for the average European family. In theory, we may value the high degree of mobility many American households have. In practice, most of those same households have no alternative to driving an average of 1,000 miles a month per vehicle in order to reach their job sites, basic shopping areas, and essential services.

Sewage Plant Expansion

In the Clean Water Act of 1972, the federal government moved, with salutary intent, to clean up the country's polluted lakes and streams. Since 1956 the federal government has provided $130 billion (in 1996 dollars) in grants to state and local governments for new sewage treatment plants and major sewer lines. Much of the money (perhaps one-third) has been spent not to remedy old problems but to provide new capacity to support new suburban growth. The federal grants have covered 75 percent of the costs of wastewater treatment plants, thus creating heavy subsidies for new development.

Redlining Black Americans

Who benefited from new suburban opportunities created? As Melvin Oliver and Thomas Shapiro have written, "Home ownership represents not only an integral part of the American Dream but also the largest component of most Americans' wealth portfolio. . . . The value of the average housing unit tripled from 1970 to 1980, far outstripping inflation. Thus households that owned homes before the late 1970s had an opportunity to accumulate wealth in the form of home equity, while those that did not missed an excellent opportunity."[6]

Though the gap had closed slowly over the decades, in 1988 homeowner-ship among blacks (42 percent) seriously lagged homeownership among whites (64 percent). Part of the gap could be ascribed to lower incomes among blacks in comparison with whites; in the 1990 census black median family income was only 58 percent of white median family income. But it is clear that the past exclusion of blacks from new suburban housing still lim-ited access (though it was much improved) to good mortgages, and the price exacted by segregated housing patterns has shrunk the black community's wealth. Blacks make up approximately 11 percent of the nation's population and earn about 7 percent of the nation's income, but own only 3 percent of the nation's accumulated wealth.

The home equity and wealth gap remains wide even though blacks with comparable education have almost closed the income gap with whites. Table 5-1 charts the median household incomes of white and black households headed by individuals with comparable educations. In 1988 black college graduates earned 80 percent of the income of white college graduates. Black householders with postgraduate degrees earned 77 percent of the income of white householders with postgraduate degrees. True income equality was attained only at the bottom of the social heap. Whites and blacks with no more than an elementary school education had virtually identical earnings.

By contrast, the gap in home equity is staggering (table 5-1). Even black college graduates and professionals have less than one-third the value of home equity that their white counterparts do. In fact, white high school dropouts typically have greater home equity than black professionals.

As mentioned earlier, segregated housing patterns add to this disparity in home equity–based wealth. Income and home values calculated for fifty-

6. Oliver and Shapiro (1995, p. 198).

Table 5-1. *Median Household Income and Home Equity of Blacks and Whites with Comparable Educational Attainment, 1988*

Thousands of dollars unless otherwise noted

Educational attainment	White median	Black median	Percentage of black-to-white
Median household income			
Elementary	7,001	6,942	99
Some high school	11,554	8,724	76
High school degree	17,328	11,534	67
Some college	27,594	21,076	76
College degree	35,068	28,080	80
Postgraduate	40,569	31,340	77
Median home equity			
Elementary	23,044	2,500	11
Some high school	22,310	430	2
High school degree	29,424	1,199	4
Some college	33,489	5,714	17
College degree	49,365	15,170	31
Postgraduate	56,373	17,796	31

Source: Adapted from Melvin L. Oliver and Thomas M. Shapiro, *Black Wealth/White Wealth: A New Perspective on Racial Inequality* (London: Routledge, 1995), table A5.2.

eight metro areas for 1990 are particularly revealing. In the Baltimore metro area, for instance, the average black homeowner had an income of $39,000 and a home worth $69,000. By contrast, the average white homeowner in metro Baltimore had an income of $55,000 and a home worth $133,000. In effect, for every dollar of income, the black homeowner received $1.68 in home value, whereas the white homeowner received $2.40. Within metro Baltimore's still segregated housing market (its segregation index was 71 in 1990), the average black homeowner got only 70 percent of the home value per dollar of income that the average white homeowner received. (See appendix table A-7.)

I have driven through many Baltimore-area neighborhoods, including many well-maintained, black middle-class neighborhoods. I know that the lesser value of black-owned homes rarely reflects the widely held white prejudice that "blacks don't keep up their neighborhoods." I also have no doubt that a black neurosurgeon joining the faculty of Johns Hopkins Medical

School could buy a home of any value he or she could afford anywhere in the Baltimore area.

What the racial home equity gap does reflect is that most black homeowners live in majority-black neighborhoods where whites will no longer buy homes. When the 74 percent of the Baltimore area's potential homebuyers that are white take themselves off the market for houses in black neighborhoods, the potential demand and competition for those homes are automatically reduced. With the demand for homes in predominantly black neighborhoods solely dependent on the buying power of the black community, increases in home value are automatically dampened.

Because metro Baltimore still has segregated housing markets, its black homeowners pay, in effect, a 30 percent "segregation tax." Black homeowners in fifty-eight metro areas typically paid a segregation tax of 17 percent in 1990. In only a handful of metro areas (including Albuquerque) did black homeowners receive about the same housing value for each dollar of income as did white homeowners. With a low segregation index (39), Metro Albuquerque is also one of the nation's most integrated communities.

In fact, relative segregation of housing markets has a statistically significant impact on the variation in segregation tax among different regions. Simple regression analysis shows that for every point increase in the segregation scale, the segregation tax increases by five-tenths of a percent. Thus it is not surprising to find that black homeowners pay little or no segregation tax in the least segregated housing markets (like Albuquerque) and the highest segregation tax in the most segregated housing markets (for example, 43 percent in metro Detroit).

Playing the "race card" has thus robbed black Americans of many of the benefits of the redefined, postwar American dream. "America can solve its housing problem or America can solve its race problem. America cannot solve both problems." While the civil rights movement struggled to unite Americans, the sprawl machine inexorably worked to divide them.

An Insider's Testimony

Perhaps the best way to sum up the full impact of the sprawl machine is to cite expert testimony from within the real estate development industry itself. Christopher B. Leinberger is the managing partner of Robert Charles Lesser & Company, the largest independent real estate advisory firm in the

country. Leinberger's firm specializes in helping real estate investors identify the hottest places to invest in metropolitan areas across the nation.
Leinberger is also a thoughtful analyst of his industry who has written per-
ceptively about the very trends he has helped to promote.

Over the past thirty-five years, Leinberger writes, what has become
the fundamental unit of metropolitan areas is the "metro core," the area in
which the vast majority of export and region-serving jobs are located.[7] First-
generation metro cores are, of course, the original downtown hubs and immediately adjacent areas. Shortly after World War II, most upper-middle
and high-end households abandoned the gracious, traditional neighborhoods around these downtown cores for new suburban communities. Re-
tailing followed into new regional shopping malls, and almost all new jobs
were being created in office complexes and new industrial parks outside the
original core areas.

The second generation of metro cores emerged during the 1960s, typically providing new office space and industrial locations two to six miles
from downtown. Examples would be the Stemmons Freeway area in Dallas,
mid-Wilshire in Los Angeles, and the area around the Northeast Express-
way in Atlanta. Typically, the prosperity of these office-oriented, second-
generation metro cores has been brief, and most are now failing. They have
fallen victim to the decline of the neighborhoods around them, in the wake
of the poverty expanding outward from inner-city ghettos and barrios, or,
merely as a result of their own inadequacies: as sterile strips of boxy, 9-to-5
office buildings with few surrounding mixed uses and amenities, they have
been unable to compete with newer, third-generation metro cores.

Edge Cities

The spectacular growth of third-generation metro cores, dubbed "edge cities," has attracted much attention.[8] All metro areas in the country, regardless
of population size, have a third-generation metro center, Leinberger claims,
and they all share a unifying characteristic: they are located adjacent to the
vast concentration of upper-middle and high-end housing districts. "All such
metro cores in the country have this characteristic," Leinberger explains,
"because the bosses live in the high-end housing districts and want to minimize their commutes and the commutes of the firm's senior management."[9]

7. Leinberger (1996).
8. Garreau (1991).
9. All quotations from Leinberger are from Leinberger (1996, pp. 203–22).

"Upper-middle and high-end housing tends to heavily concentrate in most metropolitan areas," Leinberger continues. "By understanding the limited access highway system, [and then] by placing a point in the downtown and drawing a roughly 90 degree arc that encompasses the high-end housing concentration, [one can] define the 'favored quarter.' This is where upwards of 80 percent of all commercial real estate activity and job growth took place over the past generation."

Third-generation metro cores, such as Tyson's Corner on the I-95 beltway outside Washington, the Perimeter Center outside Atlanta, and the O'Hare Airport area in Chicago, experienced explosive growth in the 1970s and 1980s. Despite only two decades of existence, by the end of the 1980s many had more occupied office space than the old downtowns.

Following the real estate slump of the late 1980s and early 1990s, many third-generation metro cores have resumed their growth, but generally at rates only slightly higher than those of their metro areas as a whole. Some even grew less rapidly than their metro rates for the first time. Leinberger identifies three reasons for the slowdown: traffic saturation, growing neighborhood opposition to further growth, and the "character" of many such edge cities. All began with a suburban character: relatively low densities with upward of 70 percent of their land area dedicated to moving and parking cars. Third-generation metro cores that are becoming denser, more urban environments with a greater emphasis on pedestrian-scale activities are still growing vigorously. Those that have retained their excessively suburban character are sliding toward stagnation as fourth-generation metro centers are now evolving in many regions.

Fourth-generation office-oriented metro cores, such as Fair Lakes on I-66 west of Washington and Plano on the Dallas Tollway, lie four to twelve miles farther out from the third-generation metro cores, always moving away from the center city. They are characterized by very low-density, heavily landscaped office campuses.

The Future of Metro Cores

What does the future hold for the different generations of core areas? Leinberger sees only three possibilities for the original downtown cores: stability, moderate decline, or severe decline. Downtowns consistently capture their share of employment in only three sectors: professional services, finance, and government. Relative stability can probably be found in a few downtown areas: Washington, Seattle, Portland, San Francisco, midtown

Manhattan, and Boston, all of which have strong employment bases in those three sectors, combined with substantial high-end housing and retail sectors serving large influxes of tourists, as well as the residents of nearby, still affluent city neighborhoods.

In the not-too-distant future, the majority of downtowns will experience a moderate decline. Some may see their retail sector flourish to a degree, buoyed by successful convention centers, sports stadiums and arenas, and tourist attractions. Yet these activities will do little to regenerate the downtown employment base. Leinberger places Denver, Baltimore, and San Diego solidly in this category. Others, such as Atlanta, Philadelphia, and Los Angeles, "could slip into the severe decline category if remedial action is not taken, because all product categories (office, industrial, housing, and retail) are in relative decline."

Severely declining downtowns—those of Detroit and Saint Louis are prime examples—have retained virtually no upper-end housing or any retail base, nor do they have any prospect of developing either. The impact of convention business or sports facilities is very limited because visitors flee the downtown immediately after the event. Office occupancy is stagnant or even declining. "In essence, there is 'no there there,'" Leinberger concludes.

Most second-generation metro centers also suffer from having "no there there." Most were created solely for the office market and have little retail or nearby high-end housing. Among second-generation metro cores, an extraordinary public investment, such as the Washington area's Metro system (which Leinberger characterizes as "the longest subway system in the world and the safest in the country") can spur office, retail, and housing development at major subway stops, as has happened around Court House and Ballston in Arlington County, Virginia, and Chevy Chase and Bethesda in Montgomery County, Maryland.

Some third-generation metro cores are "densifying" by becoming mass transit hubs, developing high-density apartments and condominiums, upgrading and expanding retail stores, and generally creating a more urban feel. The key to the success of such urbanizing metro cores as Atlanta's Buckhead area and Perimeter Center, Denver's Cherry Creek, and Country Club Plaza in Kansas City is, in Leinberger's view, that they offer "one of the few, if not the only, safe urban environments in the metropolitan area."

As noted above, however, Leinberger expects suburban-character, third-generation metro cores to decline slowly. Part of the reason is racial.

Research has shown that the white population has an aversion to shopping or living in a community where there is more than a 20 or 25 percent mi-

nority population. Whenever a community or shopping center goes over
the line, it becomes virtually 100 percent minority very rapidly. This kind
of change generally affects a metro core in the demographics of the shopping centers and malls and then the rental apartment housing stock. Both
can change very quickly.... In an overbuilt local rental apartment market,
for example, owners can offer minority occupants low rents in a better
neighborhood than they live in. Where this has occurred, the new minority residents have tended to have children who attend the local elementary
schools initially. White flight from the school district occurs, generally in a
rolling fashion as the minority children get older and enter junior and senior high school. The impact on the surrounding single-family housing,
which almost exclusively will have a majority white population, and the
office market is delayed. There has not been enough experience around
third generation metro cores to document this impact or how fast it occurs. Conventional wisdom, however, suggests that there will be a decline
in values, white flight from the neighborhoods, and a movement of office
users to alternative metro cores when their leases, which generally average
five years in length, expire.

Continuing the general theme, Leinberger believes "the underlying
reason for the growth of fourth-generation metro cores is undoubtedly fear.
In spite of the fact that violent crime has remained stable over the past 20
years ..., the perception persists that crime has become significantly worse.
Much of this perception is based on rapidly growing gang activity, which is
wrongly assumed to be a predominant factor in every minority community
regardless of its socioeconomic base. The majority white population moving to the residential districts serving fourth generation metro cores sees the
move as a way to ensure safety."

Pondering the social and environmental implications of these trends
for the future of our metropolitan areas, Leinberger foresees some grim
changes:

—The poor and working poor in central cities and inner suburbs will
become increasingly isolated from new employment growth in far-distant
fourth- and fifth-generation metro cores.

—Inner suburbs will go into a rapid decline without new jobs or the
cultural and civic institutions that still claim regional support successfully
for downtown areas.

—Declining tax bases in the central city and inner suburbs will exacer-
bate existing social problems, and state governments will step in to take over
more and more functions of the local governments and school systems.

—Urbanized land will increase at rates eight to twelve times faster than underlying population and employment growth.

—Air and water pollution and traffic congestion will all grow worse because of the nearly exclusive reliance on automobile transportation. ("If the economics of oil-based automobile transportation ever radically change," Leinberger cautions, "we will have painted ourselves into a corner with few good options.")

Though "this is both the best of times and the worst of times for our metropolitan areas," Leinberger concludes, "as a nation, we continue to ignore the negative consequences of how we are building [our metropolitan areas] where 75 percent of all Americans live." Like some atomic scientists in World War II's Manhattan Project, Chris Leinberger is clearly troubled by the kind of world he is helping to create.

6

The Poverty Machine

AMERICA KNOWS HOW to fight a successful war on poverty. In the early 1960s, when Michael Harrington was writing his classic study, *The Other America: Poverty in the United States,* which seized the attention of Jack and Bobby Kennedy, almost 39 million persons, 22 percent of all Americans, would have been classified as poor.[1]

Fighting the Elderly's War on Poverty

Of that total, 5.5 million persons were aged sixty-five and older. More than 35 percent of all elderly persons lived in poverty. Just one generation later, in 1995, the poverty rate among the elderly was down to 10.5 percent. In fact, the poverty rate among America's senior citizens was less than the poverty rate for everyone else (14.1 percent).[2] On the threshold of the New Frontier and the Great Society, more than one out of three elderly persons lived in poverty. Three decades later, barely one out of ten senior citizens was poor. By any definition, that was surely one victory in the war on poverty.

1. Harrington (1962).
2. Bureau of the Census (1970, table 502). The federal government did not officially define a poverty level until 1964, so all calculations for earlier periods are retrospective.

Expanding Social Security

The war on poverty among the elderly was fought primarily by federal government programs and policies. The first milestone was the enactment of the New Deal's Social Security Act of 1935. Nevertheless, by 1960, after social security's first twenty-five years, the average retired couple's monthly check still was barely $113, or about 28 percent of median household income that year.[3]

Beginning in the 1960s, successive Congresses and administrations boosted social security benefits dramatically. One key step occurred in 1965, when Representative Wilbur Mills, all-powerful chairman of the House Ways and Means Committee, shepherded through a 25 percent increase in retirement benefits unmatched by any increase in payroll taxes. Another occurred in 1972, when benefit levels were automatically indexed to the increase in the consumer price index (to be effective in 1975). Indexing social security benefits yielded a steady increase in the real buying power of retirement checks if, as Congress determined in 1997, the consumer price index, as constructed by federal bureaucrats, systematically overstated the real increase in the cost of living.

By 1995 the average married couple's monthly retirement benefit from social security was $1,221, or some 43 percent of median household income that year.[4] Since 1960 the typical social security check had risen 110 percent (adjusted for inflation). During the thirty-four years since 1960 the federal government had more than doubled the real value of direct cash support of elderly citizens.

Protecting Pensions

Another significant federal policy was the Employee Retirement Income Security Act (ERISA) of 1974. ERISA extended federal regulatory oversight to private pension plans, which, by 1992, covered 41 percent of all private sector workers. ERISA helped assure workers that company and union pension plans would not be abused or mismanaged but could be counted on as building blocks for their retirement years. By 1993 private pension plans were paying out $156.3 billion in annual benefits to retirees, which represented a 9,200 percent increase in total payments since 1960, when just

3. Bureau of the Census (1997, table 739).
4. Bureau of the Census (1997, tables 588, 717).

$1.7 billion was paid out to private pensioners.[5] Adjusting for a fourfold increase in inflation, the average retiree's private pension in 1993 was worth more than five times its monthly value in 1960.

With government employment approaching 18 percent of the total labor force, public employee retirement plans also played a significant role in the lives of elderly Americans. The average federal annuitant's monthly benefit grew from $107 in 1960 to $1,698 in 1996, or about 200 percent in real value. Total payments to retired state and local government retirees increased from $12 billion in 1980 to $53.4 billion in 1994, which amounted to another 150 percent increase in *total* real value in just fourteen years.[6]

Despite periodic recessions, recent decades have been characterized by steady economic growth, allowing many households to build their own retirement nest eggs. Once again, federal tax policy played an important role. Internal revenue code amendments promoted tax-deferred savings plans such as Keogh plans and individual retirement accounts ($152.4 billion in assets in 1995), and 401(k) employee savings plans ($44 billion paid out in benefits in 1993).[7]

Increasing Home Equity

The rising value of the family home also helped build retirement incomes. Until the 1997 tax reform (see chapter 13), any gain from selling one's home was subject to federal capital gains taxes. However, tax law did permit a one-time exclusion of $125,000 in capital gains for home sellers after age fifty-five. This allowed many older homeowners to convert some home equity into retirement income.

Creating Medicare

Public subsidies for the elderly were not restricted to money income. Medicare's passage in 1965 put another major building block in place. By 1994 medicare reimbursements were worth more than $4,800 a year for each elderly enrollee.[8] The program's comprehensive health coverage vastly improved the health care of seniors and alleviated the threat of major medical bills depleting their savings. Also, by relieving employers of providing high-

5. Bureau of the Census (1997, tables 592, 593).
6. Bureau of the Census (1997, tables 590, 591).
7. Bureau of the Census (1997, table 594).
8. Bureau of the Census (1997, table 161).

cost health insurance for older employees, medicare allowed many older workers to continue working in full- or part-time jobs, effectively extending their earning power.

Other Federal Subsidies for the Elderly

There have been many more in-kind subsidies for the elderly. By 1993 HUD had financed the construction of 507,500 units of public housing for the elderly. Some 1.7 million seniors either lived in federal public housing projects or received rental assistance through federal rent vouchers. Hundreds of thousands of additional housing units for elderly tenants have been built by non-profit organizations, aided by federal subsidies. In 1992, 1.2 million lower-income senior citizens were assisted by the federal food stamp program.[9] Under the Older Americans Act, the federal government makes grants to states for a wide range of social services, counseling, and recreation programs for senior citizens; the act's appropriations topped $865 million in fiscal year 1998.

Through almost four decades of successive presidents, senators, and congressmen, U.S. society has sanctioned spending the money necessary to ensure that, if retirement would not exactly bring guaranteed golden years for all Americans, raw want would be minimized and a comfortable retirement provided for most. By 1996 at least 38 cents of every federal dollar was spent on direct cash assistance, medical services, and programs for the elderly.

With the huge baby boom generation beginning to reach retirement around the year 2010, this massive commitment of society's resources cannot be sustained without significant reforms. Will Congress and the president muster the political courage to take the necessary actions? (The earlier changes are enacted, the more modest they need be.) The 1997 balanced budget agreement was not reassuring. At the last moment, President Clinton and the Republican congressional leadership backed down on Senate-enacted measures to postpone modestly the age of retirement eligibility and boost monthly medicare premiums for wealthier retirees. I am confident, however, that, crablike, Washington politicians will soon edge their way into adopting modest but essential changes rather than face the draconian cuts that continued procrastination would ultimately require. America's future retirees will not be thrust back into pre-1960s conditions. The war on poverty among the elderly, I believe, has been won permanently.

9. Bureau of the Census (1996, tables 1203, 579).

Reducing Poverty among Urban Whites

I would also argue that our nation has fought a successful war on poverty among urban white Americans. As noted in chapter 3, in urban America the 1990 census counted 10.8 million poor whites, about as many as poor blacks (6.9 million) and poor Hispanics (4.8 million) combined. But the white population of the country's 320 metropolitan areas was 140 million in all. Only about one out of every thirteen white residents of our metro areas (7.7 percent) was poor in 1990. By contrast, the poverty rate among Hispanics was 24.5 percent and among blacks 27.5 percent, or three to four times as great as poverty among whites.

Furthermore, as both my analyses and field observations and Paul Jargowsky's extensive census studies showed (cited in chapter 4), there were relatively few poor white neighborhoods. At the higher poverty level (more than 40 percent poverty rate), Jargowsky found that only 14 percent of all high-poverty neighborhoods were "white slums" (where whites constituted at least two-thirds of the residents).

I have not calculated a comparable percentage for poverty neighborhoods (more than 20 percent poverty rate) in all fifty-eight metro areas I have visited. Undoubtedly, the proportion of poverty neighborhoods in which whites constituted at least two-thirds of all residents would be somewhat higher than 14 percent.

An extreme example would be metro Pittsburgh, where poor whites outnumbered poor blacks by three to one. With the collapse of the steel industry in the 1970s and 1980s, poverty soared in both Pittsburgh itself and in the "Mon Valley" steel towns. The number of poverty tracts jumped from 82 to 144 during the two troubled decades. Categorizing poverty neighborhoods by predominant racial group (at least two-thirds of residents were of one group or another), by 1990 there were 85 white poverty tracts (twice the number in 1970), 35 black poverty tracts, and 24 mixed-race poverty tracts.

At the other extreme would be metro Memphis, where the racial proportions of poverty were reversed: poor blacks outnumbered poor whites by three and a half to one. In 1990 there were 7 white poverty tracts (the same number as 1970), 63 black poverty tracts, and 17 mixed-race poverty tracts. Thus, between my two extreme examples, white poverty neighborhoods as a percentage of all such neighborhoods ranged from 59 percent (metro Pittsburgh) to 8 percent (metro Memphis).

In regions like Pittsburgh, the growth in poor white neighborhoods reflected both the impact of major factory layoffs on traditional white, blue-collar neighborhoods and the constant tendency toward greater income segregation promoted by ever-outward suburbanization. Compared with the expansion of poor black and poor Hispanic neighborhoods, however, the growth of poor white neighborhoods in central cities and older suburbs was still relatively small.

The result is that, although poverty affects millions of white households at any given moment, it is rarely a *community* crisis for white residents of any metropolitan area. Among the seventy-five largest metropolitan areas in the 1990 census (excluding Honolulu, Hawaii), the region with the highest poverty rate among white families (9.9 percent) was Knoxville, Tennessee. The one with the lowest black family poverty rate was the Washington area, with 10.1 percent.[10] For all areas, the highest poverty rate for white families was still lower than the lowest poverty rate for black families.

Moreover, nowhere was the poverty rate for white residents even half the rate for black residents. In only two large metro areas (El Paso and Tucson) was the white (that is, Anglo) poverty rate even 40 percent of the black rate. In both those communities, Hispanics occupied the bottom rung of the economic ladder.

As discussed in chapter 4, poor whites are also rarely concentrated in poor neighborhoods. In the fifty-eight metro areas in which I have consulted, in 1990 barely one out of four poor whites lived in poverty neighborhoods, and only one out of twenty poor whites lived in high-poverty neighborhoods. For the most part, poor whites living in poor neighborhoods found either blacks or Hispanics in the majority. By contrast, one out of two poor Hispanics and three out of four poor blacks lived in poverty neighborhoods (30 percent of the latter in high-poverty neighborhoods).

To repeat, three out of four poor whites live in working-class or middle-class neighborhoods, whereas one out of two poor Hispanics and three out of four poor blacks live in poverty neighborhoods.

I repeat these facts because this disproportion is what fuels the dynamics of poverty in urban America. To be poor and white is, in general, still to be part (albeit often a marginal part) of the mainstream of white, middle-

10. The poverty rates of metro Knoxville and metro Washington are not that easy to compare. Because Washington's cost of living is 37 percent higher than the national metro average, its poverty rate is significantly understated; the poverty rate in metro Knoxville, where the cost of living is 13 percent below the national average, is somewhat overstated. In addition, located on the fringe of Appalachia, the Knoxville region has many genuinely poor people, but its statistics are somewhat ballooned by the disproportionate presence of university students at Vanderbilt and the University of Tennessee (though this latter factor would not affect the *family* poverty rate significantly).

class society with its values, expectations, and above all, access to educational and employment opportunities. To be poor and Hispanic or poor and black is, in general, to be isolated from mainstream society.

The success of the war on poverty among poor urban whites can be traced, not to some government agency's master plan, but to a core of assumptions flowing from the fact that American society is still heavily organized along lines of race and ethnicity:

—One assumption is that the majority of poor white households will live in local communities with sufficient fiscal health to provide adequate public services. Indeed, the majority of poor whites live in suburbs or in "elastic" southern and western central cities. Despite the strains felt by many older, inner suburbs, most suburban jurisdictions are in better fiscal shape than poverty-stricken central cities.

—Two, even in the face of the wrenching economic transformations that lie at the heart of much poverty in America, the majority of poor whites will live in sectors of their metro areas where most new job creation is occurring. Nationwide, 55 percent of poor whites live in suburbs outside central cities, where in the last two decades 80 percent of all new jobs have been created. By contrast, 67 percent of poor Hispanics and 77 percent of poor blacks live in central cities where low-skilled employment, in particular, has been vanishing.

—Three, the majority of poor white children will have access to better educational opportunities. Local public schools typically mirror local housing patterns. Because most poor white children do not live in poor neighborhoods, most poor white children do not attend neighborhood schools heavily attended by other poor children. Attending predominantly middle-class schools has a positive effect on educational outcomes.

The Importance of Family Structure

The issue of opportunity for children is certainly an important one. By 1995, 14 million children constituted almost 40 percent of all poor persons in the United States: 35 percent of the white poor, 46 percent of the Hispanic poor, and 47 percent of the black poor.[11] Appendix tables A-8 and A-9 show how family structure affects the incidence of poverty among children. At the same time, they highlight the most hopeful set of statistics

11. Bureau of the Census (1997, tables 736, 737).

I have yet encountered regarding urban America: of all white married couples with children, 96 percent are *not* poor; of all black married couples with children, 89 percent are *not* poor, and of all Hispanic married couples with children, 87 percent are *not* poor.

Among the fifty-eight metro areas in which I have analyzed this phenomenon, the variation in *non*poverty rates of white married couples is small, from a low of 93 percent to a high of 99 percent (appendix table A-8). The variation in nonpoverty rates for Hispanic and black married couples is somewhat greater. However, across all racial and ethnic lines the basic observation holds: the odds are nine out of ten that children in two-parent, often two-wage-earner, families will *not* be poor.

The dismal side of the argument, illustrating the "feminization" of poverty, is also summarized in appendix table A-9: of all white single mothers with children, 33 percent are poor; of all black single mothers with children, 56 percent are poor; of all Hispanic single mothers with children, 56 percent are poor. The two-parent, two-wage-earner family is the most effective anti-poverty program for children. That is not a statement of social values. That is a demographic and economic fact. It is true that many single mothers, often through great effort, are able to keep themselves and their children above the raw poverty level. Two-thirds of all white single mothers and almost half of all Hispanic and black single mothers are not poor. Nevertheless, the surest path to poverty is to be the child of a single mother.

The dramatic differences between poverty rates for married couples and for single mothers highlights a growing social concern for white and Hispanic society, one that has already become a clear and present disaster for black society. Appendix table A-10 shows the number of married-couple families for every 100 single-mother families in 1990. In the fifty-eight metro areas there were 501 white married couples with children for every 100 white single mothers with children, a ratio of 5 to 1. The ratio dropped within the Hispanic community: 310 married couples with children per 100 single female family heads, or 3 to 1. But within the black community there were only 80 married couples with children for every 100 single mothers, a ratio of less than 1 to 1.[12]

In the fifty-eight metro areas that I analyzed, the white ratio ranged from more than 6 to 1 in prosperous, highly educated labor markets such as

---

12. By 1995 these ratios had shrunk even further. In just five years, the national ratio of white married couples with children to white single mothers with children had dropped to 455 to 100; for Hispanics, to 285 to 100; and for blacks, to 77 to 100.

Atlanta, Minneapolis-Saint Paul, Washington, and south central Pennsylvania to around 4 to 1 in less prosperous, more blue-collar labor markets such as Battle Creek, Kalamazoo, Akron, Dayton-Springfield, and Youngstown-Warren. (The Ohio industrial communities all had substantial numbers of long-term immigrants from Appalachia, initially recruited for lower-skilled factory jobs that had substantially disappeared by 1990.)

Among blacks, the same economic factors are at work. High-education, high-tech job markets with substantial black middle classes (Atlanta, Fort Worth, Washington) still have slightly more married couples raising children than single mothers. Hard-hit factory towns such as Buffalo, Erie, and Muskegon have very low ratios of black married-couple families to single-mother families. However, the patterns are uneven (note Minneapolis–Saint Paul's low ratio). The variations in black family structure, however, range from social disaster to social catastrophe.

Even more dramatic is the imbalance between married-couple families and single-mother families in the poorest neighborhoods. Appendix table A-11 presents the ratio of married-couple families to single mothers in the poorest tracts (those with poverty rates higher than 40 percent) and in the rest of the metro areas excluding these poorest tracts. As a group, the poorest neighborhoods averaged only 43 married couples raising children for every 100 single mothers with their children. Throughout all the other neighborhoods of these metro areas, subtracting the high-poverty areas, the average was 347 married-couple families for every 100 single-mother households.

There was an 8-to-1 swing between the typical family structure of the poorest neighborhoods and that of all other neighborhoods. As a result, a child growing up in one of these poorest neighborhoods has little exposure to what constitutes the successful formula in adulthood for child-rearing: married-couple families. Regionwide, 90 percent of two-parent families will not be poor; even in these poorest neighborhoods, typically three-quarters of two-parent families are not poor. But in high-poverty neighborhoods a society of single mothers and their children will be the norm, and in these poorest neighborhoods three-quarters of all single mothers are poor.

The connection between these ratios regarding family structure and a population group's poverty rates can be illustrated through a mathematical exercise. Suppose that, across the fifty-eight sample metro areas, the black population had the same family structure ratio as the white population while maintaining the same relative poverty rates associated with their own group's family structure. In other words, in this hypothetical exercise 11 percent of black married-couple families would still be poor (the converse of 89 per-

Table 6-1. *Impact of Family Structure on Poverty Rates*

Community and family structure	Married couples		Single-mother families		Combined poverty rate, all families with children
	Number	Poverty rate	Number	Poverty rate	
Black community					
Black family structure	80	11	100	56	36
Hispanic family structure	310	11	100	56	22
White family structure	501	11	100	56	18
Hispanic community					
Hispanic family structure	310	12	100	56	23
Black family structure	80	12	100	56	36
White family structure	501	12	100	56	19
White community					
White family structure	501	4	100	33	9
Hispanic family structure	310	4	100	33	11
Black family structure	80	4	100	33	20

cent of black married-couple families *not* being poor), and 56 percent of all black single-mother families would still be poor. I will only vary the ratio of family structures. Instead of 80 married-couple families for every 100 single-mother families (the actual black community ratio), in this exercise I calculate poverty rates for the black community on the basis of 501 married-couple families for every 100 single-mother families (the actual white community ratio).

Table 6-1 summarizes the results. With the current black family structure, the poverty rate for black families with children is 36 percent. With the shift to a white family structure (that is, 501 rather than 80 married-couple families for every 100 single-mother families), the black family poverty rate would be halved to 18 percent. (With a Hispanic family structure, the black family poverty rate would decline to 22 percent.)

Similarly, the Hispanic family poverty rate (23 percent) drops slightly to 19 percent with a white family structure but shoots up to 36 percent under a black family structure. In like fashion, the poverty rate for white families with children is 9 percent. Applying the Hispanic family structure ratio,

Table 6-2. *Ratio of Married-Couple Families to Single-Mother Families Nationwide, 1960–95*

| Census year | Ratio married/100 single-mother | | | Ratio white married/black married |
	White	Black	Hispanic	
1960	1,539	413	n.a.	3.7
1970	1,125	197	390	5.7
1980	592	95	375	6.2
1985	500	78	252	6.4
1990	494	75	248	6.6
1995	422	63	225	6.7

n.a. Not available.

the white family poverty rate increases slightly to 11 percent, but it would more than double, rising to 20 percent, if the black population's family structure ratio were applied to the white population.

If such hypothetical calculations are set aside, empirical evidence shows a significant and persistent difference in family structure between blacks and whites. The earliest census information on family structure by racial group dates from 1960. Table 6-2 summarizes the changes over the intervening thirty-five years.

In 1965 U.S. Senator Daniel Patrick Moynihan, then a young assistant secretary of labor, wrote a confidential report to President Lyndon Johnson entitled "The Negro Family: The Case for National Action." In it Moynihan stated:

> At the heart of the deterioration of the fabric of Negro society is the deterioration of the Negro family. It is the fundamental source of the weakness of the Negro community. . . . In essence, the Negro community has been forced into a matriarchal structure which, because it is so out of line with the rest of American society, seriously retards the progress of the group as a whole.[13]

Moynihan's document was leaked to the press (probably by liberal critics of his thesis) and caused an immense controversy at the time. Yet black family structure was much less tilted toward single-mother families when Moynihan

13. Moynihan (1965).

was writing than it would be three decades later. In the 1960 census, for every 100 black single mothers there were still 413 black married couples with children rather than just 63 black married couples for every 100 black single mothers, as in 1995. In 1960 white married couples with children also dominated the white family structure much more than a generation later. In 1960 there were 1,539 white married couples with children for every 100 white single mothers, compared with a ratio of only 422:100 by 1995.[14]

Throughout earlier decades, the ratio of white married couples to single mothers was about 3.5 times that among blacks, a very substantial, but relatively stable, differential. For purposes of argument, I will assume that this roughly 3.5 to 1 differential sums up the consequences of the historical experience of African Americans in U.S. society: 250 years of slavery, 100 years of Jim Crow segregation in the South and de facto segregation in the North, the transition from rural poverty to the lowest rungs of the urban economic ladder, substantial education gaps between whites and blacks, and active discrimination in housing and job markets. I will not try to separate out the impact of all these factors on family structure. I will just assume that this is the starting point.[15]

From the 1960 census onward, however, the historic differential between white and black family structures deteriorated sharply, from 3.7 in 1960 to 6.7 in 1995. How could this be? During these very same decades America dismantled Jim Crow laws, eased racial discrimination in the job market, and, to a lesser degree, reduced de facto segregation in housing markets and public education.

Most notably, long-standing educational gaps were narrowed significantly. Table 6-3 shows the long-term achievements of African Americans in striving for educational parity with white Americans. In fact, in September 1996 the Census Bureau announced that a historic milestone had been passed. For the first time, among persons aged twenty-five to thirty-five, blacks and whites had attained the same high school completion rate. While

---

14. Hacker (1992, p. 231).

15. Note, too, that the ratio of married-couple families to single-mother families has been changing outside the United States as well, most notably in northern and western Europe. Certain demographic and economic factors are contributing to this trend across many societies. Among them are the increasing age at marriage, higher divorce rates, increasing social acceptance of having children outside marriage, women's greater participation in the paid labor force and hence greater economic independence, and, in many societies, a substantial decline in the wages of millions of male blue-collar workers. In the United States these factors are operating across all racial and ethnic lines.

Table 6-3. *Educational Attainment, Persons Aged 25–35 Nationwide, 1940–90*

Census year	Completed high school		Ratio black/ white	Completed four years college		Ratio black/ white
	Black	White		Black	White	
1940	12.3	41.2	3.35	1.6	6.4	4.00
1950	23.6	56.3	2.39	2.8	8.2	2.93
1960	38.6	63.7	1.65	4.8	11.8	2.45
1970	58.4	77.8	1.33	7.3	17.3	2.36
1980	82.2	89.8	1.10	11.5	25.3	2.20
1989	82.2	89.3	1.09	12.7	24.4	1.92

Source: Andrew Hacker, *Two Nations: Black and White, Separate, Hostile, Unequal* (Scribner's, 1992), p. 234.

the percentage of black college graduates in that age group still lags behind the percentage of white college graduates, the gap continues to close.

Disparities still exist in the quality of education provided by many central-city school systems (from which the majority of blacks graduate) compared with many largely suburban school systems (from which most white students graduate). The disparities are probably less significant among the college-educated. It is reasonable to conclude that parity in educational attainment (as measured by years of education completed) does not yet translate into parity in the skills with which each group has been equipped by their years in school. Black Americans' substantial achievements in closing the educational attainment gap are not yet matched by equivalent gains in the job market. By 1995 the median wage for black males was only 73 percent of the median wage for white males (though the gap had narrowed from 43 percent in 1940, but less markedly from the 1970s level of 64 percent).[16]

Too Few Jobs versus Too Much Welfare

Taking the long view, several measures suggest that by the 1990s many black Americans were less isolated from mainstream society and less overtly constrained in their opportunities for advancement than in decades past. What accounted for the startling deterioration in family structure associated with higher poverty rates? Two basic schools of thought have emerged on that

16. Robert J. Samuelson, "The Jobs Are There," *Washington Post*, September 11, 1996.

question, which in the 1970s and 1980s stirred up a good amount of academic debate. By the 1990s the battle lines had been drawn in Congress and statehouses across the country, one camp crying "Too few jobs," the other "Too much welfare." In fact, both groups are complaining about the same phenomenon: the rise in urban poverty as a direct result of low-skilled city residents, particularly African Americans, working less regularly than they did. The question is why? One side argues that joblessness is involuntary, imposed on the poor by sweeping economic changes; the other that it is voluntary, the product of a rational economic choice by many poor persons themselves.

For the proponents of "too few jobs," high inner-city joblessness is the result of the sharp decline in city-based blue-collar jobs. Many of these jobs vanished under the impact of technological change or global competition. In many cities they were partially replaced by new white-collar jobs. These required higher education and skill levels than disadvantaged city residents had. The skills mismatch arose. Other blue-collar jobs were relocated from central cities to their own suburbs. Low-skilled African Americans faced greater barriers than low-skilled whites in either moving or commuting to the city's suburbs. The spatial mismatch was born.

The proponents of "too much welfare" say that extensive federal welfare programs have made not working more attractive than working. Conservative scholar Charles Murray popularized this point in his influential book, *Losing Ground.* Marshaling an extensive array of statistics, Murray argued that the ready availability of welfare payments, medicaid, food stamps, and subsidized housing allowed poor families to improve their economic position by not working and instead relying on the public dole. Short-term economic improvement, however, was simply the precursor of long-term social disaster, as two-parent families dissolved, births out of wedlock increased, and succeeding generations of inner-city residents became locked in a cycle of poverty. "We tried to provide for the poor and produced more poor instead. We tried to remove the barriers to escape from poverty and inadvertently built a trap," Murray wrote.[17]

Counterattacking Murray with his own array of statistics was William Julius Wilson, the former president of the American Sociological Association, who now heads Harvard University's black studies program:

> Murray's thesis in *Losing Ground* does not begin to come to grips with the complex problem of the rising number of female-headed families and out-

17. Murray (1984, p. 9).

of-wedlock births because he overemphasizes the role of liberal welfare policies and plays down what is perhaps the most important factor in the rise of black female-headed families—the extraordinary rise in black male joblessness. . . . The decline in the incidence of intact marriages among blacks is associated with the declining economic status of black men. . . . Black women nationally, especially young black women, are facing a shrinking pool of "marriageable" (i.e., employed) black men. . . . The sharp rise of black female-headed families is directly related to increasing black male joblessness.[18]

University of North Carolina economist John Kasarda and Kwok-fai Ting, a statistician at the Chinese University of Hong Kong, have attempted to adjudicate the scholarly battle by statistically assessing the relative contribution of both factors—economic structural change and welfare dependency—to joblessness.[19] They examined trends in joblessness, poverty, and welfare for the non-Hispanic white and non-Hispanic black residents of sixty-seven large cities between 1980 and 1990. To test the skills versus spatial mismatch hypothesis, Kasarda and Ting measured the relative importance of low-skilled industries located within each city itself in 1980, the size of the city's low-skilled work force, and the degree of economic restructuring that occurred during the next decade (such as the loss of low-skilled jobs and their partial replacement by high-skilled jobs in the city itself). Residential segregation within the city, measured by a dissimilarity index, was also incorporated into the model. The impact of welfare participation was measured by its "feedback" effect on joblessness.

Low-skilled industry jobs averaged almost 42 percent of all city-based jobs in 1980; over the next decade the cities lost 15 percent of their low-skilled industry jobs. By 1990 a large skills mismatch had developed for black city residents compared with white city residents. Almost 58 percent of all jobs located in the cities were filled by workers with more than a high school education. Some 56 percent of adult white city residents had more than twelve years of education (a negligible skills shortfall) compared with only 37 percent of adult black city residents (a 21-point gap between skills available and skills required).

The researchers attempted to measure spatial mismatch by the average travel time of city residents to city-based jobs (an "imperfect measure of

18. Wilson (1987, pp. 104–05). Wilson has elaborated on his themes more recently in Wilson (1996).

19. Kasarda and Ting (1996). In addition to the information quoted, my discussion of the two schools of thought was substantially modeled on this article.

spatial mismatch," they commented). One-way commuting times of white residents to city-based jobs averaged about twenty minutes. For black city residents average commuting times were a slightly longer twenty-three minutes. This was, in part, a reflection of the loss of jobs within segregated black neighborhoods as well as the greater isolation from newer job locations within the cities.[20]

In 1990, joblessness, poverty, and rates of welfare participation were substantially higher for blacks than whites in the sixty-seven cities. About 33 percent of white women and 15 percent of white men were jobless compared with almost 40 percent and 27 percent of black women and black men, respectively. Only 14 percent of white women and 10 percent of white men fell below the poverty line compared with 37 percent of black women and 24 percent of black men. Welfare participation of black women was more than three times the welfare participation of white women. Given restrictive eligibility rules, welfare participation rates were substantially lower for both white men and black men than for women.

The question, of course, is the extent to which all of these factors contributed to joblessness. From their detailed multiple regression analyses, Kasarda and Ting concluded that "economic restructuring and the welfare disincentive paradigms are not necessarily conflicting explanations of urban joblessness and poverty. They may, in fact, operate side by side to reinforce joblessness and poverty." Furthermore,

> Resident education levels, urban industrial structure, and racial segregation all play roles in influencing skill and spatial mismatches for both African Americans and . . . whites. Urban industrial structure and racial segregation, however, have a greater impact on skill and spatial mismatches for African-Americans than for whites. In turn, these mismatches, as well as welfare program participation, contribute to urban joblessness.
>
> Skill and spatial mismatches, in general, have greater effects on joblessness among white residents than among African Americans, despite a quite strong association between spatial mismatch and joblessness for African-American women. Conversely, welfare program participation contributes more to joblessness among African-American city residents than among white residents, with the complete welfare-joblessness-poverty cycle strongest among female African Americans.[21]

20. The average dissimilarity index of black residential segregation was 66 for the fifty-eight cities.

21. Kasarda and Ting (1996, p. 409).

Kasarda and Ting also found that joblessness had its greatest impact on poverty rates among African American women and the least impact among white women. Family structure, they added, was largely to blame for this difference, "since it has been well documented that a lower percentage of African American women have working spouses." Combined with welfare programs, these fewer job opportunities and lower wages in all likelihood discourage poor African Americans from seeking employment alternatives. The solution to all these problems, Kasarda and Ting concluded, lies not only in policies designed to reduce inner-city unemployment and poverty but also in a concerted effort to mitigate spatial and skill mismatches and to reform welfare. Above all, structural barriers to job access, such as housing segregation, and the traps welfare can create for the poor need to be eliminated.

The weight Kasarda and Ting give spatial mismatch as a cause of joblessness would no doubt increase considerably if the dynamics of whole metropolitan areas were taken into account. The impact of changes in the city-based job supply on city residents alone is far from the central phenomenon. Two-thirds of all whites (including 55 percent of poor whites) now live in suburbs outside central cities where, in recent decades, more than 80 percent of new job creation has occurred (including most low-skilled job creation). Almost 70 percent of all blacks (including 77 percent of poor blacks) live in central cities, from which, as Kasarda and Ting noted in their sample of sixty-seven major cities, about 15 percent of low-skilled industry jobs vanished in just one decade.

Paul Jargowsky's metropolitan work sheds somewhat more light on the subject. Using a sophisticated statistical model to measure the factors that contribute to the growth and number of high-poverty neighborhoods, Jargowsky was first startled by the "alarming" growth rate of *all* high-poverty neighborhoods since 1970, whatever their racial composition: over this period, the number of persons living in ghettos, barrios, and slums has grown by 92 percent and their poor population by 98 percent. For the 8 million people now living in these neighborhoods, "reduced economic opportunities and social isolation add insult to the injury of being poor. Within some of these communities, the deprivation does irreparable harm." In Jargowsky's view,

the primary factors behind the increasing concentration of poverty are metropolitan economic growth and the general processes that create and sustain segregation by race and class. Metropolitan-level variables for economic opportunity and segregation [both economic and racial] can explain about four-fifths of the variation among metropolitan areas [of the number of high-poverty neighborhoods] and about the same proportion of the changes in neighborhood poverty over time. Although such factors as spatial location, neighborhood culture, and social policy may play a role, they are secondary to income generation and neighborhood sorting, which together explain most of the observed variations in ghetto poverty.[22]

The fundamental need on the policy side, Jargowsky adds, is to increase productivity and reduce inequality. "Policies that affect the spatial organization of metropolitan areas and reduce racial and economic segregation will also affect the formation of ghettos and barrios. In contrast, policies that aim to alter the culture, values, and behavior of ghetto residents are unlikely to make much difference without larger changes in the metropolitan economy and in rates of segregation."[23]

For Jargowsky, two principal factors—the level and changes in average metropolitan household incomes and the neighborhood sorting process—explain four-fifths of the variations observed in what he terms "neighborhood poverty," or the percentages of residents of all income levels in each metro area of different racial and ethnic groups that live in high-poverty neighborhoods. Assuming that the same factors apply comparably to the "concentration of poverty" (the percentages of poor whites, blacks, and Hispanics who live in high-poverty neighborhoods), I would suggest that a third factor explains most of the remaining one-fifth variation in the concentration of poverty among different metro areas: federal public housing policy.

The Impact of Public Housing Projects

There is no sadder example of the unintended consequences of a well-motivated social policy than the federal public housing program, especially in its efforts to address highly concentrated poverty. Take the case of Cleveland, which in 1990 had sixty-three high-poverty census tracts. Tracking the location of housing projects operated by the misleadingly named Cuyahoga Metropolitan Housing Authority (whose effective jurisdiction is limited to the city of Cleveland), I found a high-density housing project in or right next to every high-poverty census tract. The situation was no different in

22. Jargowsky (1997, pp. 185–86).
23. Jargowsky (1997, p. 186).

the city of Baltimore's thirty-four high-poverty census tracts. After touring more than sixty metropolitan areas, I have concluded that nothing in private housing markets compares with the intense concentration of poor minorities in federal public housing units. By the 1990s federal public housing had become the biggest poverty trap in American society.

It was not always that way. When the New Deal Congress approved the Wagner-Steagall Act, public housing was intended to be transitional housing for low-income working families. The federal government financed only the construction of low-rise, small-scale, generally attractive projects. The projects were maintained and managed by local housing authorities whose operating budgets had to be self-sustaining from the rents collected. As a result, local authorities worked hard to maintain a diversity of tenants, at least where income was concerned. Racial diversity would have been impossible since most projects were rigidly segregated in the North as well as in the South.

In many communities I have visited, some middle-aged black leaders (businessmen, agency administrators, city council members, and mayors among them) have said that "I was raised in Lafayette Terrace (Baltimore)," or "As a child I lived ten years in Techwood Homes (Atlanta)." "Is that project today the same place you grew up in?" I'll ask. "Oh, no," is the instant answer. "In my day the housing project was a real community: lots of families with the fathers going off to work every day. Today the projects are very different. Nothing but women on welfare and their children."

The shift started in Washington, D.C., in Julia Vitullo-Martin's view (many others would agree). She blames the regulations that the Department of Housing and Urban Development (HUD) imposes on public housing and the complexities added to them by Congress: "A program can start out fairly simple and straightforward and quickly become a mess."[24]

The unraveling of public housing began in the 1950s. To accommodate hundreds of thousands of low-income black migrants pouring into the nation's cities from the rural South (and to house tens of thousands of others displaced by federal urban renewal programs and urban freeway construction), many of the nation's larger public housing authorities began to build huge high-rise projects. Such projects were thought to be cheaper (they were not), modern, and beautiful, "stunning though that idea may seem today," Vitullo-Martin wrote.

24. Vitullo-Martin (1996, p. 105). This sixteen-page article is the best short history and critique of the country's public housing program I have found, and my briefer history is patterned on it.

In the 1920s Germany's Bauhaus architects had put forward a new vision for workers' housing: clean, high, pure, well-constructed buildings that rejected the false trappings of the bourgeoisie—curtains, clutter, space, individual entrances. Intent on avoiding the picturesque, the Bauhaus Modernists advocated severe horizontality in composition and perfect simplicity in design. This worked well enough when the finest materials were exquisitely crafted into housing for the wealthy, but worked deplorably when shoddy materials were carelessly employed in huge repetitive buildings.[25]

Over the decades the inherent ills of the Modernists' antihuman vision were compounded by the evolution of HUD's minimum design standards. During the 1930s and 1940s public housing projects were often better built and more attractive than privately owned, low-rent apartments and row housing in many communities. Faced with private landlords' criticisms and the ever-present federal desire to slash costs, HUD subsequently outlawed such "amenities" (HUD's term) as basements, doors on closets, ceiling fans, and individual entrances. A few communities gained HUD exemptions to upgrade their new projects by supplementing HUD funds with local support, but by the 1970s most public housing, as the saying went, "looked like public housing."

The final blow to humane, positive public housing came neither from design nor density but from congressional meddling with tenant selection standards. In 1967, Congress approved a series of reforms introduced by Edward Brooke of Massachusetts, the Senate's only black member at the time. To assist public housing tenants who were paying high proportions of their incomes in rent, the Brooke amendments mandated that no tenant should pay more than 25 percent of his or her income in rent. With incredible speed, this well-intentioned reform had terrible results, converting "a low-rent but self-sustaining program into a low-income—and eventually deeply subsidized—program."[26]

The impact of the Brooke amendments was twofold. Faced with immediate rent increases, working families found that much better housing was available for the right price in the private market. Tens of thousands of stable, working-class households quickly deserted public housing projects. With their best tenants gone, local authorities found rental income plummeting; 25 percent of welfare recipients could not cover basic maintenance and

25. Vitullo-Martin (1996, p. 107).
26. Vitullo-Martin (1996, p. 109).

management costs with their monthly stipends. For their first three decades, local housing authorities had been basically self-sufficient. In fiscal year 1969, the first year of the Brooke amendments, operating subsidies for local authorities were $14 million. By fiscal 1999, HUD's annual operating subsidies had ballooned to $2.8 billion, with federal subsidies now covering the greater share of local authorities' annual operating budgets.[27]

Directives from Washington continued to compound local authorities' problems. In 1981, seeking to focus an admittedly scarce supply of subsidized housing on the neediest, Congress required that 95 percent of residents be in the "very low income" bracket, that is, with incomes below 50 percent of the area median income. Simultaneously, Congress raised the standard rent level to 30 percent of adjusted gross income. In 1987 Congress further mandated that local authorities give preference to applicants who were already receiving other welfare assistance and had been displaced by other federal programs (such as highway construction), or who were living in substandard housing, or who were paying more than 50 percent of their income to private landlords.

The federal preference list was further expanded in 1992 to include young disabled persons. Incredibly, the new federal mandate defined "former" drug abusers and alcoholics as being among the disabled. This last congressional intrusion almost shredded the one public housing program universally recognized as successful: public housing for the elderly. Placing supposedly recovering young drug addicts (and traffickers) into apartment buildings formerly reserved exclusively for the elderly created terrifying conditions for many elderly tenants. One local housing authority official explained: "We messed it up. It was fixed and we broke it. Or Congress broke it and we let them."[28]

Private Rent Subsidies

By the mid-1970s, it was clear that the nationwide network of public housing projects had broken down. During the early years of the Nixon administration several successful experiments had been carried out providing rent vouchers for households eligible for public housing. The experiments became a full-fledged program with the passage of section 8 of the Housing and Community Development Act of 1974.

27. Data provided by HUD's Public and Assisted Housing Division.
28. Vitullo-Martin (1996, p. 109).

Section 8 subsidies took two forms: unit-based and tenant-based. Under the unit-based approach, local authorities would contract with private landlords for a specified number of units; in fact, whole private apartment complexes were often financed under section 8. Ultimately, though privately built and managed, many such "section 8 ghettos" became little different from housing authority–operated projects.

More beneficial was the more flexible use of tenant-based section 8 certificates and vouchers. A section 8 certificate allowed an eligible family to obtain private rental housing. Under a three-way rental agreement, the housing authority would pay the landlord the difference between the tenant's monthly payment (30 percent of the tenant's income) and the negotiated rent. Rent levels could not exceed HUD-established fair market rents (FMRs), which varied by size of unit and local market. Under the section 8 vouchers, tenants could opt for more expensive housing by using more than 30 percent of their income to supplement HUD's FMR ceiling.

Over the next two decades the section 8 program grew rapidly. It began by providing rental assistance to 330,000 poor households in 1976. By 1998, section 8 was aiding some 2.8 million poor households, twice the 1.4 million poor households living in public housing projects.[29] But here again the politics of race distorted the program. Administration of the section 8 program was assigned to the same local public housing authorities. The legal powers of most authorities (particularly big-city agencies) were limited to the boundaries of the government that established them. Few authorities spanned city and suburbs. Certificates and vouchers could be used only within each authority's jurisdiction. Within cities the use of section 8 certificates and vouchers often became concentrated in working-class neighborhoods already destabilized by nearby public housing projects. At the same time, section 8 was a boon for many suburban jurisdictions that had resisted building public housing projects (except for the elderly). Allocation of section 8 assistance expanded rapidly and was used in more dispersed patterns.

In 1987, in one of its rare constructive actions, Congress amended section 8 to make certificates and vouchers "portable" across jurisdictional lines. However, few local authorities aggressively promoted areawide use of this assistance since it was difficult to administer when tenants carried vouchers from one jurisdiction into another while still reporting back to the first.

By the 1990s the federal public housing assistance program was still maintaining historic, racially segregated patterns, now de facto rather than

29. Bureau of the Census (1994, table 577).

de jure. Of the 1.4 million tenants in projects, 48 percent were black and 18 percent were Hispanic in 1997. The great majority of family projects were located in central cities. Suburban housing assistance relied heavily on section 8 certificates and vouchers. Overall, in 1997, about 45 percent of all section 8 beneficiaries were white, 39 percent were black, and 15 percent were Hispanic. For poor blacks, housing assistance typically meant living in a public housing project or "section 8 ghetto" in a high-poverty city neighborhood. For poor whites, housing assistance meant receiving a rent subsidy for a privately owned apartment or house in the lower-poverty suburbs.

High-Poverty "Neighborhood Effects"

Like the nation's public housing programs, the neighborhood sorting process Jargowsky analyzes is not color blind but color coded. Is the net result just the grouping together into high-poverty ghettos and barrios of poor blacks and Hispanics who would otherwise face the same problems if they were scattered in communities with less poverty? Or do high-poverty ghettos and barrios themselves generate and perpetuate poverty?

This question has spawned a lively debate over the issue of "neighborhood effects." I believe that the preponderance of the evidence—and my own experience and observations—supports the view that poor neighborhoods are poverty machines that generate poverty itself. The much greater concentration of poor blacks and Hispanics than poor whites in poverty and high-poverty neighborhoods contributes substantially to minority poverty rates, which are three and four times the poverty rate among whites nationally.

Another old adage is that "you can take the boy out of the farm, but you can't take the farm out of the boy." Can you take the ghetto out of the boy by taking the boy out of the ghetto?

Several years ago the Urban Institute and I studied the test results of pupils from public housing households in the Albuquerque Public Schools.[30] We chose Albuquerque for two reasons. First, as its former mayor, I had excellent contacts with both the local housing authority and the public school system. This facilitated data gathering. Second, Albuquerque has an unusu-

---

30. Rusk and Mosley (1994). Our study was supported by a grant from the Carnegie Corporation of New York, the nation's leading philanthropic foundation in the field of early childhood education.

ally high number of public housing children living in middle-class neighborhoods and attending middle-class neighborhood schools. With 80 percent of the metro area's population, Albuquerque is a near-metropolitan city. Its small housing projects and rental subsidies are widely scattered across the city. Thus Albuquerque operates a quasi-regional public housing policy.

On the other side of the equation, Albuquerque Public Schools, with the nation's twenty-fifth largest enrollment, is one of only five metrowide school systems. There is a high degree of uniformity in the distribution of school resources. Albuquerque also has a predictable pattern of test score results. Outcomes mirror inputs, as measured by the socioeconomic status of the children's families, since all other inputs (per pupil expenditures, facilities, teacher qualifications, and so on) are substantially equal. Among Albuquerque's seventy-eight elementary schools, the percentage of pupils who qualified for free and reduced-price school lunches accounted for almost 80 percent of the variation in school-by-school test scores. The high correlation between socioeconomic status and test scores has been confirmed by many educational studies since the massive report prepared by sociologist James Coleman for the U.S. Office of Education in 1966.[31]

We examined the third- and fifth-grade test scores of 1,108 children from public housing over a ten-year period. The results? Having statistically controlled carefully for sex, race and ethnicity, and household characteristics, we found that for every percentage point decrease in poverty among a public housing child's classmates, that child's test scores improved 0.22 of a percentile. In other words, attending a middle-class neighborhood school with 20 percent poor children rather than a high-poverty neighborhood school with 80 percent poor children meant a 13 percentile point improvement in an average public housing child's test scores.

When we switched the focus from the school's socioeconomic mix to the school's average test performance, the results were even more dramatic. For every percentile increase in the school's average test scores, the public housing child's scores improved 0.53 percentile point. Attending a school whose students ranked on average in the 80th percentile in the national tests as opposed to a school whose students were in the 20th percentile meant a 32 percentile improvement in the average public housing child's test scores.

Good teaching makes a difference. However, champions of typical school-centered reforms should not get too excited about these last results.

31. Coleman and others (1966).

In Albuquerque (and elsewhere almost invariably) the high-performance schools all drew most of their pupils from households with high socioeconomic status. In a school with 80 percent of the children from poor households, I doubt that any combination of educational reforms and enhanced resources would produce a 13 percentile improvement in test scores (much less a 32 percentile improvement).

How much of the improvement can be attributed to what happened in that middle-class, high-achieving classroom where the public housing children spent six hours a day, 180 hours a year? How much can be attributed to what happened in the middle-class neighborhood or in the children's own households, where the children spend all the rest of their time? Our Albuquerque study could not determine. Neighborhood effects could be modest. At the very least, those children were probably exposed to standard English much more in the middle-class neighborhood than in a poorer neighborhood. Black English or Chicano English (and certainly Spanish itself) are legitimate vehicles of communication, but standard English is the language in which the child is tested and must communicate in the adult world of work.

In 1996 Hillary Rodham Clinton published *It Takes a Village,* proposing a wide range of reforms for improving the lives of the country's children.[32] At the Republican National Convention, presidential candidate Bob Dole thundered in rebuttal that Republicans believe that it takes not a village but a *family* to raise a child. In my view, it takes a family, a neighborhood, and a school to raise a child successfully. Where families are weak, neighborhoods and schools must be correspondingly stronger to compensate.

Implicitly, American society functions in a way that fulfills that formula for many poor white children. For most poor black and Hispanic children, however, the formula works in reverse. Those with the weakest families are consigned overwhelmingly to the weakest neighborhoods and the weakest schools. High-poverty ghettos, barrios, and slums are substantially the outcomes of the middle-class dispersion and disinvestment promoted by the sprawl machine. Such high-poverty neighborhoods themselves—and the neighborhood schools that struggle to serve them—become the poverty machine for the next generation.

32. Clinton (1996).

7

The Deficit
Machine

IT WAS HARD to decide which looked more fearsome, the Speaker of the House or the life-sized skull of *Tyrannosaurus rex* displayed in the Speaker's conference room in the Capitol building. It was June 1995, and Newt Gingrich was at the height of his power and notoriety. Most of his Contract with America had just been successfully rammed through the U.S. House of Representatives in the previous 100 days.

A dozen presidents of major chambers of commerce from around the country and I had remained standing until the Speaker motioned us to sit down around his conference table. They had come to Washington for a seminar on the federal budget that the association of American Chambers of Commerce Executives had asked me to organize. I had prevailed on Senator Pete Domenici, Senate Budget Committee chairman, to meet with the group.[1] The Atlanta chamber president had arranged the audience with Speaker Gingrich.

---

1. Domenici had been chairman of the Albuquerque City Commission from 1967 to 1970, just before I arrived in Albuquerque. He often talked about his experiences as "mayor" of Albuquerque, although Albuquerque did not shift from a commission-manager to mayor-council form of government until 1974. In reality, with his energy and ability Domenici exercised mayoral-type leadership even without the formal executive powers of a mayor.

Gingrich began with his standard ten-minute talk, sprinkled with quotations ranging from Alexis de Tocqueville to futurist Alvin Toffler. Then he invited questions.

"What are the prospects for real collaboration between cities and suburbs on some of the tough issues like schools and housing?" asked Jim Dunn, president of the Richmond Chamber of Commerce. Jim had been pushing regionalism in Virginia, ultimately with substantial success (see chapter 13).

"Never happen," the Speaker snapped. "Why should Cobb County or Gwinnett County, for example, get involved with Atlanta?[2] What's in it for them? The city's got too many problems. The solution for Atlanta's problems is for city government to get its own house in order. Eliminate union featherbedding. Cut the bureaucracy. Slash high tax rates that are driving families and jobs out of Atlanta. Become a lean, well-run, low-cost government like its suburbs. Then Atlanta can compete on even terms." The Speaker's imperial dictum stifled any follow-up response from the chamber executives (though several others, I knew, were actively pushing regional strategies in their communities).

"If your analysis is correct, Mr. Speaker," I interjected, "how do you explain this fact? Most major cities that annex new development have high credit ratings and low tax rates. Older cities cut off from annexing new development have lousy credit ratings and high tax rates. Let me illustrate the point with this chart."

I distributed copies of a multicolored, three-dimensional chart (see figure 7-1) that looked vaguely like the island of Manhattan. The "island" was traversed by five "avenues." Buildings of successively greater heights were arrayed along the length of each avenue. The relative heights of the buildings, I explained, represented different cities' credit ratings. The tallest buildings (AAA credit ratings) towered over "downtown." The buildings scaled back progressively in size (AA1, AA, A1, and A) until one came to the low-rise fiscal slums "uptown" (BAA1, BAA, BA1, BA, and B).

On First Avenue were represented all the "zero-inelastic cities" that since 1950 (or for decades earlier) had been unable to annex new suburbs at all. First Avenue had only one AAA tower downtown

2. Gingrich's 6th congressional district embraces part of suburban Cobb, Fulton, Gwinnett, and Cherokee Counties, known locally as the "golden crescent."

Figure 7-1. *Elasticity and Municipal Bond Ratings for America's Largest Cities*

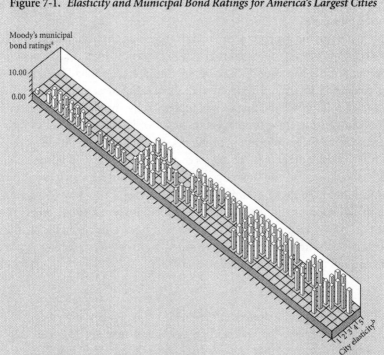

Moody's municipal
bond ratings[a]

10.00

0.00

1 2 3 4 5
City elasticity[b]

a. Bond ratings (or "building heights") range from B (1.0) to AAA (10.0).
b. 1 = zero; 2 = low; 3 = medium; 4 = high; 5 = hyper.

(Minneapolis) and only four slightly shorter AA towers (Cincinnati, Hartford, Syracuse, and San Francisco).[3] Most First Avenue buildings were squat tenements clumped uptown in the fiscal slums.

Average building heights (that is, credit quality) improved steadily along Second Avenue (low-elastic cities) and Third Avenue (medium-elastic cities, including Atlanta, which quadrupled in size

3. Both Minneapolis and Saint Paul (an AA1 rating) are traditionally major net beneficiaries from the Twin Cities fiscal disparities plan, the nation's only significant regional tax base–sharing program (see chapters 10 and 11). The assurance that Minneapolis and Saint Paul will benefit proportionally from any new commercial and industrial development in the region encourages the credit rating agencies to maintain high credit ratings for the two central cities.

during the 1950s). The great bulk of downtown high-rise towers, however, were clustered along Fourth and Fifth avenues (high- and hyperelastic cities, such as Indianapolis, Nashville, Charlotte, Houston, Raleigh, and Austin).

"I call your attention to the fact," I continued, "that there isn't a single low-rise building—that is, a low-credit city—located along Third, Fourth, and Fifth avenues. Credit ratings have little to do with having strong unions or weak unions, Republican- or Democratic-controlled city halls, commission-manager or mayor-council governments. Credit ratings substantially reflect a city's ability to defend—even expand—its market share of the regional tax base through its ability to annex new suburban growth."

The Speaker was rendered speechless.

Of course, it was all a Walter Mittyesque daydream. In reality, it was not my meeting. I was just the consultant, not a principal, at the conference table. Had I been a mayor again and part of a delegation of mayors, it would have been a different story. As it was, I just bit my tongue and let the moment pass.

The Conservative Party Line

The Speaker's approach to urban problems, however, was straight conservative party line: a city's fiscal distress was basically its own fault, thanks to profligate, undisciplined spending; the dead weight of municipal bureaucrats; and the iron grip of city employee unions. Of course, middle-class families and businesses had deserted many cities. Quite simply, they were driven out by high taxes and poor services.

Speaker Gingrich's remarks echoed the findings of a policy analysis recently issued by the Cato Institute, a right-wing, libertarian think tank located in Washington.[4] (Renowned as a voracious reader, Gingrich had probably read the report.) The analysis was apparently triggered by (or at least framed as a response to) the U.S. Conference of Mayors' call for a new $35 billion "Marshall Plan for the cities" in the wake of the 1992 Los Angeles

4. Moore and Stensel (1993).

riot. The report examined economic and population growth and fiscal policies for seventy-seven of America's largest cities.

"Unquestionably, there are regional factors at play in determining the relative rates of growth of cities," the report's introduction acknowledged. "Most of the declining cities in our survey are the once-mighty industrial centers in the Northeast and the Midwest—the Rustbelt. Most of the growth cities are in the Sunbelt, on the West Coast, and in the Southeast.... Still, the fact that for long periods of time some cities have flourished as others have been deteriorating suggests that the self-imposed policies of cities play an important role in determining their economic fates. We believe an important factor is that their spending and taxing policies are very different. Growth cities have pro-growth fiscal policies; declining cities have anti-growth fiscal policies."[5]

The study divided the seventy-seven cities into five groups based on population and economic growth during the 1970s and 1980s. The first category was highest-growth, with ten cities (for example, San Jose, Lexington, Jacksonville, Raleigh, Charlotte), then came high-growth with eleven (notably, Las Vegas, Nashville, Phoenix, Austin, Albuquerque, and San Diego), average-growth with ten (for example, Boston, Los Angeles, Houston, Dallas, San Francisco, Indianapolis), low-growth with twenty-six (such as Denver, Kansas City, Minneapolis, Seattle, Portland, New York, Atlanta, Baltimore, Philadelphia, Saint Louis, Chicago), and lowest-growth with five (Milwaukee, Buffalo, Cleveland, Rochester, Detroit).

The authors of the Cato Institute study asserted that cities "do have some direct control over their own economic fortunes. Cities in decline are victims of bad public policies that are at least *partially* self-generated" [emphasis added]. They did acknowledge that "in some case they are also victims of high state taxes." Upon comparing the fiscal policies of low-growth and high-growth cities, they concluded that low-growth cities spend, on average, $1.71 for every $1.00 of expenditures in high-growth cities; have tax burdens about 50 percent higher; impose tax burdens on families often about $1,000 higher; have much higher government payroll costs; on average, have more than twice the number of municipal employees per 10,000 residents; are much more likely to impose a local income tax; tend to rely heavily on income and property taxes for revenues, whereas high-growth cities rely heavily on sales taxes; routinely spend $1,400 more per student on education; and are characterized by a substantially higher burden in combined state and local taxes

5. Moore and Stensel (1993, p. 11).

for their residents. Consequently, through their high spending and taxes, low-growth cities promote their own decline.[6]

To restore economic vitality and capital investment to declining cities, the Cato Institute report continued, it would be necessary to bring down the costs of municipal services, and lighten the tax burdens that pay for them. This could be done, it was felt, "without sacrificing vital services." Without such measures, no amount of federal aid would be able to "reverse the decline of urban America."[7]

I agree with that very last statement, suitably amended: without basic changes in *metropolitan systems*, "no amount of federal aid can reverse the decline of urban America."

"City Problems"

The Cato Institute's perspective is widely shared. In my travels to more than ninety metro areas, I have often heard suburban officials and suburban residents upbraid the region's core city government for being wasteful, inefficient, incompetent, costly, too bureaucratic, and corrupt. High taxes or poor services are another complaint. But by far the strongest objection that suburbanites raise concerns what they call "city problems." Just what are city problems? Most often they refer to high crime and, more tellingly, poor schools. When challenged about the city's "poor schools," critics rarely provide specific facts about the competence of teachers, principals, or administrators, or pupil-teacher ratios, or the availability of textbooks and teaching aids, or the quality of school buildings. Sometimes "poor schools" does not even refer to comparative levels of expenditures per pupil. As the Cato Institute study itself observed, some city school systems have higher per pupil expenditure levels than many suburban school systems. What most suburban critics implicitly mean by the city's "poor schools," I find, is that the city system has many schools *with a lot of poor children in them.*

The real issue, then, is the social structure of the city within its metropolitan context rather than the city's specific fiscal policies. This again brings up the idea of the city's elasticity, its ability to absorb new development within its city limits. In the postwar era of low-density development, a city could only do this if it had vast amounts of undeveloped land within existing city

6. Moore and Stensel (1993, pp. 26–28).
7. Moore and Stensel (1993, pp. 37–38, 39–40).

limits (as Los Angeles did around 1950) or if it could expand through annexation (which is what three-quarters of the country's central cities did).

However, dismissing the importance of annexation, the Cato Institute remarked, "Annexation is as much a consequence of a city's economic success as it is an explanation of that success. In many cases localities have merged with central cities because it has been in their economic interests to do so. By the same token, more and more localities are now attempting to secede from declining central cities because their economic policies, such as tax rates and service costs, have grown too burdensome."[8]

The passage just quoted is a vintage example of looking at public policy through thick ideological glasses. In the mid-nineteenth century some smaller municipalities did voluntarily merge with larger municipalities for improved city services. (The mergers of Roxbury and Charleston with the city of Boston in 1857 and 1864, respectively, come to mind.) By the mid-twentieth century, however, residents of existing communities almost never voluntarily merged with larger cities unless they were beset by severe groundwater pollution problems from a proliferation of septic tanks that could only be solved by annexation into a city's water and sewer system.

Even the handful of successful city-county consolidations (a form of superannexation) occurred because a preponderance of central-city voters swung countywide elections over the opposition of many voters in unincorporated areas.[9] Other consolidations were a defensive measure against city annexation. In 1963, for example, largely rural Queen Anne's County merged with the tiny city of Virginia Beach (2,000 residents) to immunize the county against further encroachment by the city of Norfolk.[10]

Most annexations occur in one of two circumstances. First, an owner of a large tract of land may want to develop the land and needs municipal utilities and other services; annexation is the city's price for extending services. (Albuquerque, Columbus, Ohio, and Midland, Michigan, are good examples of such service-motivated annexation requests by major developers. Typically, such cities control regional water and sewer systems.) Second,

8. Moore and Stensel (1993, p. 12).

9. In the case of Nashville-Davidson County and Jacksonville-Duval County, voters of all existing smaller municipalities elected to remain independent of the larger, unified governments. The merger of Indianapolis-Marion County was the direct handiwork of the Indiana legislature, accomplished without any local referendum. In this case also, existing municipalities were exempted from "Unigov."

10. The resulting city of Virginia Beach, with 432,545 residents by 1997, is not only Virginia's largest "city" but regularly ranks at the top of the list as America's healthiest central city. Virginia Beach, of course, is a municipalized suburban county.

Table 7-1. *Elasticity Scores of Seventy-Seven Central Cities, by Growth*

Cato Institute growth rating	Number of cities	Elasticity score	Capture-contribute percentage[a]
Highest	10	32	47
High	11	29	53
Average	25	22	33
Low	26	13	−22
Lowest	5	7	−40

a. The degree to which the central city either captured a percentage of the metro area's net population growth or contributed to suburban growth by a net population loss over the period from 1950 to 1990.

some state laws give nearby cities unilateral power to annex unincorporated residential, commercial, and industrial developments without landowner approval. (Texas, Tennessee, and, in particular, North Carolina law virtually mandate such annexations.) When cities have the power to annex, they use it.

To explore annexation's possible influence on city growth and fiscal health, I assigned elasticity scores to each of the seventy-seven central cities studied by the Cato Institute, according to the methodology I developed in *Cities without Suburbs* (see table 7-1). The scores range from a minimum of 4 for the cities that were the most densely developed in 1950 and subsequently could not expand their boundaries at all (such as New York, Newark, and Detroit) to a maximum in the high 30s for those that were least densely developed in 1950 and subsequently expanded their city limits the most (notably, Phoenix, San Jose, and Tucson).

The Cato Institute's categorization by population and economic growth corresponds almost exactly to my categorization of cities by relative elasticity, or geographic expansion. The average elasticity of the Cato Institute's ten highest-growth cities is 32, which falls within the range of my hyperelastic cities (31–40). The eleven high-growth cities (average elasticity 29) fall within my high-elasticity category (25–30). The twenty-five average-growth cities (average elasticity 22) correspond to my medium-elasticity category (18–24). The twenty-six low-growth cities (average elasticity 13) correspond to my low-elasticity cities (9–17), while the five lowest-growth cities (average elasticity 7) fit firmly into the zero-elasticity category (4–8).

Table 7-1 also shows my calculation of the average "capture-contribute percentage" for the Cato Institute's city growth categories. On the average,

Table 7-2. *Elasticity Scores of Seventy-Seven Cities, by Fiscal Health*

Cato Institute fiscal rating (taxes/spending)	Number of cities	Elasticity score	Capture-contribute percentage[a]
Very low	19	30	47
Low	20	26	36
Average	15	20	5
High	21	17	3
Very high	11	10	−18

a. See table 7-1.

cities in the top three growth categories captured shares of their regions' new growth. The low- and lowest-growth cities, however, suffered substantial population losses and were net contributors to their suburbs' growth.

A city that captures a positive share of its region's growth is adding to its tax base. It is also maintaining a more socially and economically balanced population that proportionally has a less acute demand for many services. A city that is losing population and steadily contributing to the growth of its suburbs is not only losing potential tax base, but its residual population is also concentrated in low-income households that have high service needs.

Table 7-2 considers the Cato Institute's rankings of municipal fiscal health. These rankings are based on six factors: per capita city expenditures, city expenditures as a share of personal income, growth in per capita expenditures, combined state and city per capita tax burden, city tax revenues as a share of personal income, and city employees per 10,000 residents. The nineteen cities categorized as having very low taxes and spending levels per capita are, on average, hyperelastic cities that have captured 47 percent of their region's growth. In other words, low-tax/low-cost cities have maintained broad tax bases and strong middle-class populations. They have incorporated half of their suburbs into the city.

At the other end of the spectrum are eleven cities with very high taxes and expenditures per capita. They are typically zero-elastic cities that were unable to expand territorially. They have suffered a steady drain of middle-class households and tax base into their suburbs.

Each of these groupings varies greatly, of course. Social scientists typically use regression analysis to assess the interrelationship between different factors. The Cato study reports that "the correlation between fiscal variables and economic performance variables ranged between 0.3 and 0.5." (A correlation of 1.0 would mean that a city's economic performance can be completely explained by municipal tax and expenditures levels. A correlation of 0.0 would mean there is no relationship.)

I ranked the study's seventy-seven cities by economic growth and fiscal outcomes and analyzed the relationship with each city's elasticity. The correlation between elasticity and fiscal outcomes was 0.38; between elasticity and the city's growth rate, a more substantial 0.56. In short, a city's annexation policy is a somewhat better explanation for its economic growth and fiscal health than its tax levels and city service costs.

In reality, an apples-to-apples study would undoubtedly yield an even greater explanatory margin for elasticity over fiscal policy. All my elasticity calculations cover a city's territorial and population trends for four decades (1950–90). All but one of the Cato Institute's data series start in 1965 or 1970. The positive elasticity ratings of a number of major cities are based on annexations undertaken in the 1950s (for example, in Milwaukee, Atlanta, and Norfolk). Adjusting my analysis for more comparable time periods, I believe, would yield an even better "fit" between elasticity and the Cato study's assessment of economic and fiscal health.

America's Ailing Cities

A much more thorough study of the relationship of a city's demographic profile, economic base, and fiscal health was undertaken by Helen F. Ladd and John Yinger.[11] They analyzed both the hypothetical (or "standardized") and actual revenue-raising capabilities and service costs of eighty-six of the nation's largest cities for 1972, 1982, and 1988. On the revenue side, Ladd and Yinger concentrated on property taxes, earnings taxes (payroll or income), and sales taxes. To determine a city's "standardized" revenue-raising capability, they assumed that every city has the legal power to levy all three types of taxes. They also assumed that the standardized city received 50 percent of its revenue from property taxes and 25 percent each from earnings and sales taxes. The key variables then were the relative well-being of city residents (measured by per capita income) and the ability of the city to "export" its revenue-raising needs through taxes on noncity residents.

11. Ladd and Yinger (1991).

Revenue-Raising Capacity

For a sample of seventy-eight cities with comparable revenues, Ladd and Yinger hypothesized that, on average, for every dollar of city property taxes, nonresidents would pay 34 cents and city residents 66 cents. (The authors termed this an "export ratio" of 0.52.) Nonresidents paid property taxes as customers of city-based retail stores, employees in city-based offices, and consumers of city-based manufacturing goods. Nonresidents would pay a proportionate share of property taxes paid by stores, offices, and factories. The authors also calculated that of each dollar of sales taxes paid, nonresidents would pay 17 cents and residents would pay 83 cents (export ratio = 0.21). This ratio reflected the fact that households did the bulk of their shopping (at grocery stores, pharmacies, gasoline stations, dry cleaners, and the like) close to where they lived. Finally, of every dollar paid in earnings taxes (in large part hypothetical, I would remind the reader), nonresidents paid 56 cents and residents paid 44 cents, on the assumption that the typical city would still be the surrounding region's primary job center (export ratio = 1.27).

In general, the wealthier the city's residents, the greater the revenue-raising capability of city government. On the other hand, the more the city serves as an employment and retail center for its region (and manufacturing center for the nation), the greater its capability to export revenue raising onto nonresidents. Table 7-3 illustrates how these concepts applied to particular cities in 1982. Denver, Boston, and Oakland all had resident income levels higher than the average city. The residents of Atlanta, Baltimore, Detroit, and San Antonio had less than average income levels. This would mean that, on the basis of residents' income, inherently the first three cities would have higher revenue-raising capabilities than the latter three.

With regard to the second factor (the revenue export ratio), both Boston and Atlanta had notably high potential ability to raise revenues from nonresidents. Within their metropolitan areas, both are relatively small cities with large job bases. In 1980, zero-elastic Boston held only 15 percent of the regional population, and medium-elastic Atlanta 20 percent. By contrast, high-elastic San Antonio both had a high proportion (76 percent) of its region's population and the smallest manufacturing base (less than 8 percent of all workers).

From the point of view of their potential revenue-raising capabilities, Denver, Atlanta, Boston, and Oakland all had higher than average potential, and Detroit, Baltimore, and San Antonio all substantially lower than average revenue potential. These calculations were based on a standardized (or

Table 7-3. *Indexes of Standardized and Actual Revenue-Raising Capabilities of Seven Representative Cities, 1982*

City	Per capita income	Estimated export ratios	Revenue-raising capability Standardized	Revenue-raising capability Actual[a]
Atlanta	92	178	119	116
Baltimore	83	86	78	57
Boston	91	178	118	100
Denver	121	110	125	134
Detroit	83	92	80	44
Oakland	108	123	115	93
San Antonio	81	48	65	79

Source: Helen F. Ladd and John Yinger, *America's Ailing Cities: Fiscal Health and the Design of Urban Policy* (Johns Hopkins University Press, 1991), p. 57.

a. Actual taxing authority under state law.

hypothetical) package of taxes that all cities would share. As already noted, all cities were assumed to levy a property tax (50 percent of local revenues), earnings tax (25 percent), and sales tax (25 percent).

That, of course, is not the reality. Table 7-4 summarizes the cities' actual taxing powers. Only six cities out of the eighty-six analyzed levied all three taxes as the standardized model hypothesized.[12] Twenty-nine cities were restricted to the property tax alone, which accounted for 82 percent of all their tax revenues. (These were primarily in New England, New York, New Jersey, and North Carolina.) A dozen cities combined property and earnings taxes in some proportions. Thirty-nine cities depended on the combination of property and sales taxes.

For the eighty-six cities as a group, property taxes represented 53 percent of total tax revenues, other taxes (utility franchise taxes, business licenses, and the like) 20 percent, sales taxes 17 percent, and income, earnings, or payroll taxes only 10 percent. Note, too, that only eighteen of the group had some form of income, earnings, or payroll taxes, which are the principal revenue source for state and federal governments. Twelve major cities had the power to tax incomes earned in the city in full by residents and commuters alike. These were Louisville, Newark, San Francisco, Birmingham, Kansas City (Missouri), Philadelphia, Saint Louis, and five Ohio cities

12. These were Kansas City (Missouri), New York, Saint Louis, San Francisco, Birmingham, and Washington.

Table 7-4. *Revenue Mix of Eighty-Six Cities, by Category of Tax Use, 1982*

Category of tax use	Number of cities	Percentage of total tax revenues			
		Property	Earnings	Sales	Other
Property only	29	82	0	0	18
Property and earnings	3	66	18	0	16
Earnings and property	9	23	71	0	6
Property and sales	21	52	0	23	25
Sales and property	18	29	0	48	23
All three	6	28	29	18	25
Average	86	53	10	17	20

Source: Ladd and Yinger, *America's Ailing Cities*, p. 127.

(Akron, Cincinnati, Cleveland, Columbus, and Dayton).[13] Toledo, Detroit, and New York partly tax commuters, while Pittsburgh, Baltimore, and Washington tax residents' incomes but not commuters'.[14]

When real-world limitations were used to calculate cities' standardized revenue-raising potential, their taxing capacities were generally lower. Boston, Oakland, Baltimore, and, in particular, Detroit all suffered significant reductions in underlying revenue-raising capability, while Denver and San Antonio improved their positions. What do these calculations mean? They mean, for example, that, with identical tax policies (as represented in the third column of table 7-3), the city of Denver had more than 50 percent greater inherent revenue-raising capacity than the city of Detroit. In terms of the two cities' actual taxing authority under different Colorado and Michigan laws (column 4), the city of Denver was endowed with *three times* the actual inherent revenue-raising capacity of the city of Detroit. Contrary to conclusions reached in the Cato Institute study, these projections were entirely or almost entirely independent of each city government's taxing policies.

Of course, a city's actual revenues are not determined solely by its ability to collect local taxes and service fees. State and federal aid make important contributions and, on balance, partly offset disparities in local revenue-

13. Earnings taxes (including self-employment earnings and profits from unincorporated businesses as well as salaries and wages) are the primary revenue source for all Ohio municipalities.

14. In 1973, on granting the federal District of Columbia extensive home rule powers, the Congress explicitly prohibited the District government from enacting a commuter tax, basically, the only revenue limitation imposed on the District City Council that otherwise received all of the taxing authority of cities, counties, and states combined.

raising capabilities. (Ladd and Yinger undertake a thorough analysis of the differential impact of state and federal aid as well.) However, the basic picture of the revenue side of the equation has been set.

Standardized Expenditures

On the expenditure side, Ladd and Yinger calculated standardized expenditure needs by first assuming that service responsibilities are the same for all city governments. The goal was to describe external constraints on a city government's ability to provide public services. They divided public services into three basic groups: police services, fire services, and general services (including airports, public health, highways, housing and urban renewal, corrections, libraries, parking, parks and recreation, sanitation, water and sewer utilities, and, in some cities, education and hospitals). They then analyzed the impact that different environmental factors (that is, factors beyond the city government's control) had on service costs per city resident in the eighty-six cities.

Police Protection

Many factors affect the cost of police services, such as private sector wage rates (with which police departments must compete for personnel) and the percentage of commuters in the work force (who also must receive police services). However, the one factor with the greatest impact on the cost of police services per city resident was the city's poverty rate. For every 1 percent increase in the poverty rate, the cost of police services per resident increased 5.5 percent. As measured by variations from the average for the eighty-six cities, a city whose poverty rate was one standard deviation from the mean would pay 36 percent more per resident for police services; a poverty rate one standard deviation less than the mean would mean a 27 percent reduction in the cost of police services per resident. In terms of the poverty factor, then, the city of Norfolk (with a poverty rate of 19 percent) would pay 70 percent more for police protection per resident than its suburban neighbor, Virginia Beach (with a poverty rate of 6 percent).

Fire Protection

Ladd and Yinger also found a significant relationship between a city's poverty rate and the cost of fire services: one standard deviation above the average municipal rate would raise fire protection costs 27 percent, and one standard deviation below would lower fire protection costs by 21 percent. As measured by standard deviations from the means, other significant influences were the percentage of older housing (+13 percent versus −12 percent); the regional consumer price index, which influences firemen's wage levels and equipment costs (+12 percent versus −11 percent); and the proportions of higher fire-risk rental housing and retail property that had to be protected in comparison with lower fire-risk offices, factories, and owner-occupied homes.

Infrastructure

The percentage of older housing also served as a proxy for the age of a city's infrastructure. Thus cities with older infrastructure had higher costs than cities with newer infrastructure (+11 percent versus −10 percent). Interestingly, the cost of general services was also significantly affected by a city's population density. As the authors explained, "Cities with low densities face high transportation and coordination costs, whereas cities with high densities face severe congestion." Given that water, sewer, and street maintenance are included in the category of general services, low-density cities must also have high capital costs per resident. The minimum cost for general services, the authors calculated, is "at a density of about 15,800 people per square mile, well above the 1982 average of 5,468.... The cost at a density of 15,800 is about 11 percent below the cost at the average density and about 6 percent below the cost at the maximum density. All else equal, therefore, both New York with its relatively high density [23,550 people per square mile] and cities with very low densities, such as New Orleans (2,870 people per square mile) ... face relatively high costs for general services."[15]

Table 7-5 illustrates the differences in costs for ten cities and summarizes the variation in the three services across all eighty-six cities. The cost of general services in 1982 was more than twice as high in the city with the toughest setting (163) as in the one with the most favorable setting (70), but most cities were grouped within 10 percent (plus or minus) of the average (for a standard deviation of 30).

The variation across cities was much greater for police services, largely because of dramatic differences in city poverty rates. The cost per resident

15. Ladd and Yinger (1991, p. 85). New Orleans's apparent low density results from having 60 percent of its municipal area in swampland or under Lake Ponchartrain.

Table 7-5. *Indexes of Public Service Costs and Standardized Expenditure Needs, Ten Selected Cities, 1982*

Cities	Cost index			Standardized expenditure need[a]
	General	Police	Fire	
86 cities				
Average	112	159	133	115
Standard deviation	30	22	111	52
Maximum	163	710	343	214
Minimum	70	35	43	58
Selected cities				
Albuquerque	77	64	83	71
Cleveland	151	300	218	172
Houston	118	130	95	112
Kansas City, Mo.	144	106	99	126
Miami	75	280	194	114
Newark	102	710	344	214
New Orleans	113	461	110	162
Richmond	112	148	188	118
Salt Lake City	163	145	141	149
Tampa	112	141	138	112

Source: Ladd and Yinger, *America's Ailing Cities*, p. 100.
a. As an index of the 1982 index for these cities.

of police services was more than twenty times as high in the city with the harshest conditions (Newark, 710) as in the city with the most favorable conditions (Virginia Beach, 35), and the range among most cities was very wide (plus or minus 55 percent).

The variation in fire costs fell between the cost variation for general services and police service. The highest-cost city (once again, Newark, 344) had to pay almost eight times as much for the same quality fire protection as the lowest-cost city (Virginia Beach, 43). The fire costs of most cities were grouped within 25 percent (plus or minus) of the average for all cities.

In discussing variations among the selected cities, Ladd and Yinger explained:

> Albuquerque has relatively low police costs because its poverty rate [14 percent in 1980] is somewhat below average and its share of metropolitan population [80 percent] is relatively large, and Cleveland has relatively high

police costs primarily because of its high concentration of poverty [29 percent in 1980]. High poverty is also the main cause of high fire costs in Cleveland, high police costs in New Orleans, and high police and fire costs in Newark and Miami. Population density does not affect police and fire costs, but high or low densities boost the cost of general services. Miami has relatively low general service costs despite its high other costs because it has relatively low wages and because its population density, about 12,300, is near the lowest-cost density. Salt Lake City and Richmond have relatively high general service costs because their population densities, below 2,500, are extremely low. Finally, New Orleans has low fire costs despite its high poverty because it has a high value of service and manufacturing property ... which are relatively inexpensive to protect from fire.[16]

Finally, the three categories were summarized to calculate the standardized expenditure needs.[17] Standardized expenditure needs varied widely across cities (table 7-5). The highest-cost city (Newark, 214) had to spend almost four times as much per resident to provide the same level and quality of services as the lowest-cost city (Virginia Beach, 58). Again, standard deviation indicated that most cities' standardized expenditure needs were grouped within 15 percent (plus or minus) of the average city.

As with standardized revenue-raising capability, the preceding calculations do not reflect actual city expenditures and the quality of services. Service quality will vary significantly among different cities. In addition, the specific package of services that a given city government provides will vary significantly from city to city. Albuquerque operates an airport, bus system, and water and sewer systems as municipal departments, for example. In many communities these services may be operated by independent regional authorities. In like manner, Albuquerque's city government has no responsibility for health care, a function that most consolidated city-county governments must assume. Some city governments, such as New York, Baltimore, and Richmond, are responsible for financing local public schools. In most cities, local school districts are independent governments with separate taxing authority.

16. Ladd and Yinger (1991, p. 92).
17. The 1982 standardized expenditure needs were expressed as an index of the 1972 index for the same eighty-six cities. At an index of 115 in 1982, the average city had to spend 15 percent more (after adjusting for inflation) to achieve the same level and quality of services it had in 1972. In effect, further deterioration in the economic and social environment of the average city during the 1980s had upped the cost of meeting a standardized service level.

Ladd and Yinger explore real world costs versus standardized model costs as well. Their standardized models, however, were the most revealing. Combining a city's standardized revenue-raising capability with its standardized expenditure needs yielded a city's "standardized fiscal health." A city with a standardized fiscal health of 20 percent would have 20 percent more revenue-raising capability than expenditure needs. It could provide its residents with the standard quality and level of services, while cutting taxes 20 percent. Alternatively, it could maintain the same revenue level and improve the quantity and quality of services by 20 percent. On the other hand, a city with a standardized fiscal health of –20 percent would either have to slash the level of services or receive sufficient state and federal aid to cover the revenue gap.

I have spent some time here countering the Cato Institute's arguments with Ladd and Yinger's observations in order to reinforce my central point about municipal finances: the foremost reasons for substantial disparities in taxes and services among cities—and among cities and suburbs—are factors over which local officials have *minimal control.*

A city's revenue-raising capabilities are based primarily on what taxes it can collect from whom. City councils do not control that basic decision. State legislatures do. State legislatures determine what a city's basic revenue-raising authority will be. For the most part, mayors and city councils can set tax rates only within narrow, legislatively prescribed limits.

Equally important for both revenue-raising potential and service needs is the social and economic profile of the city's work force and residents within the metropolitan framework. As I have argued, in the age of sprawl, the ability or inability of a city to be territorially "elastic"—to be able to defend its market share of the region's population and economic growth through annexation—is vital. Here again state legislatures control the rules of the game. In effect, annexation is impossible in one-third of the nation (the Northeast and Middle Atlantic states). It is difficult to carry out in one-third of the nation (generally, in the Midwest and Sun Belt states that require property owner approval for annexations), and relatively easier in the remaining one-third of the nation (mostly Sun Belt states, notably Texas, Tennessee, and North Carolina).

"Geography is fiscal fate," I told an audience of several thousand in a keynote address to the national convention of the Government Finance Officers Association in June 1997. (At the convention I actually did use my three-dimensional "island" graphic of bond ratings with which, in my Walter Mittyesque musings, I had confounded Speaker Gingrich.) A city's territo-

Table 7-6. *Standardized Fiscal Health Scores for Sixty Major Cities,*
by Elasticity

Elasticity category	Number of cities	Capture-contribute percentage	Fiscal health
Hyper	10	49	6
High	8	28	−5
Medium	11	11	7
Low	11	−2	−14
Zero	20	−38	−26

Source: Author's calculations based on Ladd and Yinger, *America's Ailing Cities*, pp. 121–22.

rial elasticity roughly conforms to Ladd and Yinger's calculations of standardized fiscal health (table 7-6). Limiting the comparison to sixty central cities, I found that the twenty-nine reasonably elastic cities (medium- to hyperelastic) captured both positive shares of their regional growth (11–49 percent) and had generally positive standardized fiscal health scores. Eleven low-elastic cities, however, contributed modestly (−2 percent) to suburban growth and averaged negative standardized fiscal health scores (−14 percent). The linkage becomes acute for zero-elastic cities. They not only lost a substantial amount of their population to their suburbs (−38 percent) but had to face constant underlying fiscal crises (−26 percent fiscal health score).

Inelasticity and Incompetence

Are the Cato Institute and the hundreds of suburban officials and residents whom I have heard condemn their core city governments totally wrong? Of course not. There are demonstrable instances of waste, featherbedding, sclerotic bureaucracy, even outright corruption. Nevertheless, beyond the specific history of many inelastic cities, the sprawl machine and the poverty machine combine to create a deficit machine. Until the interlocking cycles of sprawling peripheral growth and the core disinvestment and abandonment are reversed, inelastic cities will be unable to make themselves healthy solely through what they do.

Ed Rendell became mayor of Philadelphia in 1992 at the City of Brotherly Love's lowest moment. It was bankrupt. Its credit rating had dropped so low that it could no longer market its municipal bonds. With courage, determination, and hard work, Mayor Rendell brought Philadelphia back from the brink of total collapse. Within six months, Rendell's reforms had succeeded in raising the city's bond rating from B (meaning "imminent danger of nonpayment") to BA (the "speculative investment" or "junk bond" grade).

We were chatting at a conference in Philadelphia about city-suburb relations. Mayor Rendell told me, "Back in the darkest days, our suburban neighbors told me, 'Cut back on the city unions' power. Slash city payrolls to get rid of the deadwood. Get rid of the bureaucracy. Balance the budget. Get your bond rating back. Get your house in order and then we suburbs will be happy to help out.'

"Well," Rendell continued, "I did all that. I backed the unions down. I chopped the deadwood out of the bureaucracy. I balanced the budget. I got our bond rating raised. I got Philadelphia's house back in order—and it didn't make a darned bit of difference. Our suburbs are no more ready to help now than they were before."

In this generation many central cities are sinking under the burden of too many poor people and too little tax base. In the next generation, that will be the fate of many older suburbs. To fix the deficit machine, we absolutely must change the rules regarding metropolitan housing and development patterns and add regional revenue sharing to ease the transition.

PART TWO

The Outside Game

SPRAWLING DEVELOPMENT patterns, growing concentrations of minority poor, and widening fiscal disparities define America's urban crisis. Part 2 shows how a handful of communities have adopted policies to combat these destructive forces. They have used regional land use planning to help control sprawl; regional fair-share low- and moderate-income housing to help dissolve concentrations of poverty; and regional revenue sharing to help reduce fiscal disparities.

Rather than survey the range of various state and local initiatives in growth management, affordable housing, and revenue sharing, I have focused on the best practices available. For those who follow urban affairs, my choices are not surprising: Oregon and Portland for strong regional growth management (chapter 8); Montgomery County, Maryland, for long-tested mixed-income housing policies (chapter 9); and the Twin Cities area for regional revenue sharing, though in this case, I have chosen to focus on Minnesota's recent experience in political coalition building as its most important lesson for the country (chapter 11).

In its place I have described the voluntary program devised in the Montgomery County–Dayton, Ohio, region (chapter 10). Dayton's economic development and government equity (ED/GE) plan is ten parts economic development to one part revenue sharing. Within the context of Ohio's highly fragmented system of local governance, the countywide collaborative effort is a remarkable achievement, but the minimal impact of its revenue-sharing component illustrates the limitations of voluntary intergovernmental compacts.

With suitable adaptations from state to state, these new rules for local governments would substantially reverse sprawl and the growing concentrations of poverty, and ease fiscal disparities. These three rules would, in effect, bring the built-in benefits of elasticity to inelastic cities and their older, built-out suburbs.

Actually, these rules are essential for elastic cities as well. Many elastic cities have the legal tools to control sprawling development better. Yet few actually do. The recent actions by the city of San Jose and three other California cities to adopt urban growth boundaries—and enforce their goals through supportive utility policies limiting new extensions—stand out as positive examples.

A number of communities have mandatory affordable housing requirements for all new development, but (to my knowledge) only Montgomery County, Maryland, and neighboring Fairfax County, Virginia, require that a modest percentage of the affordable housing created must be sold to the county housing authority, a crucial step in fighting the concentration of poverty. Any region would benefit from adopting Montgomery County's housing policies.

Elastic cities serve as internal revenue-sharing mechanisms, but as they mature, other communities (both incorporated and unincorporated) spring up on their outskirts. Multijurisdictional growth management and housing compacts, buttressed by revenue-sharing arrangements, are becoming more and more necessary around the Albuquerques, the Charlottes, the Columbuses, the Indianapolises. The old formula—defending your market share of regional growth through annexation or consolidation—becomes less and less effective.

Despite tripling their municipal territory from 1960 to 1990, even the fifty most expansion-minded central cities lost market share: from 65 percent (1960) to 51 percent (1990) of their urbanized populations and from 60 percent (1960) to 43 percent of their metropolitan populations.

Only two regions that I have visited successfully do it all. The first is Toronto, Canada. For four decades the Toronto region was served by Metro Toronto, a regional government. Formed in 1954 when the city of Toronto was one-half of the region's population and about three-quarters of its tax base, Metro Toronto successfully guided the metropolitan area's growth. Today Toronto is generally proclaimed North America's most livable city. (That certainly was our reaction when Delcia and I visited Toronto in November 1996.)

Metro Toronto was responsible for overall transportation and land use planning; all major infrastructure systems (water, sewer, highways, transit, regional parks); financing local public schools; and a regionwide police department. The city of Toronto and five suburban municipalities provided fire protection, maintained local streets, picked up the trash, and provided other purely local services.

Within its 240-square-mile jurisdiction, Metro Toronto carried out all the measures I would later recommend: regional land use planning, regional revenue sharing, and regional "social housing." Where subsidized housing would be located, for example, has never been a matter for local governments to decide. Social housing has always been controlled by Metro Toronto or even by the provincial government of Ontario. As a result, social housing is widely dispersed and concentration of Toronto's poorest residents is averted.

Metro Toronto's Achilles' heel is that, once established by the Ontario parliament, Metro's jurisdiction was never allowed to expand beyond its original 240-mile territory. For two decades that was sufficient, but in recent decades growth has leaped past Metro Toronto's reach. The Greater Toronto Area (GTA) now has a population of 4.5 million people scattered over 2,700 square miles.

In 1996 the Conservative party took control of Ontario for the first time in decades. Taking a page out of the Republican party's manual in America, the Tories campaigned on a platform of "less government." Fulfilling their pledge, in early 1997 the provincial government "amalgamated" the city of Toronto, its five suburban municipalities, and Metro Toronto itself into one unitary government. In the process, the Tories claimed, they had simplified local government and eliminated almost half of all local elected offices.

This was a better outcome than one alternative: abolishing Metro Toronto itself and leaving Toronto and its five immediate suburban neighbors without any overall mechanism. But the newly elected parliamentary majority rejected Metro Toronto's own preference: extend Metro's powers to the full 2,700-square-mile Greater Toronto Area. (The Tories' political stronghold is Toronto's outer suburbs.)

Instead, what was long viewed by American eyes as the model of regional collaboration (Canadian-style) has been converted into something much more familiar, a central city surrounded by hostile suburban counties (called, in Toronto's case, "regional municipalities").

The new amalgamated city of Toronto is a much healthier central city than its American counterparts. Toronto, of course, is the business and financial capital of Canada, New York, and Chicago rolled into one. Long characterized as "Toronto the Good," Toronto has been transformed from the straitlaced head of British Canada into the heart of a world city. It is populous (2.5 million residents) and amazingly cosmopolitan.[1] With approximately 10,500 residents per square mile, the new Toronto is also much more densely populated than all but a dozen U.S. cities.[2] Yet with carefully interconnected subway lines, bus routes, and a viable streetcar system, Torontonians move around readily and quickly. All the ills of city life that many Americans tolerate are refuted by Toronto.

Yet Canada no more escapes the influence of American styles in its metropolitan development patterns than it does in business or popular culture. New suburban communities springing up in the Greater Toronto Area (outside the influence of Metro Toronto) are indistinguishable from American suburbs. Whether Toronto will still be North America's most livable city in another half century is an unanswered question. There is now no counterpart to Metro Toronto to deal with the new regional challenges across a region ten times the size of that successfully managed by Metro Toronto.

The other community that has done it all is Montgomery County, Maryland. Someone might object that Montgomery County is only one-fifth of the national capital region. It is a fair objection. Silver Spring or Bethesda would never have supplanted Washington itself as Montgomery County's central city; county government does not have to contend with true inner-city problems in all their intensity. Yet Silver Spring, in particular, could have evolved into an extremely distressed area if county policies had allowed that to happen. Instead, it is simply a somewhat frayed and aging community that the county is trying hard to reinvigorate.

With 826,766 residents in 1997, Montgomery County, standing alone, would be the nation's sixty-ninth largest metro area. It offers, in the words of a former county planner, "a big enough canvas to work on." A large enough portrait of a complex urban community has been drawn on that canvas to be judged critically.

Montgomery County has its problems. The Montgomery County Public Schools are constantly struggling to meet the needs of many

---

1. In 1991, only 65 percent of Metro Torontonians reported English as their mother tongue.

2. All except New York City (23,698 per square mile) and San Francisco (15,502) have been steadily depopulating since mid-century.

minority students whose numbers are steadily approaching half the county's school population. Tragic murders occur. Yet with a poverty rate one-quarter that of neighboring District of Columbia, Montgomery County has one-twentieth the murder rate. These points serve as reminders that the world is not perfect. Yet the perfect should not be made the enemy of the good. Montgomery County is an exceptional community in which many people of different racial and ethnic backgrounds and different economic status live side by side. Any region that adopts the model policies detailed in part 2—and as practiced in Toronto and Montgomery County—will be much closer to being all that America can be.

8

Portland, Oregon: Taming Urban Sprawl

"IN THE GOOD OLD DAYS, where did Portlanders love to go to get a break from city life?" Our guides as Delcia and I toured Oregon's metropolis in February 1996 were Carl Abbott and Ethan Seltzer, two Portland State University professors.

"Sauvie Island," my hosts agreed, "a very special place . . . forty square miles of prime farmland on an island where the Columbia and Willamette rivers come together . . . just ten miles from Downtown Portland. Strawberries, pumpkins, other vegetables, dairy farms. On weekends families would come out from the city to buy fresh produce and show their children real cows and horses. Businessmen could even go duck hunting at dawn, then make it into the office by 9 A.M."

"Sauvie Island was right in the path of urban development?" (The Portland area's population had more than tripled in fifty years.)

"Yes, flat land, great views, linked by highway to Portland. Some potential flood and drainage problems, but nothing that enough money couldn't fix," Carl replied. "The turning point came in 1976 when a developer first proposed subdividing the 3,000–4,000-acre Douglas Farm."

Carl paused. "Let's go see what Sauvie Island looks like today."

Leaving Portland's skyscrapers behind us, we drove north on U.S. 30, following the Willamette River. Overshadowed by towering cargo cranes, low-slung factories and warehouses lay on either side of the highway. In a steady procession, oceangoing freighters and container ships lined the wharves of the Port of Portland on our right. Three-quarters of American wheat exported to Japan, China, and other Pacific Rim destinations passes through Portland.

Several hundred yards to the west, a steep, wooded ridge, Forest Park, rose up. A mile-wide ribbon, Forest Park stretches from almost the edge of downtown nine miles northward. A guidebook claims that, with its more than 5,000 acres, Forest Park is the largest municipal park in the world.

"What's in Forest Park?"

"Bike trails, jogging trails, even some old growth forest. It's very popular with city residents. Much of it was assembled by the city in the 1930s through tax foreclosures," Ethan explained.

Just as the Willamette veered northeastward to join the Columbia, a sign announced "Sauvie Island," pointing toward a concrete bridge arching high over the Multnomah Ship Channel. At the highest point of the bridge we had a brief, panoramic view of what had become of Sauvie Island.

It was still farmland stretching as far as we could see!

"How is this possible?"

"Senate Bill 100, Oregon's Statewide Land-Use Planning Act, passed in 1973. Aroused neighbors blocked subdividing Douglas Farm, and by 1979 Sauvie Island was placed outside Portland's urban growth boundary. It should always be farmland." Carl's faint grin betrayed a touch of pride. "Or nature preserve. Most of the northern end of the island is a wildlife refuge."

"There's the Pumpkin Patch." Ethan pointed out several reddish, white-trimmed farm buildings. "Tens of thousands of Portlanders come out here every fall to get their Halloween pumpkins. It's a real urban-rural ritual."

Our car cruised virtually alone along the two-lane road that hooked around three sides of the island. Gazing across fields and orchards, we could see downtown Portland's tallest buildings to the south and Mount Hood etched sharply against the eastern horizon. To the northeast was the truncated remnant of Mount Saint Helens, its upper 1,500 feet having been pulverized and ejected into the atmosphere by the cataclysmic eruption fifteen years earlier. Even more startling for us visitors was the sight of giant ships sailing along the Columbia River, their superstructures towering above the riverbank levee that hid their hulls.

We turned westward to cut across the island's neck. Several lookout points and parking areas punctuated the southern edge of the state nature sanctuary. Farther along, discreet wooden signs pointed up roads leading to two private duck-hunting clubs. "You should see this road before dawn dur-

ing duck season. Real traffic jams out here with cars lined up, hunters waiting to get their turn in the duck blinds," Ethan commented.

"What would prevent Sauvie Island from being turned into five to ten-
acre 'farms' with big mansions for 'gentlemen farmers,' which happens in so
many places?"

"Oregon's laws preserving agricultural land around urban areas are
really tough," Carl explained. "On this island no single property can be less
than sixty-seven acres except for a few smaller parcels that were 'grandfathered.' Land has to be actively farmed, producing at least $80,000 in an-
nual revenue. A farmer who wants to build another house must show that
the new house is essential to farming the land. No hobby farms allowed. You
know, keep a few horses but commute to your law office in Portland."

As the sun set, we turned southward back toward the city. Houseboats
lined sections of the Multnomah Ship Channel, dividing Sauvie Island from
the mainland. "That's one way to have a 'detached' house in the suburbs
without spending weekends cutting the grass!"

"A houseboat's really a lot of work, constant maintenance," Ethan cautioned. "But, you just tie up, pay your docking fee to the wharf owner, no
property taxes. Some people really like it. Portland provides for lots of different lifestyles."

Saving the Farm

Over breakfast the next morning I sought more information on Oregon's
land use planning law from two nationally recognized experts, Henry Richmond and Bob Stacey. For many years they led 1000 Friends of Oregon, the
state's leading watchdog group over land use planning and growth management. I had been praising the environmental organization's success.

"Do you know who really passed Senate Bill 100 back in 1973?" Henry
said. "A small group of conservative Republican farmer-legislators. The one
who got it started was Hector MacPherson, a dairy farmer who was a member of the Linn County Planning Commission for many years. County planning commissions might try to preserve farmland, but state laws were so
weak back then that the commissions were really powerless whenever developers waved enough money around in front of hard-pressed farmers. The
Willamette Valley has some of the most productive agricultural land in the
world. Agriculture's 20 percent of the state's economy. But Hector saw that
the farming economy—and a whole way of life—was being paved over by
urban sprawl year after year."

"The story is told," Bob interjected, "that one day Hector was driving past a neighbor's farm. A big Caterpillar was shoving the soil around. 'What ya plannin' to grow here?" Hector called out. "Houses," the Cat operator answered.

"That finally tore it for Hector," Henry continued. "He was fed up and got himself elected to the state Senate. He was determined to change state law to make exclusive farm use zoning stick."

"So, Oregon's landmark growth management law wasn't really the handiwork of liberal Democrat tree-huggers from Portland?"

Henry smiled at my gentle dig. "Oh, some of us were there at the state capitol, plugging away, but at every critical legislative juncture there was a conservative Republican farmer-legislator in the middle of the reform battle. Hector MacPherson, of course, Jim Smart and Randy Smith from Polk County, Stafford Hansell from Umatilla County. Salt-of-the-earth types with real dirt under their fingernails. At legislative hearings they spoke with the moral authority of Old Testament prophets. They're the ones who really put Oregon's land use law on the books."

"And, of course, we had Tom McCall as governor then," Bob added. "Another Republican, from an old Oregonian family. McCall had a deep feeling for what makes Oregon so special. He once said that he loved Oregon more than life itself.

"The growth management act set statewide land use goals, but the key was how strongly the goals would be interpreted and enforced. Governor McCall appointed L. B. Day, a top Teamsters Union leader, as first chairman of the state Land Conservation and Development Commission." Bob chuckled. "L. B. was a tough son-of-a-gun. He proclaimed that urban sprawl was 'a stinking cancer on the lush, green breast of the Willamette Valley.'

"L. B. drove the commission members through seventy-eight public hearings. They came out with tough interim rules. Until the state commission approved new local comprehensive plans, L. B. ruled, the statewide goals applied to all local rezoning actions. His commission had to approve all local, nonconforming proposals. That stopped a lot of quick land grabs by developers."

"I have the impression that growth management is now primarily an urban issue," I said. (That week Representative Ron Wyden, a liberal Democrat from Portland, had narrowly beaten State Senator Gordon Smith, a conservative Republican from eastern Oregon, for Bob Packwood's vacated U.S. Senate seat. Wyden's narrow victory margin was widely credited to overwhelming support by Portland area environmentalists.)[1]

1. In November 1996 Smith was elected to fill the other U.S. Senate seat vacated upon Mark Hatfield's retirement.

"No. In the last legislative session, the Farm Bureau was one of 1000 Friends' best allies in fighting the law's repeal. But with the strong, antigovernment ideology of many Republican legislators these days, statewide growth management has lost its clear, bipartisan flavor," Bob explained. "If the legislature repealed the law, 1000 Friends would probably push for a popular referendum. Oregon voters have twice solidly rejected repealing our growth management law. But we haven't had a popular vote since 1982. A referendum might be a tough fight, but I'm confident that most Oregonians want strong, statewide land use planning."

State Ends, Local Means

Strong, statewide land use planning is precisely what Senate Bill 100 provides. The legislature set fourteen statewide goals that must be met by all local governments. These cover a wide range of concerns. All local governments must encourage urban development, but only within urban growth boundaries. They must curb urban sprawl. Local plans must identify and preserve historically or archaeologically significant sites and buildings. They must set aside open space, conserve fish and wildlife habitats, protect air and water quality, and develop parks. Saving productive forests and farmlands, the bill's original objective, is a high priority.

Oregon's land use planning law extends beyond concern over the natural environment to address the human environment. All local plans must encourage the availability of affordable housing for all income groups. Local plans must promote a variety of residential densities and housing types and encourage the preservation of existing housing stock. Continued economic growth, especially for unemployed and disadvantaged persons, is another key goal. Local plans must also favor efficient, energy-saving light rail and bus systems for more densely populated areas. All must be accomplished through a process of continuous citizen participation. Senate Bill 100 gives the state's Land Conservation and Development Commission the power to review and approve (or reject) all local plans, depending on whether they conform with statewide goals.

In the rest of Oregon, county government has the key coordinating role. In metropolitan Portland, however, officials who manage the growth process are directly accountable to all area residents through Metro, the nation's only elected regional government. Metro is a state-chartered regional government that covers Multnomah, Clackamas, and Washington Counties, the city of Portland, and twenty-three other municipalities. The region's voters elect directly the seven-member Metro council and Metro's executive officer.

"The constant debate about growth issues around here is really remarkable." Our dinner companion that night was Mike Burton, Metro's current executive officer. Tall, mustachioed, good-looking, fiftyish, Burton is a former state senator with a career politician's easy presence. He was elected to his first four-year term as head of Metro in November 1994. I seconded his observation. "As just one example of what you say, I picked up this morning's *Daily Oregonian,* and what was the 'Question of the Day' in the reader poll but 'Should Portland's urban growth boundary be extended or not?' Call such and such an '800' number to vote 'yes', another to vote 'no'."

"Metro is truly unique. We're the only elected level of government in the country whose mission is really to focus on the future," Burton responded. "Oh, we have some service functions. We run the Washington Park Zoo and the Oregon Convention Center. But you could strip away all these other functions. What's really important is our responsibility for regional land use planning.

"And that's made even stronger by Metro's home rule charter, adopted by the citizens of the region in 1992," Burton continued. "Our charter gives Metro an unparalleled grant of responsibility for growth management. In section 9 our citizens direct the courts to interpret Metro's land use planning powers liberally. That's an unparalleled set of instructions for the courts."

A liberal interpretation of local government powers, I thought, is standard language in most home rule charters. Burton's larger point, though, was right on the mark: Portland Metro is indeed a unique regional government with growth management powers that are unparalleled in the United States.

Electing to Go Metro

Metro had a long gestation. For seventy years the Portland area has been experimenting with regional governance. As early as 1925 a state study commission raised the alarm that rapid, unplanned, automobile-based suburbanization was outrunning Portland's ability to annex new areas. The commission called for Portland and Multnomah County's consolidation, a proposal the Oregon legislature studiously ignored.

The postwar boom revived the concern over sprawl. During the 1950s Multnomah, Clackamas, and Washington Counties all adopted their first zoning codes. By 1961 the number of special districts for fire, water, zoning, sewers, parks, and street lighting had exploded to 218 (from just 28 in 1941). Political wars raged over Portland's aggressive annexation efforts. Suburban subdivisions struggled to incorporate as a defense against "big city" annexation.

To bring some order out of chaotic local governance, the League of Women Voters, business leaders, and other good government groups persuaded the state legislature to establish the Portland Metropolitan Study Commission (1963–71). Unlike its predecessor four decades earlier, this commission made recommendations that ultimately transformed regional governance. The study commission first helped organize a voluntary Columbia Region Association of Governments (CRAG) in 1967. Then the study commission got the legislature to set up two other regional bodies: the Local Government Boundary Commission (1969), which would adjudicate annexation disputes, and the Metropolitan Service District (1970).

From the outset CRAG was embroiled in frustration and controversy. Its original membership was composed of officials representing four counties and fourteen cities. Over the years its governing board mushroomed to delegates from five counties and thirty-one member cities. All had coequal status. Though CRAG had a good professional staff, it had neither the authority nor the ability to forge a consensus around difficult regional policy issues.

As Carl Abbott, my Portland State host, explained, "CRAG board members were often torn between what was good for the region and what would protect their own constituents from unwanted costs, programs, or development." In short, CRAG had all the virtues and defects that characterize most of some 600 voluntary councils of government scattered across the nation today. CRAG was a useful setting for local officials to convene and exchange views. Its staff produced insightful studies and thoughtful recommendations. However, CRAG acted only on the easy issues, meaning that member jurisdictions thought they had nothing to lose.

The Metropolitan Services District (MSD), on the other hand, proved to be a more promising regional initiative. The MSD was created by the Oregon legislature as a "metropolitan municipality of greater Portland," covering Multnomah, Clackamas, and Washington Counties. The MSD did not supplant county government or any of the 24 municipalities. It was only an empty governmental "box" to be filled by whatever duties the legislature or the voters approved for it.

The MSD began life uncertainly and modestly. In May 1970 the region's voters swept aside the mayor of Portland's implacable opposition and activated the MSD by a 54 to 46 margin. It was initially governed by a seven-member board of local elected officials from Portland, the three counties, and three other cities. A second voter referendum turned down the MSD's request for a general property tax levy. The MSD's first project—planning a regional solid waste disposal system—was financed by a small tax on used auto tires. In 1976, this time with Portland's agreement and voter approval of an earmarked tax levy, the MSD added a second regional function, operating the Washington Park Zoo.

In 1977 the legislature injected more direct democracy into the MSD. The state lawmakers shelved having it governed by elected officials from member counties and cities in favor of having the region's voters elect a twelve-member board and an executive officer. The legislature also gave the MSD broader taxing authority (but only with local voter approval).

As Carl Abbott remembered the change, "The legislature saw direct elections as the best, and perhaps only, way to secure an effective areawide government. Like CRAG, the mayors and county officials who served on MSD's board still looked out for their own jurisdictions first."

"Why an elected executive officer rather than hiring a professional administrator?"

"A hired chief administrator wouldn't have a political base. A city manager-type simply couldn't survive in a role as increasingly controversial as MSD chief executive," Carl responded. "The MSD needed an elected head honcho."

In May 1978 the region's voters approved the revised MSD by a 55 to 45 margin. In the bargain, the voters abolished CRAG. The newly democratized MSD took over CRAG's regional planning role, including overseeing Oregon's Statewide Land-Use Planning Act for the three-county Portland area. In 1979 the state Land Conservation and Development Commission endorsed the Portland area urban growth boundary drawn up by the MSD. The boundary line was based on CRAG staff work begun five years earlier.

There were still more setbacks (two other tax referendums were defeated). Nevertheless, under Rena Cusma, its first elected executive officer, the MSD slowly matured. Attendance at the Washington Park Zoo boomed. Buttressed by an advisory council of local officials, the MSD took over planning for federal transportation funds. In 1986 the region's voters approved a $65 million bond issue for the Oregon Convention Center, which the MSD would plan, build, and run.

In 1987 the legislature gave the executive officer veto power over council actions. The council itself began to act less like a board of directors and more like a legislative body. Finally, in 1990 the Oregon constitution was amended to allow the MSD to have its own home rule charter. Drawn up by a citizens' charter commission, the document was approved by area voters in November 1992.

The structural changes provided in MSD's home rule charter—now officially called "Metro"—were minimal; the council was reduced from twelve members to seven. Metro's state-conferred growth management powers, however, received a resounding endorsement from local voters. In the new charter the voters affirmed that regional planning would be Metro's "primary function."

The charter charges Metro with developing a fifty-year "future vision" and a "regional framework plan." Metro has the power to resolve conflicts between regional and local plans and, by ordinance, require compliance with the regional framework plan.

Growth Boundaries and Good Sidewalks

Metro is merely the framework for regional planning, however. The substance flows from Oregon's Statewide Land-Use Planning Act. Of all the goals, the most innovative is state goal 14, which requires that each municipality establish an urban growth boundary in a perimeter around each urbanized area. There must be sufficient capacity within an urban growth boundary for twenty years of anticipated growth. Indeed, within an urban growth boundary, local land use plans, zoning regulations, and the building permit process must expedite private development.

But outside an urban growth boundary, the land is reserved for exclusive farm use, exclusive forest industry use, or for parks and natural areas. The county government must prevent both suburban development and rural sprawl. No water lines, no sewer lines, no wider county roads, no permissive zoning. Oregon draws a sharp line between what is urban and what is rural.

"When it was first designated in 1979, Portland's urban growth boundary was really just an imaginary line on a map.[2] Now, almost twenty years later, you can actually see it," our tour guide, Ethan Seltzer, commented, as we had continued our drive around the Portland area. "If we were flying over the area, in many sections you could actually see the growth boundary now from the air. Subdivisions extend up to a point, then they stop, and

2. The Portland area's initial urban growth boundary added about 20 percent more vacant land to the region's already urbanized area.

farmland takes over. Actually, we're driving along part of the growth boundary now—Sunnyside Road—in northern Clackamas County."

We continued looking around. To our right—inside the urban growth boundary—were relatively new subdivisions. Denser townhouse developments alternated with more traditional, single-family, split-level homes grouped around their cul-de-sacs. But to our left—outside the urban growth boundary—were working farms.

We turned into Sunnyside itself, a new subdivision being built in the "neotraditional" style. Though there were some attached townhouses, most were stand-alone, single-family homes. However, Sunnyside felt more like a neighborhood constructed a century before. Unlike the brick or stucco ranch houses and split-levels of classic postwar suburbs, Sunnyside's houses were two and three stories, wood frame construction, with pitched roofs, garrets, and dormer windows. Many had front porches where parents could sit and watch their children play in front or greet neighbors as they passed by. Sideyards were small, and houses situated close together lined the streets.

There was something notably absent from this neotraditional neighborhood: the blank expanse of the two-car garage doors, the dominant aesthetic feature of postwar suburban houses. With rare exceptions, garages were not visible in Sunnyside. They had been tucked into separate structures at the back of the deep lots, reached by sideyard driveways or, more often, off midblock alleyways.

Sunnyside was a good effort, but perhaps (I noted to myself) with a design shortcoming: its sidewalks. In more conventional suburban fashion, Sunnyside's sidewalks were narrow and flush to roll curbs. In effect, they were unusable by pedestrians, a seemingly small but crucial design issue that will significantly reduce casual contact among neighbors.

I had come to appreciate the importance of good sidewalks years earlier when we lived in a genuine "traditional" neighborhood in Washington. Our sidewalks in Barnaby Woods were set back from the curb about five feet. The setback was sufficient to provide a flat ribbon of concrete unbroken by drive pads and to allow stately old elm trees to line both sides of the street, creating a cool green canopy along its entire length. Parallel-parked cars provided further separation from automobile traffic.

The sidewalks in Barnaby Woods were little highways of neighborhood activity. Having been taught *never* to step into the street, toddlers to teenagers played up and down the sidewalks. Young mothers rolled baby carriages along. Elderly residents walked their dogs. Working men and women walked to and from bus stops morning and evening. All we lacked was neighborhood shopping within easy walking distance; the nearest neighborhood grocery store was a half mile away. (Sunnyside residents, I could see, would also be auto-dependent for all shopping.)

The poet Robert Frost once wrote (perhaps ironically) that "good fences make good neighbors." He had it wrong. Good sidewalks make good neighbors. With good sidewalks, neighbors are thrown together in casual encounters all the time.

Typical postwar suburban subdivisions isolate residents from one another. Where they even exist, sidewalks usually serve only to prop up curbs (as, unfortunately, Sunnyside's new sidewalks do). Wide, empty streets encourage fast traffic. Typical subdivision residents live in self-contained cocoons—either driving their cars in and out of two-car garages or disappearing into family rooms and fenced backyards.

In pursuit of the American Dream suburban-style, many Americans have bought into the notion that a big house on a big lot is a satisfactory substitute for being part of a real neighborhood. Public space disappears. Private space reigns. Residents only become "neighbors" when they take some specific action to get together—such as a car pool or an occasional backyard barbecue.

Picture This!

My sense of what constitutes a well-designed neighborhood is clearly shared by a majority of Portland area residents. Several days after my auto tour, I met with Portland City Commissioner Earl Blumenauer (now a member of Congress, having won Ron Wyden's vacated seat). He gave me a copy of *Picture This!* It was the final report of a "visual preference survey" commissioned by Metro, Tri-Met (the three-county transit authority), the city of Portland, and a dozen other local governments.

During several weeks in 1995 more than 3,000 Portland area adults and 1,500 youth participated voluntarily in thirty-five sessions conducted by Nellesen and Associates, an architectural and planning firm based in Seattle and Princeton. They were shown more than 200 pictures of commercial areas, neighborhood streets, and houses and were asked to grade their visual preferences on a scale of −10 to +10.

The results? Despite the fact that two-thirds of participants were Portland suburbanites, typical suburban shopping centers (even high-design efforts) uniformly were graded negatively. No amount of cosmetic design could hide the reality of acres of parking lots and the visual monotony of shopping center storefronts. By contrast, with their parallel parking, street trees, and variegated building styles, older city commercial streets graded positively.

The same was true for neighborhoods. Typical suburban subdivisions with low-slung homes widely spaced, one to five to an acre along curving streets or around cul-de-sacs, were graded negatively; even some very tony-looking, upper-income subdivisions were rejected. By contrast, tree-arced city streets (with good sidewalks), lined more densely with two- and three-story frame houses, brick townhouses, or even modest one-story bungalows (with screen porches) graded very positively. The highest-rated residential neighborhood was a street scene from Toronto with thirty to forty dwelling units per acre.

Picture This!, as Nellesen and Associates themselves emphasized, was merely an expression of visual preferences. How much do visual preferences actually govern consumer preferences in the Portland area? ("A lot of suburban areas around here look like everywhere else despite our growth management policies," Metro's Mike Burton had told me.) What the suburban dream has been selling successfully for decades is not just two-car garages, backyard barbecues, all-electric kitchens, and modern bathrooms. It has also been selling social uniformity and escape from "city problems."

Segregation and Revival

The Portland region has not been exempt from racial and economic segregation, I reminded a Portland City Club audience to whom I spoke the day after my auto tour. Portland's African American population is relatively small; it amounts to some 3 percent of the region's population (the same proportion as the Albuquerque area). However, as of the 1990 census, the degree of racial segregation was surprisingly high. On the dissimilarity index scale of 0–100 (with 100 representing total segregation), the Portland region measured 66. (Albuquerque's index was 39.) By this statistical measure, the Portland area was as racially segregated as the Dallas-Fort Worth, Columbus (Ohio), or Washington metro areas.

One-quarter of the Portland region's 41,000 African Americans lived in just six majority-black census tracts across the Willamette River from downtown in the city's Albina area. The poverty rate in those six tracts was 30 percent in 1970; by 1990, the poverty rate had risen to 38 percent.

In fact, race aside, the number of poverty neighborhoods with more than

20 percent poor residents had grown from twenty-three in 1970 to thirty-eight in 1990, including several now-poverty neighborhoods in suburban Gresham, Beaverton, and Forest Grove. Of the twenty-three poverty neighborhoods in 1970, over the next two decades the poverty rate had increased in eleven, was stable in five, and had declined in eight neighborhoods.

"Your growth management policies are admirable, but you need to adopt more rigorous requirements for mixed-income housing development," I advised the City Club audience. "Some communities require that 15 or 20 percent of all new construction be affordable housing.[3] Over the past two decades such a mixed-income housing policy for the Portland region would have resulted in another 10,000 moderate-income homes and apartments for working-class households and another 5,000 units acquired by a regional low-income housing assistance program. This would have been sufficient to close down Columbia Villa and other public housing projects or to convert them to mixed-income housing."

Nevertheless, measured statistically through the 1990 census, the concentration of poverty in the Portland area was more moderate and the isolation of poor households was less extreme than in most other metropolitan areas. By the same dissimilarity index, but this time measuring the segregation of poor households (regardless of race), in 1990 the Portland area measured 27, the lowest of all metropolitan areas with more than 1 million residents.[4]

Poverty neighborhoods in the Portland area *felt* different as well. As we drove through Albina and other poor neighborhoods in February 1996, they did not look like poverty neighborhoods we would see in other cities. There were too many signs of revival: renovated homes, new townhouses, and refurbished stores. In fact, our visit to Portland in February 1996 may have been one of the few occasions when my analysis was truly the victim of old data. Six years had passed since the 1990 census had identified Albina as Portland's poorest neighborhood. By early 1996 the Portland economy was booming. The region's urban growth boundary had been in place for seventeen years. Both were dramatically transforming inner-city Albina.

Seven months after our visit, the *Sunday Oregonian* provided conclusive documentation of Albina's resurgence.[5] From 1990 to 1995 the total

3. See chapter 9 on Montgomery County, Maryland.
4. The fact that three out of four poor persons were white but were not highly segregated contributed to the Portland region's low economic segregation index.
5. Jim Barnett and Steve Suo, "Albina: Up or Out?" *Sunday Oregonian*, September 8, 1996. Information and comments about Albina are drawn liberally from this article.

value of all commercial, industrial, and residential property in Albina rose from $1.4 billion to $2.6 billion. In just five years Albina's homes, stores, and factories had almost doubled in value.

Targeted public investment had made its contribution. The newspaper estimated that since 1986 government agencies had committed at least $145 million to programs designed to move low-income residents into jobs, homes, or business ownership in Albina. A red-hot real estate market, however, had pumped eight times as much value into Albina's homes and stores. Since 1990 at least 844 properties, the reporters found, had "flipped," meaning they were bought and resold within twelve months.

In 1990 city inspectors counted 700 derelict buildings in Albina. At that time some buildings' values had sunk so low that it would have cost more to bring them up to code than leave them vacant. Other buildings were seized by the county for unpaid taxes. The real estate boom hastened the rehabilitation of hundreds of dilapidated properties. Where once banks would not lend, today they welcome customers, the article reported. By September 1996 the number of derelict buildings had dropped to 100. The demand for investment property in Albina is so great that the city sells lists of derelict buildings for $10 apiece.

How was such a revival triggered in Albina? "Government and volunteer social programs can take credit for planting the seeds of renewal," the article observed. "The urban growth boundary can take credit for herding people inward. Community patrols can take credit for standing toe-to-toe with crime. . . . But the gains blossoming in Albina these days have much more basic roots: *profit*. In five years, a booming real estate market has done for Albina what fifty years of government and social programs alone could not."

In the 1990s Albina's revival is not unique in the Portland region. New investment is flowing into older blue-collar suburbs such as Gresham, Milwaukie, and Oregon City. The *Oregonian*, I think, understated the urban growth boundary's impact. By controlling peripheral growth the urban growth boundary has turned market demand inward. Albina, Gresham, Milwaukie, and Oregon City are reviving because of Metro's growth management policies. The "inside game" succeeds because the "outside game" succeeds.

Progress brings new problems, of course. "As home values rise, Albina's poorest residents are finding it harder to rent, much less buy," the *Oregonian*'s story noted. "The inner-city's revival is walking hand-in-hand with gentrification. Most home loans are made to whites, encouraging a shift in

Table 8-1. *Change in Segregation Indexes in Metro Portland High Schools, 1989–98*

Racial or ethnic group	Percentage of students		Segregation index	
	1989–90	1997–98	1989–90	1997–98
All minorities	13.6	17.7	39.0	30.5
Black	4.7	4.1	65.7	62.5
Hispanic	2.5	6.1	30.0	27.0
Asian	5.4	6.4	39.1	36.4
Native American	1.0	1.0	43.7	32.2

the racial character of Portland's largest African-American community. As Albina residents celebrate their long-awaited shot at economic redemption, some wonder: As we save our neighborhood, will we lose our neighbors?"

It is certainly a fair question, but it can be overdramatized. Despite a 33 percent poverty rate among Albina's black residents in 1990, more than half were already homeowners. They have benefited from what few black homeowners experience nationally, a sustained increase in the value of their home. In the five-year period, home values at least doubled in each of Albina's thirteen neighborhoods.

The newspaper also found that credit is flowing more readily to black homeowners. More than 260 African Americans applied for home loans in 1994, an increase of 50 percent over 1992.[6] During the 1990s, however, housing prices have increased four times as fast as the average incomes of Albina residents. According to the *Oregonian*'s calculations, in 1990 nine out of ten Albina properties were affordable for its residents. By 1995 only six out of ten were still affordable. Low-income renters—black and white—faced a growing squeeze.

School enrollments offer some measure of trends in racial segregation between census reports (table 8-1). In *Cities without Suburbs* I had calculated segregation indexes for all public high schools in the nation's 320 metro areas for 1989–90. The school segregation index for black students in Portland (66) matched the region's housing segregation index (also 66). (With-

6. Applications from whites rose 53 percent, to 2,645, in the same period, and were approved at a slightly higher rate. As a result, more than 80 percent of the increased lending activity from 1992—both in dollars and number of loans—involved white buyers.

out a court-ordered school desegregation plan for the Portland area, school enrollment patterns would be expected to mirror housing patterns.) Seven years later, the level of school segregation had dropped for all racial groups, including for black students, who saw it fall from 66 to 62. The change reflects changing housing patterns, of course. The diminished isolation of black students, for example, was due both to white regentrification of areas of black concentration (such as Albina) and to the steady movement of blacks into other neighborhoods throughout the Portland region.

Growth Boundaries and Housing Affordability

Until the 1990s, the affordability of housing had not been a pressing regional issue. From the original legislative debates in the early 1970s onward, critics argued that urban growth boundaries would artificially inflate land costs, thus reducing housing affordability and inhibiting economic development. During the urban growth boundary's first decade, Portland's urbanized population grew 14 percent while urbanized land grew only 11 percent. (Portland was one of the few urban areas in which population grew faster than land use.) New suburban areas had about 4,500 residents per square mile, about three times the typical density of new suburbs in the 1980s.

Until the mid-1980s, the Oregon economy languished as forest products, the state's leading industry, weathered a fifteen-year slump. With modest amounts of land available within the urban growth boundary and slow economic growth, area housing costs went down relative to national inflation for much of the period.

To evaluate the impact of the urban growth boundary and Metro's Housing Rule, the 1000 Friends of Oregon and the Home Builders Association of Metropolitan Portland jointly studied trends in the Portland housing market for 1985–89.[7] They found that the public policies had achieved their goals:

—Multifamily housing construction increased to 54 percent of all new housing in the region during 1985–89. Before the Housing Rule, multifamily housing (apartments, row houses, duplexes, four-plexes, and so on) rep-

---

7. Metro's Housing Rule requires that each of the region's three counties and twenty-four municipalities adopt comprehensive plans that allow for a construction mix that includes at least 50 percent apartments and townhouses. In addition, the Housing Rule sets minimum target housing densities of ten units per buildable acre in the city of Portland and six to eight units per buildable acre for most suburban areas. The Housing Rule was based on the premise that restricting development to smaller lots would result in more affordable housing.

resented only 30 percent of the region's planned, twenty-year supply of new housing.

—Lot sizes (and prices) on new single-family housing had been lowered. About two-thirds of the new homes were being built on lots smaller than 9,000 square feet, whereas the average lot measured 13,000 square feet for new housing already approved under local zoning plans in effect before the Housing Rule's enactment. Homes on large lots (larger than 9,000 square feet), on average, cost twice as much as homes on small lots (smaller than 7,000 square feet).

—Both policies helped manage regional growth while promoting affordable housing. During the five-year period, if the same amount of development had occurred under densities prevailing before the Housing Rule took effect, it would have consumed an additional 1,500 acres, an area in excess of two square miles. Because of the savings in land use realized, another 14,000 housing units could be built within the urban growth boundary. In communities throughout the region, the density of new development increased by 13–32 percent over levels before the Housing Rule, the most significant gains being in single-family development.

In terms of overall affordability, the study found that 77 percent of the region's households could afford to rent the median-priced two-bedroom apartment while 67 percent could afford mortgage payments on the median-priced two-bedroom home, and 43 percent could afford the median-priced three-bedroom home. "Without state-mandated housing policies," the study concluded, "[local] zoning would exclude low and moderate income housing from some communities, and the Portland area would likely be suffering from the same 'affordability crisis' other fast-growing areas are now experiencing."[8]

By the time of our visit in February 1996—a half-dozen years after both the 1990 census and the Housing Rule study—the Portland area was clearly drifting toward a crisis over affordable housing that extended well beyond the Albina neighborhood. The trigger was rapid economic growth. The long, forest industry–based recession was a memory. High-tech industry was "bustin' out all over." Some $13 billion worth of new high-tech plants for corporate heavyweights such as Intel, Fujitsu Microelectronics, and LSI Logic was under construction.[9] Unemployment had dropped to less than 4 per-

8. 1000 Friends of Oregon and Home Builders Association of Metropolitan Portland (1991).
9. In fact, in 1995, for the first time in Oregon's history, forest products were supplanted as the state's leading industry by Portland's high-tech companies.

cent. The "local" labor force was tapped out, and new jobs were being filled by newcomers moving from around the country.

With the sudden, heavy demand for new homes created by the new-comers (especially former Californians with substantial home equities to reinvest), housing prices had been shooting up. The *Washington Post* reported that "the median price of a single-family home had risen from $64,000 in 1989 to $139,900 in 1996. During that same period Portland has gone from being ranked by the National Homebuilders Association as one of the most affordable U.S. cities for housing to being the fifth least affordable city."[10]

Amid the rising concern over housing costs, Portland Metro and several other local groups sponsored an affordable housing conference in September 1997. Attention focused mainly on Maryland's Montgomery County, whose long experience with affordable housing policies I had championed in my visit to Portland (as I have everywhere). For almost a quarter-century, Montgomery County laws have mandated that at least 15 percent of major new construction be sold or rented at prices within the reach of low- and modest-income households (see chapter 9). Veterans of Montgomery County's path-breaking housing policies (including Bernard Tetreault, long-time head of its Housing Opportunities Commission; Eric Larson, zoning administrator of the moderately priced dwelling unit policy; and Gus Baumann, former chairman of the planning commission) made effective presentations. In the aftermath, Portland Metro began seriously considering whether to require mixed-income housing in all major new development in the Portland region.[11]

10. William Claiborne, "Cracks in Portland's 'Great Wall,'" *Washington Post*, September 29, 1997, p. A1. Aside from the fact that the survey figures report home sales for metro areas rather than just cities (as the *Post* article stated), the National Homebuilders Association's national "housing affordability index" must be approached with caution. Calculated each quarter, the index is highly volatile, matching median income estimates (soft data) with median prices of single-family homes sold (harder data). During the 1990s, other western boomtowns—Salt Lake City, Denver, Albuquerque, for example—also emerged as "least affordable housing" regions like Portland. The factors were the same: rapid influxes of job-seeking workers (holding wage rates down) put sudden pressure on housing markets that could not expand as rapidly. The impetus for Portland and Albuquerque's booms was the same: multibillion-dollar new Intel plants. As boomtown conditions recede, such housing markets adjust back to their more regular equilibrium.

11. Metro's authority to adopt such measures is well tested. In November 1996, for example, Metro enacted ten ordinances to help implement its regional framework plan, among them an ordinance banning any further retail stores in excess of 60,000 square feet on industrially zoned land. In other words, no more Sam's Club or Costco warehouses or Home Depots. Metro's goals were many: conserve industrial sites for future Intels, reduce vehicle miles traveled ("big box category killers" rely on fifteen- to twenty-mile commuter sheds), and strengthen smaller retailers (particularly in pedestrian- and transit-friendly commercial areas). Though the measures were hotly

After the conference, Portland Metro wrestled with what additional measures to take to generate construction of more affordable housing. The Metro Council adopted a series of financial incentives and eased certain regulatory requirements that were barriers to lower-cost housing. However, the Metro Council backed away from adopting a Montgomery County–type "inclusionary" zoning ordinance mandating a minimum level of affordable housing in all new developments. Responding to pleas from homebuilders and some local governments, it announced a one-year delay to allow local groups to develop their own voluntary affordable housing initiatives. If voluntary local plans did not show promise of major results, the council warned, it would resume consideration of an areawide mandatory zoning ordinance.

I believe that Portland Metro will have to adopt just such a decisive measure. From the evidence of public school records, even as racial and ethnic segregation is diminishing, economic segregation (at least among the school-age population) appears to have risen during the prosperous 1990s. From 1989–90 to 1997–98 the percentage of low-income elementary school children in a four-county region receiving free or reduced-price school lunches increased substantially, from 24 percent to 33 percent. I have calculated dissimilarity indexes regarding the distribution of these low-income pupils throughout the region's 266 public elementary schools. In the eight-year period the economic segregation index among elementary school children increased slightly from 37 to 40, suggesting that residential segregation of low-income families (at least, those with school-age children) is increasing as well.

How could the percentage of low-income schoolchildren be increasing in the midst of the Portland area's thriving economy? The reality is that boomtowns have downsides as well as upsides. Many of the newcomers migrating into the region are filling low-wage retail and service-sector jobs that leave their families still eligible for free or reduced-price lunches.[12] The irony of continued want in the midst of record low unemployment was highlighted in a cover article entitled "The Revenge of the 'Baristas'" that analyzed the expansion of low-wage jobs in the boomtown economy.[13] ("Baristas" is a slang term coined by Hispanic immigrants for jobs as bartenders, waitresses, and busboys in Portland's yuppie bars and restaurants.)

---

debated, the Metro Council approved the measures, and the area's cities and counties must conform to the new rules.

12. The nationwide eligibility cut-off levels were 135 percent and 185 percent of the poverty level ($16,036 for a family of four in 1996) for free and reduced-price lunches, respectively.

13. Metroscape (1996).

Of course, with such a substantial increase in low-income schoolchildren, the modest rise in the segregation index might have been higher in another metro area that did not have Portland's activist growth management and affordable housing policies. Conventional housing industry practices nationwide promote greater economic segregation. Without changing the local ground rules, the Portland area is likely to follow the national trend.

Revisiting the Urban Growth Boundary

Portland's boom spurred Metro to make yet another assessment of the existing urban growth boundary. By the early 1990s Metro had begun an extensive program to update its long-range regional plans. It forecast that the four-county area (including Clark County, Washington) would grow by an additional 1.1 million people during the next fifty years, for a total of 2.5 million people. Furthermore, the region's population would have a much older average age by the year 2040, a lower average household size, and a more diverse racial and ethnic makeup. By 1996, however, just five years later, the region had already added almost 40 percent of the population growth expected for the next fifty years. Most of the inventory of vacant land within the original urban growth boundary had been used up.

Even though the best plans can be overcome by events and must be modified further to accommodate new realities, it is instructive to examine the Portland area's planning process. An early step was Metro's development of four alternative "concepts for growth" in June 1994. The base case anticipated no change in current development patterns and densities. Under the base case, the current urban growth boundary would have to be expanded by about 120,000 acres (a 50 percent increase) to accommodate new population. The three alternative concepts assumed new local, state, and federal land use and transportation policies. Concept A would expand the boundary modestly while promoting higher-density development. Concept B would seek to absorb all population growth within the current boundary at much higher densities and with the most intensive public transit system. Concept C projected that much of the region's growth would be directed toward relatively compact "satellite cities" outside, separated from the urban growth boundary by extensive greenbelts; the remaining growth would be absorbed within the current boundary.

Metro held 182 public meetings with local government officials and citizens. To supplement these presentations, Metro produced a video and made it available through area Blockbuster Video stores and libraries. It mailed a tabloid and questionnaire, featuring multicolored maps of the alternative concepts, to all 550,000 households in the Portland area. More than 17,000 questionnaires were mailed back, 10,000 with additional written comments beyond the choices checked off on the questionnaire.

The Metro staff consolidated all sources of information and reaction into a "recommended concept." Among the major provisions, the staff recommended that the urban growth boundary be expanded by 14,500 acres during the fifty-year period. The average lot size for new single-family homes regionwide would be 6,650 square feet, or 6.5 units per net acre. The ratio of single-family to multifamily homes would be 62 percent to 38 percent (compared with the current 70:30 ratio). One-third of the buildable acres would allow mixed uses and two-thirds would remain in single-use categories such as residential or industrial. About 19,300 acres of currently developed urban land would be redeveloped for more intensive uses, while open space would be conserved in 14 percent of the boundary area.

In effect, Metro's recommended concept was a melding of concept B and concept C, with the satellite cities renamed "neighbor cities." It envisioned twenty-five town centers throughout the metropolitan region, each with its own downtown offering shops and services within walking or biking distance from nearby housing. Most of the nine "regional centers" projected would be built along the light rail lines linking major suburban municipalities to downtown Portland. The recommended concept was adopted by the Metro Council in December 1994.

However, pressures kept building within the urban growth boundary. In early 1997 the Metro council amended the "urban growth reserve" area from 14,500 acres to nearly 19,000 acres, including 2,500 acres of current farmland (the latter over Executive Officer Mike Burton's strong objections). By late 1997, the council was poised to extend the urban growth boundary formally into some portion of the reserved lands. Burton recommended an expansion of 3,000–4,000 acres. Don Morissette, a conservative Republican who is the only builder-developer on the council, proposed a boundary expansion of 8,000–10,000 acres. Adopting a middle ground was Metro council's presiding officer, Jon Kvistad, who stated: "I think we're looking at a 6,000-acre expansion this time. I know that it's not very politically correct to expand the urban growth boundary, but we have to do it."[14] In compari-

14. Beyond the vocal opposition of many environmentally concerned groups and citizens, all twenty-four area mayors, including the mayors of municipalities abutting the current boundary that would likely annex any new development within the expanded territory, testified against boundary expansion.

son with the rate of uncontrolled sprawl in other communities, Kvistad observed, "our 6,000 acres is not very much. It is just a pittance."[15]

Finally, in November 1997 the Metro Council voted 5–2 to add less than 4,000 acres (about 6 square miles) to Portland's existing 342-square-mile urban growth boundary. (The two dissenting voters, Morissette and Kvistad, felt the expansion was too little.) As Metro Councilor Ed Washington, whose District 6 includes Albina, explained his vote for the small boundary expansion, "We are having redevelopment in my district for the first time in forty years; we don't want to lose it."

Individual Goals, Community Means

Beyond the statistics, beyond official planning documents, beyond consultant studies, the best evidence of the success of Portland's growth management policies is the quality of life in so much of the region. It is found in Forest Park and Sauvie Island and in other parkland and natural areas to be acquired through the $138 million bond issue for open space acquisition approved by the voters of the three-county area in November 1995. It is found in strong, healthy city neighborhoods such as Hawthorne, Northwest Twenty-Third, and Irvington. Even the poorest neighborhoods, such as the majority-black Albina area or Brentwood-Davlington, do not exude the odor of despair, decay, and abandonment so typical of poverty neighborhoods in other cities that are being sucked dry by uncontrolled urban sprawl. Indeed, with its growth management policies, the Portland area is clearly experiencing an economic resurgence in many of its "traditional" neighborhoods within the city and some older suburbs.

Downtown Portland is also being rejuvenated. Of the many vibrant, interesting downtowns I have visited and admired—such as downtown Baltimore, Pittsburgh, or Cincinnati—Portland certainly relies more on public transportation than the others. Tri-Met's east-west light rail line and extensive bus routes converge on Portland's downtown transit mall; some 45 per-

---

15. As indeed it is. To place the issue in some perspective, anticipating a 50 percent growth in population by 2040, the Portland region plans to urbanize an additional 8 percent of its land. By contrast, the Detroit region projects only 6 percent population growth by 2020 but will consume 40 percent more land. Farmland conservation? The 2,500 acres of farmland the Portland region will take forty-five years to convert would be paved over in the state of Michigan in just ten days (on the basis of estimates of the South East Michigan Council of Governments and the Michigan Society of Planning Officials).

cent of all workers and shoppers in downtown Portland enter by public transportation, bicycle, or on foot. By contrast, more than 80 percent of users of downtown Baltimore, Pittsburgh, or Cincinnati arrive one per car. And, with another $445 million bond issue just approved, Portland's light rail system will be extended south from downtown into Clackamas County (with hopes for a future northward extension across the Columbia River to Vancouver, Washington).

Yet, beyond transportation distinctions, each of these other downtown areas feels fragile and threatened, even threatening, at night. These downtowns are surrounded by poverty neighborhoods. By contrast, Portland's downtown is surrounded by strong, mixed-income neighborhoods. There is a depth and solidity to downtown Portland that compels confidence in its future.

There is much to praise about Portland, and in my talk to the City Club, I had more praise for Portland's achievements than for any other of the seventy communities I had visited. Beyond even the value of its growth management policies, I concluded, the Portland community exemplifies an ideology that can breathe hope into our nation's despairing cities.

"Living now in Washington, D.C.," I told the audience, "I am bombarded daily by the ideology of the so-called 'Conservative Revolution.' But it seems to me that this revolution is based on two false propositions.

"The first is that as a society we Americans are overtaxed . . . that if we just get government off our backs, we will all prosper. Well, as a matter of fact, an annual study done by the Organization for Economic Cooperation and Development [OECD] shows that all national, state, and local taxes add up to slightly more than 29 percent of our gross domestic product. That is the second lowest tax level of any of the twenty-three member countries. We are slightly more taxed than Australians and slightly less taxed than the Japanese (who don't have big military forces to support). Our level of taxation is far below, for example, that of the Norwegians, the Swedes, or the Dutch, whose tax levels approach half their gross domestic product.

"Yet another report of the OECD," I continued, "shows that the United States has the widest income disparities of any economically developed society and that income inequality in our society is growing rapidly. I think that these two trends—a low tax level and growing economic inequality—are related. This trendy ideological notion that we are overtaxed has one clear sponsor and one clear beneficiary—the already rich. Public taxation is the vehicle through which we can afford collectively what most of us, unlike the rich, cannot afford individually.

"As a region, Portlanders have been willing to tax themselves for things that are important to you—for example, $134 million for parklands and wildlife preservation, $445 million to expand your light rail system. In a nation where many communities are consuming the seed corn of their future through blind adherence to antitax apostles, Portland's example is important.

"The second false proposition is that government cannot do anything right," I continued. "It is particularly ironic to hear that philosophy expressed by elderly persons. Thirty years ago the largest group of poor Americans consisted of the elderly. Through tremendous improvements in social security, medicare, federal private pension regulation, poverty among the elderly has been almost abolished. Almost 38 cents of every federal dollar is spent on aid to the elderly. The elderly are better off today as a group than the rest of American society. It's just wrong to claim that government can't do *anything* right. Having largely eliminated poverty and want among the elderly is just the first of a long list of things that government has done right.

"But the people of this region are a constant example of citizens who recognize that some individual goals can only be achieved through collective action, and that government is the vehicle for such collective action. Time and again you have reaffirmed that faith: in your three different referenda authorizing Metro's powers, in your constant participation in the regional planning process, in key bond votes to provide the money to achieve important land use and transportation goals.

"You are constantly engaged in the struggle to balance individual rights and individual initiatives with community goals and communal effort. There are no permanent 'right' answers. The task is always to keep pursuing the proper balance. But Portland serves as the school for America. You teach us that our most precious inheritance is precisely government of the people, by the people, and for the people."

Portland has, of course, a better way to convey what I took thirty-five minutes to tell that City Club audience. Three months later Mike Burton, Metro's executive officer, and I were sharing the podium at an Albuquerque Chamber of Commerce retreat. Mike was asked to comment on the Goals for Albuquerque, a community-wide "visioning" process in which a dozen committees involving several hundred volunteers had participated for over a year.

"We produced a wonderful Goals for Albuquerque report but very little has actually happened since," the local questioner complained.

"How long was your goals statement?" Mike asked.

"About 200 pages."

"Well, for starters, that is probably 199 pages too long," Mike responded. "We express our vision for Portland in just two sentences:

Everyone can always see Mount Hood.

Every child can walk to a library.

An almost electric charge surged through me on first hearing Portland's vision statement. As I thought more and more about it, the more layers of complexity the simple words contained. "Everyone can always see Mount Hood." Of course, that did not mean everyone would have a big picture window facing eastward. It meant that everyone could always look through forty miles of urban air and see Mount Hood clearly. Controlling sprawl. More buses and trolleys, fewer autos. Clustering homes, stores, and offices in walkable communities. Less air pollution.

And "Every child can always walk to a library." This is not a statement of the American Library Association's wildest dream, but a vision in which all children (and their parents) would feel safe from bad traffic and bad people on the streets, that many stores, schools, parks, and playgrounds as well as the library would be within walking distance, that all children would *want* to walk to a library. Is it any wonder that the Intels of the world are flocking to Portland?

9

Montgomery County, Maryland: Mixing Up the Neighborhood

MARYLAND'S MONTGOMERY COUNTY, lying outside Washington, is the nation's sixth richest county—and as I drove along River Road on a warm, sunny Saturday afternoon in mid-June, it looked every bit that wealthy. Leaving behind imposing country houses set back a quarter mile from the road, behind their white, horse farm–style wooden fences, I passed through the upscale, white-and-gray trim stores of Potomac Village, then turned right up Falls Road. To the left, the Falls Road Golf Course was moderately crowded, a public course masquerading as a private country club. To the right, the red brick manorial buildings and spacious grounds of the private Bullis Prep School were deserted that day. Colorful banners advertised soccer and lacrosse clinics that, on summer weekdays, would fill acres and acres of well-manicured playing fields with the sons and daughters of many of the national capital's most successful and powerful people.

I turned left off Falls Road onto Eldwick Way, the golf course still on my left. A half mile's drive up this country lane, a low brick sign in the center of a tastefully landscaped traffic island announced my destination: Fallswick. Turning into the Fallswick neighborhood, I cruised slowly past large homes, pulled into Lost Trail Way, parked in a space marked off around a landscaped berm at the end of a cul-de-sac and, walking down the gently sloping street, set off to interview the neighbors.

As I surveyed the 9500 block of Lost Trail Way, I noticed a paved path running between two houses. Fifty yards down the path was a four- or five-acre lake, surrounded by a discreet, wood-and-wire fence to keep toddlers out. It was certainly an attractive, well-maintained neighborhood amenity. New-mowed lawns carried right down to the water's edge. The lake served as the neighborhood's principal storm drainage facility. Whether it also doubled as a recreational lake, I could not tell.

Talking with the Neighbors

Returning to Lost Trail Way, I began to canvass the homes along the 9500 block. Each was different, yet basically the same. All were large, detached, two-story, brick colonial homes with peaked roofs and relatively narrow sideyards. Color schemes varied: red brick, white brick, cream-colored brick, gray brick; red shutters, black shutters, gray shutters. Attached two-car garages extended either left or right from the houses. Landscaping was similarly varied, yet almost all yards were immaculately groomed. These were expensive homes even for Montgomery County, probably around $500,000–$550,000 each.

One of the verities of the American way of life is that, no matter what hour a political candidate or neighborhood canvasser selects, most people are not home. This Saturday afternoon was no exception. But, working up both sides of the two-block street, I developed a rough profile of the residents of Lost Trail Way, using a "neighborhood satisfaction survey" as a tool to gather information.

A grandmother from Taiwan, living with her divorced son (an employee of Hughes Communications) and two grandchildren . . . a Chinese American physicist at the Applied Physics Lab, his wife, and two young children . . . a white woman, too busy with two young children to talk . . . two different homes where the women of the house, through security intercoms, indicated no interest in being interviewed . . . the military attaché of the Spanish Embassy, his wife and three children . . . the teenage son of a Korean couple who owned a beer and wine delicatessen in the District of Columbia . . . a white couple in their mid-thirties with one child, who just moved into the neighborhood five months earlier . . . an Asian American couple with two children (he worked as a computer consultant, she as a part-time administrator of her local church) . . . another young Asian American man, a bookkeeper, living with his two parents . . . a young white man.

There were seven houses with no one home and few visual clues: a proliferation of basketball backboards in the driveways, Jewish mezuzahs on a couple of front doors, and one house belonging to a University of Michigan graduate (judging by the doorbell, which played a stanza of "The Victors," the Wolverines' fight song).

I reached the 9400 block of Lost Trail Way, where the housing type shifted from detached, single-family houses to large, elegant townhouses. These cost about $350,000–$400,000 each. One- or two-car detached garages, thrusting forward from the townhouses, dominated the streetscape. A peculiar design. Yet walking up to each front door, I realized that the arrangement created more privacy for the front yards and little patios tucked behind the detached garage structures. Again, each property was well landscaped. If anything, the townhouse residents seemed to invest more of themselves into their patio gardens. Probably a greater proportion of "empty nesters" lived here, though all the townhouses were three- and four-bedroom units.

I began my survey again. A white attorney with two teenage children . . . another white family . . . a white management consultant, his wife (manager of the local furniture store), and their grown son (a computer consultant) . . . another Jewish household (judging by the religious symbol on the front door) . . . an Asian American household, busily greeting young guests to a child's party . . . a white vice president of Lockheed Martin, the huge defense contractor, which has its headquarters in Montgomery County . . . two more Jewish households (again with religious symbols displayed; Congregation Har Shalom and the Washington Hebrew Congregation's Julia Bindman Center both lie within a mile of Fallswick) . . . a realtor, originally from a South Asian country, watching his two young girls bicycling around the landscaped island at the end of the cul-de-sac . . . another Asian American household . . . a white couple, a phone call cutting short our conversation before I could find out more about them . . . another white couple . . . a red-haired young woman (more likely the family's daughter) who declined to be interviewed . . . a retired army colonel (white) now serving as a defense industry consultant . . . a white vice president of a local biotech company, his wife (a radiologist in private practice), and their twenty-three-year-old son, a student at the nearby University of Maryland . . . another young white woman . . . the largest townhouse on the block with a substantial sideyard, with a notice to call a certain telephone number "in case of emergency" (a doctor's house? a plumber's?) . . . ten townhouses with nobody home, though one with a "for sale" sign in front was already "under contract."

I reached the end of the 9400 block. The housing style changed once more. Tidy, more compact, two-story brick townhouses, in two rows obliquely angled to each other, formed the head of the cul-de-sac. They were separated from the rows of larger townhouses only by grassed alleys. These were clearly more modest, but still tastefully done units, each with two or three bedrooms. The most visible difference between these townhouses and those of their neighbors was that they lacked private garages. Residents' cars were parked in marked spaces either in front of the units or perpendicular to the landscaped berm in the middle of the cul-de-sac (where I had parked). Though closer to the street than any other homes, the shallow front yards were also neatly landscaped and well cared for. Whatever their market value, I already knew that these homes sold for about $80,000 each.

I continued the canvass: an African American couple, she calling out instructions to him about how to drive their two young children to the local library branch . . . a Taiwanese computer consultant, with wife and eight-year-old daughter . . . another African American woman, little girl tugging at her skirt, declining to be interviewed . . . a white loan manager at a local credit union and his wife (salesperson for the Yellow Pages) . . . a woman from El Salvador with a nine-year-old son (she worked as an assistant in a private laboratory) . . . another black woman in her mid-thirties and her six-year-old son; she was a customer service representative in the Metro system's special paratransit service for the mobility handicapped but hoped to shift to a job with county government . . . a fourth African American household, a woman and her eleven-year-old son; she was an accounts payable supervisor for a local land development company . . . four households with nobody home.

The longest conversation took place with a young white mother with two children of preschool age. Her son and an older playmate (the son of the Salvadoran woman) were playfully brandishing their Super Soakers at the two little girls riding their bicycles around (daughters of the South Asian realtor across the street). Throughout the conversation, the young daughter clung to her mother. Her husband, she told me, worked in computer operations at the headquarters of Fannie Mae, the mortgage market giant, the nation's largest financial institution, which is headquartered in Washington. She herself took occasional assignments organizing auctions of property confiscated by the U.S. Customs Service. They had lived in their townhouse for more than eight years.

"How do you like the neighborhood?" (One of my standard questions.) "Would you say that you are very satisfied, somewhat satisfied, somewhat dissatisfied, or very dissatisfied?"

"Oh, very satisfied," she replied emphatically.

"What do you like best about the neighborhood?"

"Everything . . . it's clean . . . quiet . . . safe . . . a good mix of different people . . . friendly."

"Does your son go to Wayside Elementary?"

"Not yet. He's still at Potomac Village, a private preschool. But I've heard wonderful things about Wayside," she added.

"How would you rate Montgomery County government: very satisfied, somewhat satisfied, somewhat dissatisfied, very dissatisfied?"

"I have no complaints. I don't get involved."

I thanked her, and began to turn away.

"Do you know that all these townhouses are 'MPDUs'?" The question seemed to explode eagerly from her.

I confessed that I did know about the MPDUs, or moderately priced dwelling units. (Indeed, they were the reason for my neighborhood survey.)

"These thirteen townhouses are all MPDUs," she continued, waving her hand at the two rows of smaller townhouses. "Eight years ago my husband had just graduated from college and was working for the government. He wasn't earning half of what we earn now so we qualified for an MPDU. We entered the lottery the county conducted to allocate them. Our number was pulled out, and we bought this townhouse.

"It's been great for us," she continued. "Oh, with two children now, our townhouse is a bit small. Now that we're doing a lot better, we're saving up our money. If we moved up today to the kind of house I'd really like, though, I'd probably have to go back to work full time. I wouldn't trade the opportunity to stay home with my children now for any dream house. So we'll wait for the ten-year grace period to be up and hope to sell this house afterwards for a good enough price that we can buy a bigger home without my having to go back to work full time."

(If MPDU purchasers sell their townhouse within ten years after the first purchase, I had read in the county's program description, the resale price must still fall within control levels. After the ten-year period, when they can sell at market price, the owners have to split any equity increase with the county's revolving Housing Initiative Fund. This young couple was waiting out the ten-year period before putting their townhouse on the market in order to benefit from any price increase.)

"You know that five of these thirteen townhouses are owned by the county?" she asked, indicating, with unerring accuracy, which five belonged to the Montgomery County Housing Opportunities Commission (HOC). Three of the HOC units, I knew, were federally financed "public housing units" whose tenants qualified at the lowest end of the income scale. The other two the county dubbed "McHomes," subsidized by a special county fund; typically, their residents were slightly higher up the income scale.

"How are your neighbors?"

"Fine," she replied. "Oh, there was one that caused some trouble some time back, but they're gone. I'm sure that the county moved them out. The county keeps a pretty careful eye on things."

"How about maintenance on the properties?"

"The county keeps up their property, and we owners keep up ours. Of course, the Homeowners Association takes care of all the common areas and picks up all the trash as well. I think that our fees in these townhouses are actually higher than the fees paid by the owners of bigger houses." It was the first real complaint that she'd had. (As a "homeowner" of five townhouses, the Housing Opportunities Commission pays the requisite assessments to the Fallswick Homeowners Association on behalf of its tenants.)

"The MPDU program is a great program," she concluded. "It's given us a chance." Indeed, the MPDU program had given a real chance to thirteen families in Fallswick, both the eight owner-occupant families like hers and the five renter families of the HOC-owned townhouses.

In all the interviews only two other neighbors mentioned the MPDUs. The retired colonel was "a little apprehensive when I first moved into the neighborhood, but it's turned out OK." (His judgment was not based just on being a neighbor located four doors from the nearest MPDU. He also was an officer of the Homeowners Association.) And the realtor expressed the thought that his own property might appreciate a little more in value if the MPDUs were of the same quality. "They look just fine from over here," he noted from his front yard, "but up close you can see that they're not of the same quality of construction.

"However, the county's housing laws are the best laws we have," he observed. "I haven't lived in a lot of places in this country, but overall Montgomery County is a very good place. Montgomery County stands out."

The Moderately Priced Dwelling Unit Policy

Within Montgomery County, the Fallswick subdivision is not unique. Much the same social diversity is found in many mixed-income housing developments, such as Normandie Crest, Deer Park at Fairland Green, or North Sherwood Forest, scattered throughout Montgomery County. Among Ameri-

can communities, Montgomery County stands out for its integrated neighborhoods, integrated both by racial and ethnic group and, most uncom-
monly, by income class.

The level of economic integration is not the result of any progressive
business ethic among local developers and builders (although several builders active in Montgomery County have become national champions of
mixed-income communities). Montgomery County's neighborhoods have
mixed-income housing because Montgomery County law requires it.

The county government has the nation's most progressive mixed-income housing laws, in particular, the Moderately Priced Dwelling Unit Ordinance, adopted in 1973. By law, all new subdivisions in Montgomery
County must contain a mix of housing for different income groups: 85 percent market rate (at whatever income levels the developer targets) and 15
percent priced for moderate-income households.[1]

Though Montgomery County was the earliest, a number of communities now have mandatory mixed-income housing laws. What sets Montgomery County apart is the extra mile county government travels in its
commitment to mixed-income housing. The county government requires
builders to give first right of purchase for one-third of the MPDUs to the
Montgomery County Housing Opportunities Commission, the county's
public housing authority. For almost a quarter century Montgomery County
has not built public housing projects for low-income families. Its Housing
Opportunities Commission simply buys standard new housing in regular
new subdivisions—up to 5 percent of all that is built by private developers—as an inventory of rental units for its low-income families.[2]

A "Big Box" Government

To understand how this happened one must look at the special role of county
government in Maryland. From colonial days onward, county government
has been Maryland's primary form of local government. State law provides
for the creation of municipalities, but relatively few Marylanders actually

1. The county sets the maximum eligible income at 65 percent of the county's median household income. In other words, moderate-income households fall within the lowest third of the population economically.
2. Fallswick fulfilled the formula exactly. By my count, Fallswick contained fifty-five detached
homes, twenty-six market-rate townhouses, and thirteen MPDUs (five owned by the county housing authority).

live within municipalities. There is, of course, Baltimore City (1997 estimated population: 657,256), which is, however, organized as its own county
government as well. There are also the cities of Annapolis (33,234), Frederick
(46,227), Hagerstown (34,633), Rockville (46,019), Gaithersburg (45,361),
and 149 other smaller municipalities.[3]

However, Baltimore County, which geographically almost surrounds,
but is a separate jurisdiction from Baltimore City, has 720,662 residents (1997
estimate) and no municipal governments whatsoever. With budgetary control over the unified, countywide school system, county government is the
only local government in Baltimore County. Likewise, in fast-growing
Howard County (1997 estimated population: 228,797), county government
stands alone. In fact, classifying Baltimore City as a county rather than a
municipality (as an "independent city," city government exercises all county
powers), only about one-quarter of Maryland's 5.1 million residents live
within municipalities.

Montgomery County is a prime example of a "big box" community.
Under Maryland law, Montgomery County, like all counties, has a single,
unified, countywide school system. With over 128,000 students, the Montgomery County Public School system is one of the nation's twenty largest
and clearly one of the best. Under another state law enacted in 1927, county
government exercises exclusive planning and zoning control throughout the
495-square-mile county, except for the cities of Rockville and Gaithersburg
and five small villages whose existing zoning powers were grandfathered.
(These seven municipalities total only about 12 percent of the county's population.) Though there are nominally seventeen municipalities within Montgomery County, county government is the only local government of real
consequence.[4] Well-known areas such as Bethesda and Silver Spring are just
place names, not incorporated municipalities; county government is their
residents' only government.

For decades Montgomery County was primarily a suburb of Washington. By 1950 the county population was still just 164,401 residents; about
three-quarters worked in Washington. Median family income was $5,259
(about one-third higher than the District of Columbia's median family in-

3. All municipal populations are based on the 1996 census estimates, except Baltimore City.
4. Montgomery County's empowerment by the Maryland legislature has led to perhaps the
nation's most comprehensive growth management system. Key elements are the long-range "wedges
and corridors" comprehensive plan, the annual growth policy, the Adequate Public Facilities Ordinance (linking subdivision approval to the orderly construction of public facilities), and the transferable development rights program (to help preserve one-third of the county as agricultural land).

come). Though middle-class subdivisions were beginning to spring up, at midcentury many Montgomery County residents still paid nonresident tuition to send their children to the more prestigious (and still racially segregated) public schools in the District of Columbia.

Over the next two decades, however, Montgomery County boomed. Thousands of high-quality professional and technical jobs were created at Bethesda Naval Hospital, the National Institutes of Health, the National Bureau of Standards, and other federal installations. By 1970 the county's population had ballooned to 522,809. More than half now worked at jobs located in Montgomery County itself. Average incomes were high; median family income was $16,710, now almost 75 percent higher than in the District of Columbia. The racial cleavage was also clear. The District's population was 65 percent black; Montgomery County's population was 92 percent white.

The Campaign for Affordable Housing

County government was highly respected, activist, and progressive. In response to a vigorous campaign conducted by the League of Women Voters, Suburban Maryland Fair Housing, and other citizen groups, the county council adopted a model Fair Housing Ordinance. The county acted several years before Martin Luther King's assassination fueled congressional support for passage of the Civil Rights Act of 1968.

By the end of the 1960s, a severe shortage of affordable housing had developed in the county. The economic boom, subdivision restrictions, and a temporary moratorium on new water and sewer connections had caused the price of building lots to accelerate much faster than general inflation. To maintain profitability in the face of curtailed volume, builders were constructing the largest and most profitable houses possible on virtually irreplaceable land. The prices of both new and existing housing escalated rapidly. Price escalation, civil rights advocates feared, could well negate the practical effects of the new Fair Housing Ordinance. An adequate supply of low- and moderate-income housing, the groups recognized, would be essential to achieve meaningful racial integration. They set out to secure county policies to diversify the local housing supply. It was a goal that, even in progressive Montgomery County, would take six years of constant effort to achieve.

The affordable housing advocates' first strategy focused on designating land as suitable sites for subsidized housing developments. In 1967 they persuaded county council member Ida Mae Garrott, a former League of Women

Voters president, to sponsor an amendment to the county's zoning ordinance. The amendment would require developers of "new towns" or "planned neighborhoods" to set aside land on which the county itself would build subsidized housing for low- and moderate-income families. The county attorney, declaring that such a requirement would be "conditional" zoning, promptly derailed the proposal.

Retreating in confusion, the housing advocates spent two years searching for both a new approach and more planning and legal expertise. "Fair housing" had been a civil rights issue argued largely on moral grounds. "Affordable housing" raised complex economic and technical issues. The Montgomery County groups allied themselves with the Metropolitan Washington Planning and Housing Association for professional assistance. Fortified by a grant from the Taconic Foundation, a key supporter of the national civil rights movement, in January 1970 the coalition established the Montgomery County Project for Low- and Moderate-Income Housing.

Meanwhile, the county's pending updated general plan contained two new proposed policies in the "housing element." First, the plan proposed it would be the county's official policy to seek "to house its total labor force as well as those families of low- or moderate-income that were currently living in the county." Second, the county would ensure "the economic feasibility of providing housing for all income levels" by ensuring "the provision of low- and moderate-income housing as part of all large-scale development, and as an option in smaller-scale development."

By mid-1970 the fair housing groups had succeeded in persuading the county council to adopt the proposed housing policy goals. The target shifted then to amending the county's zoning code to require low- and moderate-income housing in all new subdivision construction in Montgomery County, a path-breaking concept for the United States.

At this crucial juncture a startling political development occurred. Running on a unified platform, including a commitment to meet the housing needs of low- and moderate-income families in Montgomery County, Democratic candidates were elected to all seven county council seats in that November's election. The lone incumbent carryover, council member Garrott, became council chair. She immediately urged the housing advocacy groups to develop and submit a proposed ordinance.

After eight months the citizen work group, fortified by volunteer attorneys from one of Washington's top law firms, submitted their proposal. In all new housing developments of fifty or more units, they proposed, 20 percent must be moderately priced; one-third of the so-called MPDUs would be acquired by the county's Housing Opportunities Commission for low-income tenants. To compensate builders for developing one-fifth of their land at below-market potential, builders could negotiate a "density bonus" to allow them to build 20 percent more units on the site than conventional zoning would permit.

Initially positive about the proposal, several council members became skittish in the face of harsh criticism from the Development Advisory Board, a county-appointed group to represent development interests. Zina Greene, a key staff member for the housing advocate groups, remembers the Development Advisory Board well; "In our first meeting they were rude and outrageously inaccurate. . . . They were sure that they could prove that this was a hare-brained, do-gooder effort that certainly couldn't work. After all, if it were possible to build moderately priced housing, their attitude was that they would already be doing it."[5]

"Anyway," Zina continued, "the Development Advisory Board members argued that people like to live with their own kind and wouldn't buy housing in neighborhoods with economic diversity. . . . They even went so far as to warn the County Council about the 'kind of people' who would come to Montgomery County from the 'city' if such housing were available. Their vehement attack hung heavily over some Council members."

With the council's enthusiasm flagging, weeks dragged into months of delay. Only two council members publicly supported the proposal: Ida Mae Garrott and Norman Christeller. Of the five remaining members, one had never supported it, two were worried about citizen association opposition, and the remaining two had been shaken by the vehement criticism of the Development Advisory Board. The proposal had yet to be even formally introduced. Most critically, Garrott's year as council chair had expired, and a new chairperson might never schedule the proposal for introduction.

To that point the housing coalition had always approached council members in a very collegial manner. Now the housing coalition took a calculated risk. In late February 1971, the coalition prompted local newspaper and television to criticize the council's delay editorially. Council members were enraged at both the editorials and the coalition. How could council members be criticized when they were working so hard and were so committed to good government? But after their pique had passed, the legislation was formally introduced and public hearings were scheduled for early summer.

---

5. Memorandum, Zina Greene to the Metropolitan Washington Planning and Housing Association, October 4, 1972, pp. 53–54. Much of my early history of the MPDU ordinance is drawn from this document.

Now the coalition's effort shifted to mobilizing broad public support. The League of Women Voters and Suburban Maryland Fair Housing's educational efforts went into high gear. They distributed 30,000 educational flyers and circulated petitions of support. A speaker's bureau made dozens of presentations, using a slide and tape show. In a two-day workshop Congregations United for Shelter organized support from thirty local churches.

The grass-roots campaign came to a head in four public hearings in June and July 1972. More than seventy-five business, civic, religious, and housing groups testified in support. Most critical was the support expressed by three very respected homebuilders in the county. They cited current development procedures and showed how the density bonus could reduce costs sufficiently to allow them to build small housing units within the maximum price ceiling.

Opposition arguments fell into three broad categories. Though agreeing with the need for more affordable housing, the Maryland Suburban Home Builders, the Apartment House Council, and several builders argued for a voluntary rather than mandatory program. Several civic organizations objected to the density bonus provisions, fearing a shift in the single-family home character of their neighborhoods. Several opponents questioned the need for more affordable housing at all.

This final objection was countered effectively by the coalition's release of a new survey of local businesses. The county had embarked on an aggressive economic development program to diversify the local economy. It projected an increase of 90,000 jobs over the next decade. The survey showed that the projected increased employment base would generate a demand for 70,000 new housing units. Of the total, the occupational profile suggested, about one-third would have to be moderately priced, and about 10 percent would require public rent subsidies. Indeed, providing affordable housing to complement the county's economic growth and diversification was the central theme of the coalition's public education campaign.

Through the four hearings, buoyed by so much public support, council members increasingly warmed to the program. Council member Christeller took on passage of the MPDU ordinance as a personal crusade. Many months of careful drafting and compromise, however, still lay ahead. The MPDU percentage, for example, was reduced from 20 percent to 15 percent. Both buyers and renters would be subject to maximum income limits set by the county Department of Housing and Community Development. (Originally 80 percent, the upper ceiling for qualifying is now 65 percent of the county's median household income.) Rent limits would be controlled for twenty years.

Sale and resale prices for MPDUs would be controlled for five years (extended later to ten years). A portion of profits from the first resale after expiration of price controls would be recaptured by the county's revolving Housing Initiative Fund. The county's Housing Opportunities Commission would purchase one-third of the MPDUs for deep-subsidy households.

The county executive opposed the proposed ordinance, threatening a veto. The bill would have to have the support of at least five council members to be veto-proof. The final ordinance also had to be crafted to withstand potential court challenges. Above all, proponents were concerned that the MPDU requirement might be judged an unconstitutional taking of the builder's property; the density bonus would be a key defense against constitutional challenges.

Councilman Christeller pressed down hard. Finally, on October 23, 1973, the county council unanimously enacted the revised bill and overrode the county executive's ensuing veto, and on January 21, 1974, the Moderately Priced Dwelling Unit Ordinance became law. Its champions hailed the new ordinance as "the nation's first 'inclusionary' zoning law."

Because land previously subdivided did not contain density bonuses, all pending subdivisions were exempt from the new MPDU requirement. The first affordable housing built under the program was offered for sale to qualified purchasers and the HOC in 1976.

The MPDU Law's Impact

For two decades the Moderately Priced Dwelling Unit Ordinance has helped define how the housing industry does business in Montgomery County. The MPDU program has long since become part of the normal business climate for private builders in Montgomery County. Over the years county officials and builders have worked closely together to improve the program. One amendment in 1989 allowed builders to increase the allowable sales price by 10 percent to allow for design improvements that would make MPDUs more compatible with surrounding units (such as brick facings). Another change currently under consideration is to apply MPDU requirements in very low-density communities (that is, less than one dwelling unit per acre) whenever the property is served by public water and sewer systems.

"MPDU has been good for the county and good for the builders," Eric Larson, the county's MPDU administrator, observed, "and we have to give a lot of credit to the builders for making the program work."[6] During times of

6. Conversation with the author, June 1994.

soft housing markets, for example, some builders have even constructed MPDU allocations (for which there is always strong demand) in advance of their market-rate housing, bridging the slump in the market.

The policy has had a significant impact on the creation of affordable housing in Montgomery County. Through 1997, private developers had built 10,110 housing units under the MPDU policy; these included 7,305 sale units and 2,805 rental units. In the face of some limitations on funds available for purchase, over the years the HOC purchased more than 1,500 units. (Nonprofit organizations, which can now purchase units as well, own another 38 units.) The MPDU policy has been the HOC's largest source of scattered-site rental units for public housing families.

In a five-year period studied (1992–96), developers working under the MPDU policy built 123 rental units and 1,599 sale units. Of the new homes for sale, 8 percent had one bedroom, 23 percent had two bedrooms, and 69 percent had three or more bedrooms. The average sales price was $83,706 in 1996, which is a bargain in a county where the median housing value was $208,000 in 1990.

Turning to the characteristics of MPDU home purchasers, 41 percent were white, 22 percent black, 28 percent Asian, and 7 percent Hispanic. The average household income of MPDU buyers was $27,754 in 1996; only 6 percent of the purchasers even approached the program's income ceiling of $39,900 for a family of four.

When the MPDU program was being debated, a common anxiety expressed was that mixing low- and moderate-income housing (translation: low- and moderate-income *households*) into higher-income neighborhoods would drive down the price or dampen the appreciation of higher-end housing.

Updating an earlier study, in 1998 the Innovative Housing Institute (begun in 1996 by HOC's retired executive director, Bernard Tetreault) examined trends in resale prices of 1,012 nonsubsidized dwellings sold between 1992 and 1996 either within or next to fourteen subdivisions with subsidized housing. Eight were located in Montgomery County and six in neighboring Fairfax County, Virginia (which had adopted its own affordable dwelling unit policy in 1990). The study found that

> Overall, there was no significant difference in price trends between nonsubsidized homes in the subdivisions with subsidized units and the market as a whole—whether measured at the zip code or county-wide level.
>
> Furthermore, there was no difference in price behavior between nonsubsidized houses located within 500 feet of subsidized housing and those farther away in the same or an adjacent subdivision.

Even the price trends of those non-subsidized homes located immediately adjacent to a subsidized dwelling (either next door, back-to-back, across the street, or within 25 feet) were unaffected by their proximity.

"In sum," the study concluded, "the presence or proximity of subsidized housing made no difference in housing values as measured by relative price behavior in a dynamic market."[7]

The Innovative Housing Institute researchers also conducted structured interviews with fifty-six residents of nonsubsidized homes located close to subsidized units in both counties (plus four MPDU owners).[8] The survey found that twenty-eight households were "very satisfied" with the neighborhood, twenty-five were "satisfied," and only four were "a bit dissatisfied" or "very dissatisfied." When asked what they liked best about their neighborhoods, thirty-eight spoke of good neighbors, safety, peace, and quiet. Location, amenities, and good maintenance were mentioned by twenty-four respondents. Only fourteen of the fifty-six respondents specifically mentioned the subsidized units. Of these, six had negative comments (ranging from traffic congestion and overdevelopment to unsupervised children and teenage behavior).

In assessing the study's findings, it is important to remember the overwhelming middle- to upper-middle-class setting of the subsidized housing. Only 15 percent of the housing units are subsidized in the Montgomery County subdivisions and only 20 percent in the Fairfax County subdivisions. The two counties' housing authorities acquire 5 percent and 7.5 percent, respectively, of the units as rental properties for low-income households. Where middle-class households are so dominant, low- and modest-income households blend right in.

The Full Range of Housing Programs

The MPDU program, administered by the Department of Housing and Community Development, was not the county's first foray into the housing field. In 1966 the county council established the Housing Authority of Montgomery County. Initially, the agency was a typical federally supported pub-

7. Innovative Housing Institute (1998), p. 5.
8. The IHI researchers adapted the open-ended-field interview form that I had earlier used for my neighborhood interviews in Fallswick.

lic housing authority. Coming into the field relatively late, however, it was able to avoid the mistakes of earlier public housing programs, particularly building large, higher-density projects. The housing agency's earliest activities were building conventional (but relatively small) projects. The family projects ranged in size from 19 to 76 units. Projects for the elderly were slightly larger (96 to 160 units). Two projects mixed younger families and elderly households.

In 1974, as the MPDU policy was coming on line, the county council reorganized the agency as the Housing Opportunities Commission, with Tetreault as its executive director. The restructured organization took on an additional mission as the county's housing finance agency. It would be responsible for all forms of housing support for both low- and moderate-income households.

By fiscal year 1999 the Housing Opportunities Commission's budget had grown to $118 million. The diversity of its revenue sources reflected the diversity of its programs. Only one-third of its budget was federal grants: $8.7 million for operating subsidies for the 1,579 public housing units HOC owned and operated (the largest number acquired under the MPDU policy) and $30.6 million for section 8 rental assistance certificates and vouchers paid to Montgomery County landlords on behalf of 4,095 low-income tenants. Eleven of the public housing units were in the process of being purchased by their tenants (the latest of scores of instances in which HOC has successfully helped public housing tenants become homeowners.)

Interest on the HOC's mortgage revenue bonds yielded $33.4 million (or 28 percent of the agency's budget). These bonds had been issued to build or purchase another 3,067 nonfederally subsidized units under the HOC's "Opportunity Housing" program. (These included housing units dubbed "McHomes" for households whose incomes were just above the federal eligibility ceiling.) Of these the HOC directly managed 977, and it had placed another 2,090 under private management. Another 1,108 units were not owned by the HOC but fell within the program's guidelines.

The agency received $35.2 million in rental income from its various properties, half of which covered mortgage payments on HOC-owned properties. Finally, $9.9 million came from county government appropriations earmarked for special activities or was generated internally from HOC operations (including almost $1 million in net cash flow from HOC properties).

In all, in fiscal 1999 HOC owned or administered 9,849 houses, townhouses, and apartments for low- and moderate-income households. In addition, the agency monitored 35 privately owned multifamily properties with over 8,300 units that had been financed using the federal low income tax credit. Under the federal guidelines, 20 percent of the units were set aside for low- and moderate-income households.

What is most important about the totality of the HOC's programs is the degree to which low-income housing is spread around the county. The county planning department divides the county into eighteen planning areas. With a countywide poverty rate of 4.2 percent in 1990, HOC-assisted housing accounts for between 1.9 percent and 6.8 percent of all housing units in fifteen of the eighteen planning areas. The exceptions are downtown Silver Spring (where HOC units represent 11.6 percent of all housing units), Bethesda-Chevy Chase (largely built-out before the 1970s), where HOC has only twelve units, and the northern third of the county that is permanently protected as farmland. (Even in the rural areas, HOC has 151 highly scattered housing units, 1.2 percent of the total housing supply.)

Saving Farms by Saving Cities

As much as I have studied Montgomery County, it did not all come together for me until I participated briefly in the Ultimate Farmland Preservation Tour in February 1998. Organized primarily by the Michigan Farm Bureau, the five-day bus tour brought ninety Michigan farmers, public officials, and citizen activists to Maryland and south central Pennsylvania to study those states' farmland preservation programs and, in Montgomery County, its mixed-income housing programs as well.

The group's stamina and motivation were amazing. Arriving after a twelve-hour bus trip from Lansing to Gaithersburg, they still had the energy for a three-hour dinner meeting, peppering county representatives with detailed questions about Montgomery County's transferable development rights and mixed-income housing programs. County officials explained that two decades earlier the county's comprehensive plan had designated the northern third of the county (almost 90,000 acres) as permanent farmland. Initial "agricultural zoning" had required minimum 5-acre lots for each housing unit. Recognizing that such small lot size was promoting rural sprawl rather than farmland protection, in the 1980s the county planning commission raised the minimum requirement to 25 acres—but left the rezoned farmland with residual development rights. In other words, a 100-acre farm would have the right to have four housing units on it but would retain sixteen units of transferable development rights (that is, marketable for off-site construction but not buildable on-site). Some 40,000 acres were now protected by permanent development restrictions as the result of sale of transferable development rights.

Our presentations came to life when the ninety participants climbed onto their buses the next morning to tour Hallowell, one of the earliest communities developed under these policies. Hallowell had been a 400-acre farm but was located within the county's planned urban development zone. As "farmland," it still carried its vestigial zoning of one housing unit for every two acres; in light of topological and drainage restraints and right-of-way requirements, existing zoning would have permitted only about 150 housing units to be built.

Standing on the steps of the bandstand in the middle of Hallowell's neighborhood park on a sunny, crisp February morning, William Hussmann described what had happened. "I am chairman of the Montgomery County Planning Commission now," Hussmann explained, "but back then I was the agent for the Hallowell developer. In this hot housing market, it was much more profitable to develop many more housing units on the land. We asked the county planning commission to upgrade the zoning to three or four units per acre. 'We want more intensive development, too,' the planning commission replied, 'but we are not going to upgrade the zoning. If you want to build more housing units, go buy transferable development rights from farmers in the agricultural protection areas.'"

To the knowing smiles and chuckles of the Michigan farmers, Hussmann described haggling on front porches and at kitchen tables with local farmers over buying their farms' development rights. Ultimately, he purchased 750 development rights from thirty-five different farms at about $3,000–$4,000 per development right. This raised Hallowell's development potential to 900 homes.

Complying with the county's MPDU ordinance, the developer set aside the required allocation of affordable housing units, earning a 22 percent density bonus and raising the land's development capacity to 1,100 units. As an integral part of the new community, the developer built 130 MPDUs and then donated sixty unused development rights to the Housing Opportunities Commission for it to construct additional affordable units. (The then-chairman of the planning commission sponsored downzoning the HOC-built townhouses from sixty to forty units, a move, Hussmann speculated, that was "purely political" in preparation for the former chairman's unsuccessful bid for the elected county executive post.)

The end result was that Hallowell was developed as a community of

1,080 single-family homes and townhouses (including 130 MPDUs) and one forty-unit HOC-owned rental complex. Eighty-seven of the MPDUs were owned by moderate-income households and forty-three by the HOC for low-income households. Thirty of the forty rental units were occupied by moderate-income households as well and only ten by low-income households.

From the social perspective, Hallowell was home to a wide range of residents of different racial and ethnic groups and varying income levels. Fifty-three low-income households had been integrated smoothly into this overwhelmingly middle-class community. They were not otherwise obliged to seek low-rent housing in communities like Silver Spring or Langley Park that were already experiencing substantial pressures from lower-income households moving out of Washington into older housing.

From the environmental perspective, homes for 1,120 new households had been created in an urban environment, easing market pressures on further conversion of farmland. The thirty-five farm families had received about $2.5 million in compensation for their development rights—not tax dollars but private dollars. By controlling zoning densities in both the sending areas (the farms) and the receiving area (Hallowell) within a strong housing market, Montgomery County had successfully privatized the cost of permanent farmland preservation.

Over the next hour, as the Michigan group walked and drove along trimly landscaped streets of single-family homes and townhouse complexes, Hussmann challenged us. Which are the owner-occupied MPDUs? Which are the HOC-owned MPDUs? We could not tell. Often we could not even separate out the MPDUs from the market-rate townhouses. Unlike Fallswick, where the MPDUs were grouped together (though tastefully) in one block, market-rate townhouses, owner-occupied MPDUs, and HOC-owned MPDUs were all mixed together. Even the HOC's forty-unit rental complex was simply an architecturally compatible string of townhouses along a street near Hallowell's elementary school and community playground.

That morning, I believe, most of the Michiganders on the tour truly grasped the connection made by the battle cry of Jack Laurie, president of the Michigan Farm Bureau: "To save our farms, we must save our cities."[9]

In mid-1996 I was chatting with Tetreault, who had resigned after twenty-four years as the HOC's executive director to organize the nonprofit Innovative Housing Institute. The institute's mission is to help local govern-

---

9. In the months after the Ultimate Farmland Preservation Tour, the Farm Bureau's leadership forged a strong political alliance with Detroit mayor Dennis Archer, Grand Rapids mayor John Logie, and the mayors of Michigan's other ten largest cities.

ments and housing authorities understand the value—and, as Bernie said, noting the steady demise of federal housing support—the *financial necessity* of income-integrated housing. Through the institute, Bernie is developing videos, slide shows, model procedures and ordinances, and training materials to spread the Montgomery County success story to other communities.[10]

"You know," Bernie said, "over those years the HOC was transformed from a typical, small public housing agency managing 400 project-based apartments to a multifaceted housing developer, mortgage financier, property manager, social services provider, and rental agent. By the time I left, we were managing more than 4,000 housing units and administering another 4,000 federal rent certificates and vouchers.

"But our greatest achievement," Bernie continued, "was the degree to which we developed mixed-income housing . . . low- and moderate-income households living in the same neighborhoods with high-income families."

"Yes, I have driven and walked through some of those neighborhoods, such as Fallswick out in Potomac," I said.

"It's funny," Bernie mused. "A place like Fallswick is the kind of neighborhood where the mixed-income concept works best. The whole idea seems to go down better, the wider the gap between the market rate and MPDU houses. Where there is not much difference in value between market rate and MPDU units, market-rate homeowners sometimes show more animosity toward the MPDU and HOC residents. They feel more often that the subsidized households are getting an unfair break that they had to work for themselves. Maybe among higher-income residents there is more sense of noblesse oblige."

"Higher-income homeowners may also recognize that there is not any danger of the modest proportion of MPDUs 'flipping' the neighborhood," I added. "In a place such as Fallswick, there is no prospect that other low- or moderate-income households will be moving in. The thirteen MPDU properties are all there will ever be."

"You may be correct," Bernie said. He grinned. "Do you know what's the best measure of how scattered our mixed-income housing is? The HOC has a line item in its annual budget, about $350,000, I think. It's used to pay annual membership assessments on behalf of our tenants to over 200 private homeowner associations. Just like every other homeowner, the housing authority pays to have the grass mowed in the street medians and private parks or hire lifeguards for the community swimming pool."

10. In October 1997 I joined the board of directors of the Innovative Housing Institute.

Summing Up

The MPDU policy and the full range of the county's low- and moderate-income housing policies and programs have helped the county accommodate—even encourage—a remarkable social transformation. In 1970 Montgomery County had the look of a classic suburban county: wealthy and white (95 percent). By 1990 it had a "rainbow" look: 12 percent black, 7 percent Hispanic, 8 percent Asian. In 1970 the countywide poverty rate was 3.5 percent; by 1990 the nominal poverty rate had inched up to 4.2 percent (but about 5.8 percent, adjusted for its higher cost of living).

Two close twins of Montgomery County are its Northern Virginia neighbor, Fairfax County, and Oakland County, Michigan, outside Detroit (see table 9-1). They are comparable in geographic areas, population, and, adjusted for metro Washington's higher cost of living, average income level and poverty rate. They were also almost identical in racial composition a generation ago; all three were 95 to 97 percent white.

But there the similarities end. With sixty municipalities and townships and a relatively weak county government, the Detroit suburb is a "little box" area while both the Washington suburbs are "big box" governments. Both of the Washington suburbs had moved far along the road to achieving racially integrated neighborhoods and schools by 1990.[11]

With its aggressive mixed-income housing policies, Montgomery County maintained a low and stable level of economic segregation during the two decades (its dissimilarity index was 27 in 1970 and 28 in 1990). By contrast, Fairfax County (from 22 to 31) and Oakland County (from 27 to 38) experienced steadily rising levels of segregation of poor households.[12]

The Montgomery County Public Schools have worked hard to promote diversity without resorting to widespread busing for racial balance. They have relied on the county's diversified housing policies and periodic adjustments in school attendance zone boundaries. The county school system's

11. Specific data on racial enrollment patterns for the Fairfax County Public Schools for 1989–90 were not supplied by the state of Virginia to the National Center for Education Statistics, the source of my nationwide study. However, high school enrollment patterns would adhere closely to housing patterns countywide.

12. Ironically, the Fairfax County Council had adopted its own affordable dwelling unit (ADU) policy before Montgomery County's MPDU policy in the early 1970s. However, Fairfax County's mixed-income housing ordinance was overturned by the state courts, which ruled that, under the Dillon's Rule doctrine, Fairfax County lacked specific state authorization for the measure. Not until 1990 did the county government, having secured special permissive legislation from the Virginia General Assembly, reenact its ADU ordinance.

Table 9-1. *A Tale of Three Counties*

Demographic data	Montgomery County, Maryland	Fairfax County, Virginia	Oakland County, Michigan
Geographic area (square miles)	494.6	395.6	872.7
Total population, 1970	522,809	454,275	907,871
White (percent)	95	96	97
Black (percent)	4	4	3
Asian and other (percent)	1	0	0
Total population, 1997	826,766	914,259	1,166,512
White, 1990 (percent)	72	77	88
Black, 1990 (percent)	12	8	7
Hispanic, 1990 (percent)	7	6	2
Asian, 1990 (percent)	8	8	2
Other, 1990 (percent)	1	1	1
Cost-of-living index, 1989	137	137	99
COLA-adjusted household income, 1989 (dollars)	49,640	50,334	56,059
COLA-adjusted poverty rate, 1989 (percent)	5.8	4.8	5.9
Municipal governments (with planning and zoning powers)	8	0	60
County planning and zoning powers (as percent of county residents)	88	100	0
School districts	1	1	29
Black housing segregation index, 1970	48	51	91
Black housing segregation index, 1990	39	38	76
Black school segregation index, 1990	34	n.a.	81
Segregation index of the poor, 1970	27	22	27
Segregation index of the poor, 1990	28	31	38

Source: Author's calculations based on census reports.
n.a. Not available.

record and policies are not without their critics. However, balance and diversity within Montgomery County's unified "big box" school system is light-years ahead of the pattern within the multiple "little box" school districts in Oakland County and Westchester County, New York, outside New York City,

Table 9-2. *High School Segregation Indexes in Three Counties, 1989–90*

Racial or ethnic group	Montgomery County, Maryland (20)[a]		Oakland County, Michigan (41)[a]		Westchester County, New York (42)[a]	
	Percent	Index	Percent	Index	Percent	Index
All minorities	37.6	27	15.8	64	33.5	51
Black	15.7	34	11.2	81	18.7	63
Hispanic	8.1	32	1.4	54	9.6	56
Asian	13.7	22	2.5	44	5.2	34
Native American	0.3	23	1.0	65	0.1	79

a. The number of high schools in each county.

as shown in table 9-2. For every racial and ethnic group, Montgomery County's high schools are substantially more integrated than Westchester County's. One cannot even talk about degrees of "integration" in Oakland County; its public high schools are two to three times more segregated than Montgomery County's for every minority group except Oakland County's very small Hispanic student population (who are 67 percent more segregated than Hispanics in Montgomery County schools).

Montgomery County is not exempt from the social trends of contemporary America. County officials and residents alike are conscious of substantial economic differences between the poorer eastern part of the county (for example, Silver Spring, Takoma Park, Aspen Hill) and the wealthier western portion (Bethesda, Chevy Chase, Potomac, Gaithersburg, Germantown). All of the county government's planning and zoning efforts have not prevented the steady filtering of older housing in eastern Montgomery County down the household income scale.

However, Montgomery County has not compounded the damage of such market trends through its own housing policies. More than two-thirds of HOC-assisted housing units have been built or acquired in the wealthier western parts of the county. County policies have prevented a steeper decline in the eastern county while bringing much greater racial and class diversity to the western county than laissez-faire market trends would ever have produced. Montgomery County's more egalitarian social fabric is the direct result of its Moderately Priced Dwelling Unit Ordinance and other mixed-income housing policies and programs.

10

Dayton, Ohio's ED/GE: The Rewards (and Limits) of Voluntary Agreements

THE TOWNSHIP SYSTEM may have been an excellent way to settle the Ohio frontier in the eighteenth century, but having so many small governments certainly made it more difficult to manage a complex urban society 200 years later, Montgomery County (Ohio) administrator Don Vermillion thought as he contemplated the problems faced by the Dayton area in mid-1989. The city of Dayton was slowly dying, and Montgomery County was starting to decline with it. Only fifteen to twenty years earlier, the Dayton area had been one of America's most prosperous manufacturing centers. Since then the area had lost 45,000 high-wage, blue-collar jobs, or more than one-quarter of its industrial employment. Traditional mainstays of the region's economy had cut back or closed down. General Motors had dropped from 40,000 to 20,000 jobs. Dayton Tire and Rubber (2,000 jobs) and Dayton Press (3,000 jobs) had vanished, leaving behind only memories of better days and realities of polluted "brownfields."

National Cash Register (NCR), Dayton's flagship company, had released 20,000 employees. Almost as troubling was the possibility that NCR and Dayton's other four Fortune 500 companies might be swallowed up by outsiders in the wave of corporate mergers sweeping Wall Street. A source of Dayton's civic strength had always been its homegrown corporations. Absentee owners would never have the same civic and philanthropic commitment to the Dayton area as chief executive officers headquartered just up the street.[1]

With economic hard times, many younger residents had moved away, and few new families migrated into the area. Having peaked at about 608,000 residents in 1970, Montgomery County's population had fallen to about 575,000 people two decades later. The city of Dayton had lost a quarter of its inhabitants; its loss accounted for the entire county's population drop. Most of Dayton's suburbs had continued to grow in both population and jobs, sustaining a perception of suburban well-being and further distancing them psychologically from the city's problems.

Vermillion felt this sense of well-being was an illusion. Wealth had moved to the fringes of Montgomery County and was leaking into neighboring counties, especially Greene County, the site of Wright-Patterson Air Force Base. The base commander had promulgated a new rule requiring defense contractors to have major offices within a fifty-mile radius of the base; the "fifty-mile rule" was spurring an office boom along the Interstate 675 corridor rather than in downtown Dayton. The region's most rapidly growing area was Greene County, where Bellbrook and Beavercreek had become the newest top-of-the-line communities. The newly opened Fairview Commons Mall in Beavercreek along I-675 was already drawing shoppers away from older commercial areas in Montgomery County. Average household incomes in Beavercreek were one-quarter higher than in suburban Kettering, Montgomery County's second largest city, and more than twice Dayton's average household income.[2]

Interjurisdictional economic competition had always been fierce among Ohio's cities, villages, and townships—Ohio was known as "the Home Rule State"—and there were certainly a lot of local competitors. Within Montgomery County alone there were nineteen municipalities: Dayton, a dozen

---

1. In 1991 AT&T acquired NCR, converting it into AT&T's "GIS Division." The locus of decisionmaking for Dayton's largest private employer moved from just two miles away from the Montgomery County Courthouse to AT&T's headquarters on Manhattan's Avenue of the Americas, only 550 air-miles from Dayton but light-years away in terms of local commitment. By 1996, among Dayton's largest homegrown corporations only Mead Corporation maintained its independence and Fortune 500 ranking (256). However, the pendulum was swinging back. IBM restored the "NCR" name and announced plans to spin NCR off as an independent company.

2. Ironically, Kettering could have been part of Dayton. In 1954 Van Buren Township asked to be annexed by Dayton. The city refused, and the spurned township incorporated as the new city of Kettering.

suburban cities, and six suburban villages. Many were former townships that had incorporated to frustrate annexation by the city of Dayton. There were still twelve surviving independent townships, now almost fully empowered municipalities in all but official form. Including county government itself, Montgomery County counted thirty-two separate local governments, roughly one for every 18,000 residents. In addition, the county's 105,000 schoolchildren attended seventeen public school systems plus a plethora of private and parochial schools.

The area's political balkanization had been the focus of much local attention in recent years. In 1986 the Community Factors Evaluation Study, funded by the Dayton Area Progress Council and conducted by Wright State University, found the region's business image was suffering and that efforts to attract new or expanding companies were faltering as a result of duplicate development efforts and political infighting among the region's many local governments. Cleveland State University had prepared a second study for a county-appointed citizens board; this Citizens Financial Task Force Report had projected growing fiscal problems for local governments. Both urged the creation of a new, more cooperative way to pursue economic development. A chamber of commerce committee had recently encouraged the county to investigate tax sharing as a way to promote regional economic development.

Vermillion saw a possible way to make it happen. The Ohio legislature had just authorized Ohio counties to adopt an additional one-half percent sales tax. For Montgomery County, the tax would yield an estimated $210 million in revenues over the ten-year period authorized. The three Montgomery County commissioners had already called for a long-term, cost-cutting fiscal plan. Using the new revenues to retire high-interest bonds, upgrade law enforcement facilities, and rebuild depleted general fund reserves would rank high on the commissioners' list. Perhaps, however, buttressed by these studies, Vermillion could persuade them to set aside some of the money as a cooperative economic development fund. If there were enough money— perhaps $5 million a year—it might be sufficient incentive for most of Montgomery County's local governments to sign on to some tax-sharing arrangement as well. A quid pro quo, Vermillion thought. To qualify for economic development grants, a local government would have to agree to revenue sharing. It might just work.

Could the tough political controversies ahead for such an unusual initiative be overcome? Vermillion wondered. He himself was relatively young (thirty-four years old) with only one year as Montgomery County administrator behind him. He was a professional public manager, however, trained in the University of Kansas's renowned public administration program, and had already served as city manager of suburban Miamisburg. One of the essential tools of a successful city or county manager is skill in providing leadership behind the scenes. Vermillion knew that he had an excellent county commission. Commission president Paula MacIlwaine was a former League of Women Voters president. Commissioner Charles Curran, a former state senator, understood regional issues well. Commissioner Donna Moon, a former Kettering school board member, realized that faster economic growth was needed to sustain good public school systems. The county commission was progressive, open to new ideas, and, Vermillion felt, willing to move in new directions.

Forging Regional Collaboration

And so it was. That summer the county commission enacted the local option sales tax for a ten-year period, effective in October 1989. Of the $210 million in projected revenues, the commissioners earmarked $140 million for debt reduction, general fund reserves, and law enforcement facilities. However, they set aside $5 million a year, or a total of $50 million, for an experimental countywide economic development program. (They also reserved $20 million to be split between an affordable housing fund and an arts and cultural fund, both for the entire county.)

The commissioners recognized that the greatest political hurdle would be to get all the other local governments to participate. Township and municipal officials might reject any program promoted solely as a county government initiative, the commissioners believed. County government would need some other organization to take the lead publicly in shaping the program.

The Community Cooperation Task Force might be just the group, they decided. It was a sort of civic advisory board recently organized by the Dayton Area Chamber of Commerce at the behest of the Montgomery County Township Association. The townships had wanted the new group to help mediate annexation disputes with area municipalities. The Community Cooperation Task Force included the mayor of Dayton, three suburban mayors, the three county commissioners, three township trustees, one township clerk, one village council member, three private sector members (a CEO of a large construction firm, a university president, and a newspaper editor), and five area school board members. If the group's focus could be shifted from inherently bitter annexation disputes to a more constructive, cooperative agenda, the Community Cooperation Task Force would be the perfect broadly based team to help forge an agreement among so many diverse local governments historically jealous of their independence.

In August 1989 the county commission invited the Community Cooperation Task Force to take the lead in developing a joint economic development and tax-sharing program. Tom Heine, the Dayton chamber of commerce president, would serve as facilitator. After five months of struggling with the technical complexity of the task, the task force volunteers finally asked county staff to undertake the necessary analysis, develop a tax-sharing methodology, and report back regularly to the task force. Reluctantly, for it was still wary of adverse reaction to a "county-driven" program, the county set up a technical advisory group composed of Vermillion, the county's budget director, and the county's economic development director; three leading businessmen in the area; William Dodge, an outside strategic planning consultant; the director of Ohio's State and Local Government Commission (who had studied other tax-sharing models); and a Wright State University professor, Jack Dustin, also an expert in tax-sharing programs.

The technical advisory group reached agreement quickly on two major points. Though some local government officials on the task force had wanted access to the economic development fund without participating in tax sharing, the two programs were tied together. And though Dayton wanted a tax-sharing distribution formula based on relative need (using per capita income, unemployment and poverty rates, and tax effort as measures), the technical advisory group agreed on using simple population percentage as the distribution formula.

The real struggle revolved around the tax-sharing contribution formula. First, what revenues would be shared? How much? The members of the technical advisory group were very familiar with Minnesota's fiscal disparities plan. (Vermillion himself had first studied the program at the University of Kansas.) They decided, however, against the Twin Cities' formula because it involved sharing growth only in the commercial and industrial property tax base; the technical group felt that it was equally important to share growth in the residential property tax base. Moreover, incremental growth should be based both on new investment and the appreciation of existing property if the program was to put a dent in fiscal disparities.

When the technical group presented its initial recommendations to the task force, some of the task force members, particularly township representatives, were troubled by the formula, since it focused on property taxes alone.

They asked that a second advisory group (the technical advisory subcommittee) be organized to broaden the base of local government involvement. The technical advisory subcommittee brought to the table two township administrators and four city managers; all but one had not been involved in the prior discussions. (In all, nine of the county's thirty-one local governments—those with the largest populations and largest shares of commercial and industrial development—were involved directly in one of the two advisory groups.) With Wright State's Dustin assisting in the discussion of various alternatives, the local officials sought to hammer out a revised tax-sharing formula with the three county administrators.

City and township members challenged again the idea of sharing tax revenues at all; "government equity" ought to be abandoned. They argued that nobody (even the wealthiest communities among them) had surplus revenues to share and that revenue sharing would penalize the more "efficient" local governments to reward the "inefficient." Where would the shared revenue really come from? How fast would the commitment build up? Each was fearful of giving up too much. City and township members urged that most of the revenues from the county's half-cent sales tax increase should just flow through to local governments rather than fund the county's regional initiatives. Reluctant to oppose outright the county's effort to foster cooperative economic development efforts, however, the city and township members did not walk out of the talks.

For two months they argued back and forth. City and township administrators constantly sought to limit the amount of tax revenues shared. County administrators wanted a tax-sharing pool large enough to equal the county's $5 million a year economic development fund. The two sides could not compromise. Finally, the county yielded. Residential property included in the contribution formula would be limited to 25 percent of the increase in assessed valuation, and the contribution to the pool would not exceed the previous year's property tax growth. Even with these concessions, the group could not reach unanimity, and the debate moved back to the broader-based task force.

It was now December 1990, and the county's timetable was running out. The county had wanted to implement the economic development and revenue-sharing plan in 1991, after the first year of the new tax collections, but major issues were still unresolved. Township officials were particularly upset. Including only property taxes in the formula, they felt, favored municipalities over townships. In Ohio payroll taxes account for 50 to 85 percent of municipal revenues, but cannot be levied by townships, which are dependent on the property tax for more than 80 percent of township revenues. If cities and villages did not have to share part of their largest revenue source (payroll taxes), why should townships share theirs (property taxes)? Moreover, though property taxes most accurately reflect place-specific new investments, in Ohio property taxes are heavily earmarked for specified purposes, such as police, fire, and road improvements. Property taxes are also subject to sunset provisions; they must be reauthorized periodically by local voters. The amount of property tax that could actually be pooled was questionable.

The Task Force compromised; growth in payroll taxes would be added to the pool as well. The maximum contribution for any jurisdiction would be capped at 13 percent of the growth in payroll and property tax revenues. It was decided that the base year from which incremental growth in taxes would be calculated would always be only three years before the year of distribution. Municipal and township administrators alike were very concerned that a large increase in the tax base early in the program—from a major business expansion, for example—would leave their jurisdiction a net contributor for the remaining life of the program. They demanded that the base year be recalibrated every year. A sliding base year would keep the amount of pooled revenues from ever growing very large. In general, the difference between the contribution and distribution formulas would result in net distributions for declining, stable, or slow-growth jurisdictions and net contributions for fast-growth jurisdictions.

The final plan was dubbed the ED/GE plan (Economic Development/ Government Equity). The Community Cooperation Task Force recommended that the Montgomery County Commission adopt the ED/GE plan. It was publicly launched at a chamber of commerce dinner in January 1991. The county commission then set a deadline of July 1, 1991, for local governments to sign up.

Last-Minute Compromises

Major hurdles still remained. Even after the kick-off dinner several city managers remained concerned that their suburban cities would end up in a precarious position if they were constantly net contributors but received no offsetting economic development funds for projects in their communities. (The precarious position they feared was probably more political than fiscal in nature.) They threatened to reject the program.

The city of Kettering played a key leadership role among the suburban municipalities. Al Jordan, Kettering's assistant city manager, had been an early supporter of the ED/GE negotiations. Now he was balking. Dustin and Jordan met for lunch. "Kettering's an aging suburb now," the Wright State professor argued. "In the next decade you'll begin facing some of Dayton's problems: continuing job losses from GM's DELCO division, retail customers deserting Kettering's stores for new malls and strip centers in Greene County, aging housing stock and infrastructure, more fixed income households. Kettering will need the economic development grants to help attract new jobs to offset the losses. You might even be a net recipient of revenue-sharing funds as the end of the decade approaches."

Jordan was not persuaded. "It's hard to support the program when it's sure to cost us scarce tax dollars right away. What do we say to our citizens? How do we explain what the money was for? What do we do if we come up seriously short in the city budget?"

Dustin returned to his office and returned a phone call from one of the chamber of commerce committee members, who informed Dustin of an emergency meeting with the disaffected municipalities. "Kettering's still balking," Dustin casually mentioned to the chamber leader. "They're afraid of losing revenues."

The next day, when Dustin arrived at the emergency session, Jordan whispered to him, "Whatever you said, it worked." After more than a year of negotiations, Kettering had tried to offer an entirely new program. Chamber of commerce president Tom Heine, the task force's chairman, was not about to see all the effort go down the drain. Were Kettering and others worried about loss of revenues? Heine hammered out a final compromise. Any jurisdiction that had been a net contributor for three straight years was assured of having an economic development grant approved every third year for an equivalent amount of money. This "settle-up" accord would hold net contributors harmless. (Of course, it would also make moot any net effect of revenue sharing.)

Though twenty-seven of the local governments originally executed contracts, four municipalities filed suit, stalling ED/GE's implementation. On June 25, 1992, the Ohio state supreme court let stand lower court rulings rejecting all the municipalities' claims, and the program was officially implemented in the fall of 1992, after communities had been given time to recommit to the program.

As of mid-1996, twenty-eight of Montgomery County's twenty-nine townships and municipalities had voluntarily signed a nine-year contract with the county to participate in the ED/GE program.[3] Vandalia, one of the four jurisdictions that sued unsuccessfully to block the program, remains the sole holdout. Adjacent to the Dayton International Airport and located at the interchange of I-70 and I-75 ("the crossroads of America"), Vandalia is booming economically.[4]

Economic Development Collaboration

After such a long and arduous gestation, how has the ED/GE program actually performed? Its goals are lofty: to create and retain jobs in the county; enhance jurisdictional and county tax bases; compete successfully as a region in national and international markets; and share the benefits of areawide economic prosperity among all jurisdictions in the county.[5]

Each year Montgomery County has allocated $5 million to the economic development fund from the special countywide sales tax. Grants are awarded to (or through) participating governments to establish or expand commercial, industrial, and research facilities and to create and preserve employment opportunities. The fund supports primarily public infrastructure improvements critical to particular economic development projects, but it has also funded other legally allowable activities that foster economic development.

Each year 85 percent of the allocation ($4.25 million) is committed to projects in individual jurisdictions. Another 10 percent ($500,000) is reserved for special projects to take advantage of "newly emerging economic opportunities." A final 5 percent ($250,000) is reserved for "unexpected economic opportunities or threats that occur between funding cycles."

Certain policy guidelines and selection criteria, recommended originally by the Community Cooperation Task Force, are considered in evaluating applications for funding. The grant awards are approved annually by the county commission on the basis of the recommendations of the ED/GE advisory committee. The committee consists of fifteen members (six representing cities and villages; four representing townships; three private sector members; and two county commissioners). Dayton and Kettering have per-

3. In the 1990s Mad River and Madison Townships merged with the cities of Riverside and Trotwood, respectively.

4. Vandalia's mayor had led the dissenting municipalities. In the next election, however, a strong supporter of regional cooperation almost upset her.

5. Montgomery County (1991).

manent seats; other membership rotates annually among different participating governments.

The ED/GE advisory committee assesses project proposals on the basis
of their potential to retain or expand local businesses or attract new businesses from outside Montgomery County. The advisory committee gives
priority to proposals that create or help retain jobs, preserve or enhance the
local tax base, and have a private business as a committed end user.

The ED/GE program emphasizes sectors that have high growth potential within the regional economy, such as aerospace and avionics, automo-
tive components, communications, computer information technology, health
care, manufacturing research and development, and transportation-related
activities (for example, warehousing and distribution).

Special consideration is given to collaborative efforts that involve two
or more communities or that encourage growth in areas already served by
basic public infrastructure, such as water and sanitary sewer lines or existing roads. Projects are encouraged to leverage other public and private investment and should not substitute economic development funds for other
funding. They must be ready to begin implementation (typically within six
months of approval, with a completion date within twenty-four months).
Finally, the advisory committee strongly discourages projects that would
simply relocate businesses from one jurisdiction to another within Montgomery County.

New Jobs, Retained Jobs

What has been the economic development fund's impact? After seven funding cycles (1992–98) the results "on the ground" are impressive. Drive past
General Motors' new Clear Coat Paint Line Facility at the GM Truck and
Bus Plant in the city of Moraine. In 1992–93, $1 million in ED/GE funds
helped expand the plant, thereby retaining an estimated 3,500 jobs and creating another 65 new jobs. General Motors had been considering closing the
Moraine facility and moving its operations to Shreveport, Louisiana, or Lin-
den, New Jersey.

Out in the city of Huber Heights, $530,000 in 1992 helped build an
access road connecting a state highway with a new industrial park to accommodate ABF, a trucking firm, and this effort kept 600 jobs and created 400
more. A former department store in Kettering had closed. Some $650,000 in
ED/GE funds for site and leasehold improvements helped convert the aban-

doned store into a new telephone order-taking center for Victoria's Secret, creating 1,000 new jobs.

Other ED/GE investments are not as visible as a GM plant, a trucking company's marshaling yard, or a Victoria's Secret catalog center but have been just as crucial to the region's economy. With 22,000 military and civilian personnel, the Dayton area's primary employer is Wright-Patterson Air Force Base.[6] In 1994 ED/GE provided $135,000 to fund a local task force to defend Wright-Patterson against any cutbacks or even outright closure being considered by the Defense Department's Base Realignment and Closure Commission. "Wright-Pat" suffered no major cutbacks in the 1995 round of defense cuts. As a result, the base was available to serve as the high-security site of the Bosnian peace talks later that year, giving rise to the "Dayton Accords," a more substantive source of worldwide publicity for the Dayton area than hosting a Super Bowl or Miss USA pageant.

By September 1998 the economic development fund had gone through seven project funding cycles and committed over $34 million to 152 projects. ED/GE money had been matched by over $1 billion in other local, state, and federal funds, and private investment. The county's 1997 summary of ED/GE's achievements stated that 26,058 existing jobs will be retained, and 16,009 new jobs are expected to be created through the projects funded thus far. Taken at face value, the ED/GE program had been fabulously successful; the cost in ED/GE grants had been about $2,100 for each new job created. By contrast, in its wildest dreams, Detroit's federally bankrolled Empowerment Community program hopes to create 6,800 new jobs in its target zone at a federal cost of $300 million in grants and tax incentives—which translates to some $44,000 per new job created.

Reviewing the ED/GE program's glowing results, my thoughts wandered back to my years as mayor of Albuquerque (1977–81). I had worked closely with Albuquerque Economic Development, our community's private sector–based organization for promoting business. During those years we had persuaded many national corporations—Intel, Signetics, Honeywell, for example—to set up new manufacturing plants in Albuquerque.

In particular, I remember our negotiations with Ethicon, a subsidiary of Johnson & Johnson, the country's leading medical supply company. Ethicon was interested in building a new plant in Albuquerque to produce ultrasterile surgical sutures. Their proposed site lay south of the city limits

---

6. In 1946 Wright-Patterson's employment had peaked at 49,000 military and civilian personnel.

on a rolling bluff overlooking the University of New Mexico's South Golf Course, a visually spectacular location. The Ethicon Plant would also be the first tenant of the city's proposed South Valley Industrial Park located near the poorest, almost semirural, traditionally Hispanic neighborhoods in the Albuquerque area.

Laying in new city water and sewer lines was essential to opening up the site for industrial development, yet the city's regular policies would have required Ethicon to pay utility extension charges that would have added about $1.2 million to the plant's cost. Ethicon proposed that the cost of utility expansion be covered by a federal urban development action grant (UDAG). Complying with the federal program's conditions, Ethicon was willing to hire 75 percent of its future employees from the South Valley.

The problem was that Albuquerque did not qualify as a UDAG community. Like many cities of the Sun Belt, Albuquerque had rapidly annexed new, middle-class suburban neighborhoods into the city. Even though it had a large number of poorer neighborhoods, Albuquerque's citywide poverty statistics were too low for the city as a whole to qualify for the grant.

At that time the so-called Sun Belt–Rust Belt rivalry was in full swing. Unlike many other Sun Belt mayors, I did not object to seeing the bulk of federal antipoverty funds targeted on cities in the Northeast and Middle West. As a former civil rights and antipoverty staffer with the Washington Urban League, I knew that such cities had far greater social and fiscal problems than Albuquerque. (Moreover, I knew that, with Kirtland Air Force Base and Sandia National Laboratories, Albuquerque actually received defense dollars that far outweighed any shortfall in our "fair share" of federal antipoverty funds.) Rather than support an all-out Sun Belt assault on Frost Belt–favoring distribution formulas, I suggested that a modest slice of UDAG funds be earmarked for "pockets of poverty," a notion that appealed politically to my fellow Sun Belt mayors. We successfully lobbied Congress and the Carter administration to amend UDAG eligibility criteria. And Albuquerque became the first community to receive a "pocket of poverty" UDAG grant: $1.2 million earmarked for utility extension costs into the city's South Valley Industrial Park.

Within several weeks of receiving the UDAG grant, I found myself turning over the ceremonial shovelful of dirt at the groundbreaking of the new plant. Some eighteen months later the plant went into production, ultimately hiring 500 workers. Ethicon met all its local hiring commitments and has been an exemplary employer and civic citizen.

Was the $1.2 million UDAG grant essential to the plant project? At the time Johnson & Johnson executives claimed that it was. Johnson & Johnson's initial $9 million investment, however, dwarfed the UDAG grant's contribution. And Albuquerque's primary attraction was not inexpensive land but a labor pool that was reasonably well educated, highly motivated, and not unionized. (In the late 1980s Ethicon's Albuquerque employees rejected an effort by the Teamsters Union to organize the plant by a more than 2 to 1 margin.)

Did the $1.2 million really "create" 500 new jobs in Albuquerque in 1980? Did $34 million in ED/GE grants really "create" 16,009 new jobs in Dayton–Montgomery County, and "retain" another 26,058 existing jobs in 1992–98? Who knows? Probably a hard-nosed evaluation would downgrade both programs' claims significantly. But by any standard, the economic development fund has been a successful economic tool in Dayton-Montgomery County.

Limited Revenue Sharing

The government equity fund has also been a great success from the perspective of most local finance officers, whose goal is to minimize revenue sharing's impact. Because of the cap on contributions and the sliding base year, the amount of incremental revenues shared through the government equity fund has been modest. By the sixth year, fiscal 1998, the total funds redistributed in any one year had grown to only $712,680, contributed by fourteen of the twenty-eight participating jurisdictions; over the first six years a total of $2,902,262 had been distributed.

The government equity fund has had a modest redistributive effect. Over the first six years, communities with high fiscal capacity were, in fact, net contributors. The city of Oakwood contributed a cumulative total of $148,246; Miami Township, $190,125; Washington Township, $285,208; the city of Miamisburg, $412,161; the city of Centerville, $394,290; and the city of Kettering, $793,681. Communities with low fiscal capacity were, in fact, the largest net recipients, with Jefferson Township receiving $124,427; the city of Huber Heights, $271,371; the newly consolidated city of Riverside, $281,546; the city of Trotwood, $336,731; Harrison Township, $418,138; and the city of Dayton, $1,189,089.

As the above summary demonstrates, however, the actual impact of revenue sharing through the government equity fund is indeed modest. About a half-million dollars a year in shared revenues is a tiny fraction of the total budgets of the twenty-eight participating governments. County administrator Vermillion himself candidly characterized the government equity fund as "symbolic" revenue sharing.

The voluntary, locally negotiated Government Equity program amounts to about $1 a year per resident of Montgomery County in shared revenues. By contrast, the nation's largest, state-mandated, regional revenue-sharing program—the Twin Cities fiscal disparities plan—has grown to over $150 a year per resident of the seven-county, 186-municipality Minneapolis-Saint Paul region.

Moreover, even consistent net contributors to the Dayton area's government equity fund are being made whole over time through the eleventh-hour "settle-up" provision, under which no jurisdiction will contribute more to the government equity fund than it will receive from the economic development fund. The first "settle-up" occurred in 1995, with others to follow in 1998 and 2001 (the ED/GE program's final year). With annual economic development fund allocations being ten times the size of the annual equity fund's pool, "settle-up" will be an easy commitment to fulfill.

Other Regional Collaborations

However, the true value of the ED/GE program is that it has opened the way to an unusual level of intergovernmental cooperation in Montgomery County. Local officials cooperate constantly in the administration of the program, in particular, through service on the ED/GE advisory committee, which evaluates annual project applications.

Concurrent with ED/GE's authorization, in 1989 the county commission established the Dayton/Montgomery County Housing Commission (now the Affordable Housing Fund). Its mission was to develop regionwide approaches to meeting the need for low- and moderate-income housing. With an annual allocation of $1 million in county sales tax funds, by 1998 the Housing Commission had leveraged $7.5 million into $97 million of private mortgage commitments and renovation loans.

In the same year, the county commission also established the Montgomery County Regional Arts and Cultural District (MCRACD) to focus on the public side of arts funding, with an allocation of $1 million per year as incentive funds for the arts. Over the first six years (1990–95) MCRACD provided $3 million in operating support for fourteen arts and cultural organizations, such as Dayton Public TV, the Dayton Philharmonic, and the Museum of Natural History; made over 100 small, one-time grants to art and cultural groups, totaling $877,000 (and generating another $802,000 in matching funds from other sources); contributed $2 million for a new Metropolitan Arts Center in Dayton, which leveraged another $6.5 million in city and state grants; and spent $455,000 to promote a merger of Arts Dayton and the Miami Valley Arts Council into Culture Works, a regionwide United Way for the arts, which will also provide management and technical assistance to local arts organizations. In all, an independent evaluation estimated that from 1990 to 1995 MCRACD's $6.4 million investment had had an aggregate economic impact of $21.3 million on the Miami Valley economy.[7]

In the economic development arena, beyond ED/GE itself, the economic development directors from all thirty jurisdictions have joined forces in the I-70/I-75 Development Association. In 1995 a regional sports council was established to strengthen the area's professional minor league sports.

Even recent head-to-head battles have lost some of their traditional bare-knuckles, take-no-prisoners character. In the mid-1990s Kettering and Dayton were locked in fierce competition over the location of Banc One's credit-processing facility. To ensure that Banc One's bank office operation would remain in Montgomery County, ED/GE laid $1 million of incentive funds on the table, available regardless of which local city was chosen by bank officials. However, advisory committee members pressured both cities to work out a supplemental tax-sharing agreement. Kettering won out, but is now sharing a percentage of the payroll taxes collected with Dayton in partial compensation for 600 jobs shifted from the city.

Replicating ED/GE

The ED/GE program is important for the lessons it provides for other communities. The lessons were drawn for me by Jack Dustin, ED/GE's academic godfather and now a member of Wright State University's Department of Urban Affairs:

> Linking economic development funding to tax sharing gives local governments a powerful incentive to discuss tax equity as an objective of cooperative and coordinated economic development. Politics is politics, of course, and there is always some behind-the-scenes political horse-trading on

7. Stock (1996).

project proposals. However, local government sponsors must identify what benefits their proposed projects bring to the county as a whole. The selection process favors projects with broad impact. The application and selection process keeps regional impact at stage center. ED/GE sends a clear message: each local government's fortunes are tied to their neighbors' well-being.

An areawide authority can best provide leadership in getting communities to opt into a tax-sharing plan. County governments represent, for example, a higher level of authority over local governments and have a history of promoting equity and cooperation. But tax sharing needs to be conveyed in a nonthreatening way. Working through other organizations, such as chambers of commerce, universities, or private consulting firms, helps facilitate the decisionmaking process. If the facilitating group is seen as balanced and fair and is well respected, it can inhibit parochial interests and discourage 'get even' inclinations among local governments.

Pondering the strong resistance encountered in ED/GE's negotiations, Jack continued:

> Even when coupled with economic development funding, tax sharing is a risky step for local governments. . . . In effect, local governments need to be asked how they think tax sharing can work and then a consensus must be developed.
>
> The technical details of developing tax-sharing formulas are best left to fiscal, tax, and legal professionals. . . . Most business persons and other community leaders have neither the time nor the technical expertise to formulate complex formulas.
>
> Sound methodology will be important in establishing only a baseline of who contributes and who receives. . . . Contributions to a regional tax pool will be based more on negotiation than pure mathematics. . . . Differences in perception of fairness between municipal, suburban, and township representatives may require modifying the "ideal" formula to keep the coalition of communities together.
>
> Despite a powerful economic incentive, local governments will seek to minimize their contribution to a tax-sharing pool. As a result, some provisions to minimize financial burden, regardless of fiscal capacity, will have to be considered. If regional cooperation is a worthwhile goal of local governments, as almost all claim it is, then some cost should be expected and acceptable.

The county administrator, Don Vermillion, highlighted the most crucial lesson for me in a conversation in 1996. "The key is having elected officials with vision and political courage," he observed. "These qualities are just as important for those who must stay with the program as those who make the original decision. We've had six different county commissioners since ED/GE began. Majority control has shifted from Democrats to Republicans. We've had several tough fiscal years when other tax receipts were falling and there were lots of budget pressures on behalf of more traditional county programs. But all the commissioners have stuck by ED/GE, the affordable housing fund, the regional arts fund.

"'We've seen our larger community improve as the result of working together rather than working against each other,' they've said. 'We're going to keep on with these collective efforts.'"

Lessons of ED/GE

At least two principal lessons can be drawn from this chapter. The first relates to the enormous complications of achieving meaningful collaboration among multiple units of local government in "little box" regions.

As a speaker and consultant who is often described as a proponent of "metropolitan government," I have occasionally been admonished by my hosts to "remember, David, that here in Connecticut [or Ohio . . . or North Carolina . . . or Texas . . . or whatever state I am visiting] we have a very strong commitment to home rule." Well, *everybody* in this nation has a strong commitment to home rule, if that phrase is understood to mean the desire of citizens to have a say in what happens in their local community. How that basic democratic need is satisfied simply varies in scale from community to community and state to state. In Albuquerque, New Mexico (1996 population: 420,000), city council candidates campaign door-to-door in council districts that average about 45,000 residents; groups of neighbors numbering a few hundred to a few thousand band together in nonprofit neighborhood associations in order to carry out voluntary community projects or influence their city government. In Kent County, Michigan (1997 population: 539,000), with thirty-four independent municipal and township governments, Grand Rapids mayor John Logie has calculated that there are 637 local elected officials—one for about every 845 residents—and 100 more than are elected, Mayor Logie notes, to run the U.S. government.

A state's basic system of local government is something that has rarely been determined in living memory. It has simply been inherited from the past, often shaped by historical circumstances that preceded the creation of the very states and localities affected.[8] Ohioans have not only 88 counties and 942 municipal governments but also 1,314 township governments because that is the hand that history dealt them.

No Ohioan of the twentieth century (or even the nineteenth century) decided that townships should be a primary form of local government. The Continental Congress decreed that the Ohio Territory should be divided into townships when it enacted the Land Ordinance of 1785 (under the authority of the Articles of Confederation). The Continental Congress needed to pay off the officers and soldiers of the victorious revolutionary army as expeditiously as possible with the grants of western lands promised. The Congress adopted the scheme offered by Thomas Hutchins. In 1764, as a young captain in the Sixtieth Royal Regiment, Hutchins had made an expedition to the Ohio. He had conceived of a plan of military colonies north of the Ohio as protection against the Indians, based on an almost Roman-like sense of order.

Appointed as first geographer of the United States as reward for his services during the revolution (he sided with the rebels), Hutchins headed a corps of surveyors that divided "the said territory into townships of 6 miles square, by lines running due north and south, and others crossing these at right angles, as near as may be. . . . The plats of the townships respectively shall be marked by subdivisions into lots of one mile square or 640 acres, the same direction as the external lines, and numbered from 1 to 36."

One-seventh of the lots were reserved by the Congress to fulfill its commitments to the officers and soldiers of the Continental Army. Additional lots were allocated by lottery to fulfill the individual states' promised bounties to their revolutionary militias. "Lots Nos. 8, 11, 26, 29, in all townships . . . were reserved to the United States for future sale"—the fiscal salvation of the fledgling central government.

The geographer's whole design was eagerly embraced by the New England delegations, especially Massachusetts and Connecticut, which had long organized their own states into townships. Despite cession of most of their western claims, they saw the Ohio Territories as extensions of themselves. Indeed, they had insisted that the Land Ordinance declare that "there shall

8. Slicing the democratic pie into smaller and smaller pieces is no guarantee of greater citizen participation. For the "big box" Albuquerque Public Schools, voter turnout averages 8–10 percent, while voter turnout for the nineteen school districts in "little box" Kent County, Michigan, averages 5–6 percent—neither turnout exactly a shining example of grass-roots democracy.

be reserved the lot No. 16 of every township for the maintenance of public schools." And in light of its proposed Western Reserve, Connecticut had insisted that townships there be laid out Connecticut style—five miles on a side rather than six.[9]

When the Ohio Territory was organized as a state in 1803, the survey townships ordained by the Continental Congress were converted into actual local governments. Township government built and cared for country roads, maintained the peace, and promoted local economic development. Townships gave rural citizens instruments of local government below county governments (though in southern and western states, county governments alone sufficed to meet rural citizens' need for representative democracy; again, county government was a function of *their* historical traditions).

For several generations, more densely settled municipalities viewed surrounding townships largely as land banks. Ohio municipalities annexed township lands when annexation served municipalities' needs. With the advent of rapid suburbanization after World War II, however, many townships were no longer composed of just farms and open lands. Townships themselves had become semi-urbanized communities with sophisticated local governments. Covetous of their positions, township officials increasingly resisted annexation. The Ohio legislature, in turn, strengthened townships' independence, eroding the annexation powers of municipalities and, in 1991, endowing townships with home rule status.

In Ohio the result was not only a highly balkanized political map (to 2,344 local general governments can be added 666 independent school systems) but the emergence of what Jack Dustin terms an ethic of highly competitive "civic individualism." Local communities competed—often bitterly—both to secure the tools that would support economic growth (canals, roads, railroads, tax abatement powers) and to attract and hold on to private businesses. How and when do such local governments reverse course and say they must no longer compete but must learn to work together? How do they come to share rather than lock themselves in fierce interjurisdictional competition and continue to bid away the benefits of regional economic growth?

Vertical intergovernmental revenue sharing is widespread. Throughout the United States the federal and state governments provide more than one-third of all local government revenues. Of $721 billion (fiscal 1994) in local

---

9. South of the Ohio River, in the lands claimed by Virginia, the Carolinas, and Georgia, those states' system of organizing local government into much larger counties rather than by smaller townships prevailed.

government revenues direct federal grants-in-aid totaled about $30 billion and state aid (including pass-through federal funds) totaled about $212 billion.[10]

Horizontal revenue sharing between local governments is far less prevalent. There are scattered examples of negotiated, bilateral revenue-sharing agreements between two governments. The city of Louisville and Jefferson County, Kentucky, have a multiyear "compact" to split local income tax revenues. The city of Charlottesville and Albemarle County, Virginia, split the growth in property taxes in return for Charlottesville's "no annexation" pledge. And there are numerous situations in which county governments collect local option taxes and redistribute them to municipalities under a negotiated formula; Georgia's "local option sales tax" would be an example. Another would be Monroe County, New York's apportioning sales tax to Rochester and twenty-nine other local governments and eighteen school districts.

By contrast, local *multijurisdictional* revenue sharing is very rare. All cases I know about are based on sharing revenues derived from incremental growth. One prominent example was spurred by construction of a new home stadium for the National Football League's New York Giants. In 1972 fourteen New Jersey townships created the Intermunicipal Tax Sharing Account to share revenue from the development of the Meadowlands sports complex in Hackensack, New Jersey; the program distributes approximately 40 percent of the growth in property tax revenues. Under a recent Ohio state law, Akron and Springfield have established successful joint economic development districts with local townships; in return for extension of municipal utilities to township-based industrial parks, the city collects payroll taxes from new industries while the townships harvest increased property taxes in a win-win arrangement.

Dayton-Montgomery County's ED/GE program is the nation's best example of a voluntary revenue-sharing compact among multiple local governments. Given the region's highly fragmented local governance, the ED/GE program is a significant achievement; the fruits of greater cooperation, rather than competition, on economic development issues have been substantial.

Limitations of Voluntary Compacts

Yet the second lesson of this chapter is that, in spite of herculean efforts, ED/GE's tax-sharing impact is negligible. To achieve significant regional rev-

10. Bureau of the Census (1997, tables 478, 482).

enue sharing (as described in this chapter), regional land use planning (as in chapter 8), and regional mixed-income housing (as in chapter 9) across multiple jurisdictions that jealously guard their local sovereignty, the legal ground rules under which they operate need to change.

The federal government can shape local government responsibilities to a limited degree. Through Congress and the federal courts the federal government can define local governments' responsibilities regarding those rights guaranteed their residents as national citizens; the Civil Rights Act of 1964, the Voting Rights Act of 1965, and the Americans with Disabilities Act of 1990 are excellent examples. Congress, of course, can also attach reasonable strings to its grants-in-aid to local governments. Federal writ follows the federal dollar.

But how local governments are organized and what respective powers they have are the domain of state governments. The U.S. Constitution is silent on the issue of local government; therefore, under the Tenth Amendment, determining the form and duties of local government is a power reserved to the states. The problem is that U.S. legislatures rarely exercise their authority to deal constructively with the growing complexity of governance in metropolitan areas. Typically, legislatures give considerable deference to local governments and local authority, heavily influenced by the American enshrinement of "home rule." (Home rule arguments become paramount, however, only when it suits legislators' political and ideological convenience.)[11]

Chapter 11 presents a case study of the regional reform movement in the Minnesota legislature. The reformers have been addressing all the key issues highlighted in the preceding chapters: urban sprawl, the concentration of poverty, fiscal disparities, fair share affordable housing. But Minnesota reformers have not tried to create broad, authorizing statutes to encourage voluntary cooperation among local governments. They have decided to change the statutory rules of the game. And they have demonstrated that success is based on building political coalitions among central cities, older suburbs, and rural areas appealing to the oldest motivation in the political book: raw, political self-interest.

11. Under the Canadian constitution, provincial governments have full authority over the conduct of local government affairs. In contrast to American state legislatures, Canadian provincial parliaments are much more robust in the exercise of their constitutional responsibilities regarding the form of local governance. Provincial governments not only established Metro Toronto (further combining and reorganizing municipal governments in the process), but also decreed regional arrangements for Montreal, Winnipeg, Edmonton, Vancouver, and several other Canadian urban areas.

11

Minneapolis-
Saint Paul, Minnesota:
The Winning Coalition

MYRON ORFIELD LOOKS as if he stepped out of a casting call into an updated remake of *Mr. Smith Goes to Washington,* Frank Capra's 1939 classic film of a small-town Everyman confounding the forces of reaction and privilege in the U.S. Congress. Lean, Nordic-handsome, six-foot-two, with a boyish earnestness to match Jimmy Stewart's original screen portrayal, Orfield is a four-term, Democratic Farmer Labor (DFL) party state legislator from Minneapolis. In his thirties, married, and father of a young son, Orfield is a true son of Minnesota. His Minnesota roots reach back three generations to his grandfather, Anders Ortfjeld, who emigrated from Trondheim, Norway, to a farm near Bellevue, Minnesota, in 1880.

The youngest of six children of a Minneapolis insurance agent, Orfield still lives in the Lyndale-Farmstead neighborhood that he grew up in and that he now represents in the Minnesota House of Representatives. After graduating from the University of Minnesota with a degree in history and political science, he studied American history at Princeton, then got his law degree from the University of Chicago in 1987. When not in the Minnesota legislature, he has taught courses on Fourth Amendment issues and legislative process as an adjunct professor at the University of Minnesota and Hamline University law schools.

A local newspaper profile has characterized Orfield as "more bookish than charismatic . . . [with] an academician's reserve. At public meetings, Orfield is more apt to give tutorials than speeches."[1] (And with a rapid-fire delivery, I might add. Orfield's verbal style sharply contrasts with the "Outstate" Minnesota languor so deftly captured in the 1996 film *Fargo*.) Orfield is a polite, but persistent, debater, controlling his emotions under even the harshest public attacks. One is sure that he was raised in the best "Minnesota Nice" tradition.

In short, Myron Orfield does not look or act like what he really is: the most revolutionary politician in urban America.

Orfield has forged the first enduring political alliance between the nation's declining central cities and older, threatened, blue-collar suburbs. A few academicians and journalists may have pointed out that urban poverty is spreading from inner city to inner suburb, but Orfield has developed the most compelling and comprehensive documentation of this trend and translated it into effective political action. The political coalition he has organized between legislators from Minneapolis-Saint Paul, their declining blue-collar suburbs, and what Orfield terms "developing, low-tax-capacity suburbs" has become a dominant force in the Minnesota legislature. Orfield has split the suburbs politically.

"Orfield's political strategy is the first new idea on the urban scene in many years," Tony Downs, the Brookings Institution's renowned urban guru, has noted. "He's making a vital contribution."[2]

Maps as Political Tools

Orfield has also pioneered a new political tool: maps. To be specific, multicolored maps that, jurisdiction by jurisdiction, trace the decline of central cities and many older, inner-ring suburbs and the rise of affluent outer-ring suburbs. In place of the typical personal attacks on one's opponents that masquerade today as "negative campaigning," Orfield has substituted "fact attacks." With the help of staff from the legislature and state planning agencies, Orfield has produced plenty of maps—300 of the Twin Cities area alone. "No matter how skeptical listeners are," the same newspaper profile commented, "Orfield perseveres with more maps, more data, more explanations.

---

1. "Urban Visionary or Suburban Villain?" *Saint Paul Pioneer Press*, April 17, 1994, pp. 1b–2b.
2. Conversation with the author, April 22, 1996.

His detractors tire, retreat, and devise new assaults. Orfield, the Energizer Bunny of urban policy, keeps going and going and going."

Orfield is spreading the gospel of alliances between central cities and older suburbs—and his mapping acumen—across the country. Since his political breakthrough in the Minnesota legislature, he has been invited to speak in dozens of metro areas. With local foundation support, the non-profit group Orfield heads has mapped metrowide economic and social trends in Atlanta, Baltimore, Chicago, Cleveland, Detroit, Gary-Hammond, Grand Rapids, Los Angeles, Miami, Milwaukee, Philadelphia, Pittsburgh, Portland, Seattle, San Francisco, and Washington.[3]

The case Orfield's maps make for regional reform is graphic and compelling. Equally important, his credibility as a successful politician who has converted analysis into public policy makes him an even more effective expert witness in presenting his own material. Though focused on the Twin Cities, his first book, *Metropolitics,* lays out a comprehensive case for regional policy reforms.[4] Looking census tract by census tract across the 7 counties and 187 municipalities that form the bulk of the Twin Cities region, Orfield charts the widest array of demographic, educational, economic, and fiscal trends. The list ranges from poverty among children under the age of five to the allocation of state highway funds. It is truly a checklist of critical concerns that would add up to a comprehensive portrait of vast disparities in many metropolitan areas. Public policy activists and concerned citizens anywhere can use *Metropolitics* as an analytical starting point for their own communities. *Metropolitics* serves as a detailed road map for analyzing and understanding most urban regions in America.

Orfield's political odyssey began with his first campaign for the legislature in 1990. He faced heavy political odds. "Though someone on every block knew one of my relatives," he says, he was just twenty-eight, a political unknown, and facing better-known Democratic party insiders. He first won the DFL nomination, then the general election by knocking on every door in his district (some 17,000 doors) three times, asking residents for their vote and listening to their concerns.

"I grew up in Lyndale-Farmstead, but I was really shocked when I started going around the entire legislative district. I found a lot of people who were

3. Orfield's mapping operations outside Minnesota were initially carried out through the Metropolitan Area Program, a nonprofit subsidiary of the National Growth Management Leadership Project. In 1998 MAP was established as a separate, nonprofit organization, the Metropolitan Area Research Corporation, on whose board of directors I serve.

4. Orfield (1997).

really hurting, a lot of poverty. And it was getting worse," Orfield told me later. "The neighborhoods were changing fast for some reason, and something had to be done."

A Freshman Legislator's Debut

After his surprise victory, Orfield entered the Minnesota House of Representatives as the most junior of freshman legislators. Both houses were solidly under DFL control in 1991–92, Orfield's first term. Orfield's DFL colleagues held about 60 percent of the seventy-three House seats and thirty-six Senate seats from the Twin Cities area. All of Minneapolis and Saint Paul's seats and almost half the suburban seats were held by DFL members. Slightly more than half of suburban seats were filled by Independent-Republicans (IR).[5]

Like most state legislative bodies, the tradition in the Minnesota legislature is that freshmen should be seen, not heard, and must vote right (that is, with their party's leadership). But the young representative leaped right into the fray in his first session. Concerned about the rising poverty he had seen in his district, Orfield introduced and passed a bill to study the economic health of the Twin Cities and its inner-ring suburbs.

In the 1992 session Orfield's next bite at the apple was a tougher task. A metrowide system for financing sewers and sewage treatment plants had been created years ago. All householders in the Twin Cities region were being assessed a uniform fee for systemwide debt service, varying only by the size of each customer's sewer hook-up. As a result, householders and businesses in established core communities were forced to pay for new sewer extensions and treatment plant expansions on the urban fringe at the same rate as the residents of the new suburbs. In Orfield's eyes, many of the region's poorest households were subsidizing the creation of elite, suburban enclaves for many of the region's wealthiest residents.

In January 1992 Orfield introduced the Metropolitan Infrastructure Stability Act. He urged the legislature to overturn the uniform regional debt service system and require new developments to cover the true costs of their

---

5. In Minnesota both national political parties have recast their state-level images. The Democratic Farmer Labor party was formed by a coalition of all of Minnesota's rich tradition of left-of-center political parties just after World War II, a merger in which Minneapolis's youthful mayor, Hubert H. Humphrey, played a key role. After a crushing legislative defeat in 1974, the state's Republican party restyled itself the Independent-Republican party, trying to distance itself from Watergate and the disgraced President Richard Nixon.

own sewer expansion. Developers and suburban officials howled and succeeded in rapidly killing the Senate version. With the active support of the
Local Government Committee chairman, however, Orfield's bill reached the
House floor. In an eleventh-hour compromise, Orfield and his supporters
agreed to withdraw the bill in return for a commitment of $400,000 in state
funds for the University of Minnesota to make an independent study of
freeway and sewer financing.

Having once been a freshman legislator myself in New Mexico, I can
attest that passing even study bills is no small achievement. But Orfield, the
"Energizer Bunny," was not content to wait for the results of the two studies.
He had already embarked on his own exhaustive analysis of Twin Cities regional trends. He had an excellent mentor right at hand. Myron's older
brother, Gary Orfield (now a Harvard University professor) had long been
the nation's leading academic authority on school desegregation. An advocate of metrowide education strategies, Gary told his younger brother to
focus on census tract data, particularly poverty rates among children. What
the young legislator found would ultimately stun the Twin Cities area.

Twin Cities' Decline

For decades Minnesotans had prided themselves on the notion that they
were exempt from the social problems that afflicted other urban communities. To begin with, the Twin Cities region saw itself as a prosperous and
racially homogeneous society. In the 1990 census, the 2.5 million-resident
Twin Cities area was 91 percent white. The region's median family income
($43,252, the 1990 census reported) ranked twenty-ninth highest among all
320 metro areas, while the region's 8 percent poverty rate fell far below the
nation's 12 percent level.

The Twin Cities area also had a long and proud history of progressive
government. Neither Minneapolis nor Saint Paul had ever fallen under the
sway of big-city machine politics. The respected Citizens League was just
one of many "good government" groups that embodied a high level of civic
activism.

For a generation the Twin Cities area had been held forth as one of the
nation's models of regional governance. In 1967 the Minnesota legislature
had created the Metropolitan Council to bring some coherence to development planning for a region fragmented into 7 counties and 187 municipalities and townships. The "Met Council" was composed of seventeen citizens

appointed by the governor, drawn from districts into which the region was divided. Supported by an excellent professional staff, the Met Council had been empowered by the legislature to coordinate regional airport policy, devise a regional sewage collection and treatment system, and develop regional land use policies. In the 1970s the Met Council successfully encouraged suburban communities to accept some subsidized housing. And, though not administered by the Met Council itself, the Twin Cities region benefited from the legislatively established fiscal disparities plan (1971), the nation's most significant regional revenue-sharing program.

In his research, however, Orfield discovered that during the "me decade" of the 1980s the Twin Cities had fallen prey to urban blight. Despite regional prosperity, poverty rates within the central cities were climbing. The 1990 census had reported poverty rates of 16.7 percent for Saint Paul and 18.5 percent for Minneapolis, both more than twice the regional poverty rate. In just a decade, the percentage of children receiving free lunches in the Minneapolis Public Schools increased from 33 percent to 52 percent. Across the Mississippi River (narrow so far north), in the Saint Paul Public Schools, the rate had increased from 28 percent to 55 percent.

But, as Orfield has told many audiences, "when poverty is seen as 'just an inner-city problem,' it has no political legs. It's when poverty becomes a suburban problem that you can do something politically." So Orfield shifted his analytic focus to the Twin Cities suburbs. He found that fortune smiled on only a part of suburbia: a band of suburbs to the south and west, which Orfield dubbed the "Fertile Crescent." Lying along Interstate 494, the Twin Cities' beltway, and stretching from Eagan on its eastern end to Maple Grove on its western terminus, the Fertile Crescent accounted for only 27 percent of the region's population but 61 percent of its job growth. Benefiting from the transfer of 88 percent of state and federal road construction funds during the 1980s, the Fertile Crescent's commercial and industrial tax base had soared 240 percent (compared with a 143 percent increase for the rest of the region). By 1992 the Fertile Crescent's commercial and industrial tax base per household was 62 percent higher than that of the rest of the region. The Fertile Crescent's median household incomes were 45 percent higher than the average of other communities.

Another quarter of the region's population lived in the "inner-ring" suburbs. Built up in the early postwar years, blue-collar suburbs such as Columbia Heights and Brooklyn Park were hurting. They lagged the Fertile Crescent by every indicator: they had captured only 18 percent of the region's new jobs, their household incomes were 30 percent below the Fertile

Crescent's, and they had only two-thirds of the Fertile Crescent's property tax base per household (even after the revenue-shifting impact of the fiscal disparities plan).

Most ominous was the rapid increase in economically stressed households in the inner-ring suburbs. During the 1980s, the number of married couples with children had dropped by one-quarter, while the percentage of single mothers had escalated to almost one-fifth of all families. Eleven percent of all inner-ring children lived in poverty, well below the 32 percent child poverty rate of the central cities but almost three times the percentage of poor children in the Fertile Crescent. Clearly, the sprawl machine in the Twin Cities area was victimizing inner-ring suburbs as well as Minneapolis and Saint Paul.

Building the Metropolitics Coalition

Orfield captured all these trends (and many more) in his maps and set out to recruit allies. It would, he realized, be difficult to persuade many suburbs "even if they were *in extremis*." "Allying politically with the cities," he later told me, "is foreign to their world view . . . a sort of political degradation to them." Throughout 1992, Orfield carried his maps and arguments to more than 100 meetings, first with individuals, then with larger groups. He targeted three key constituencies: community development corporations, church organizations, and inner-ring suburban officials.

During the autumn months, Orfield met regularly with inner-city community development corporations, Legal Aid representatives, and other neighborhood activists. He led them carefully through an understanding of regional development trends and their dire effects on inner-city communities. Orfield's maps graphically confirmed what many inner-city activists had long suspected: huge public expenditures were subsidizing the growth of exclusive communities on the metropolitan fringe to the severe detriment of central-city neighborhoods.

Getting inner-city groups to embrace a suburb-oriented reform agenda was a difficult task, however. Too often around the country the typical response is "Just send *us* more money to rebuild *our* neighborhoods." To many inner-city activists, regional strategies look like another plot to dilute black or Hispanic voting strength and undermine their own influence and position. At last, however, the Twin City groups committed their support for a package of regional reform bills, in particular, the proposed regional fair share housing act.

A second crucial component of the budding coalition was added when the North Metro Mayors Association (NMMA) publicly endorsed Orfield's reform package. The NMMA is an organization of northern suburban communities that banded together in 1982. Its membership includes both inner-ring suburbs and outer-ring communities that are rapidly developing new residential subdivisions. With most business expansion occurring in the Fertile Crescent, however, these modest-income bedroom communities lack adequate commercial and industrial tax bases to deal with the fiscal demands of rapid growth.

Throughout 1992, Orfield courted NMMA members in both individual and group meetings. By January 1993, on the eve of the legislative session, the NMMA was ready to act. At a large public meeting Orfield again displayed his maps and outlined his plans. The NMMA and its seventeen member cities endorsed his program. Their support would be crucial since these suburban cities had twenty-six House members (compared with only eighteen from Minneapolis and Saint Paul).

It was about this time that I first came in contact with Myron. One wintry afternoon just before Christmas 1992 I received a call from a youngish-sounding state legislator from Minnesota. He had heard about a book I was writing, *Cities without Suburbs*, from George Latimer, former mayor of Saint Paul and new chairman of the National Civic League, to whom I had sent a manuscript version. Could I send Myron a manuscript copy as well? I readily did.

I heard nothing further until four or five months later. My telephone rang one late spring morning. "Dave, this is Myron. I just finished reading your book last night. It proves all the things we have been fighting about up here. I sat down on my stairs for a moment to start to read it, and I got so engrossed that I didn't get up until I finished it.[6] Boy, I only wish that I had read it before the legislative session. But we had a lot of excitement here. Let me tell you about it."

The Battle Is Joined

And what a story Myron had to tell! His previous effort to reform the way the regional sewer system was financed had been criticized as too narrow.

6. Myron is not only a speed-talker but probably a speed-reader. However, Delcia did enjoin me that, if I wanted people to actually read *Cities without Suburbs*, it should not be long. At just 130 pages, my first book fit her formula.

For the 1993 session he proposed a broad package of six bills, collectively called the Metropolitan Community Stability Act. The bills were designed to promote fair share housing, reform the Met Council, tighten the regional land use planning system and reform the tax code affecting agricultural lands, strengthen the Met Council's role in transportation planning and transit services, reinvest more funds in inner-city revitalization, and stiffen the work requirements in Minnesota's welfare system. From Myron's retelling (and the evidence of dozens of news articles I subsequently reviewed) it was clear that the Metropolitan Community Stability Act—with its centerpiece, the fair share housing bill—had been a major battleground in the Minnesota legislature's 1993 session.

The Comprehensive Choice Housing Act (CCH) had been carefully devised with the advice of inner-city community groups, housing advocates, and the northern suburban mayors throughout the previous fall. It directed the Met Council to set "fair share" affordable housing goals for each of the area's 187 local communities. Communities would be credited for their existing supply of affordable housing. Minneapolis, Saint Paul, and many older, blue-collar suburbs would already have their "fair share," and the CCH's provisions would have no further effect on them.

For nonconforming communities, however, the CCH imposed three requirements: reduce unreasonable barriers embedded in restrictive zoning codes, development agreements, and practices; support public or private affordable housing providers; and ensure that affordable housing would continue to be affordable to low- and moderate-income renters. Communities that failed to make progress faced stiff penalties—the loss of general state financial aid, a freeze on state-assisted road and sewer construction, and prohibition on access to tax-increment financing.[7] In light of the severity of these penalties, the bill provided that final housing goals would be set by an administrative law judge, assuring local governments of due process (a political condition of the North Metro Mayors Association's support).

Finally, the bill directed that the Met Council focus its compliance activities first on those communities farthest from meeting their fair share goal. This "worst go first" rule assured some wavering blue-collar suburbs

7. Tax-increment financing permits a local community to front-end construction costs by bonding against a future revenue stream from properties whose value would be enhanced by the project. Instead of distributing enhanced property tax yields to the local school district or other public agencies, a city government will retain the "incremental" tax collections in a special category ("a tax-increment district") to pay off the bonds. Tax-increment financing had been a popular device of some Fertile Crescent cities to finance their own commerce-creating beltway interchanges.

that the Met Council would not follow a path of least resistance and load up their cities with even more low- and moderate-income housing; the primary targets would be the wealthy communities of the Fertile Crescent.

Throughout the four-month session the legislature battled over the Metropolitan Community Stability Act package. Voting blocs formed according to whether or not legislators thought their districts would benefit. Minneapolis, Saint Paul, the blue-collar suburbs, and rural areas with a poor tax base would clearly benefit. Of the forty-five House members from these regions, all but six were DFL. Orfield and colleagues worked strenuously to secure support from the six IR representatives from these areas; in the end, only one Republican House member (from inner-ring Saint Louis Park) voted for the housing bill. In the face of implacable opposition from Fertile Crescent IR members, Orfield concluded later, "it was simply too difficult for these [inner-ring] Republican members to oppose their normal allies on so controversial an issue."[8]

Most of the controversy surrounded the housing bill. The DFL-controlled legislature potentially had the votes to pass the housing bill and the other measures in Orfield's package. However, one big vote loomed ahead, that of popular IR Governor Arne Carlson. Early in the session Governor Carlson announced that he would be guided by the Met Council's views. Orfield took heart. In drafting the housing bill Orfield had made dozens of changes suggested by the Met Council staff. "By the time the bill was introduced," Orfield would write, "it was as much the council's bill as ours."[9]

But as Fertile Crescent opposition intensified, IR appointees on the Met Council wavered. Having supported the housing bill when first introduced, the Met Council now backtracked. Then, after the *Minneapolis Star Tribune* thundered editorially, "The Met Council Takes a Housing Dive," the council reversed course yet again and testified in support.

A Gubernatorial Veto

Governor Carlson's vote, however, would ultimately be determined not by the Met Council's position but by straightforward partisan politics. In mid-April the IR legislative caucus held a tumultuous closed-door meeting with the governor. Veto the housing bill, they told him, or we will not sustain any

8. Orfield (1997, p. 116).
9. Orfield (1997, p. 117).

of your other vetoes in the DFL-controlled legislature, particularly, the DFL-sponsored campaign finance reform bill that Carlson, a potent fund-raiser facing a reelection campaign, strongly opposed.

After the IR caucus meeting, Governor Carlson's opposition crystallized, and he issued a letter on April 23 outlining his objections to the housing bill and urging its withdrawal. The term "barriers to affordable housing" was not well defined, the governor claimed. The bill failed to deal with "the single most destructive barrier to low-income housing—land cost." It infringed on local governments' home rule prerogatives while overexpanding the Met Council's powers. Finally, the bill relied excessively on penalties rather than on incentives (he ignored the fact that his budget-cutting administration had already rejected any new spending or tax incentives).

Orfield and his colleagues countered the governor's objections and sought any possible compromise. The governor's door had shut. The much-amended Comprehensive Choice Housing Act passed the House 79 to 51, eleven votes short of overriding the promised veto. All but four DFL members voted in favor. (The four DFL dissenters all represented Fertile Crescent constituencies.)

The housing bill's supporters sought to create a veto-proof strategy in the Senate. They would graft the housing provisions into the omnibus state government appropriations bill. The governor would not veto the whole state appropriations bill over the housing provisions, they reasoned.

But they were wrong. After an IR-sponsored motion to delete the housing provisions failed by a single vote, the Senate had passed the appropriations bill. But, during the House-Senate conference committee in the session's waning hours, the governor's chief lobbyist made clear Carlson's unbending opposition. To each offered compromise, the lobbyist intoned, "That is a veto item." Finally, at 2:30 A.M., with all hope of compromise dead, the housing provisions were extracted from the appropriations bill.

Senate supporters made one last effort. The House-passed CCH was brought back to the floor and amended to meet all the governor's earlier objections. The result, Orfield later wrote, was "a toothless housing bill [that was] essentially a 'request' (without penalties) to communities to remove their housing barriers." The modified CCH was passed in the session's final hours, and just as promptly vetoed May 23 by the governor.

A few other parts of the Metropolitan Community Stability Act had fared somewhat better. A provision protecting farmers in urbanizing areas from storm sewer and road assessments became law, the last surviving provision of a more sweeping Metropolitan Land Use Policy Act. The package's welfare reform component passed as well, raising monthly stipends for single, able-bodied adults from $203 to $408 in return for twenty hours a week working at minimum wage in jobs that would rehabilitate depressed neighborhoods.[10]

However, the package's transportation planning bill was also vetoed. It had required the Met Council to assess whether traffic congestion could better be solved by expanding public transit than by building new or wider roads. In addition, each highway expansion would have to be evaluated for its impact on linking core area residents with expanding job opportunities out in the urban fringe. The bill was supported by the Met Council, the Minnesota Department of Transportation, and, in Orfield's phrase, "virtually every imaginable interest group." But it fell victim to the Fertile Crescent's paranoia that the Met Council's expanded powers might lead to some kind of fair share housing regulations or new curbs on development.

Falling short by just one vote—the governor's—obscured what a remarkable maiden session the coalition between the inner city and the inner ring had. A strong fair share housing bill, transportation and transit planning reform, limitations on farm infrastructure assessments and tax-increment financing, and welfare reform had all passed. The coalition had fallen apart on only one issue: the bill to convert Met Council membership from gubernatorial appointment to direct election. Fierce lobbying by the state's association of counties persuaded rural DFLers that an elected Met Council would shift too much power to the Twin Cities area to the detriment of rural interests. With its rural votes fading away, the coalition was unable to get the Met Council reorganization bill to the floors for a vote in either legislative chamber.

After such a bitterly fought legislative session, Governor Carlson was willing to extend one small olive branch. He agreed to appoint a state commission, the Advisory Commission on Metropolitan Governance, to be co-chaired by Orfield and state Senator Carol Flynn (DFL-Minneapolis), who had sponsored the advisory commission notion. The seventeen-member commission would meet in the interim, then report its findings and recommendations for action in the 1994 session.

10. Welfare rights and inner-city organizations had strongly protested the measure. However, Orfield noted, the bill was "enormously popular among the middle-class suburban legislators" and passed unanimously as part of the omnibus health and human services act. Costing an estimated $25 million over its first two years, the program was not funded, however.

A Visit to the Twin Cities

The advisory commission's opening session in mid-September was the occasion of my first of four trips to the Twin Cities area. Myron and local supporters put together an extensive schedule for me and Neal Peirce, a veteran nationally syndicated columnist and coauthor of *Citistates,* another strong call for regionalism.[11] The highlight was the public forum Neal and I shared at the Landmark Center, a nineteenth-century Romanesque castle in downtown Saint Paul. It was my first direct exposure to the vibrant climate of civic participation that characterizes the Twin Cities region. The 250-seat auditorium was filled to capacity for a lunch-hour lecture series.

Neal outlined the central thesis of the just-published *Citistates,* namely, that communities must work together as a whole region in order to compete effectively in the emerging global economy. (After hearing Neal's arguments and talking further with him during that trip, I myself began to focus more on the issue of regional economic competitiveness.)

I followed with the themes of *Cities without Suburbs,* illustrated with extensive data about the Twin Cities area itself. Discussing the "Point of No Return" always grabbed an audience's attention. How did the Twin Cities measure up? Major population loss? Minneapolis down 30 percent, Saint Paul down 13 percent. Disproportionate minority population? Minneapolis 23 percent minority, Saint Paul 27 percent. This was not very high by many cities' standards, but within such an overwhelmingly white regional population, the central cities were clearly becoming catch basins for minorities. City-suburb income ratio? Minneapolis 84 percent, Saint Paul 78 percent. Well above the critical 70 percent threshold but both trending steadily downward.

"Unlike a Hartford, Newark, or Detroit, for example, the Twin Cities numbers are not horrifying," I told the Landmark audience, "but they make me just plain mad. I see the patterns I've described above and say 'Darn! These people ought to be doing a better job. They've got so much going for them.'" But I had also learned my new lesson well from Myron. I continued:

> This decline is rooted in the very patterns of ever increasing suburban sprawl that have dominated American lifestyles over the past forty years. And my analysis is too simplistic. It is not just the traditional central cities that are victimized by this steady process of withdrawal and abandonment by the

11. Peirce and Johnson (1993).

middle class. As state Representative Myron Orfield and his legislative allies have shown so convincingly, older, inner-ring suburbs are victimized as well. What we too superficially classify as "inner-city" problems are spreading out into older, blue-collar suburbs.

I reminded them that these older suburbs have fewer assets to call upon to fight growing crime, poverty, and family disintegration. Unlike the great old cities, these suburbs do not have prestigious neighborhoods where wealthy people still choose to live or the endowment of wonderful parks, museums, and other civic facilities that are the legacy of past glory, or downtown areas that are employment centers for the region. Although the Twin Cities area and the state had pioneered some of the most notable initiatives in building a metropolitan *community*, I told them that they had let wise policies slip away. To get back on track, they had to address a key, but simple, question:

> Is the Twin Cities area going to continue to become a society increasingly
> segregated by income? Are the most advantaged going to keep segregating
> themselves more and more in enclaves of privilege farther and farther out?
> Are the most disadvantaged going to be segregated more and more in de-
> caying inner-city neighborhoods and declining inner-ring suburbs?

The choice they faced, I said, was whether to strengthen their sense of community or continue down a path of ever more fragmented governance: "Fragmented governance promotes fragmented citizenship—the withdrawal of the middle class from the practice of civic responsibility and the isolation of the poor from the example of personal responsibility."

Then I drew upon an anecdote that tells of three medieval stonemasons who were once asked what they did. The first said he was paid to cut stone. The second stated that he applied his talent and skill to extract extraordinary shapes from blocks of marble. The third smiled and said simply, "I build cathedrals." The Twin Cities had the conditions and the right tools, I told them. If they had the courage and the vision, they, too, could build a cathedral.

Expanding the Metropolitics Coalition

Myron and his colleagues needed no cathedral-building guidance from me. Between sessions they recruited allies from the Twin Cities religious community. The strongest support came from the Saint Paul Ecumenical Alliance, which sponsored two large public rallies in February 1994 supporting the regional reform movement. Shortly thereafter the Joint Ministries Project in Minneapolis signed on, followed by the Interfaith Action Organization and the Metropolitan Interfaith Coalition for Affordable Housing. Guided by Archbishop John Roach's powerful public statements, the Catholic Office for Social Justice was particularly influential in developing suburban support for fair share housing.

By mid-1994 the coalition building took on new institutional solidity with the formation of the Alliance for Metropolitan Stability. The alliance brought together church groups, environmental organizations concerned about managing growth, inner-city antipoverty groups, and neighborhood associations. Funded by local foundations, the alliance became a focal point for rallying broadly based political support for the regional reform agenda.

The Advisory Commission on Metropolitan Governance, however, had not proved to be the "watershed" I had prophesied. Characterized by the same partisan politics that divided the legislature, the advisory commission was unable to reach agreement on hot issues such as fair share housing or expanding the fiscal disparities plan. After several months of meetings, its only significant recommendation was that the legislature end the semi-independent status of three regional agencies—the Regional Transit Board, the Metropolitan Transit Commission, and the Metropolitan Waste Control Commission—and make them operating divisions of the Met Council. The advisory commission also recommended the direct election of Met Council members, but by so narrow a margin that the recommendation would carry little political weight.

The growing base of public support for the regional reform agenda was softening some of the Fertile Crescent's opposition. In the wake of a bitter public controversy over fair share housing in Maple Grove, one of the fastest-growing Fertile Crescent cities, three IR House members introduced the Metropolitan Poverty Reduction Act of 1994, immediately dubbed "Orfield Lite" by the press.

The suburban IR bill was a pastiche of different provisions. To promote affordable housing, it proposed reducing the building materials tax on low-income housing developments and better coordinating existing affordable housing programs and funding. It recommended support for a pilot project in Eden Prairie, another Fertile Crescent city that was already planning such a local initiative. And "Orfield Lite" would strengthen the region's "reverse commute" programs, under which more than 2,000 central-city workers were being transported daily to Fertile Crescent job sites. (Reverse commuting programs are often easily embraced by suburban officials. In effect, their message to inner-city residents is "Come work here—just don't try to live here.")

The forces behind fair share housing praised the housing provisions of the Metropolitan Poverty Reduction Act, despite their modest impact. It represented a significant change in Fertile Crescent rhetoric, Orfield thought. Whereas the previous position had been "nothing, no time, never," the conservatives' bill represented "a symbolic acceptance of suburban affordable-housing policy and regional responsibility for the problems of the city and older suburbs."[12]

The killer provision of the "Orfield Lite" package, however, was that its IR sponsors tied the housing provisions to Governor Carlson's sweeping reform of the state's troubled workmen's compensation program. They argued that the state's costly workmen's benefits hurt job creation. Cutting those costs would greatly help to create more jobs, reduce unemployment, and revitalize inner-city neighborhoods.

Workmen's compensation had become a litmus test issue in Minnesota politics. For a generation, a DFL-labor union alliance had squared off against an IR-business coalition. Both sides were unyielding. When IR sponsors refused to support their own modest housing proposals without full enactment of the governor's workmen's compensation reforms, the Metropolitan Poverty Reduction Act was pronounced "dead on arrival" in the DFL-controlled 1994 legislative session.

Looking for opportunities for compromise, the pro-housing coalition reintroduced the previously vetoed Comprehensive Choice Housing Act. Public support had grown. Beyond the church coalitions, the League of Women Voters, and other community organizations, the Association of Metropolitan Municipalities, representing 85 percent of the region's population, endorsed the bill. The *Minneapolis Star Tribune* editorialized eight times in support, while three times the *Saint Paul Pioneer Press* called editorially for a housing compromise.

The governor's opposition was unyielding. In desperation, the pro-housing forces unilaterally stripped the bill of the penalty provisions and passed it on straight party-line votes. Governor Carlson just as promptly vetoed it for the second straight year, despite the fact that the penalties (his principal objection) had been dropped. Orfield commented that the governor's game was one that no one could win.

12. Orfield (1997, p. 129).

The regional agenda had moved forward with one modest success. The advisory commission had introduced its bill to elect Met Council members and place the three regional agencies directly under the council. An elected Met Council faced fierce opposition from both the Association of Metropolitan Counties (which feared loss of county government power in Hennepin, Ramsey, and other metro counties) and the statewide county association, which argued again that a more powerful regional government would dry up state aid for outstate Minnesota. The counties' lobbying efforts stripped at least ten DFL votes from Orfield's coalition, and the measure was defeated on the House floor by a 65 to 64 vote.

However, there was bipartisan support for the advisory commission's second recommendation: folding the independent regional agencies into the Met Council structure. The defeated bill was called back to the floor, stripped of the elected council provisions, and passed overwhelmingly.

So ended the second session of "Metropolitics" (as Orfield had begun to call the coalition). Again, in the short 1994 session, the coalition had succeeded in passing a regional fair share housing bill, to be frustrated by the governor's veto. The effort to convert the Met Council from a gubernatorially appointed state agency to a popularly elected regional government had failed by the narrowest of margins. With the addition of the three regional agencies, however, the Met Council would have operating authority over regional road, transit, and sewer agencies with a combined annual budget of over $400 million. Second only in budgetary size to Hennepin County itself, the Met Council had been turned into a more powerful force for regional unity. Most important, for the first time in its history the Met Council combined all major land use planning and transportation responsibilities. With its greatly expanded powers, if the Met Council could be converted into a directly elected body, or the governor's appointees shaken out of their conservatism, the Met Council could exercise tremendous power on behalf of regional reforms, Orfield judged.

Strengthening Regional Tax Base Sharing

The 1994 election brought new challenges to Metropolitics. Faced with a weak DFL candidate, Governor Carlson won a landslide reelection for a second term. Nor was Minnesota otherwise exempt from the Republican tide that swept the nation. Though the state Senate was not up for reelection, IR candidates scored major gains in the House. The DFL lost thirteen seats, bringing the House to sixty-nine DFL members and sixty-five IR members. Six DFL seats were lost in inner-ring and low-tax-capacity outer-ring suburbs, and two DFL incumbents lost their seats in Fertile Crescent districts.

The elections did not seem to have been influenced directly by the legislative battles over the regional reform package. Nevertheless, Orfield and his allies had lost the DFL-based margin needed to pass a housing bill. Any success for the regional agenda would have to be based on issues that could attract some IR votes, especially among newly elected freshman representatives from inner-ring swing districts. Orfield turned his efforts to revising the region's fiscal disparities plan.

The fiscal disparities plan has been the Twin Cities region's greatest claim to fame among progressive "good government" circles for a generation. It is worth examining its history and impact at some length before turning to the reform efforts in the 1995 legislative session.

The fiscal disparities plan was enacted by the Minnesota legislature in 1971 (by a one-vote margin in the House), but court challenges delayed its implementation until 1975. Fertile Crescent legislators have made repeated efforts ever since to repeal the program.

The Met Council has described the plan's rationale succinctly:

> From a regional perspective the Twin Cities is one economy. Large commercial-industrial developments tend to concentrate in a few locations, drawing workers and clients from a market area that is larger than the city it is located in. Access to these concentrations, primarily highways, is a prime determinant of where these developments locate. Cities with such access are the ones most likely to get commercial-industrial development.
>
> Since the property tax is the primary source of local government revenues, certain types of development—office space, headquarters buildings, up-scale housing—are attractive because they typically generate more revenue than it costs to serve them. Not all cities can expect to attract such development, but most participate in financing the regional facilities serving these developments. The ideas underlying tax-base sharing is to allow all cities to share in the commercial-industrial development that is, to a large extent, the result of the regional market and public investments made at the regional and state levels.[13]

13. Metropolitan Council (1995).

The law requires all taxing jurisdictions in a seven-county area, including 186 cities, villages, and townships, 48 school districts, and about 60 other taxing authorities, to contribute 40 percent of the *increase* in the assessed value of commercial-industrial property into a common pool. (A community's pre-1971 assessed valuation is totally exempted.) The pool is taxed at a common millage, and revenues are redistributed among all local governments on the basis of each jurisdiction's population and its "tax capacity" (per capita market value of commercial and industrial property) in relation to the regionwide tax capacity. A jurisdiction with below-average tax capacity receives a relatively larger distribution from the regional pool, and a jurisdiction with above-average tax capacity receives somewhat less.

By 1998 the annual fiscal disparities fund had reached $410 million, almost 30 percent of the region's total commercial-industrial property tax collections.[14] Among cities, villages, and townships, 137 were net recipients, while 49 were net contributors. Over the years the net contributors had consistently been the Twin Cities' wealthiest suburbs, such as Bloomington, Minnetonka, Eden Prairie, Edina, and Plymouth. Giant shopping malls, office towers, garden-like industrial parks had sprouted vigorously along the interstate highways that cut through these Fertile Crescent cities or lay adjacent to the Minneapolis–Saint Paul International Airport.

The major recipients were Saint Paul, many inner-ring suburbs in Hennepin and Ramsey Counties, and virtually all towns and villages lying well beyond the suburban beltways. Fueled by its downtown office boom, Minneapolis moved from largest net recipient in 1980 to second largest net contributor in 1990. (Its $19 million net contribution in 1991 represented 6.5 percent of its total commercial and industrial tax capacity.) With the devaluation of its downtown office buildings during the 1990s bust, however, by 1995 Minneapolis was once again the second largest net recipient.

Orfield and his allies made an abortive attempt to expand the fiscal disparities concept in the 1994 session. Their Metropolitan Reinvestment Act would have included residential property in regional tax base sharing for the first time. The bill specified that all cities would keep the full tax base on

---

14. The relative value of the shared pool has fallen from a peak 31.8 percent of all commercial and industrial property taxes in 1992. Commercial and industrial assessed valuation and rates fell in some communities, often because of court rulings in contested assessments. In its first year (1975) the shared pool represented 6.7 percent of commercial and industrial valuation. By 1998, the polled revenues distributed reached $410 million (about 28 percent of all commercial and industrial property taxes).

all homes up to $150,000 in value, but any increment above $150,000 would be contributed to a regional pool. Orfield calculated this would have yielded a net $113 million for redistribution in 1994.

The differential impact of residential tax base sharing, if anything, would be greater than the redistribution of the commercial and industrial tax base under the existing fiscal disparities plan. Measured by population, only 24 percent of the region's cities would contribute to the remaining 76 percent. Most net givers would be in the Fertile Crescent; the net recipients would be Minneapolis and Saint Paul, inner-ring cities, and outer-ring suburbs with a low tax capacity. Even after the tax pool, however, the Fertile Crescent would have high tax bases to support local services.

Unlike the existing fiscal disparities plan, however, the pooled funds would not be redistributed for general government services. The funds would be targeted toward housing issues. One-third of the pool would be allocated to suburbs that had not met affordable housing goals; they could either use the funds to provide the housing locally or turn implementation over to the Minnesota Housing Finance Agency. Two-thirds of the pool would flow to cities that had already exceeded their fair share of affordable housing. They could use the funds for reinvestment in and redevelopment of declining neighborhoods.

Introducing the bill late in the short session, Orfield had admittedly not prepared the political ground well. The usual suspects—Fertile Crescent legislators and Governor Carlson—quickly lined up in violent opposition, but some of the presumed beneficiaries were critical as well. Saint Paul and many northern suburbs were convinced they would receive more back than they contributed, but they really preferred to get their money back without housing-related strings attached.

As political support eroded, the sponsors cut the strings loose and placed the housing-based revenues directly into the fiscal disparities plan. This attracted enormous support; the revised bill had, in Orfield's words, "the momentum of a rodeo bull in a steel chute."[15] Faced with certain veto, however, the bill became trade bait. Senate leadership killed it in exchange for votes on a controversial measure for decommissioning a nuclear power plant. They promised to support tax-sharing reform in the 1995 session.

For the 1995 session Orfield upped the ante. The abortive 1994 effort had shown that, with the right formula, regional tax sharing was a political silver bullet. Orfield decided to move for approval of a Metro Fair Tax Base

15. Orfield (1997, p. 139).

Act that would create a unified regional tax base and redistribute almost $1 billion, which was four times the impact of the fiscal disparities plan. The bill would require net recipient cities to use half the tax base received as the basis for a property tax cut. "The Metro Fair Tax Base Act offered recipient cities and their politicians exactly what American politicians always promise," Myron commented to me, "a tax cut and better services."

The North Metro Mayors Association held a summit meeting and quickly declared its support, as did virtually all member groups of the Alliance for Metropolitan Stability. Major efforts were made to wean IR representatives from low-tax-capacity suburbs away from the Fertile Crescent–dominated IR caucus, particularly an IR House member from low-tax-capacity Anoka, whose House predecessor a generation before had been a key sponsor of the original Fiscal Disparities Act. To no avail. Hardball tactics within the IR caucus prevented any early IR support.

Faced with across-the-board rejection by potential IR recruits and widespread controversy fanned by incendiary television news coverage and right-wing talk show hosts, the sponsors scaled the bill back. They decided to leave the existing commercial and industrial-oriented fiscal disparities plan untouched. Then they scaled back residential coverage first to home values over $150,000 (the 1994 bill's level), then to home values over $200,000, finally to just new *growth* of the residential tax base above $200,000. The concessions would shrink the annual pool to just $44 million but shift the ratio between net givers and net recipients from 26–74 to 17–83, which would bring more legislators into the ranks of supporters. These compromises allowed moderate members of both parties to support the bill but by no means reduced the violent opposition from the Fertile Crescent.

"Take no prisoners" was the order of the day in both camps. Opponents vilified Orfield and his allies as "communists" and "Marxists." Noting that the original fiscal disparities plan had been enacted in 1971 with key Republican support, proponents countered that the Metro Fair Tax Base Act, as now amended, was simply "a gentle enhancement of a good Republican idea." Expert studies volleyed back and forth.

After long and acrimonious hearings and floor debate, the scaled-back Metro Fair Tax Base Act passed the House 71 to 63. All DFL members except four from high-tax-capacity districts voted in favor. In a key move three IR representatives from low-tax-capacity districts joined in support. After a procedural misadventure, the bill passed the Senate 36 to 30. The weakened Metro Fair Tax Base Act was, of course, promptly vetoed by Governor Carlson.

A Compromise Housing Bill

After Governor Carlson's reelection and the loss of key DFL seats in the House, Orfield had despaired of getting meaningful fair share housing legislation past the governor's veto pen. State Senator Ted Mondale (DFL-Saint Louis Park), son of former Vice President Walter Mondale, stepped into the breach. In negotiations through the summer and fall of 1994, Mondale and Curt Johnson, Governor Carlson's former chief of staff and newly appointed Met Council chairman, labored to devise a regional affordable housing bill acceptable to the governor.[16]

The result was the Metropolitan Livable Communities Act, which was introduced at the outset of the 1995 session. The initial bill gave the Met Council the power to "negotiate" affordable housing goals with all regional jurisdictions in order to carry out the Met Council's Regional Blueprint. (The twice-vetoed Comprehensive Choice Housing Act would have allowed the Met Council to set such goals through an administrative hearing procedure.) Mondale and Johnson adopted a variation of the failed Metropolitan Reinvestment Act's provisions for pooling the tax base. Rather than pool home values above $150,000, the new bill would require each jurisdiction to pool all home values above an amount equal to twice the value of the jurisdiction's average home. The result would have created a modest pool of funds (about $2.4 million in the initial year) that would have grown slowly but steadily over time. Local jurisdictions could choose either to send their contributions to a regional affordable housing fund or to administer their contributions themselves to meet their own jurisdictions' negotiated targets. If they already met their targets, the funds would be used to upgrade deteriorated housing stock. Two of the bill's other provisions would promote broadly defined environmental cleanup goals and fund a $5 million model low-income housing project.

"The Mondale-Johnson compromise," Orfield would observe, "was just the beginning" of compromise.[17] House IR leaders still thought the bill too strong and demanded further concessions. First, pooling taxes on high-value homes was made voluntary. Mondale and Johnson argued that there would still be incentives for local jurisdictions to contribute, above all, because the

---

16. Johnson is also a regular collaborator in the series of community studies known as Peirce Reports and is a principal of the Citistates Group, with which I am affiliated.

17. Orfield (1997, p. 151).

bill authorized the Met Council to take into consideration local nonparticipation in its allocation of sewer and road funds. Second, power over the proposed housing pool (to the extent that any community voluntarily contributed) was shifted from the Met Council to county governments. With that concession, counties that should have more affordable suburban housing (for example, Hennepin and Carver) probably would not, and counties that would (for example, Ramsey and Anoka) probably should not. The only metro county well positioned to use the fund would be Dakota County (which I believe has one of the most progressive suburban housing authorities in the nation).

As the Metropolitan Livable Communities Act reached the floor, there was little controversy left. Weary of the long battle, the two metropolitan dailies hailed the bill and called for its approval. It would give the Met Council the statutory authority to negotiate goals and the ability to withhold infrastructure grants from cities that did not participate voluntarily in the regional housing program. The bill passed handily, and, at long last, a regional affordable housing bill was signed into law by Governor Carlson at the close of the 1995 session.

"In the end," observed Orfield, who had carried the battle for suburban affordable housing for so long, "the victory was more symbolic than substantive (much like the 1957 Civil Rights Act, the weak precursor of the 1964 act). The [Metropolitan Livable Communities Act] broke the deadlock, and the basic approach of the [Comprehensive Choice Housing Act] was accepted. Like the 1957 Civil Rights Act, the Metropolitan Livable Communities Act was a platform on which a stronger and more enforceable act can be built." Orfield concluded, "It also put the southwestern suburbs on notice: if things do not happen under the voluntary system, fair housing forces will be back."[18]

An Elected Met Council

Both sides, however, rested during the 1996 session, in part out of exhaustion, in part to let implementation of the compromise housing bill get started. In 1997, however, the Metropolitics coalition enacted what Orfield would call "the most important measure yet": popular election of Met Council members. Defeated in the 1994 session, making the Met Council account-

18. Orfield (1997, p. 152).

able not to the governor but to the citizens directly was a cause that had since gained new support. Thanks to the Metropolitics coalition's successful expansion of the Met Council's powers, the Met Council's $418 million budget in fiscal 1997 was second only to that of Hennepin County among Minnesota's local governments. The Met Council's property tax level was $107 million, and it had $687 million in bonded indebtedness. The council designates where all major roads will be built, annually constructs tens of millions of dollars of new sewer projects, runs the transit system, and supervises the airport authority. The cry for ending "taxation without representation" had gained new force among many more conservative legislators.

The elected Met Council bill passed both the House and, surprisingly, the Senate. (State senators traditionally feared that, with much larger constituencies than senate districts, elected Met Council members might become more politically influential than state senators.)

Governor Carlson's press secretary predicted another veto. The governor, he said, objected to adding another layer of "elected bureaucracy." He also objected to public financing of Met Council election campaigns (about 10 cents per voter, the bill's proponents pointed out).[19] Though expressing some support, Curt Johnson, the current Met Council chairman, observed: "I worry that if you start electing people to these positions, it will be difficult and often impossible to get the members to look across the jurisdictional lines and consistently vote for what makes sense for the whole region."[20] "No Met Council could be more 'parochial,'" a Minneapolis Star Tribune editorial countered, "than the present body, which consists wholly of gubernatorial appointees who must constantly toe the governor's line on regional issues or risk getting immediately fired."[21]

"Signing the bill would be consistent with his votes in support of an elected Metropolitan Council back in the early 1970s, when Carlson served as a member of the Minnesota House.[22] The ideal of regional government of the people, by the people, and for the people that Rep. Carlson embraced then deserves no less support from Gov. Carlson now."[23]

19. Contributions from land developers, homebuilders, and contractors played major roles in Minnesota politics. Six of the Met Council's seventeen members in 1997 were land developers.

20. "House OKs Bill to Elect Met Council Members," Minneapolis Star Tribune, May 7, 1997.

21. "Metro Democracy: Carlson Shouldn't Get in the Way," Minneapolis Star Tribune, May 13, 1997.

22. As a state representative, Arne Carlson had sponsored an elected Met Council bill in 1971 and voted for similar bills in 1973 and 1975.

23. "Metro Election: One Step Down, Two to Go," Minneapolis Star Tribune, May 9, 1997.

On May 15, 1997, Governor Carlson vetoed the bill despite his earlier support of an elected Met Council when he was a legislator. It was yet another proof of the adage "where you stand depends on where you sit." Responded Representative Orfield: "The bill will be brought forth again."

Lessons of Metropolitics

Metropolitics is a continuing process, of course, a story without a last chapter. But Orfield and his allies have already taught urban America some vital lessons, above all about the real political arena in which regional reform movements must be prepared to do battle: the state legislature. Even though citizens may believe that local home rule is sacrosanct, throughout the nation local government is, in reality, "the child of state government." State legislatures control local governments' scope of powers, particularly in the areas of tax policy and land use planning and development regulation. "Home rule" states (like Ohio) afford local governments broad flexibility. "Dillon's Rule" states (like Virginia) maintain a tight rein over local governments.

In a democratic society all sovereignty ultimately flows from the people. I have heard it argued that the voters in federal elections, state elections, and local elections are all the same people with presumably the same personal values and self-interests. That is true. How can a state legislature be expected to do collectively what local governments would not do individually if both are accountable to the same voters? How can legislators be expected to overcome the intense factionalism of highly fragmented urban areas?

I was led to the best answer by a historical reference made by a forgotten speaker at a conference I attended but can no longer identify. As so often happens, it is one of the Founding Fathers who provided the crucial insight, in this instance, James Madison's Federalist Paper 10, arguing for approval of the newly proposed Constitution of the United States. As Myron's brother, Gary, summarized Madison's argument,

> James Madison wrote that the best way to cure the evil of narrow factions pursuing narrow interests that undermine the interest of the broader community is to expand the scope of the community. By bringing a wider diversity of interests into a larger government, he said, there would be less likelihood of the tyranny of a narrow majority and greater likelihood of a full debate leading to the pursuit of broader community-wide interests. Madison reasoned that "the smaller the society" devising a policy, the more

likely that a local majority, not balanced by other forces and considerations, will "concert and execute their plans of oppression."[24]

In highly fragmented metro areas, without the creation of an elected regional government like Portland Metro, there is no public body to speak to the interests of the entire region. It is only at the state level that local citizens' interests are placed in a framework that addresses their interests as citizens of the entire state or of a substate metropolitan region. State legislatures *must* serve as regional policy bodies because they are the only ones that can. Legislatures must set new ground rules for how the myriad local governments must share common responsibilities for common problems.

The second lesson from Metropolitics is that communities seldom make progress on hard, divisive issues through friendly, consensual agreement. They do so by building political coalitions. And those coalitions are most durable when based on each member's political self-interest—that is, their perception of the interests of the constituencies they represent. The glue that held Metropolitics together was social, economic, and political self-interest.

"The politics of self-interest were particularly apparent in the housing bill," Orfield observed about the legislative battles:

> The decisive suburban political support was largely defensive in character. Civil rights and access to opportunity were an important part of the housing bill's rationale. But most suburban members—and city members, for that matter—supported fair housing, largely to protect their communities from an "unfair" burden of low-income housing and from future neighborhood decline. These members were resigned to the fact that their communities had poor people. They believed that the [Fertile Crescent] must also accept their fair share of poor residents and accompanying social costs.[25]

The third lesson is that the mathematics of local self-interest would by and large provide Metropolitics coalitions with the potential to win. University of Minnesota geographer John Adams has shown that almost every large metro area is characterized by "the Favored Quarter," a slice of the region where most high-end commercial and residential development occurs. In Chicago, the Favored Quarter is the northwestern suburbs around Schaumberg

24. Orfield (1996).
25. Orfield (1997, p. 116).

and Hoffman Estates. In Memphis, the Favored Quarter extends through East Memphis to Germantown and Collierville. In Atlanta, the Favored Quarter grows out through the Buckhead area of North Atlanta into Cobb County. And so on, in almost every metro area that I have visited.

In three short years Minnesota's Metropolitics coalition racked up a remarkable legislative record. It enacted three fair share housing bills, approved a new regional revenue-sharing formula pooling tax revenues from high-end housing, restructured regional sewer and transportation agencies with annual budgets totaling $400 million, changed the tax code, expanded the Met Council's powers, and converted the Met Council from an appointed to an elected body. The coalition most often was stymied by one vote: Governor Carlson's. Only his vetoes prevented more sweeping redefinition of regional benefit sharing and regional burden sharing.

Portland may be the nation's model for regional land use planning and growth management. Maryland's Montgomery County may offer the widest range of exemplary mixed-income housing policies. The Twin Cities fiscal disparities plan may be the nation's most extensive regional revenue-sharing program. But the Minnesota legislature has been engaged in the battle over all the crucial regional issues. And Orfield and his colleagues have shown how to put together the winning coalition. Metropolitics itself is the most important regional reform model in the nation.

PART THREE

Changing the Rules of the Game

PART 2 OUTLINED policies that have proved effective against urban sprawl, concentrated poverty, and fiscal disparities. What Portland, Montgomery County, Maryland, or Minnesota have accomplished is not unique. Other examples could be cited from other communities.

However, these are probably the best, in part because these communities have had almost a quarter of a century's experience with a regional growth boundary, a countywide mandatory mixed-income housing policy, or a regional tax-base sharing program. Their long-term success makes them all the more persuasive and reliable models for other states and communities to adopt and emulate.

What rules need to be changed or what the new rules should be seems clear enough. What is lacking is the political will to act in state legislatures, county courthouses, and township and city halls around the country. Part 3 focuses on the coalitions needed to move the political system to act. Chapter 13 provides case studies of faith-based movements (the Northwest Indiana Federation of Interfaith Organizations), business-driven groups (Virginia's Urban Partnership), the role of activist academics (the Ohio Housing Research Network), and grass-roots citizens' groups (Rochester's Metropolitan Forum). Attention is also given to the vital role (and limitations) of philanthropic foundations in helping finance reform movements, and also to the many city mayors (whose constituents have the most to gain) who, like reluctant warriors, generally stand on the sidelines of regional reform movements.

But first chapter 12 recounts the halting efforts to redirect federal public housing policy, an example of good intentions gone terribly awry. For three crucial decades federal public housing policy has been the greatest promoter of economic and racial segregation in America's urban areas.

12

Changing Federal Public Housing Policies

AT FIRST THE television screen showed puffs of smoke shooting from the base of the giant shape. Then the explosive cloud billowed outward, engulfing the lower half of the multistoried structure, which shuddered and then slowly crumpled downward into a huge pile of dust and rubble.

It was 1972, and the television pictures might have been of the failed launching of a giant Saturn 5 rocket. But all the launches succeeded, carrying U.S. astronauts to their rendezvous with the moon. Each rocket would recede like a flaming meteor in reverse and, shortly thereafter, vanish from earthbound view. Within minutes the space capsule would break free of Earth's grip, carrying the hopes of the human race soaring into the heavens.

No, this was not the launching of a moonshot on the television screen. This was an image of humankind's hopes, gripped by the hard, earthly realities of poverty and discrimination, crumbling into dust. This was the dynamiting of the massive, high-rise, Pruitt-Igoe public housing project in Saint Louis. Headlining network broadcasts across America, the demolition of Pruitt-Igoe was one of the era's unforgettable images.

What stunned many viewers was that Pruitt-Igoe was not some decades-old structure, now technologically obsolescent. The apartment complex had been built only seventeen years before, in 1955, and had been lauded for its state-of-the-art design by federal and local housing officials and community leaders alike. The design won an award from the American Institute of Architects.

Why were these buildings being destroyed so soon? Very simply, Pruitt-Igoe had spawned an untenable social environment. With Saint Louis's poorest families warehoused in its multistory towers, civilized life in Pruitt-Igoe had disintegrated. Fear and violence ruled the dimly lit hallways and stalked dirt expanses littered with broken glass surrounding the buildings.

Pruitt-Igoe was much more than a failure of architecture or property management. It was the failure of a concept: the belief that the most poverty-stressed families could be housed successfully in such high concentration. After experimenting with several management approaches, the Saint Louis Housing Authority and officials from the federal Department of Housing and Urban Development reached a painful conclusion. Pruitt-Igoe could never be made to work. It was better to level it than to continue trying to make it a suitable environment for mothers to raise young children.

Demolishing Big Mistakes

It took HUD twenty-three more years to really learn the lesson of Pruitt-Igoe. Not until 1995 did major demolition of high-density public housing projects begin again. On local television I watched Baltimore's Lafayette Courts and Lexington Terrace implode in seconds. They had become familiar to me during my many visits to Baltimore while I researched and wrote *Baltimore Unbound*.[1]

Closer to home, wrecking balls leveled Ellen Wilson Homes, a bleak complex of thirteen barracks-like apartment buildings in Southeast Washington, on the edges of upscale Capitol Hill. And out of my personal viewing range (demolition of public housing no longer making network news), the Vaughn Apartments in Saint Louis (next to the vacant Pruitt-Igoe site) came tumbling down, joined by Newark's Christopher Columbus Homes, Chicago's notorious Cabrini-Green and Henry Horner Homes, and two-score other projects, including the granddaddy of them all, Atlanta's Techwood, the nation's first public housing project, built in 1936.

By the end of 1996 HUD had approved the demolition of nearly 43,000 units in the nation's worst public housing complexes, "a 4-year pace," proclaimed a HUD booklet issued during President Clinton's reelection campaign, "that dwarfs the 20,000 units demolished in the previous 10 years

1. Rusk (1995).

combined."[2] HUD Secretary Henry Cisneros set a target of 100,000 units to be demolished by the year 2000.

In part, many demolitions were made possible by a technical change in federal law. At the behest of low-income housing advocates, Congress had stipulated that no unit of public housing could be demolished without one-for-one replacement by a new project. Soaring construction costs and intense local controversies over new sites slowed the cycle of demolition and replacement to 1,600 units a year by the early 1990s.

Progress was paralyzed in a gridlock of good intentions. On the one hand, nearly everyone recognized that, in Cisneros's words, "change is needed. Concrete high-rises have become half vacant shells, scarring the urban landscape. Other projects are beset by crime and gang activity. The very names of some places—Cabrini-Green, Robert Taylor Homes, Desire—haunt the American imagination."[3] On the other hand, public housing's most enthusiastic champions could count four other eligible poor persons for every tenant in existing units. They resisted any reduction in the supply of public housing units, however miserable the social and physical living conditions in many projects might be.

While HUD lobbied the Congress for permanent changes in authorizing legislation, Cisneros achieved a temporary breakthrough in the appropriations committees. For fiscal 1996 Congress allowed a suspension of the one-for-one rule (a measure subsequently carried over into fiscal 1997). This action legally freed HUD to act.

Perhaps even more significant was a major shift in HUD's own philosophy toward public housing. While noting that public housing projects provided essential shelter for 1.3 million of America's poorest households, HUD asserted that

> the current public housing system is plagued by deeply rooted, systemic problems. . . . Perhaps the most destructive of these fundamental problems is that public housing concentrates the very poor. Misguided policies that required housing authorities to restrict assistance to the poorest Americans have robbed public housing communities of the working families whose example is so crucial. The average income of the public housing communities has fallen from 35 percent of area median income in 1990 to less than 17 percent today. This concentration of poverty has left much

2. U.S. Department of Housing and Urban Development (1996, p. 9).
3. HUD (1996, p. 1).

urban public housing prey to an array of economic and social problems that destabilize families and neighborhoods.

In addition, public housing is itself concentrated in high-poverty neighborhoods. The politics of project location have led to the physical, social, and racial isolation of public housing in many cities, cutting off the residents from jobs, basic services, and a wide range of social contacts.[4]

"We've learned our lesson," Secretary Cisneros swore at the demolition of the Vaughn complex in Saint Louis. "We're changing the model."[5] How was the model being changed?

—Designed as bare, utilitarian boxes and constructed on an inhuman scale, many public housing projects stood out from their surroundings and stigmatized the families that lived there. The new model would replace failed high-rises with lower-density townhouses and garden-style apartments more compatible with surrounding neighborhoods.

—In keeping with the "Garden City" ideal of the 1950s and 1960s, many projects were sited in massive "superblocks" that cut off city streets and inhibited normal circulation within the community. Under the new model, urban street grids would be reintroduced, and "defensible space" strategies would be used to enhance community safety.

—Starved for operating funds, many projects had become simply warehouses of poverty, isolating the community's poorest households from educational and training facilities, employment opportunities, and essential services. Under the new model, supportive services designed to foster self-sufficiency would become integral parts of public housing developments.

—And, most important, for two decades federal policy had given preference to the poorest of the poor, excluding from public housing working families "who are the role models and social glue of stable communities." Under the new model, high-density projects would be replaced with more human-scale, mixed-income communities. A proportion of former tenants would be provided rent vouchers to be used throughout the region while many of the new units would be marketed to attract working, middle-income families. "Any effort to reverse the social consequences of concentrated poverty in public housing," HUD stated, "must include a reassertion of the paramount importance of income integration so that the very poor can live next door to working class families."[6]

4. HUD (1996, p. 5).
5. HUD (1996, p. 9).
6. HUD (1996, pp. 11, 27).

If You Build It, Will They Come?

Attracting working-class families to live next door to public housing tenants: that is the crux of the challenge for HUD's new model for public housing communities. If you build it, will they—middle-income households—come?

Putting the "new model" into practice in Baltimore provides an instructive guide to the evolution of the thinking of both local and federal public housing officials—and the useful role played by a class action suit in federal court.[7] In my judgment, Baltimore's Inner Harbor is the most successful downtown redevelopment project in the country. It is a jewel, however, set in a precarious setting, immediately surrounded by some of the highest poverty areas in the city. In the 1950s the Housing Authority of Baltimore City (HABC) built four massive, high-rise, family public housing complexes— Lexington Terrace (677 units), George P. Murphy Homes (758 units), Lafayette Courts (807 units), and Flag House Courts (487 units)—that, west to east, ring downtown and the Inner Harbor. "Our city leaders' worst nightmare," a veteran civic activist once confided to me, "would be two or three high-visibility shootings right down here in the Inner Harbor. All these people," he said, sweeping his hand toward the Inner Harbor, thronged with festive tourists and happy local sports fans, "could disappear overnight."

With $193 million in federal HOPE VI grants from HUD, plus $65 million in state funds and $35 million in city funds, HABC is tearing down and recreating the four public housing developments. "We want to use this largest, one-time chunk of federal cash available in the 1990s to rebuild our city," Van Johnson, HABC's HOPE VI director, told me in October 1998.

Lafayette Courts is the first "new" community completed. Although the architecture is new and attractive, the renamed Pleasant View Gardens is a

---

7. In 1995 the American Civil Liberties Union filed a class action suit, *Thompson* v. *HUD*, charging that HUD, the Housing Authority of Baltimore City, and the city of Baltimore had maintained a racially segregated public housing program for decades. Any litigation can create harsh feelings among the parties, and this suit was vigorously pursued by the ACLU. Nevertheless, the basic facts were uncontested, and all parties shared basic values and similar goals. As remedy, the ACLU sought additional section 8 rent vouchers to substitute for the 16,000 project-based units owned by HABC. The vouchers could be used by low-income city residents for rental housing anywhere in metro Baltimore, achieving complete deconcentration of HABC tenants. The case was settled in early 1996, elaborating on plans HUD and HABC had already initiated to dismantle HABC's four major housing projects under the HOPE VI program. The settlement added 1,342 new HUD-financed rent vouchers, plus additional state and city funds for homeownership opportunities, to be used by HABC tenants to secure rental housing in "non-impacted areas": census tracts with less than a 10 percent poverty rate and less than 25 percent African American residents.

traditional public housing community with some new bells and whistles attached. A central goal of this earliest HOPE VI grant was to reduce project density by 60 percent. That was certainly achieved. The high-rise towers were "imploded" in 1995 and replaced by 228 townhouses and a 110-unit, four-story apartment building for senior citizens by mid-1997.

Over 90 percent of the residents of Pleasant View Gardens are very low-income households. Only 27 of the townhouses (all of which were quickly sold) are owner-occupied. However, HABC and HUD set a low income ceiling for the new homeowners: 60 percent of the city's median family income (which means the owners must fall in the lowest quarter on the region's income scale). Another 103 of the townhouses are legally organized into a condominium arrangement in hopes that the more successful tenants can graduate into owning their own units.

Lexington Terrace's redevelopment represents a more decisive step toward a mixed-income community. The 677 units in five high-rise and twenty-five low-rise properties were leveled in July 1996. By fall 1998 construction had begun on 203 townhouses for public housing tenants and 100 for-sale townhouses to be known as "The Townes at The Terraces." (A prominent sign along Martin Luther King Jr. Boulevard advertises "new homes from the $40s"; about $60,000 is the top sale price, Van Johnson tells me.) With no model townhouse even completed for inspection by potential homebuyers, there are already contracts on 90 percent of the sites. To qualify, buyers cannot exceed 115 percent of the city's median family income (in other words, about twice the maximum income of purchasers at Pleasant View Gardens.) Thus, for the Terraces, the income mix has shifted to 67 percent public housing tenants and 33 percent moderate-income homeowners. The Terraces will be ready for occupancy in 1999.

Flag House Courts will be yet another step forward. Sometime in 2000 all 487 units in three high-rise and fifteen low-rise buildings will be demolished. In accordance with the consent decree in the federal law suit, the redevelopment plan will include a maximum of 125 public housing rental units and a minimum of 125 market-rate units. Purchasers of the market-rate units will not be subject to maximum income ceilings. For the new Flag House Courts the income mix will be at most 50 percent public housing tenants and 50 percent market-rate homeowners.

The redevelopment plan for the George P. Murphy Homes probably goes as far as HUD and Congress will allow in shifting the income mix away from 100 percent public housing tenancy. After the Terraces project is completed and reoccupied, 758 units in four high-rise and twenty low-rise buildings of Murphy Homes and twenty-three two-story buildings of adjacent Emerson Julian Gardens will be demolished. They will be replaced by 210 single-family homes in the form of townhouses and detached two- and three-story buildings. Seventy-five units scattered throughout the new community will be reserved for public housing tenants. The remaining 135 homes will be sold to moderate- and middle-income households. In short, for the last project, the income mix will shift to 35 percent public housing and 65 percent moderate-income (that is, subject to some income ceiling) and market-rate households (subject to no income ceiling).

Architecturally, the new Murphy-Julian homes should have strong market appeal. They are designed by UDA Architects of Pittsburgh, one of the nation's most renowned "new urbanist" firms. Having demonstrated its creative talents in designing many HOPE VI projects for housing authorities around the nation, UDA Architects was selected by the Disney Corporation to design the "pattern book" for Celebration, Disney's 5,000-home "new urbanist" community near Orlando, Florida. (Celebration will be twenty times the size of Seaside, Florida, the real-life set for Jim Carrey's fantasy movie, *The Truman Show*.) "Socially and architecturally, the new Murphy-Julian homes will be a transforming event for Baltimore," Van concluded.

Despite the dramatic reduction in concentration of poor households at specific sites (for example, a hypothetical 90 percent reduction at Murphy-Julian homes), redeveloping public housing projects has not led to casting displaced poor households out onto the streets. First of all, many high-density public housing projects had become so inhospitable that many otherwise desperate households would not live in them. (As of January 1997, for example, at least three years before planned demolition, 40 percent of units at Flag House Courts were vacant.)

For families actually needing temporary or permanent relocation, HABC has filled the gap with rent vouchers or relocation into small, HABC-owned scattered-site units. The shortfall of public housing units at Pleasant View Gardens was filled by 345 rent vouchers and 168 projected ownership opportunities in nonpoverty neighborhoods throughout the region and 50 small, scattered-site HABC-owned units in nonpoverty areas. The reduction of 1,639 public housing units in the remaining three projects would be offset by 1,452 new rent vouchers (used regionwide) plus 188 new units built at several other city locations with state and city funds.

Van Johnson and I toured Pleasant View Gardens on a crisp October 1998 morning. HABC's HOPE VI chief glowed with understandable pride as we drove slowly along streets lined by new, brick-faced, two-story townhouses. Some blocks echoed Baltimore's trademark rows of white stoops leading up to each front door. Other blocks broke up the traditional theme with more varied placement of townhouses. The twenty-seven owner-occupied townhouses, though all grouped along an exterior street, were architecturally indistinguishable from the HABC rental townhouses.

As we drove down streets and around New Hope Circle (the neighborhood's focal point), Van pointed out different community facilities: a large brick and glass community health facility operated by the Greater Baltimore Medical Center; a multipurpose community building housing the management office, a police substation, and community meeting rooms; a large day care center for 120 children, complete with colorful playground; and an even larger youth development center managed by the Boys and Girls Club of Central Maryland, including a computer learning center, multipurpose rooms, and a gymnasium.

"And Pleasant View Gardens is one of HUD's new 'Learning Communities,'" Van added. "Every townhouse is equipped with a computer and Internet hook-up."

"Well, if an almost 100 percent public housing community can create a successful social environment, Pleasant View Gardens certainly ought to be the place," I responded. "Personally, I'll still put my money on Murphy-Julian Homes."

"Yes," Van smiled. "You really have to get the income mix."

The Three As and Three Ss

The key to success in luring middle-class families back to inner-city neighborhoods, I heard urban consultant Marc Bendick Jr. tell an Allentown, Pennsylvania, audience, is to satisfy the three As and the three Ss.[8] The three As are ready *access* to high-quality job centers—a condition easily fulfilled by the locations of Lafayette Courts and Lexington Terrace, adjacent to Baltimore's Johns Hopkins Medical Center, Inner Harbor, and revitalized downtown, or the Village at Techwood (in downtown Atlanta), or Cabrini-Green (just north of Chicago's Loop); high-quality *amenities* in the neighborhood, a combination of both quality design features (restoring street grids, attractive landscaping and street furniture) and new facilities (parks, recre-

8. Bendick was project director and author of Committee for Economic Development (1995).

ation centers, new shopping areas); and high *affordability* of the redeveloped housing destined for middle-income buyers and renters, a difficult balance that HUD, local authorities, and private developers must strike between sales prices and rents low enough to attract middle-income clients seeking bargains and prices high enough to meet the public and private cashflow and profitability requirements.

Harder to satisfy—and much more critical—are, according to Bendick, what middle-class households seek in terms of the three *Ss*, beginning with adequate internal *space* within the new apartments and townhouses. That issue will be within the private developers' control only if HUD, housing authorities, and private financiers are truly prepared to meet competitive market standards in the new, mixed-income developments.

Next are quality *schools*, the critical decision point for most middle-class families with children. This will prove to be a very difficult hurdle even in developments such as Atlanta's Village at Techwood, where local authorities are committed to creating a new magnet elementary school. Despite enhanced curricula and showcase facilities, the proportion of children from low-income households will probably have to fall below 20 percent to 30 percent before middle-class parents will be convinced that the local school provides a suitable environment for their own children. In light of the typical 60-40 target income ratio in HUD's HOPE VI developments, achieving predominantly middle-class enrollments will be impossible if they are drawn solely from the HUD communities' own populations. The key to success may be enrolling a high proportion of middle-class children of downtown office workers into nearby magnet schools.

Last, and most important, is *safety*. Public housing has created its own variation of Gresham's law: bad neighbors drive out good neighbors. Private housing around major public housing projects often declines because of rising crime, delinquency, and neighborhood vandalism. Unless the new developments create an environment of safety and security, HUD's vision of mixed-income communities will rapidly evaporate.

Perhaps the most dramatic shift in federal policy has occurred in the selection of public housing tenants. As an example of past good intentions terribly misplaced, in 1992 Congress opened up senior citizens' complexes to disabled applicants of any age. Most remarkably, the new federal law defined the disabled as including supposedly recovering alcoholics and drug addicts. The results were predictable. Aggressive young men and women, sometimes still actively engaged in drug trafficking, destroyed the atmosphere of peace and safety in many senior housing projects. Tenant satisfaction plummeted, and elderly tenants began to leave voluntarily, a previously unheard-of phenomenon.

Civilizing the Projects

Today HUD's guiding philosophy is that "public housing is a privilege, and it would be wrong to subordinate the safety of decent, law-abiding public housing residents in favor of the very residents who are terrorizing their neighborhoods." Local housing authorities are urged to screen out potential applicants with recent criminal records and evict tenants engaged in drug and other criminal activity. As President Clinton proclaimed in his 1996 State of the Union address, "From now on, the rule for residents who commit crimes and peddle drugs should be one strike and you're out."

In many housing authorities, significant improvement has occurred. Faced with a sudden severe crack epidemic, Georgia's Macon Housing Authority instituted a tougher crime strategy in 1989 that included one of the country's earlier One Strike policies. People applying for admission to public housing faced strict screening procedures: in 1995 about 280 applicants out of 1,000 were denied admission because of their criminal history. In 1989 the Macon Housing Authority evicted 59 residents for drug-related activities. By 1995, after six years of effective screening and strict lease enforcement, evictions for drug-related offenses had dwindled to only 8 cases. In a 1994 survey of over 100 resident leaders, more than 80 percent reported feeling safe in their community.

Similar trends are reported in Toledo, Ohio, by the Lucas Metropolitan Housing Authority. As a result of tougher tenant screening policy, 330 out of 2,300 applicants were rejected for criminal history in a recent twelve-month period. After a One Strike eviction policy was implemented in 1994, drug-related evictions rose from 0 in 1993 to 41 in 1995. As a result of these and other anticrime activities, incidents of drug-related crime dropped by one-fourth between 1993 and 1995; reports on non-drug-related crime plummeted by two-thirds. By 1995, 76 percent of surveyed residents reported feeling safe, an increase from 46 percent in 1993.

Many public housing projects are located in—and have helped create—America's poorest, most crime-ridden neighborhoods. Not all crimes committed in public housing communities are perpetrated by public housing residents. In New Haven, for example, 85 percent of those arrested on public housing property in the late 1980s did not live there. Likewise, 77 percent of persons arrested on Cincinnati's public housing property were not public housing residents.

HUD has added funds to fight public housing crime at the street level. HUD's public housing drug elimination program has provided grants to more than 500 community-based anticrime initiatives in public housing developments nationwide. The grants put additional police on public housing beats, support resident patrols, give young residents positive alternatives to gangs and drugs through diversion and prevention efforts, and make "defensible space" improvements to public housing facilities.

Operation Safe Haven targets federal, state, and local law enforcement agencies, public housing staff, and residents to stamp out the worst infestation of gangs, drugs, and violent crime in public housing projects and surrounding neighborhoods. In its first two years, Operation Safe Haven resulted in more than 8,000 arrests and the confiscation of $3 million in drugs, almost $2 million in cash, and more than 1,000 weapons.

Dramatically reducing crime in public housing communities has a twofold positive impact. Nobody has a greater stake in reducing the violence and chaos of crime-ridden public housing communities than their current residents. But improving both the image—and reality—of neighborhoods with high percentages of public housing households is the key to attracting middle-class households back to future mixed-income developments.

Cisneros's Legacy

"HUD's Cisneros to Leave a Legacy of Public Housing Reform," headlined the *Washington Post* story. Cisneros had just announced his resignation in late November 1996 after four years as, in my view, the most successful of the ten secretaries of Housing and Urban Development since the cabinet agency was formed in 1965. It is ironic that public housing reform was seen as Cisneros's principal achievement. Through two terms as mayor of San Antonio, Cisneros had paid minimal attention to San Antonio's public housing program. Upon his designation as President-elect Clinton's HUD secretary, he had to seek out several local public housing administrators and tenant activists for a crash course in public housing issues.

I could readily understand Cisneros's inattention to public housing as mayor of San Antonio. I acted the same way as mayor of Albuquerque, and I, unlike Cisneros, was a full-time chief executive. Albuquerque Housing Services was a line agency under the mayor's office. Under San Antonio's council-manager system, Cisneros was a part-time mayor presiding over city council meetings. San Antonio's public housing agency was an independent authority.

But in the eyes of both Cisneros and myself, public housing really functioned as a federally operated program in a local setting (almost like a Veterans Administration hospital). HUD rules and regulations governed almost all decisions. During the 1970s and 1980s there was little room for local flexibility. Mayors allocate time and attention to issues they have to decide. No decisions, no time and attention.

Cisneros and I also shared another common experience. We had both been mayors of Sun Belt cities that aggressively annexed large shares of sprawling regional growth. He had been born in San Antonio at the outset of the postwar suburban era and had witnessed its vast transformation. As Cisneros told me in December 1994, when we were collaborating on an essay on regionalism in which he recalled the small, compact world of San Antonio in the 1950s, with downtown at its center: "At that time only half-a-million people lived in the entire area—80 percent within the city's 70 square miles."[9]

Cisneros explained how San Antonio escaped the fate of many other American cities after the Second World War: the state's liberal annexation laws allowed it to expand and follow its sprawling suburban development. In this way, San Antonio increased its municipal territory nearly fivefold, adding more than 260 square miles and bringing in new middle-class subdivisions, shopping centers, offices, and industrial parks:

> Through expansion the city remains home to over 70 percent of the metropolitan area's population and has maintained a strong middle class, a broad tax base, and a high municipal bond rating. . . .[10]
>
> Through annexation, the city of San Antonio *is* largely its own suburbs. But the Detroits, the Clevelands, the Hartfords—for many inner-city residents of such cities, achieving the American Dream requires opening up to them all the metropolitan area's resources and opportunities.[11]

9. HUD published the essay as a series of pamphlets by the secretary. See Cisneros (1995).

10. By 1990 metro San Antonio's three-county area had over 1.3 million residents. The urbanized core covered 438 square miles (75 percent within San Antonio's expanded city limits).

11. Cisneros (1995, pp. 3–4).

Metropolitan solutions, regionalism, linking cities and suburbs, ending the economic and social isolation of inner cities—these were persistent themes sounded by Cisneros throughout his years at HUD, particularly during his first two years, from his confirmation hearing onward. Yet Cisneros's intellectual commitment to metropolitan strategies (the "outside game") was constantly counterbalanced by the greater emotional and political attractiveness of community development strategies (the "inside game"). Part of the inside game's appeal was rooted in Cisneros's own local history. San Antonio's traditional Anglo-dominated politics had been reshaped by the organizing activities of COPS (Communities Organized for Public Service), a local arm of Saul Alinsky's Industrial Areas Foundation. Working through Catholic parishes and largely Hispanic union locals, COPS had helped forge San Antonio's Hispanic residents into an effective political force. COPS had been a key part of the coalition that elected Cisneros as San Antonio's first Hispanic mayor. Cisneros knew firsthand the political muscle of grass-roots movements, but he also knew how rarely poor neighborhoods escape the grip of poverty.

Another part of the inside game's appeal, however, was purely bureaucratic. Since the National Housing and Demonstration Cities Act of 1965, community development was one of HUD's significant bureaucratic missions. The signature institutions of the Great Society's War on Poverty were independent community action agencies that were often at political odds with city hall. The model cities program had been Lyndon Johnson's way of cutting the mayors directly into a piece of the antipoverty action. Spawned by the community action program, neighborhood associations continued to play key planning roles in model cities, but local model cities bureaucracies were direct agencies of city government.

To take the Great Society logo off the program, in 1974 the Nixon administration recast model cities as community development block grants (CDBGs). Postured as more flexible block grants, CDBGs had enough conservative camouflage (plus city hall support) to survive the Reagan years. Though CDBG funding had eroded, by the time of Cisneros's arrival in 1993 the CDBG program still amounted to $2.5 billion. With a young and aggressive Andrew Cuomo as assistant secretary for community development, HUD's own inside game would always demand attention and support.[12]

12. At the outset of the second Clinton administration Cuomo became the eleventh secretary of Housing and Urban Development.

Clinton White House: Playing the Inside Game

Finally, and most important, the White House had chosen to play the inside game. President Clinton's earliest congressional defeat had been the stinging rejection of the new administration's $15 billion "economic stimulus package" in mid-1993. Faced with unanimous Republican opposition, the Democratic-led Congress backed down. The economy was already rebounding from the 1991–92 recession, some argued. More telling was widespread characterization of the package as "just another pork barrel for big city mayors." Critics cited a document compiled by the U.S. Conference of Mayors of ready-to-go projects in different member cities. The Conference of Mayors staff naively believed the document would demonstrate persuasively both the pressing needs of cities and their ability to spend new federal funds quickly. Instead, the mayors' conference inadvertently created Exhibit A for the opposition. Among the hundreds of proposals were an outdoor ice skating rink, a swimming pool, and midnight basketball—all "antirecession" projects widely derided by conservative pundits and congressional opponents.

In the aftermath of that defeat, the White House searched for some strategy to help big cities that could gain a modicum of conservative support. It settled on the idea of federally sponsored "enterprise zones," a largely Republican notion that had been ardently championed by Jack Kemp, the Bush administration's HUD secretary. With a facility that Republicans were to rue by the time of his 1996 reelection campaign, Clinton embraced Republican ideology on enterprise zones, added $1 billion to the previous array of proposed federal tax incentives, and rechristened the package "empowerment communities."

In late 1993 the White House secured congressional approval for the new program, and HUD launched the contest for what was dubbed "the last big federal giveaway." Throughout 1994, hundreds of cities and rural areas packaged their proposals. On December 20, 1994, Cisneros announced the winners: New York, Detroit, Chicago, Atlanta, Baltimore, and Philadelphia-Camden. These were designated "empowerment communities," and each was awarded $100 million cash grants and an estimated $200 million in tax incentives. Smaller cash grants and lesser tax incentives were awarded to Los Angeles and Cleveland as "supplemental empowerment zones" and to Boston, Houston, Kansas City, and Oakland as "enhanced enterprise communities." Almost 100 cities and rural areas were awarded $3 million grants and their target neighborhoods were dubbed "enterprise zones."

As a loyal soldier of the Clinton administration—and with genuine enthusiasm—Cisneros set forth to administer the new empowerment community and enterprise zone program.

Since taking office, however, his main goal had been to gain congressional approval for a major redirection of HUD's programs, particularly, the troubled public housing program. HUD had fallen into political scandal and bureaucratic disarray during the Reagan years. During the Bush years Secretary Jack Kemp had labored mightily to clean out the Augean stables. For the first time in a dozen years the Democrats controlled both the White House and Capitol Hill. The moment was right, Cisneros believed, to push for wide-ranging reform of all HUD's authorizing legislation.

The draft legislation went far beyond seeking reforms solely in public housing policy. HUD sought congressional authorization to raise significantly the eligibility ceiling for the FHA's mortgage insurance program, to secure greater flexibility for community development block grants, to promote greater homeownership, and to expand a host of other HUD programs. HUD organized a coalition of a wide range of interest groups to support the omnibus bill. In early 1994 hearings began before friendly, Democratic-controlled subcommittees in the House and Senate.

The Godfathers Strike

By the late summer of 1994 the legislation was reaching the critical stage. The vote on the omnibus bill would come first in the House. The legislative path was tricky, as HUD was trying to achieve parallel reform language in both authorization and appropriations legislation moving through the House. Particularly sensitive were HUD's proposals to raise the FHA's maximum mortgage insurance limits. This proposal was actively opposed by the Mortgage Insurance Companies of America (MICA), Washington lobbyist for major private mortgage insurers. The private mortgage insurers provided "Cadillac insurance" (mortgage insurance for homes above FHA's limit). The higher FHA's ceiling, the lower their members' profits, as MICA saw it. For all the controversial measures in the omnibus bill, raising FHA's ceiling was the only provision that drew highly organized opposition.

August 20, 1994, was a truly historic day—the founding meeting of the National Partners in Homeownership, another of Cisneros's major initiatives. "Everybody was there—all the top brass from the National Association of Home Builders, Fannie Mae, Freddie Mac, all the leadership of the home building and home financing industry in one room for the first time," one HUD participant remembered. "Except MICA. They were represented by some third-level staffer."

Unbeknownst to HUD, at that very moment, all of MICA's big guns were on Capitol Hill, lobbying members of the House Appropriations Subcommittee on HUD. Midway through the National Partners in Homeownership session, Cisneros was called out of the room to take a call from Representative Louis Stokes, subcommittee chairman. A few minutes later he returned, ashen-faced. "MICA's pressure is too great," Stokes told Cisneros. "The Appropriations Subcommittee's going to have to cave in and not raise FHA's mortgage limits in the money bill."

It was a tableau right out of *The Godfather*. While Al Pacino prays publicly at the baptism of his newborn child, his henchmen are out slaughtering the opposition. In this case, given the realities of legislative warfare, a henchman was dispatched to pray at the baptism while the industry's godfathers were off on their murderous mission.

The omnibus authorization act and the HUD appropriations bill, with conflicting FHA provisions, both passed the House. The Senate speedily agreed to the HUD appropriations. If the omnibus bill were now approved by the Senate, as legislation enacted later, its higher FHA ceiling would prevail. To achieve its ultimate goal, MICA would have to make an all-out effort to defeat the omnibus bill.

"Drop raising the FHA ceiling from the bill," some HUD insiders argued. "The rest of the bill will just sail through. We can fight the FHA battle another day." "We've come this far together," others argued. "We should not break faith with any members of our coalition by dropping any part of the omnibus bill. Besides, Senate leaders assure us that they have enough votes to pass the omnibus bill even over MICA's opposition."

Cisneros decided to press for Senate approval of the House-passed omnibus bill with its higher FHA ceiling. The Senate Democrats were right. They did have the votes, if they could just get the omnibus bill on the floor. But getting a vote scheduled was the problem. The Senate was deadlocked over Clinton's health reform bill. The Republicans were determined to deny the president even a face-saving vote on a greatly scaled-down version of the administration's ambitious health care reform. They filibustered day after day to block a health care vote.

Under the Senate rules, when a filibuster blocks action on the regular agenda, any other Senate business, in order to be considered, must be placed on the consent calendar. That required unanimous consent. MICA lobbied its supporters to block unanimous consent on the omnibus housing bill.

One Republican senator would withhold unanimous consent, citing some minor issue. HUD would negotiate a compromise, then find another Republican senator with yet another minor objection. HUD was dying the death of a thousand cuts. Each time HUD met a critic halfway, it could not get closer to its goal: a floor vote. Finally, Senator Phil Gramm, already positioning for his 1996 presidential run, made it clear that he was unalterably opposed to the omnibus bill and would never assent to its being placed on the consent calendar.

In mid-October Congress adjourned. The omnibus housing bill died on adjournment. It had never reached the Senate floor. Key congressional Democrats, one HUD insider recalled, were "amazingly complacent." "Don't worry," they said. "We've held all the hearings necessary. After the 1994 elections, we'll just reintroduce the omnibus housing bill and run it right through."

Cisneros's Finest Hour

On Election Day the political earthquake struck. From Maine to California the ground beneath congressional Democrats shook and heaved. By midnight a yawning chasm had swallowed the Democratic majorities. The Republicans captured the Senate 53 to 47 for the first time since 1986. By a margin of 230 to 204 the Republicans ended forty years of Democratic control of the House of Representatives.

The headlines highlighted the most visible leadership changes. Bob Dole replaced George Mitchell as Senate Majority Leader. Newt Gingrich was handed the Speaker's gavel, but not by his predecessor, Tom Foley. Foley had not even made it back to the 104th Congress, dumped by his Spokane constituents after twenty-eight years.

From HUD's perspective, the changes were, if anything, more stunning. Gone as chairman of the House Banking, Finance, and Urban Affairs Committee was Representative Henry B. Gonzalez, a long-time member whose first job had been with the San Antonio Housing Authority.

There were, of course, no Republican members who had ever chaired House committees and subcommittees. Moreover, with freshmen and sophomores (first elected in 1992) composing more than half of the Republicans, key leadership roles fell to virtual newcomers. Chairing the housing subcommittee was Representative Rick Lazio from New York, beginning only his second term.

It was not just that the new Republican majority lacked institutional memory. They gloried in that fact. Many had been elected on an explicit anti-Washington platform. Many not only did not know the facts; they did not want to know the facts. They had their agenda. And the central item on that agenda was to cut back the size and scope of the federal government. Within two weeks of the election, the Republican leadership announced their immediate targets: abolish five cabinet departments: Commerce, Labor, Energy, Education, and HUD.

Running scared after the stunning election results, the Clinton White House sharpened its own ax as well. The White House budget cutters, it was reported, had HUD on the administration's kill list. In the 104th Congress HUD would not be fighting for passage of the aborted omnibus housing act after all. HUD would be fighting for its very existence. It would be Henry Cisneros's finest hour.

The shadow of the gallows concentrates the mind marvelously. Drawing together the best ideas of an able cadre of young assistant secretaries, Cisneros launched a preemptive strike. On December 19, 1994, Cisneros announced a sweeping "Reinvention Blueprint" of HUD. (His press conference came the day before the much-anticipated award of empowerment community and enterprise zone grants.)

Believing both in the critical nature of HUD's mission and the need to carry it out more efficiently and effectively, Cisneros proposed three major reforms. First, consolidate more than sixty major HUD grant programs into three "performance funds" decentralized to states and local governments. HUD would "preapprove" local plans to ensure compliance with national goals. Second, convert the Federal Housing Administration into an independent but government-owned Federal Housing Corporation, consolidating its many statutory programs into a few broad, flexible activities directed to three general markets: single-family homeownership, multifamily rental housing, and health care facilities. And third, totally transform the nation's public housing program. Cisneros pulled every page out of the Republican book except that chapter advocating total abolition of the federal government's housing assistance for the poor.

He vowed to create a real launching pad for families trying to raise themselves from squalid conditions and improve their lives. His blueprint for reinventing HUD would create housing certificates to give public housing residents a genuine market choice between public housing and the private rental market; break the monopoly of local housing authorities over federal housing resources by forcing housing authorities to compete in the marketplace with private landlords to attract renters with housing certificates; give preference to families that are moving toward self-sufficiency by already working or participating in "work-ready" and education programs; and end inner-city blight caused by many public housing projects by accelerating the demolition of uninhabitable and nonviable properties. Nor would new developments be targeted exclusively at the very poor.

Over a three-year transition period HUD would get out of the direct funding of public housing by converting project-based public housing subsidies to tenant-based rental assistance. During fiscal 1996 and 1997 HUD would deregulate more than 3,000 well-performing local authorities, work to reform more than 100 severely troubled authorities, and, for 10 to 15 of the most troubled local authorities beyond any reasonable hope of improvement, divest them of their properties and management control. During fiscal 1996 HUD would consolidate all public housing funds into a Capital Fund and Operating Subsidies Fund. States and localities could opt to receive all housing funds as housing certificates. By fiscal 1998 all former project-based public housing subsidies would be completely portable housing certificates awarded to eligible low-income households.

Even by the standards of the Republicans' Contract with America, Cisneros's proposals were a bold stroke. More important, HUD's reinvention blueprint came just six weeks after the Republicans' stunning election victory. Beyond rattling their sabers at HUD, congressional Republicans had not had time to develop their own plans.

Cisneros drew on his close personal ties to President Clinton and Vice President Al Gore to get their imprimatur on HUD's reinvention blueprint. "The reinvention of HUD," Cisneros stated, "flows from the work of the National Performance Review [Vice President Gore's 'reinventing government' initiative], the most sweeping and ambitious effort to revitalize the Federal Government in half a century."

Cisneros had blunted the assaults on HUD. It would be another matter to sell his reinvention plan, which was "viewed with skepticism by many conservatives and near horror by some liberals."[13] The new Republican majority's first budget action was a harbinger of things to come. Congress slashed more than $15 billion from the federal government's fiscal 1995 budget already in effect; $7.2 billion, almost half the cuts, was taken away from HUD alone. Most was in funds for section 8 certificates and vouchers.

13. Guy Gugliotta, "Doubts on Reinvention: GOP Casts Skeptical Eye on Housing Overhaul," *Washington Post*, March 9, 1995, p. A19.

Republican budget cutters argued that not a single poor person would be evicted and put out on the street as a result. Technically, they were correct. The money was as yet "uncommitted." It was still on its way from HUD to 3,400 different local housing authorities. But it was the first time since the inception of the section 8 program that the flow of rent subsidy funds was being reduced. The pipeline of rental assistance was drying up. Cisneros called the rescission "callous and short-sighted."

"We have been waiting for a sound proposal," said Senator Christopher S. Bond (R-Mo.), chairman of the HUD Appropriations Subcommittee. "What is touted as a 'reinvention blueprint' is more press release than working plan." Bond also expressed doubts about HUD's plan to deregulate local housing authorities and voucherize completely all housing assistance. Bond feared that deregulating a "good stock" of public housing could cripple many authorities and also questioned whether vouchers, which "cost twice as much" per family as public housing, could serve as many people as the current system.[14]

Senator Bond's criticisms were echoed by influential groups such as the National Association of Housing and Redevelopment Officials (NAHRO), the Washington-based trade association of the country's 3,400 local housing authorities. While always seeking greater flexibility under federal regulations for local authorities, NAHRO opposed Cisneros's proposal to phase out federal operating subsidies for its members over a three-year period. In response, HUD modified its plan in early 1995. Smaller public housing authorities (PHAs) (less than 100 units) would enter the new world of 100 percent tenant-based subsidies by fiscal 1998; medium-sized PHAs (100–250 units) by fiscal 2000; the larger PHAs (more than 250 units) by fiscal 2002. This would allow larger PHAs to renovate many of their larger projects to compete for voucher-bearing tenants and middle-class households.

Of Cisneros's three original initiatives, two failed to leave the starting gate. Combining all HUD programs into three "performance funds" and converting the FHA into the FHC never even received a hearing in the Republican-controlled Congress. Transforming public housing, however, was another matter.

Transforming Public Housing

Total voucherization of public housing assistance was not seriously considered. As I had written in *Baltimore Unbound*, "the philosophy of Cisneros's

---

14. Gugliotta, "Doubts on Reinvention."

plan [that is, voucherization] should appeal to the new Republican congressional majority. The politics of Cisneros's plan probably will not."[15] Suburban-based Republican members of Congress were not about to unleash a diaspora of black and Hispanic housing project residents into private rental apartments in their suburban districts.

But much of the rest of HUD's proposals for reforming public housing were attractive. After months of negotiation and debate between HUD and Capitol Hill, Representative Lazio reported out the United States Housing Act of 1996.

—The new bill consolidated dozens of public housing funds into two block grants for PHAs, one for capital investment and the other for operating expenses. This wiped out in one stroke dozens of regulatory bottlenecks that crippled the administration of the federal public housing program for years.

—The new bill provided permanent authority for PHAs to use rehabilitation funds to demolish deteriorated projects rather than rebuild them at immense cost. It also authorized housing authorities to give rent subsidy vouchers to tenants in condemned public housing complexes so they can move to privately owned housing instead of waiting for years for a new public housing complex to be built.

—The bill softened rent preferences for the poorest households, repealed the Brooke amendment setting rents at 30 percent of tenants' incomes, and lowered the marginal tax on tenants' additional earnings—all measures designed to attract working-class families back to public housing.

The United States Housing Act of 1996 passed the House of Representatives by a vote of 315 to 107 on May 9, 1996. The final vote obscured how bitterly House members had fought over key details. A floor effort to reinstate the Brooke amendment failed by a relatively narrow vote of 196 to 222, with some Republicans swayed by Democratic fears that repealing it would enable housing authorities to raise rents well beyond the ability of poor tenants to pay and thereby lead to evictions and homelessness.

Overall, the bill was a triumph for Cisneros. The House bill headed to a House-Senate conference committee for reconciliation with a less sweeping and "softer" Senate-passed bill. Cisneros said he was "looking forward" to working with House and Senate conferees "to create a public housing reform bill that can be signed by the president."[16]

15. Rusk (1995, p. 145).

16. This quotation and the material in the previous paragraphs are drawn from Guy Gugliotta, "House Votes for Overhaul in Housing," *Washington Post,* May 10, 1996, pp. A1, A23.

The bill's substance was more favorable than its timing. In 1992 candidate Clinton had pledged "to end welfare as we know it." The Republican Congress overcame Democratic opposition to send President Clinton the welfare reform bill in early August, just before the Democratic presidential convention. In the face of strong liberal opposition and the resignation of three high-level administrators at the Health and Human Services Department, Clinton signed the welfare reform bill.

Conservative Republicans were also determined "to end public housing as we know it." The wide-ranging reforms just enacted were too complicated for campaign-year sound bites. They needed a simple, easily explained symbol. The House conferees demanded that any compromise House-Senate bill repeal the Wagner-Steagall Act, the New Deal legislation that had launched the federal public housing program.

That was too much for the White House. President Clinton's signature on the welfare reform law wiped out a sixty-year federal commitment to provide the country's poorest families with a basic minimum income. The president was not about to tear down another New Deal monument. Cisneros invoked a sure presidential veto if the final package contained Wagner-Steagall repeal. Influential senators made clear their opposition and ability to block any such action. Once again, when Congress adjourned in mid-October for the final weeks of the 1996 campaign, a comprehensive public housing reform law died.

"Issues of race, class, and poverty remain the unresolved agenda for America," Henry Cisneros wrote me in December 1996, as he was preparing to leave office. With his departure (and that of Labor Secretary Robert Reich), the Clinton administration lost its strongest champions of the poor.

Efforts to transform the federal public housing program moved forward, but on flimsy legal foundations. Suspension of the one-for-one replacement law, greater local flexibility in using federal capital funds, authority to develop public housing as part of private mixed-income developments, greater rent flexibility, repeal of federal admissions priorities to attract more working families—all were legally permissible only because the fiscal 1997 HUD appropriations act had provided one-year authority for these policies. Without a comprehensive housing bill, continuing reforms down this path would be dependent upon language in the annual appropriations acts suspending permanent laws on the books.

For a strategy that would systematically shift poor black families—mostly mothers and children—out of inner-city projects into voucher-subsidized private rental housing located in nonpoor neighborhoods, there was not only no congressional consensus, there was hardly any support at all.

The Death of Moving to Opportunity

That was brutally demonstrated in the sad history of HUD's Moving to Opportunity national demonstration project. With special appropriations from fiscal 1992 and 1993, HUD originally planned to conduct a careful, ten-year study of combining vouchers and intensive counseling to enable a small number of families living in high-poverty areas to find housing in low-poverty areas. In each of five major metropolitan areas—Baltimore, Boston, Chicago, Los Angeles, and New York—130 public housing families would receive vouchers and special intensive counseling, another 130 would receive vouchers and normal counseling support, and a third group would serve as the control group. Test families would have to move from high-poverty neighborhoods (more than 40 percent poverty) to low-poverty neighborhoods (less than 10 percent poverty). In fiscal 1994 HUD hoped to expand the program to additional families in the test communities. The goal was to study definitively the impact that low-poverty communities have on the employment, income, education, and social well-being of poor, inner-city families.

In the five metro areas the small projects quietly got under way. Then all hell broke loose surrounding the Baltimore project. Political campaigns had begun for the Baltimore County commission. Moving to Opportunity was an irresistible target for several conservative candidates. They began beating the tribal drums. They raised the specter of hordes of black public housing residents from Baltimore City invading hard-pressed, largely white, working-class suburbs in eastern Baltimore County. Right-wing talk show hosts jumped aboard. Angry protest meetings were organized in Essex and Dundalk. HUD, city, and county officials (who had quietly agreed to cooperate) came under public siege.

Finally, Maryland's U.S. senators, Barbara Mikulski and Paul Sarbanes, stepped in. Though card-carrying liberal Democrats, they were alarmed during an election year. The fact that Moving to Opportunity's rules would prevent any participants from moving into moderate-poverty communities such as Essex and Dundalk carried no weight with the senators. They were not interested in trying to quell racial fears with facts. They were interested in eliminating the issue. Through Mikulski's membership on the Senate Appropriations Committee, they canceled Moving to Opportunity's $149 million for fiscal 1994, shifting the money to a noncontroversial program. They had heard the voice of the people, they claimed, and had killed Moving to Opportunity (though the five already funded projects continued).

"Boy, it's tough when even your supposed friends won't stand up for what's right," said one HUD insider. "Cosmetics aside, the congressional message was clear: 'We don't want to hear anything more about HUD programs to move poor blacks into white neighborhoods.' Frankly, where HUD has been able to move decisively against segregating poor blacks, it has been in response to federal court orders. Whenever HUD has sought legislative support for fighting racism, the Congress has backed off."

Breaking the Impasse

As I noted in 1995, Cisneros's proposals to convert all public housing assistance to a client-based voucher system might be very attractive ideologically to the new Republican congressional majority, but I doubted that the politics of dispersing poor, often minority, households into suburban areas would appeal to that majority.

In an early draft of this book, in 1996, I projected again that:

> The federal housing dollar is shrinking. Balancing the federal budget by fiscal 2002—while leaving social security and medicare substantially untouched—makes big cuts in HUD's housing assistance programs unavoidable. And they are politically weak. The only major constituency for conventional public housing is NAHRO and its local housing authority membership (although the construction trades are always ready to lobby for construction and major renovation funds). Private owners of project-based section 8 apartments may be a more formidable interest group. They, after all, are private investors and, unlike local housing authorities, make political campaign contributions.
>
> And there is *no* political constituency for the policy that makes the most sense: Cisneros's proposal to completely voucherize whatever federal housing assistance remains. Poor families receiving housing vouchers must be among the most powerless groups in American society, and poor households that do not now but might receive vouchers in the future exist merely as bloodless abstractions in the eyes of many politicians. After all, no family will be put out on the street, the budget cutters assured their congressional colleagues in rescinding $7 billion in HUD's section 8 budget for fiscal 1995.

In October 1998 the Republican Congress and President Clinton agreed on a $500 billion appropriations bill for fiscal year 1999. The bill included

$24.5 billion for HUD without cutting any HUD program. Most significant was an increase of $2.7 billion for section 8 rental assistance, providing an increase of 90,000 rent vouchers over the previous level—the first increase in four years.

In a "Dear Colleague" letter I received, HUD Secretary Andrew Cuomo commented that "in 1996, the *New York Times Magazine* ran a cover story called 'The Year That Housing Died,' describing the consequences of the halt over the previous few years in issuing new rental assistance vouchers. Today I believe that 1998 could well be labeled 'The Year That Housing Was Reborn.'"[17]

In addition to funds for 90,000 additional vouchers in fiscal year 1999, Cuomo noted, Congress authorized another 100,000 vouchers in fiscal year 2000 and an extra 100,000 more in fiscal year 2001.

"Under the deconcentration provisions of the bill," Cuomo continued, "more moderate-income working families will be admitted to public housing in lower-income developments, while at the same time lower-income families will be given the chance to move into higher-income developments [through rent vouchers]. . . . HUD will also be allowed to continue tearing down failed public housing projects and replace them with new townhouse-style developments, through the HOPE VI program [whose annual appropriation was boosted from $550 million to $625 million]. . . . These reforms implement President Clinton's visionary plans to transform public housing from segregated ghettos of poverty and despair into economically integrated communities of opportunity."

So clearly both the *New York Times* and I were overly pessimistic—at least, temporarily. The booming American economy, feeding the tax increases enacted in the 1990 and 1993 budget agreements, ballooned federal revenues so much that "balancing" the budget was achieved not painfully by 2002 but painlessly by 1998.[18] In such flush times the Republican-controlled

17. Letter from Secretary of Housing and Urban Development Andrew Cuomo, October 8, 1998.

18. In an op-ed column in the *Washington Post* William G. Gale, a senior fellow at the Brookings Institution, wrote that "the projected surpluses are substantial, roughly $1.5 trillion over the next decade. But they arise from the peculiarities of government budget accounting, which focuses on annual cash flows, not from underlying economic reality. Over the next several decades, because of the pressure that retiring baby boomers will put on Social Security and Medicare, the government faces large economic deficits, rather than surpluses. Even with no tax cuts [as proposed by Congressional Republicans], the accruing surpluses will not be sufficient to pay for future liabilities. . . . Put differently, if the government kept its books like a business, it would show a shortfall under current circumstances, not a surplus." "A 'Surplus' We Need," *Washington Post*, October 16, 1998, p. A27.

Congress aped the self-styled conservative stereotype of past Democratic-controlled Congresses. The opening of the fiscal floodgates had begun earlier in 1998 with enactment of a $220 billion highway and transit assistance bill, and the fiscal tsunami carried HUD's programs right along with it.

Such largess will likely be seen in a different light when the American economy inevitably cools again, and Congress begins to deal seriously with the consequences of the aging baby boom on social security and medicare. However, the concept of deconcentrating the poor through a combination of vouchers, demolition of massive projects, and modest mixed-income redevelopment appears to be embraced by a significant congressional majority. If HUD meets its target of 100,000 high-density units demolished by 2000, the next census should record a significant reduction in high-poverty neighborhoods.

That will be good news indeed for America's ailing cities—and for many victims of the poverty machine.

13

Building Regional Coalitions

"THIS PLAN ONLY affects the unincorporated areas of Lake County. This matter only concerns 'south county' residents." The chairman of the Lake County (Indiana) Plan Commission was clearly upset. He had expected a routine meeting of the twelve commissioners to approve the proposed Lake County comprehensive plan. There had been no controversy and little public interest in the plan; only a dozen citizens had turned out at the plan commission's previous public hearing in mid-June 1996.

Now, two weeks later, the planning commissioners were confronted by a delegation of about fifty determined citizens. And the group was not just large, it was very different from the smattering of developers, builders, and bureaucrats who were regulars at plan commission meetings. This group was about evenly divided between blacks and whites, a rare enough occurrence in Northwest Indiana (the nation's most racially segregated metro area, according to the Census Bureau). Also, these were mostly Protestant ministers, Catholic priests, rabbis, a Muslim imam—all leaders of the Northwest Indiana Federation of Interfaith Organizations. They had driven down from Gary, Hammond, and East Chicago to the county seat in Crown Point for this meeting.

"We disagree," responded the Reverend Victor Davis, pastor of Gary's Spirit of God Fellowship Church. The former Iowa Hawkeye running back, still trim and athletic, warmed to his argument. "We don't feel this plan addresses urban sprawl. We feel that sprawl needs to be reversed or stopped. Suburban sprawl into rural areas lures residents from Gary, Hammond, and East Chicago, eroding their tax bases, and leading to further deterioration of infrastructure. And older suburban communities often take the greatest hit as development continues in the cornfields. The interfaith federation asks that action on the plan be postponed until another hearing is held in Gary or Hammond so that 'north county' residents can have their say," Reverend Davis concluded.[1]

Though obviously annoyed, plan commission members agreed to postpone action until their August meeting in order to hold the hearing requested. It was a modest request and only a small concession, hardly on the order of a "shot heard round the world." But out of small events—a weary Rosa Parks refusing to move to the back of that Montgomery, Alabama, bus, for instance—mighty movements can grow. The federation's very appearance that night marked an opening shot in a new phenomenon. Urban church activists were beginning to challenge the sprawl machine.

The Churches

The interfaith federation was, itself, a relative newcomer. Its church-based constituent groups had existed in Chicago's Indiana suburbs for some years: the United Citizens Organization of East Chicago, the Interfaith Action Coalition of Gary, and the Interfaith Citizens Organization of Hammond. But traditional political rivalries and race had kept apart the movements in East Chicago (48 percent Hispanic), Gary (80 percent black), and Hammond (78 percent white).

Joining together across jurisdictional and racial lines had created a potent political force in Lake County. Using civil rights–style political action, the federation blocked relocating the county juvenile courts from Gary to Crown Point. More impressively, they overcame the determination of two federal district judges to move the federal courthouse out of Hammond. Their grass-roots muscle was further highlighted in April 1996 when the federation mobilized more than 1,000 members of their congregations for a public rally at the Hammond Civic Center. The mayors of the three cities were all present as well as most other prominent Lake County politicians.

---

1. "Urban Group Wants Decision on County Plan Delayed," *Hammond Times,* July 2, 1996.

"We must change the way we think about this region," Reverend Davis urged at the rally. "We are a single metropolitan region, with a shared history and a shared economy. We must act as an entire region on critical issues like the need for a regional transportation system and a tax-base sharing system to address growing tax rate disparities."[2]

Higher tax rates in Gary, Hammond, and East Chicago were also critical concerns of Inland Steel, USX's Gary Works, Amoco, and Northwest Indiana Public Service Company, the region's major industries. With giant facilities anchored in the lakeshore communities, they were the deep pockets called upon to bail out the poverty-stricken cities. "We're going to lose one of these industries very soon if we don't address the inequities of the tax system," Tom Reis, another federation member, warned.[3]

The local church coalitions themselves were members of a larger movement, spearheaded by the Chicago-based Gamaliel Foundation. Patterning its organizing approach on the teachings of the late Saul Alinsky (whose Industrial Areas Foundation had been organizing working-class neighborhoods since the 1930s), the Gamaliel Foundation had organizers and affiliates in seventeen communities. Its target communities were Chicago and its depressed southern suburbs, Joliet, Peoria, Iowa's Quad Cities, Detroit, Saginaw, Minnesota's Twin Cities and the Iron Range, Saint Louis and East Saint Louis, Cleveland, Columbus, Cincinnati, Milwaukee, Racine, Buffalo— almost a roll call of the Midwest's hardest-hit industrial areas.[4]

All the local church alliances in Northwest Indiana had had their neighborhood victories. Some had even reshaped major policies and programs of their city governments. But year after year they could see their communities declining in spite of their efforts. Stable middle-class families moved away. Remaining residents were proportionally poorer and poorer. Local stores closed. Salvation Army stores replaced supermarkets and pawnshops replaced pharmacies. Factories large and small would close down overnight. City services declined even as tax rates went up. Crime, drugs, and booze flourished. What was happening? Why could they win battles but never win the war?

Myron Orfield laid out the full picture for a national meeting of Gamaliel's organizers in December 1995. Using Minnesota's Metropolitics to illustrate his points, he showed how sprawling development patterns, increasing segregation by income class, continued racial discrimination, local

---

2. "Leaders Address Region's Ills," *Hammond Times*, May 1, 1996.
3. "Leaders Address Region's Ills."
4. The seventeenth community was Oakland, California.

fiscal disparities, and other factors flowed together to constantly defeat grass-roots efforts to stabilize inner-city neighborhoods. The Gamaliel staffers were very impressed, particularly Paul Scully, assigned to support the Northwest Indiana movement. He invited Myron and me to Gary for a two-day workshop for 150 ministers, lay leaders, and business representatives in early June 1996.

The Metropolitan Summit for Redevelopment was hailed by the local papers. The *Gary Post-Tribune* called the summit "a giant step toward promoting a broader understanding.... The twin centers of dispute these days—landfills and casino money—are just the latest targets in a war that has seen issues come and go. They are no more or less important than other problems that have divided the industrial north from the suburban and rural south. Each side views its needs as being greater than those of the other, but truthfully they are linked to each other. Only the most narrow vision fails to recognize that an apple is only as strong as its core."[5]

The *Hammond Times* sounded a similar theme. "Promoting 'Buffington Harbor' as the site of a spanking new riverboat casino cannot alter the fact, unpalatable as it may be to some, that it really is in Gary, whose hospitality they want to enjoy, whose resources they want to exploit, but whose public mention they want to shut out.... That mentality has to be reversed. It is a mentality of escape; and there is no escape."[6] Local leaders, the *Times* concluded, should focus on the problems of the region as a whole.

Two weeks later the federation won a temporary pause in the Lake County comprehensive plan's apparently well-greased path to approval. But an emotional battle royal was shaping up over the site of a new county landfill. The issue would pit north county against south county again.

Battling the Garbage Dump

Over the previous year the Lake County Solid Waste Management District had evaluated possible sites. By a hotly disputed 12 to 11 vote, the district board had approved a 560-acre site in the midst of farmland in Eagle Creek Township on the county's southern boundary. As an alternative site they rejected the "J-Pit," an abandoned sand quarry on the Gary-Hammond boundary.

5. "North vs. South: Lake County's Regional Feud Must End," *Gary Post-Tribune*, June 21, 1996.

6. "No Town Is an Island," *Hammond Times*, June 25, 1996.

The Eagle Creek site, however, required a county zoning change and was fiercely opposed by South County Residents Opposed to Dumps (SCROD). The group prevailed with the plan commission, which, composed almost entirely of south county commissioners and residents, voted 12 to 0 against the Eagle Creek site at its August meeting. Heavy lobbying by the federation convinced the Lake County Council to reverse the planning group's action by a 4 to 3 vote in late September. The swing vote was cast by the county councilwoman from Hammond. She switched in the last seventy-two hours because she tried, but failed, to get assurances that Gary's J-Pit would not be used if the Eagle Creek location was rejected: "I could not get these assurances. I live near the J-Pit. I need to protect my environment. I have no choice."[7]

SCROD was incensed. It promised further court challenges. A meeting was held to consider having the southern townships secede from Lake County, perhaps joining rural (and white) Newton County. (Secession would require an amendment to the state constitution, experts advised.) Letters to the editor bombarded the papers. Some were sorrowful in tone: "When will the day come when our leaders' foresight is greater than the vision of a garbage mountain stuck in the middle of pristine farmland?"[8]

Others letters were spiteful, even hateful, especially those criticizing the Reverend Rick Orlinsky, the priest of Saint Catherine of Siena in Hammond and a leading federation spokesman. A South County resident wrote: "I, too was at the county council meeting where the Rev. Rick Orlinsky led his three busloads of north Lake County followers to endorse the murder by poison and pollution of south county children and residents. If he is a spokesman for the Catholic Church, then they can no longer preach pro-life because of this crude messiah of the north who has discredited his church. Strip off your cassock, Orlinsky, and put on your grave digging clothes, because once the dump is operational, you'll be able to bury a lot of south county residents who you despise."[9]

7. "Council OKs Landfill Rezoning," *Hammond Times,* September 27, 1996.
8. "A Chance to Show Unity Was Lost," *Hammond Times,* October 14, 1996.
9. "Priest Helped Put South County at Risk," *Gary Post-Tribune,* October 23, 1996. More serious were the efforts to silence Father Orlinsky through political pressure on the Catholic Church. The *Hammond Times* revealed ("Church Asked to Muzzle Priest," December 8, 1996) that, before the landfill vote, a South County councilman had contacted Bishop Dale Melczek, who had refused to intervene. The bishop said that Orlinsky was speaking on behalf of Interfaith, not the Catholic Church. "While Melczek makes a strict distinction between the diocese and Interfaith," the *Times* reported, "he speaks highly of the group, which receives some of its funding from the Campaign for Human Development, an arm of the National Conference of Bishops. 'They fund self-help groups

Responded one grandmother in Gary: "I speak for a group of citizens who never wished a 'dump' on anyone. We have been dumped on by so many different things, we know what it is to be taken advantage of and ignored. The funny thing was, there was no one to care, to offer help, until we had to come to grips with it ourselves. Our cancer rate is very high, so are those of heart problems, breathing problems, etc. For our children and our grandchildren, the future looks rather bleak. We can't survive another dump [in Gary]."[10]

Amending the Land Use Plan

Throughout the months of pitched battle over the landfill, the Lake County comprehensive plan plowed its way inexorably forward. The federation thought it had a commitment for a new hearing to be held in north county; a plan commission staff member rescheduled the hearing for Crown Point again as "the most centrally located point." The federation boycotted the hearing in protest. At the same August meeting, when the plan commission (with its central and south county membership) voted unanimously to oppose the Eagle Creek landfill, its members also recommended unanimously that the county council adopt the comprehensive plan.

The next round, however, belonged to the federation. "Against long odds," the *Hammond Times* reported, "urban activists won a temporary victory over suburban sprawl [September 3] . . . when the County Council narrowly voted to defer a vote on the plan until the federation leaders have a chance to voice their concerns and suggest changes."[11]

Aided by a volunteer city planner, the federation weighed in with three pages of proposed amendments by mid-October. The *Hammond Times*, which had praised the federation's metropolitan summit and had endorsed the Eagle Creek landfill site, came unglued. "Wanted: Red Light along I-65," its banner headline screamed. "Economics of Envy," it editorialized. The federation's proposed amendments are "a document dripping with unconcealed hostility toward the south part of the county. . . . It is not so much a

---

that assist the voiceless in expressing themselves on public policies,' Melczek said. 'That is what [Interfaith] is doing.'"

10. "Interfaith Group Acted with Best Interest of People," *Hammond Times*, November 3, 1996. More than 500 families lived within a half-mile of the J-Pit on the Gary-Hammond border; only seventeen families lived that close to the Eagle Creek site in south county. Indeed, tipping fees from the Eagle Creek landfill would provide $4 million to clean up and close Gary's existing municipal dump.

11. "Vote Deferred on Plan for Land," *Hammond Times*, September 4, 1996.

plan for equitable development as a declaration of war. . . . The unabashed aim is to stop the wheels of progress in south county and to force them to come to the north."

The *Times*'s editorial vitriol was easily exceeded by the county council's sole representative on the plan commission: "I think the Interfaith people should mind their own damn business, take care of their churches and their communities, and keep their youth away from crime. We don't stick our nose into Gary or Hammond or East Chicago. Why should they stick their nose into the unincorporated areas?" Commenting on the federation's call for "fair share" affordable housing in new subdivisions, the south county councilman concluded, "Those people can't afford these homes. They can't even afford a gallon of paint."[12]

The federation was stung. Its proposed amendments, in its view, had been modest and moderate; within the group, members who wanted no further development in south county had been argued down. It had recommended that the county wait to approve any new roads until the Northwest Indiana Regional Planning Commission completed the regional 2020 transportation plan. The federation had suggested that the amount of farmland immediately rezoned for residential development around southern Cedar Lake, Lowell, and unincorporated Saint John Township be reasonably limited to that necessary to accommodate the next ten years of projected population growth. It had recommended deleting proposals for new industrial zoning and holding commercial rezoning along Interstate 65 and U.S. 231, in the county's southern section, to a maximum of twenty acres. The federation had opposed a county proposal to have developers of new south county subdivisions contribute to an "off-site" affordable housing fund; instead, it argued for a minimum of 10 percent affordable housing as an integral part of new subdivisions.[13] "There is nothing radical, divisive, vengeful, or extreme about this document," the federation argued in an op-ed response to the *Times*.

Nowhere does it talk about killing development in south Lake County to force development into Gary, East Chicago, and Hammond. In fact, the

12. "Wanted: Red Light along I-65," *Hammond Times*, October 20, 1996.
13. "Off-site affordable housing will tend to concentrate low-income housing in one particular area and actually increase exclusionary effects," the federation argued in its amendments. "On-site affordable housing will encourage inclusionary developments and reduce the heavy burden on one community." The federation's proposal was drawn from my metropolitan summit presentation on Montgomery County, Maryland's moderately priced dwelling unit policy (see chapter 9).

document talks about preserving and stabilizing the second ring of suburbs such as Highland, Griffith, Lake Station, and Merrillville, the communities most at risk from the current development trends. These
communities are already seeing the same patterns of decline experienced
by their northern neighbors in the last two decades. The only difference is
that these towns don't have the industrial tax base to fall back on when
their residential tax base slowly erodes. . . . If we follow the blueprint produced by the plan commission, what will [the *Times* propose] to protect
the property values of its readers in [these suburbs]? What about their property rights?

The issues we are working on and the solutions we are proposing are
in the interest of the entire region. They aim to promote stability in the
suburbs, redevelopment in the cities, preservation of agricultural space,
economic diversity in our housing, and tax rate equity between municipalities.[14]

The federation concluded its statement by challenging the *Times* to work
with it to convene a conference to discuss its proposals "for the Lake County
plan and the future of Lake County" in a gathering of the mayors, town
managers, city council members, planners and county officials from the cities and suburbs for "a rational and factual conversation about the danger-
ous development trends taking place in our region and the solutions to deal
with them."

And that, indeed, was the path taken. Recognizing that there was little
public understanding of the consequences of suburban sprawl—and less
political support within the county council—the federation opted for longer-
term education rather than short-term conflict. When pro-plan supporters
geared up for another donnybrook public hearing in mid-December, the
federation's president, the Reverend Vincent L. McCutcheon, announced:
"We will not participate in an event designed to provoke a north/south con-
frontation." Instead, the federation held a countywide prayer breakfast "to
promote understanding and fellowship." Successfully persuading the county
council to attach an amendment to the comprehensive plan requiring a consideration of potential amendments in June 1997, the federation watched
quietly as the county council adopted the plan at its December meeting.

14. "Officials of Interfaith Federation Criticize *Times* Editorial," *Hammond Times*, November
1996.

A Legislative Victory (Indirectly)

The year's battles had one other immediate result. Success caused the federation to become a principal target in a key Lake County legislative race. Running for a vacant, traditionally Republican House seat in south county, the Republican candidate broadcast a flyer that claimed the federation was "a political action group for North Lake County Democrats. They seek the environmental and economic destruction of South Lake and Porter Counties. Interfaith already controls four of the seven members of the Lake County Council. *They are now supporting a Merrillville Democrat for State Representative.* If they are successful, Democrats will control the Indiana State house. Interfaith's Gary and East Chicago allies will be in charge of important House committees and gain even greater control of South County." For the future of "our families and businesses," the flyer urged, the district's residents should vote Republican.

"It's funny," mused Paul Scully, the federation's senior staffer, in a conversation with me several weeks after the election. "The federation never even talked to the Democratic candidate, much less actively supported him. But he won, and his victory did shift control of the Indiana House. So, I suppose, in a way, we did gain greater influence."

It had been a bruising short course on the politics of regional development. The landfill battle was somewhat familiar ground for federation veterans. But the vehemence of the response to their proposed land use plan amendments startled federation leadership. The message was clear: "Stick to your own sandbox and we'll tolerate you . . . barely. Mess with our turf and we'll cut your heads off."

Breaking into a Closed System

Decisionmaking within the sprawl machine was a closely held process, the federation realized. Legally, the county council's planning and zoning powers apply only to unincorporated territory. Lake County's eighteen incorporated municipalities conduct their own planning and zoning. It was, perhaps, understandable that the plan commission was dominated by residents of south county, where most unincorporated land was found, but that precluded strong voices asserting that south county sprawl had a direct impact on north county stability and vitality.

The system was infused with conflicts of interest. Most striking was the revelation by the *Gary Post-Tribune* that the plan commission's staff director was himself an investor in a proposed subdivision within two miles of the Eagle Creek landfill site.[15] He had been a "ferocious" critic of the landfill, had blasted it as a potential safety hazard, and had voted against the Eagle Creek site as a member of the Lake County Solid Waste Management Board. Now he declared his twenty-four-townhouse Tucson Subdivision to be "a nice little project. We have sewer, well water, sidewalks and full utilities. . . . We are on the opposite side of Interstate 65. The highway's elevated there so you couldn't see the landfill if it was 400 feet high."

Swapping his planning director hat for his developer hat, he remarked: "Do I think I'm exposing them [future homeowners] to anything? I hope not. The water is chlorinated and there are all kinds of safeguards." Referring to the prospect of protracted litigation before the Indiana Department of Environmental Management and in the state courts, the planning director–developer perhaps reflected the typical attitude of area developers: "People are still safe building down there for a little while because you never know. Even if they prove me wrong, they've still got all this litigation to go through so they have another five years."

It was as if the federation's recommendations were written in a foreign language, the federation found. By the standards of communities with active growth management policies in place, the federation's proposals were exceedingly modest. They proposed no urban growth boundaries as in Portland, Seattle, or San Jose; just do not rezone more farmland than you need, they suggested. They were not seeking to ban further freeways or highways, but simply asking local authorities to wait for the transportation planners' study. Their minimum target of 10 percent affordable housing in new subdivisions was well below Montgomery County, Maryland's 15 percent or the 20 percent minimum required in Fairfax County or Loudoun County, Virginia (hardly radical hotbeds).

Most vexing was that the principal beneficiaries of the federation's amendments would probably not be Gary, Hammond, and East Chicago, but the band of older suburban communities south of them, which had traditionally been antagonistic to the three cities. The concern was based, in part, on data I developed for the federation's metropolitan summit in June 1996. It showed that several major suburbs had already joined the downward income trend taking place in the three cities (table 13-1).

15. "Residential Developers Undaunted by Landfill Concerns," *Gary Post-Tribune*, November 10, 1996.

Table 13-1. *Change in Relative Household Income in Lake County, 1970–90*
Percent

Area of county	Household income as percentage of metro mean	
	1970	1990
East Chicago	83	69
Gary	88	69
Hammond	113	82
Griffith	116	108
Highland	128	118
Hobart	113	107
Lake Station	95	81
Merrillville	133	112
Whiting	90	76

Source: Author's calculations based on census reports.

The federation's opposition to new industrial zones along Interstate 65 and U.S. 235 was, indeed, designed to encourage industrial reinvestment in vacant industrial sites in the three cities, which were already served by shipping on Lake Michigan, extensive rail lines, and Interstates 80 and 90. But the federation's desire to restrain new commercial development was designed to "ensure the viability of U.S. 30 as the commercial hub," the corridor five miles south of Gary and Hammond where the shopping centers and regional malls were the core of the tax bases among the first ring of suburbs.

Assessing their six months' effort, the federation realized that it was still too vulnerable politically. Inner-city groups had to do more than just argue for the interests of inner suburbs. They would have to enlist suburban congregations actively in the federation's ranks. In early 1997 they stepped up efforts to reach out to suburban churches. They also moved to repair relationships with the local press, particularly the *Times*.

Recruiting Suburban Support

The 1997 metropolitan summit of Northwest Indiana showed how far the federation had come in spreading the message in just one year. The first metropolitan summit had been held in inner-city Gary. The second metropolitan summit took place in suburban Merrillville in the commercial heart of Lake County. The first summit was sponsored solely by the federation. For the second summit, the federation was joined by the Calumet District of the United Methodist Church, the Roman Catholic Diocese of Gary, the Jewish Federation of Northwest Indiana, and the Merrillville Clergy Association. At the first summit most of the 150 participants were residents of Gary, Hammond, and East Chicago. At least half of the almost 300 participants in the second summit were residents of first-ring—and even second-ring—suburbs.

The program was packed with information and provocative ideas. Indianapolis Mayor Stephen Goldsmith keynoted the conference, emphasizing the necessity for regional collaboration. john powell, director of the University of Minnesota's Institute on Poverty and Race, talked quietly but eloquently about race in America. Memorably, he quoted South Africa's Bishop Desmond Tutu: "It is very difficult to wake up a man who is pretending to be asleep."

The federation had commissioned Myron Orfield's Metropolitan Area Program to map trends in Northwest Indiana. With a dozen multicolored maps based on census data, tax records, and school reports, Orfield hammered away at uneven development patterns, rising child poverty, and growing fiscal disparities affecting both the cities and many first-ring suburbs.

My initial role was to reemphasize Orfield's themes. The Lake County economy has revived modestly, with lower-paying service jobs steadily substituting for higher-paying industrial jobs. Unemployment is lower, but the concentration of poverty grows and spreads outward from central cities to many older suburbs. Though racial barriers are slowly dropping, economic segregation is growing because of prevailing patterns of new development. New investment in new subdivisions and shopping centers is largely offset by disinvestment in older communities. Without strong land use policies, today's winners become tomorrow's losers. Ultimately, all of Lake County loses.

After the box lunch break, it was my task to offer a six-point action plan for "overcoming uncontrolled suburban sprawl in Northwest Indiana." The first recommendation was that the Lake County Council should adopt a strong, sprawl-controlling, comprehensive land use plan that includes urban growth boundaries. Lake County's reform movement should seek a tricounty alliance with concerned groups in neighboring Porter and LaPorte Counties and recruit allies throughout the state (thus the invitation to Indianapolis Mayor Goldsmith). Second in order of priority, reformers should press the Indiana legislature to adopt a strong, Oregon-type land use law.

Third, the new Lake County plan should require a modest amount of low- and moderate-income housing in all new subdivisions in unincorporated areas. Fourth, the land use plan should be buttressed by a special tax-base-sharing district for unincorporated areas. Existing municipalities would only qualify for revenues from the tax base pool by adopting land use, zoning, and mixed-income housing ordinances that were consistent with county policies. Recommendation five was that the Lake County Council develop a transportation policy to support a comprehensive land use plan, including a countywide tax levy to support an expanded, multicommunity bus system. ("Transportation problems do *not* have transportation solutions," I cautioned. "They have land use solutions.")

The last recommendation was that "grass-roots coalitions make land use and transportation planning a more open, democratic process." Membership on the Lake County Plan Commission should be diversified to reflect the stake of older, northern communities in future development patterns. County government should increase the plan commission's budget to allow it to hire disinterested, full-time, professional staff. Membership on the Northwest Indiana Regional Planning Commission should be reformed to reflect one-person, one-vote principles; vital transportation decisions are currently weighted against larger urban population centers. Above all, grass-roots coalitions should make the Lake County comprehensive land use plan *the* key issue in 1998's county council elections.

The conference participants went into breakout sessions to plan the next steps. The Reverend Dan Estes, president of the Merrillville Clergy Association, led the report session. What will the business community do? What will the political leadership do? What will the faith community do? Enthusiastic and committed, Reverend Estes gathered pledges for specific next steps.[16]

A Spanish refrain cautions, "Entre dicho y hecho hay gran trecho" (there is a big gap between what is said and what is done). The Northwest Indiana Federation of Interfaith Organizations has a long, hard path ahead of it. But if new alliances can indeed be forged across racial lines, across class lines, across city and suburb boundaries in metro Gary-Hammond, Indiana, the nation's most racially divided metro area, such alliances can be forged anywhere.

16. The success of their organizational efforts is illustrated by the fact that the third metropolitan summit, held in June 1998 in the largest Lutheran church in suburban Merrillville, attracted 1,500 participants. The newspaper reported that the line of cars waiting to turn into the church parking lot that Saturday afternoon extended a mile and a half down the road.

Over the two-year period, the efforts to curb Father Rick Orlinsky's advocacy through political pressure on the Catholic Church hierarchy had been the ugliest episode of the federation's campaign. Fortunately, the local bishop had stood fast in support of the activist priest. In fact, more vigorous advocacy was developing within the Catholic Church nationally. In early 1996 Anthony M. Pilla, bishop of the Diocese of Cleveland, issued an extraordinary message titled "The Church in the City." After a sophisticated analysis of the impact of suburban sprawl and out-migration from central cities and many inner suburbs, he turned from demographics and economics to theology to show that a common mission links the urban and the suburban church.

It would not be enough to promote mutual philanthropy and interactions between city and suburban parishes. The Catholic Church was targeting issues—sprawl, fiscal disparities, segregated housing—that required political action. Although the church had a role to play, it could not address these issues by itself but would have to join with many others in that undertaking. Bishop Pilla urged his supporters not to be bowed by a sense of hopelessness in the face of a challenge of enormous magnitude, "involving deeply rooted attitudes and beliefs." "If anything," he said, "reason for hope is greatest when we face reality. So let us face it, and let us join with our neighbors, public officials and community leaders in the hopeful undertaking of building a new urban future for Northeast Ohio."[17]

Bishop Pilla's potential influence clearly reaches beyond Northeast Ohio. In 1996 he became president of the National Conference of Catholic Bishops. In fact, at their national leadership meeting in December 1996, the Gamaliel Foundation's Catholic activists voted to encourage Bishop Pilla to push his views more forcefully with his fellow bishops.

The Business Community

"The Regional Competitiveness Act is the first thing I've seen in 30 years that can work to bring municipalities together," said former Virginia Governor Linwood Holton, spokesman for the Urban Partnership.[18] In the 1996 session the Regional Competitiveness Act passed both houses of the Vir-

17. Pilla (1996, p. 5).

18. "Momentum Builds as Regions Form Partnerships," *Urban Impact* (Virginia Center for Urban Development, Fall 1996).

ginia General Assembly by overwhelming majorities. "As a symbol of the General Assembly's willingness to implement the concept," Holton said, "they've already put $3 million into the Regional Incentive Fund despite the fact that they didn't have anything extra to play with."

The Urban Partnership had sought first-year funding of $10 million, rising to $100 million by the third year. Holton expressed his confidence that the General Assembly would fully implement the legislation by allocating, in an always-cautious politician's parlance, "an appropriate amount into the fund."

Other state legislatures have provided incentive funds for intergovernmental cooperation, and the ultimate impact of Virginia's law may well depend on the size of the incentive available.[19] But what is fascinating about Virginia's Regional Competitiveness Act is the way policies and services are ranked for local collaboration. In order to qualify for any incentive funds, a "regional partnership" must collaborate on joint undertakings earning at least twenty points under the new law. The law specified the maximum points the state agency managing the program can assign to different activities: regional revenue sharing, ten; education, ten; human services, eight; local land use, eight; housing, eight; special education, six; transportation, five; law enforcement, five; economic development, four; solid waste, four; water and sewer services, four; corrections, three; fire and emergency medical services, three; libraries, two; and parks and recreation, two.

There would be no "soft path" to regionalism in Virginia. Cities and counties would not be able to qualify with a laundry list of less controversial services and infrastructure compacts. In fact, the top-rated items virtually mirrored the dictum of Don Hutchinson, president of the business-based Greater Baltimore Committee, who has said, "If regionalism isn't dealing with land use, fiscal disparities, housing, and education, regionalism isn't dealing with the issues that really matter."[20]

The Regional Competitiveness Act was not the Urban Partnership's only achievement. Five of seven bills it sponsored were enacted, including broad authorization of revenue and tax base–sharing agreements among local governments, authority for the Virginia Housing Development to finance mixed-income housing throughout the state on an 80-20 formula, and several other housing-related measures. A proposed constitutional amendment to remove

19. By 1998 the General Assembly had raised the appropriation to $10 million.
20. Remarks made at the meeting of the Regionalism Task Force of the Greater Baltimore Committee, September 30, 1996.

the referendum currently required for counties to enter into revenue and tax base–sharing agreements was carried over to the 1997 session.[21]

Forming the Urban Partnership

Remarkable as the Urban Partnership's success was in its initial legislative foray, the group's history and membership were equally noteworthy. The partnership was formally organized in July 1994 after a year of discussions between the political and business leadership of Virginia's major cities. Core members were the mayors, city managers, and chamber of commerce presidents of fifteen major Virginia cities. Lending additional business muscle were top executives from many of the state's major corporations, among them Bell Atlantic, Crestar Financial, First Union Bank, Norfolk Southern, Virginia Power, and American Tobacco Company. Cochairs were Jean Clary, chairman of the statewide Virginia Chamber of Commerce, and Mayor James Eason of Hampton. Staff support was provided by Neal Barber, a veteran Richmond chamber staff member, and Virginia Commonwealth University's Center for Urban Development. With major business support as well as local government contributions, the partnership raised a $375,000 war chest and targeted the 1996 legislative session. "The basic premise of the Urban Partnership is simple," announced Jean Clary. "Virginia needs healthy cities for a healthy economy."

The emergence of the Urban Partnership in Virginia and its philosophy came as no personal surprise. Over the previous two years I had been invited to Richmond, Norfolk, and Roanoke over a dozen times for speeches and workshops by the Richmond Chamber of Commerce, Forward Hampton Roads, and other business and civic groups. I sounded all my themes of city and suburban interdependence, illustrated with census data for each community, themes that were further documented by excellent local scholars such as William Lucy of the University of Virginia and Michael Pratt of Virginia Commonwealth University.

My most useful contribution, however, may have come as lead witness before Governor Douglas Wilder's Advisory Commission on Revitalization of Virginia's Urban Areas in July 1993. In comparison with the highly fragmented northern states, local government in Virginia could be characterized as the "big box" model. With more than 6 million residents, Virginia

---

21. In an antitax climate, the legislature narrowly rejected the proposed amendment in the next session.

has only 95 counties, 41 independent cities, and 189 town governments (which are part of their surrounding counties). Its 136 school districts are coterminous with—and fiscally accountable to—counties or independent cities.[22]

The General Assembly, however, had dealt Virginia's forty-one independent cities a cruel blow when in 1979 it required that any further city annexations had to be approved by the county government affected. "Affected" is, perhaps, too mild a word, for under Virginia's unique system, "independent cities" are not part of the surrounding counties. When an independent city annexes unincorporated territory, it takes everything away from the county. The county loses residents and tax base. Students shift from county schools to city schools. The county assessor, county treasurer, county clerk, the county sheriff—all see their budgets and staffs shrink. It is not surprising that, since 1979 only Danville among Virginia's largest cities has succeeded in getting county approval for proposed annexations.

Losing Out to North Carolina

From 1979 onward (that is, after the General Assembly's freeze on annexations), I told the governor's advisory commission, one can document the steady population, income, and fiscal decline of Virginia's principal cities, especially by comparison with North Carolina's principal cities, which exercise the nation's most liberal annexation powers. During the 1980s average city incomes had slid eight percentage points lower, to an average of only 85 percent of suburban incomes for Virginia's five primary central cities. By contrast, North Carolina's five primary central cities had maintained an average of 107 percent of their suburban incomes. North Carolina's major cities all had AA+ or AAA credit ratings. Wall Street was slowly downgrading Virginia's cities.

Most important, while the real income growth of North Carolina's city residents (22 percent) had clearly swamped Virginia's city residents (9 percent), as entire metropolitan areas the real income growth rate of North Carolina's "elastic" regions (22 percent) had steadily outstripped Virginia's "inelastic" regions (16 percent). Clearly, city and suburbs were economically intertwined.

22. By contrast, with 5 million residents, Wisconsin has 57 counties, 583 municipalities, 1,267 townships, and 430 independent school districts.

I was able to make the lesson more tangible in Norfolk in a talk to For-ward Hampton Roads in October 1993. "Several years ago you set a goal of landing a major league sports team for the Hampton Roads area. What progress have you made?" Hampton Roads was not among the final five for two new National Football League franchises, I reminded the audience, con-fessing that I had just served as a consultant on Charlotte's bid. "As a region, Virginia's Tidewater-Richmond axis has the population and economy to be considered among the finalists. You haven't yet shown that you can pull to-gether the resources of all your communities in order to compete." I pre-dicted that Charlotte would be awarded its NFL franchise and speculated that Jacksonville could well be the other choice. To almost no one's surprise, the next day the NFL announced its choice of the Carolina Panthers. Thirty days later, to almost everyone's surprise, it awarded the second coveted fran-chise to the Jacksonville Jaguars (ranked second in my study ahead of Balti-more, Saint Louis, and Memphis).[23]

My data had given Virginians hard evidence of what they already felt: Virginia was losing ground to North Carolina. The theme was carried for-ward in further research commissioned by the partnership. "In three of the six metropolitan regions of Virginia, earnings per private sector job have fallen (Norfolk-Virginia Beach-Newport News, Charlottesville, and Roanoke). North Carolina regions have lost no ground," the partnership reported. "Family poverty rates increased in five out of six central cities in Virginia from 1970 to 1990. In North Carolina family poverty rates declined in central cities in five of its six metropolitan areas."[24] It was all quietly gall-ing to Virginia's pride.[25]

Another research presentation by William Lucy and David Phillips of the University of Virginia also captured the partnership's attention. Many neighborhoods in suburban counties were declining as well. Beyond the evident erosion of the central cities, population and income were declining in many parts of older suburban counties. For example, during the 1980s Henrico and Chesterfield Counties, which abut Richmond, lost population in almost one-half and one-quarter of their census tracts, respectively. Simi-larly, median family incomes as a percentage of the Richmond regional av-

---

23. In recounting this history to later audiences, I told them, "You've just heard me pull the old politician's trick: 'Shoot at anything that flies; claim anything that falls.'"

24. Lucy and Phillips (1994, pp. 8, 10).

25. Located between Virginia and South Carolina, North Carolina was once described as "a vale of humility between two mountains of conceit."

erage fell in 71 percent of Henrico's census tracts and 63 percent of Chester-field's.[26] Urban decline was not a phenomenon of only growth-constricted core cities. High-end growth was also moving outward, from inner counties such as Henrico and Chesterfield to outer counties such as Hanover and Goochland.

Hammering Out the Legislative Agenda

In mid-1994 the partnership formed its committees and went to work. The Research and Issues Development Committee commissioned a wide-ranging set of "policy scans" and struggled to thin out long laundry lists of policy proposals into a recommended legislative agenda. The Government Affairs Committee charted a sustained lobbying strategy targeted on the 1996 General Assembly session. The committee called for "bold, significant, and dramatic" recommendations that would be "the top legislative priority of our member localities."

In December 1994 the partnership held an urban summit in Richmond, attended by 400 business and political leaders from across the state.[27] Business leaders emphasized that all parts of a region need to be healthy for the region to be competitive in a global economy. Keynote speaker Anthony Downs of the Brookings Institution emphasized that "it is up to suburban leaders to change attitudes about mutual interdependence and mutual membership in a single metropolitan community." Representative Norman Sisisky observed that "our destinies are linked together whether we like it or not."[28] Cooperation is the key, he emphasized, and the best solutions are ones that are hammered out in meetings rather than mandated.

What was in danger of being hammered out of committee meetings, however, was active business participation. Several chief executives, accustomed to more of a command psychology, were becoming restless with the more leisurely pace set by their public partners, particularly some of the city managers. Particularly vexing was the reluctance of many governmental members to address major reforms on jurisdictional issues. "We've been looking at regional cooperation when a real major barrier to significant progress is the artificial political boundaries that separate city from county or city

26. Lucy and Phillips (1994, pp. 7, 9).
27. "Counties Already Feeling Cities' Ills," *Richmond Times-Dispatch*, December 9, 1994.
28. "Expert: Growth Patterns Lead to Suburban Linkage with Central Cities," and "Common Themes from a Congressman and Business Leaders," *Urban Impact*, February 1995.

from city," one executive stressed.[29] Ultimately, however, the innate caution and stubborn turf protection of mayors and managers prevailed. Aside from suggestions that independent cities could revert to town status—and by becoming part of counties again, regain annexation powers—the partnership members could not agree on basic governance reforms.

After the second urban summit the following June in Norfolk, the Urban Partnership settled on its seven-point agenda for the 1996 legislative session. The initial program, staff director Neal Barber wrote me later, was "modest against your standards."[30] Like all good lobbyists, the partnership realized that the best lobbying is done before the beginning of the session. General information and summaries of its research had been sent to all legislators that spring. Personal visits and phone calls were made to all legislators (often by major business leaders) after the partnership's board approved its legislative program. Throughout the summer and fall, follow-up visits were made with General Assembly members and candidates to reinforce the importance of the proposals. Postelection visits were made to successful candidates between mid-November and mid-December to reinforce the partnership's message.

As noted above, the Urban Partnership's initial legislative proposals met with remarkable success, far more than is typically experienced by the Virginia League of Municipalities or the Virginia Association of Counties. It was business leadership that made the difference.

Building Regional Business Coalitions

Business leaders are practically the only natural constituency for regionalism. Business groups tend to think in terms of economic regions and labor market areas. This is particularly true of local chambers of commerce. Most are regional bodies, though there may be subunits for smaller jurisdictions.

The nature of local business leadership is changing dramatically, however. With its big steel plants and refineries, Gary-Hammond-East Chicago

---

29. "Common Themes from a Congressman and Business Leaders."
30. Letter to the author March 4, 1996. I had made a presentation to the Partnership's Governmental Affairs Committee in February 1995, hoping to help it focus its priorities. I had urged that it focus on the high concentration of poverty in older city and inner-suburb neighborhoods. I urged the partnership to lobby Virginia's congressional delegation to support HUD's proposed transformation of public housing, seek to convert Virginia's "fair share" housing law from permissive authorization to mandatory requirement, and have the General Assembly establish Minnesota-type tax base–sharing programs in all metro areas. Though their final legislative package addressed these priority concerns, the partnership (probably realistically) set more limited goals.

is the exception. In many regions dominant industrialists are gone: moved, merged, or bankrupt.

Akron is a good example. For half a century Akron was the rubber capital of the world, and "Big Rubber"—Firestone, Goodyear, B. F. Goodrich, and General Tire—ran the town. At the end of World War II, the Big Four employed 70,000 workers in the Akron area. In the next four decades the Akron area lost tens of thousands of tire and rubber jobs. By 1995 only Goodyear maintained a major presence (5,000 employees). Bridgestone/Firestone had shrunk to barely 900 employees; B. F. Goodrich to less than 600. Acquired by Michelin, General Tire had closed local operations completely.

In his 1967 film debut, *The Graduate,* young Dustin Hoffman received one word of poolside advice from his father's business partner: "plastics." It was Akron that took the advice to heart. Akron has now successfully converted from the world's rubber capital to the world's polymer capital with more than 400 companies engaged in plastics research, development, and production. But they are all relatively small-scale operations. Not one polymer company ranked among the Akron area's fifty largest employers in 1995. Big Plastic cannot gather in one room and shape the Akron area's future; Big Plastic does not exist.

In Akron and many other communities, the core leadership of the chamber of commerce is no longer a region's major manufacturers. Local business leaders now generally come from businesses more dependent geographically on the local market: the gas, electric, and telephone companies; locally owned banks; local newspapers; even major hospitals (which act like for-profit businesses more and more). Such companies are important, but they do not command the power that major industrialists once had to get things done at city hall or in state capitols. The era has passed when, for example, a single captain of industry, John Patterson, chairman of National Cash Register, could imperiously demand that Dayton throw out its mayor and city council and establish the nation's first commission–city manager form of government in 1914.[31] Acting in coalitions, however, as

---

31. Those days are not altogether gone, however. Founded in 1906, Kellogg, the country's largest breakfast cereal company, grew up in Battle Creek. The Kellogg Company and the Kellogg Foundation (the United States' second richest) needed new headquarters buildings. "We're not going to invest $70 million in a new building in the midst of a dying, Midwestern industrial city," William LaMothe, Kellogg Company's CEO, in effect, announced in 1982. "We're tired of all the constant, petty bickering between the city and suburban Battle Creek township. Either you two merge or we're out of here and off to the Carolinas." That giant corporate hammer pounded out a new political alignment. City and township merged into one (by a 9 to 1 vote in the city, 3 to 1 in the township). The consolidated government set a uniform tax rate for its new unified tax base: a

Virginia's Urban Partnership shows, business leadership can still wield clout. And harnessing such business groups to regional reform is a key to political success.

Perhaps the next significant, statewide, business-driven regional reform movement is emerging in Pennsylvania, where a statewide Alliance of Midsized Cities began forming in 1996. It may fill a crucial power vacuum, for Pennsylvania politics has traditionally been dominated by "everyone else against Philadelphia and Pittsburgh." In the crunch, the needs of Pennsylvania's "third-class cities" are often ignored.

Now CEO-dominated business groups such as the Lehigh Valley Partnership, the Lancaster Alliance, Scranton Tomorrow, the Erie Conference on Community Development, and the Greater Johnstown Committee are joining together. "Our common bond is that we are all local business leaders deeply concerned about the future of our cities," explains Tom Wolf, president of Better York and a leading voice of the nascent statewide alliance. "However, we've come to realize that what happens *inside* our cities is largely determined by what happens *outside* our cities. While we are right to appreciate the virtues of our system of local government, the future health of our county will be determined in large part by how we address the issue of regional interdependence now."

Speaking of his own York County, Wolf continued: "We will never solve regional problems like traffic congestion by purely local action. We will never develop a rational land use plan for the region if we continue to rely exclusively on local planning efforts. And we will never assure our region of long-term prosperity if we continue to condemn our older communities to make do with declining tax bases, increasing poverty, and long-term economic stagnation."[32]

In the fall of 1996 I was invited to give several speeches in Lancaster, the Lehigh Valley, and York. For Better York I undertook a larger task, writing a "York Report," which was published as a twenty-four-page tabloid by the York *Daily Record*. The report targeted three key problems:

---

30 percent tax increase for former township property owners, a 30 percent tax cut for former city property owners, including Kellogg and other major industries. Rather than just pocketing the tax cut, however, Kellogg contributed an equivalent amount to a new economic development fund. Several dozen other companies followed suit. Matched dollar for dollar by the Kellogg Foundation, their contributions built a $10 million economic development fund over the next five years and helped trigger a major revival of the Battle Creek economy.

32. "For Renewal, County Must Consider Some Regionalizing," *York Daily Record*, November 20, 1996.

—Urban sprawl: in the past thirty years York County had lost 30 percent of its farmland to suburban development.

—Concentrated poverty: though just five miles square, York City housed 91 percent of the county's poor minorities.

—Fiscal disparities: York City had less than half the tax base per capita of suburban Spring Garden township.

With slight shifts in data, the York Report might have described conditions in Lancaster, Reading, Allentown, and all of Pennsylvania's midsized cities as well.

The York Report laid out a program of land use reforms, regional revenue sharing, mixed-income housing, and policies to spur a socially balanced restoration of York City's historic neighborhoods. To Better York's leadership, however, I argued their top priority should be to control sprawl. With many neighborhood homes abandoned, once-strong neighborhood shopping areas closed down, and nearby factories long gone, often to the suburbs, the results of suburban sprawl were painfully apparent to the residents of all of Pennsylvania's central cities and of most boroughs.

Controlling the sprawl, I argued, would help revive central cities, boroughs, and many inner suburban townships by gradually turning development away from greenfields toward established communities. There would be many potential allies, including Pennsylvania's growing environmental movement, in the campaign for a strong statewide land use law. "Regional land use planning tends to be a vehicle for regional fair share affordable housing and regional revenue sharing anyway," I pointed out. "Strong state laws like those of Oregon and Washington set fair share affordable housing as one of the state goals, and revenue sharing can be developed as the 'glue' that helps build support for growth management." In early 1997 the business leaders' Alliance of Midsized Cities made it their top priority to work for a strict, statewide land use law such as Oregon's, and they began the long, arduous task of building legislative support.

Universities

Surrounded by the whirring and clicking of television cameras and press photographers assembled in the Rose Garden in August 1997, the president of the United States beamed. With short strokes from a couple of dozen pens, President Clinton signed the compromise budget and tax bills that would balance the federal budget by the year 2002. The ceremonial pens were handed to congressional leaders and administration stalwarts as mementos of the momentous occasion.

At least one souvenir pen should have been handed out to a small band of academic researchers in Ohio. They were the true authors of one important tax reform in the 1997 budget-balancing law: repeal of virtually all capital gains taxation on sales of private homes. But the academics did not get a pen. Nor were they even invited to the Rose Garden ceremony. Back home in Ohio, they would have to be content with having leveraged a superb piece of policy research into a major change in national policy.

Both President Clinton and the Republican candidate, Senator Bob Dole, had embraced repealing capital gains on home sales during the 1996 campaign. Dole's proposal was part of the Republicans' determination to roll back capital gains taxes across the board. The president's proposal was cast as a broad appeal to the interests of middle-class homeowners, another example of the centrist stance that would carry him to second-term victory. His words, however, cloaked the true origins of the proposal: two words that would be absent from the presidential campaign, "urban policy."

Key Housing Research

The idea of exempting home sales from capital gains taxation had been advanced by its original authors as a tool for slowing suburban sprawl and reinvigorating the demand for older housing in central cities and inner suburbs. The key research had been carried out by the Ohio Housing Research Network, a branch of the Ohio Urban Universities Program. Throughout 1992 researchers from seven state universities, led by Tom Bier of Cleveland State University, had pored through county court house records.[33] They had tracked every sale and purchase of a home in the counties surrounding Ohio's seven largest cities in 1991. Their research yielded important insights into metropolitan housing markets. First, 80.5 percent of all sellers (city and suburban) took advantage of the capital gain provision—that is, they "rolled over" any capital gain by buying a new house equal to or greater in value than the house they had just sold. Second, of the 80.5 percent of homesellers who bought more expensive homes, 84.2 percent moved farther out from

33. The members of the Ohio Housing Research Network are the University of Akron's Center for Urban Studies, the University of Cincinnati's School of Planning, Cleveland State University's Urban Center, Ohio State University's Department of City and Regional Planning, the University of Toledo's Department of Geography and Planning, Wright State University's Center for Urban and Public Affairs, and Youngstown State University's Center for Urban Studies.

the region's urban core; only 15.8 percent moved inward toward the city center to purchase their next home. Third, of the 19.5 percent who bought less expensive homes, 36.1 percent moved inward toward the center. This number was 2.3 times greater than those who met the capital gain rollover requirement.

"By requiring homesellers to purchase a home priced at least equal to the one sold in order to shelter their capital gain," the Ohio researchers wrote, "Section 1034 [of the Internal Revenue Code] obstructs movement to lower-priced homes (and rental units), and it penalizes people who are forced to make such a move. In urban areas where the geographic pattern of home values is one of increasing value with distance from the center, the provision encourages movement out and away from the center, and discourages movement toward it, which exacerbates urban decline." In other words, the provision reduced the options for sellers who move inward by 38 percent, the researchers concluded. Hence, they argued, "Section 1034 should be changed to remove the tax penalty against sellers who move down in price."[34]

Selling Homesellers Tax Reform

The policy recommendations that flowed from this insightful work were simple and straightforward, and I was determined to spread the word around Washington policy circles. An opportunity came in March 1994, when Michael Stegman, HUD's assistant secretary for policy development and research, asked me to organize a round table on regionalism. Attendees would be two dozen members of the Urban Policy Report Working Group: representatives from the White House staff, the Council of Economic Advisers, the Office of Management and Budget, the Treasury, and a half dozen other cabinet departments. (The most important participant, it turned out, was the Health and Human Services Department's David Garrison, who became a real champion of capital gains tax repeal on home sales.) I invited Tom Bier, Myron Orfield, and Jefferson Davis, a Connecticut legislator leading the regionalism effort in his state, to make presentations. With his quiet, factual, clear presentation, Bier, in particular, stirred the audience's interest.

However, there is a season for all things in Washington, and despite my fairly persistent efforts to push the Ohio researchers' home sales capital gains tax exemption forward, it did not catch fire immediately. After the Republican takeover of Congress following the 1994 elections, the Contract with

---

34. Ohio Housing Research Network (1994, p. iii).

America's pledge to cut capital gains taxes 50 percent across the board dominated the political debate. Democrats were rather solidly opposed, seeing
the House Republicans' plan as another giveaway to the wealthiest rather
than real help to middle-class families.

"A compromise that would leave the overall capital gains tax unchanged,
but eliminate capital gains entirely on sale of homes ... would be good fiscal
policy, good urban policy, good environmental policy, good family policy,
and good politics," I told Senator Pete Domenici, influential chairman of
the Senate Budget Committee and the most popular figure in New Mexico
politics.[35] It would be good fiscal policy because "the federal treasury collects only about $3 billion a year from capital gains tax on home sales be-
cause four out of five homesellers reinvest any gain in a new house of equal
or greater value. *In short, the tax's impact on homeseller/homebuyer conduct
is several times greater than its actual impact on federal revenues.*" It would be
good urban policy because "the capital gains tax adds to the abandonment
of older city neighborhoods and older inner suburbs. It is possible that repeal
might [substantially increase] the demand for central-city/older suburban
housing. This could do far more to revitalize older, distressed communities
than empowerment and enterprise zones can ever dream of."

Furthermore, it would be good environmental policy because "America
is overhoused, and urban sprawl is gobbling up agricultural land voraciously.
... Removing an obstacle for households to buy down or become renters
diminishes the incentive to move out, eases development pressures on the
periphery, and strengthens use of existing neighborhoods and infrastructure." It would be good family policy because "their home is typically a family's
biggest investment and asset, yet current tax policy locks that value away
from a family's use (unless they take out a home equity loan). Not penaliz-
ing homesellers for buying a cheaper home or becoming renters allows them
interest-free liquidity. Families could invest in starting a new business, pay
for further education or training (for parents or children), or otherwise reinvest their funds. It opens up more options for families to manage their
own lives better in an ever-changing world." And it would be good politics
because a "repeal of the capital gains tax on homesellers primarily targets
working-age, middle-class households, whose modest wealth is largely tied

35. This and subsequent quotations are from the author's memorandum to Senator Pete
Domenici, January 23, 1995.

up in their home, rather than wealthier households who invest in stocks, bonds, art works, and other such items."

Whatever the strength of other arguments, the good politics of exempting homesellers from capital gains finally took hold in the middle of the presidential campaign. In August 1996 Tom Bier suddenly received a flurry of calls from White House and HUD officials asking for additional copies of his research report. President Clinton publicly launched the proposal en route to accepting the Democratic nomination in Chicago. Debated sporadically, the proposal was the closest thing to "urban policy" discussed in the campaign and was presented to the Congress as part of the administration's fiscal 1998 budget request.

Universities as Regional Reform Organizers

The success of the Ohio Housing Research Network's efforts illustrates just one role that universities play in the regionalism movement: they conduct research of direct concern to public policy issues. Through conferences and workshops, university-based programs also build broad understanding of critical issues among a wide range of participants. Many, such as Michigan State University's Urban Affairs Department or Wayne State University's College of Labor, Urban, and Metropolitan Affairs, conduct regular training programs for business leaders and public officials and administrators. Portland State University's Institute of Portland Metropolitan Studies is engaged in conducting leading-edge analyses of developments in that region. Virginia Commonwealth University's Center for Urban Studies provides key staff support for Virginia's Urban Partnership.

One of the most comprehensive and coordinated university-based projects being conducted on a statewide basis is the Ohio Urban Universities Program. Supported by both the Board of Regents of the statewide system and a line-item appropriation from the state legislature, the program links local research efforts by the major state universities in Cleveland, Columbus, Cincinnati, Akron, Dayton, Toledo, and Youngstown.

I had twice been in the Cleveland area through the sponsorship of Cleveland State University. In mid-1995 Tom Bier secured a grant from the Urban Universities Program to support my visiting and speaking in the other six major metro areas. The goal was to sound some common themes throughout the state: the impact of uncontrolled sprawl, decline of central cities,

growing distress in many inner-ring suburbs, the growth of poverty neighborhoods, the need for regional strategies.

Throughout the fall of 1995 and the spring of 1996 I traveled to the six
other communities. The Housing Research Network members took me under their wing, organizing a wide range of activities. Each visit featured a
major lecture on campus for students, faculty, and citizens alike, but the
professors organized many other events as well: speeches at established civic
forums such as Columbus's Metropolitan Club or the annual luncheon of
Toledo's Corporation for Effective Government, breakfast or luncheon presentations to business leaders or groups of local elected officials, editorial
board briefings, interviews on the local public television or radio station,
and in each community a two- to three-hour windshield tour by car so that
I could put some real-life images behind the data I had amassed or the reports they had sent me.

The themes I sounded and the data I presented were no surprise, certainly not to the professors. Their own studies had often called attention to
the same trends. In many respects, I was simply the "hired gun," the "national expert" brought in to give visibility to community conditions their
own work had previously highlighted. And I certainly learned a great deal
both about and from each community. My Ohio tour was a wonderful postgraduate course in the problems of urban America (at least, Midwest-style).

In May 1996, with all the visits completed, we all took stock at a statewide, one-day conference held in Columbus. It was billed as the Ohio Regional Forum on Land Use and Development Patterns. About 100 persons
attended from the seven metro areas: professors, local officials, key state
agency personnel, a half-dozen state legislators, several journalists. Most had
been involved in the local meetings.

We reviewed common statewide trends, beginning with unchecked urban sprawl. In one generation Ohio had consumed land at almost five times
the rate of population growth, a ratio second only to that of Michigan and
Pennsylvania. The suburban areas around every metropolitan city in Ohio
were more sparsely settled than the national average for suburbs. The next
trend was city decline. All of Ohio's central cities except still-annexing Columbus had lost population and dropped further down the income scale.
Ohio's city-to-suburb income ratio ranked the third worst among all the
states, and its fair share of poverty index was the sixth most burdensome. In
the area of racial segregation, Ohio's metro areas averaged the second worst
in housing markets and the fourth worst in public schools. As for the concentration of poverty, more than 82 percent of the state's poor African Ameri-

cans lived in poverty neighborhoods, compared with 34 percent of poor whites (a comparatively high percentage for poor whites and a reflection of widespread factory layoffs in recent decades). The number of poverty neighborhoods had grown by 50 to 100 percent in every metro area.

Today's Winners Become Tomorrow's Losers

But most important were the data on the decline of older suburbs along with the cities. If "today's winners become tomorrow's losers," "tomorrow" had arrived decades ago in Cleveland and East Cleveland. It was now arriving for many of Cleveland's inner suburbs ringing the high ground around the lakeshore cities: Bedford Heights, Garfield Heights, Maple Heights, Parma Heights, and Warrensville Heights, among two dozen declining suburbs. Suburban Norwood, North College Hill, Reading, and Sharonville, for example, were following Cincinnati's slow downward slide, as were West Carrollton, Shiloh, and Englewood, among others, in the Dayton area.

With its aggressive annexations, Columbus, Ohio's capital and now most populous city, had stabilized its economic position (at about 85 percent of the regional average household income). However, suburban Whitehall's average income had plummeted, while Gahanna, Grove City, Reynoldsburg, and Blacklick Estates were trending downward. Even Upper Arlington, long Columbus's premier suburb, could be destabilized by the emergence of New Albany, now the region's recognized top-of-the-line new town. A similar story was being played out in all of Ohio's metro areas. Somewhere between two-thirds and three-fourths of its atomized suburbs were on a downward demographic and economic path as development patterns spawned Ohio's own "favored quarters."

Our joint yearlong campaign had clearly heightened awareness of regional trends and reform needs, the Housing Research Network members judged. When, just a few weeks later, Governor George Voinevich appointed a new state commission to study ways to preserve Ohio's fast-vanishing farmland, the organizers felt it was a direct reflection of the year's work. The campaign had succeeded in pushing the regional reform agenda forward.

Of course, state-supported universities do not formally lobby causes in state legislatures (except on behalf of their own budgets). But political movements are driven by ideas, as Speaker Newt Gingrich so effectively demonstrated in projecting his controversial college-based television lectures into the Republican takeover of the U.S. House of Representatives. College and university faculties are key groups shaping the ideas driving regional reform movements, and, in their individual capacities as community citizens, academics can be found at the heart of almost all civic reform movements.

Grass-Roots Citizens' Groups

In September 1995, Rochester, New York, hosted golf's Ryder Cup competition. Pitting an all-star team of U.S. professionals against Europe's best golfers, the Ryder Cup was billed as one of the world's premier sporting events, just behind the Olympic Games and international soccer's World Cup. It brought an estimated 30,000 spectators and 1,400 journalists for a week to Rochester, generated an estimated $40 million in revenues, and showcased Rochester's Oak Hills Golf Club to hundreds of millions of television viewers around the world. With the European golfers storming from far back to win seven of eight last-day matches and eke out a half-point victory, longtime fans pronounced this Ryder Cup the most exciting ever.

The Reality Cup

In the weeks leading up to and through Ryder Cup week, the Rochester area was also the venue for the Reality Cup, an event designed to showcase not the face of wealth and prosperity in Rochester, but the city's struggling community, and to bring attention to the poor throughout the county. Among the events staged for the Reality Cup was a challenge to the winning Ryder Cup squad for eighteen holes of miniature golf, with the proceeds to go to charity. The Reality Cup cocaptain was a Catholic nun whose House of Mercy serves 5,000 needy people a year. When asked what she thought was the best part of her game, Sister replied "the windmill." (Having been beaten by the Europeans, a chastened team of American pros packed up quickly and moved on to the next PGA tour stop without taking up Sister's challenge.)

A Corporate Citizenship essay contest was also held for the fifty-two corporations that anted up $12 million in fees for corporate hospitality tents at the Oak Hill Country Club. Essays were to describe the corporation's contributions to the solution of local community problems in 500 words or less, typed double-spaced on plain white paper. The winning CEO would receive a plaque, a cash prize, and an all-expenses paid tour of Rochester neighborhoods, including lunch at the House of Mercy. (Not surprisingly, there were no corporate entrants.) A steady stream of thoughtful and thought-provoking op-ed articles and letters were also sent to the editors of supportive metropolitan dailies and specialized weeklies.

Of all the Reality Cup events, my personal favorite was "Other Half Tours—A Self-Guided Tour of the Greater Rochester Community." The tour pamphlet laid out in gently ironic tones the daily tragedy of many American cities.

Anyone can show you the glitz and the glitter or the quaint country towns of the World's Image Center [Rochester's slogan]. But you are more than a tourist to us. We want you to feel at home like you live here. So here are some local spots that can help you understand our community.

1. The first stop is in the Town of Pittsford, the host of this year's Ryder Cup. At the center of the town find the Phoenix Hotel Building. This former hotel was a well-known stop on the "underground railroad," the network that assisted runaway slaves during the time of slavery in America. It was also the time that Pittsford had its highest concentration of African-American residents. But Pittsford is not alone in maintaining its racial homogeneity. [Pittsford is now 98 percent white.] While the city of Rochester is over 40 percent African-American or Hispanic, only one of the twenty suburban towns has a minority population greater than 4 percent.

2. Next drive out route 31 to Perinton and see the Wegman's Supermarket and the Top's Superstore under construction across the street. Altogether that's nearly 200,000 square feet of groceries! Contrast this with the availability of groceries in the city. Wegman's has just closed two stores and the city has spent nearly 3 million tax dollars supporting efforts to bring food to its residents. All this in the town that is the home of what national business publications describe as the country's best grocery chain!

3. Now take route 590 north to route 104 west and get off at the Seneca exit. Welcome to the town of Irondequoit. Find Rogers Elementary School at 219 Northfield Street. Check out the basketball courts behind the school: the nets and hoops and backboards were taken down because too many kids from the city were coming across the border to play basketball. It's a perfect symbol of problem solving in a county with 1 city, 20 towns, 10 villages, and 19 separate school districts.

4. Now drive south into Northeast Rochester. In this section of the city, young men are 60 times more likely to be murdered than people living elsewhere across the community. If you are at the 500 block of Clinton Avenue you are within a fifteen-minute walk of roughly 70 percent of the murders that occurred across the county in the past three years.

5. Turn east and head for the North Street Recreation Center. It's one of the city's excellent recreation facilities and it's in the heart of this troubled section of the city. Just don't go there in the evenings after eight or on Sun-

days. It won't be open. Despite all the discussion of the importance of recreation and other services, it's mostly a 9 to 5 world. Opening the centers
late at night is a problem that just can't be solved.

6. Now go across the inner loop, that not-so-natural boundary between the business district and the places where most people live. Here's
where you'll find the problems that can be solved. Like at the War Memo-
rial, the home of Rochester's hockey team, the "Americans." The "Amerks"
owners will soon be the beneficiaries of a $500,000 investment by the City.
Or consider the community development money that has gone into the
Hyatt Hotel or the High Falls area. And see the construction site of the new,
publicly funded baseball stadium to replace the one in Northeast Rochester, the home of the Rochester Redwings.

7. Here is an example of economic development that is worth its own
stop. Find the Rochester headquarters of Monro Muffler. The president of
the corporation has been doing "pride in Rochester" public service an-
nouncements. One reason he may be happy is that, in his deal with the City
of Rochester, in exchange for locating his headquarters in the city, the company won't pay any city taxes for ten years and won't pay its full share for
twenty years. The city did, however, get the PSAs.

8. Well, it's time to head back toward the golf course. Head out East
Avenue and see how the community of Susan B. Anthony and Frederick
Douglass grew. Drive out to Oak Hill Country Club, the site of the Ryder
Cup, which is expected to bring 30–50 million dollars to town and from
which, as the head of the Chamber of Commerce said, many poor people
will benefit because the hotels and restaurants where they work will be
filled for the whole week.

The Reality Cup activities drew the ire of the chamber of commerce
and a number of Rochester area citizens. The Reality Cup did seem to stub
its toe when New York City's controversial Reverend Al Sharpton virtually
invited himself to a Rochester rally, drawing a torrent of negative letters to
the editor, and then at the last minute decided not to show up. But an editorial in the *Democrat and Chronicle* probably best summed up the Reality
Cup's message and the reaction of many area residents. Those who had staged
the Reality Cup, it said, were merely reminding everyone of "the reality of
poverty in Rochester," reminding them of all those who "won't be attending
the Ryder Cup. Not with tickets selling for $1,000 and up," who have to work
two jobs to make ends meet, have no health insurance, no paid vacation, no
pension.

And that's all the Reality Cup people are saying. They've gone out of their way to say they don't oppose the Ryder Cup itself. Go ahead and have the party. Have a good time. But after the celebrities have gone home and the corporations have folded up their $200,000 hospitality tents, remember the reality of [those] people. . . .

If Rochester can mobilize for an international golf tournament, it can also mobilize to provide health care for the working poor, get its big businesses more involved in the education of poor children and train people for jobs that pay a living wage.[36]

The Metropolitan Forum

The "party-poopers" who staged the Reality Cup, said the editorial, were actually "the ones most likely to get something done." Indeed, the event was the idea of an energetic and creative group of people calling themselves the Metropolitan Forum. With no budget (aside from small contributions from members) and no staff, but with the power of their ideas and vision, the Metropolitan Forum has been pushing forward the need for regional strategies to deal with sprawl, fiscal disparities, and concentrated poverty.

Key members include Jim Gocker, an attorney; Ralph Sell, deputy director of the Center for Governmental Research; Bob Bonn, former employment and youth services director for the Rochester Urban League and now a health agency executive; John Klofas, a criminology professor at the Rochester Institute of Technology; and Mary Anna Towler, editor and publisher of *City*, Rochester's alternative weekly. The weekly paper, in particular, has kept up a steady stream of stories about the social and economic costs of the region's fragmentation.

Like all of New York State, the Rochester area is an exceptionally difficult institutional and political environment in which to champion regionalism. Since 1963, article 9 of the state constitution has set forth a "Local Government Bill of Rights." As a practical matter, local governments are guaranteed that there will be no change in local government boundaries without a vote of approval by residents of any city, town, or village affected. The geopolitical map of New York State has been frozen for almost half a century. As a consequence, given each region's sprawling development patterns, older communities are doomed to a slow, steady decline. The state has

36. "After the Party's Over," *Rochester Democrat and Chronicle*, August 27, 1995.

fifty-seven counties outside of New York City (whose five boroughs are really counties). Of the fifty-seven principal municipalities in each county, some forty-four lost population and fifty-six lost income in relation to their neighboring towns over the period from 1950 to 1990. The only principal municipality in any county in New York that was stronger regionally in 1990 than it was in 1950 was the spa and racetrack community of Saratoga Springs. State law guarantees that at the heart of every urban region will be a city growing weaker and weaker with each decade.

Rochester's institutional rigidity is compounded by partisan political conflict. Rochester Mayor William Johnson, former Urban League chief, is one of the few African American mayors to publicly espouse regional strategies. Johnson, a Democrat, is stymied at every turn by the Monroe County Republican party. Fearing that Johnson, the region's most popular political figure, might challenge the Republican Monroe County executive in a future election, the county Republican party has put out the word to suburban town and village governments: Don't cooperate with the city of Rochester on anything! No joint purchasing agreements, no mutual aid compacts, no regional public works projects—much less any collaboration on the really tough issues dealing with sprawl, fiscal disparities, housing and education.[37] The only headway Mayor Johnson has made is through negotiations with the few suburban jurisdictions headed by Democratic officials.

Nevertheless, the constant, creative agitation of the Metropolitan Forum has moved the public debate over regionalism forward. And its efforts in Rochester have met with a sympathetic response in urban communities in Upstate New York. In 1996 an all-but-bankrupt Utica City agreed to Oneida County's "regionalizing" the city-owned water system and auditorium. The Syracuse mayor and Onondaga County executive have publicly explored various forms of city-county consolidation or joint review. Joel Giambra, Buffalo's elected comptroller, publicly champions that city's merger with Erie County.[38] A "thruway alliance" seems to be developing critical support for major governance reforms in New York State.[39]

---

37. From an earlier era, the Rochester area does still have the Morin-Ryan Plan, a county–local government tax sharing agreement, in place. A supplemental agreement, distributing additional sales tax revenues, was added for 1995–99.

38. In 1997 Giambra commissioned the Rochester-based Center for Governmental Research to assess merger possibilities. Rejecting outright consolidation as infeasible, the institute recommended that Buffalo contract Erie County to take over delivering about 90 percent of municipal services. Without anticipating any rank-and-file downsizing, the institute estimated that Buffalo could save 9 percent to 15 percent of its budget just by eliminating duplicative administrative layers and cutting down on Buffalo's high costs of city officialdom.

39. The growing interest in regionalism was certified by the success of the Chautauqua Con-

Where such growing ferment over regionalization in New York will ultimately lead is an open question. Years ago a famous *New Yorker* magazine cover depicted the United States as seen from New York City, with Brooklyn and Queens lying humbly in the foreground, and Manhattan dominating the Earth, while just west of the Hudson River the rest of America disappears as terra incognita. New York's approach to local governance reform mirrors that *New Yorker* cover. Past state commissions have been composed exclusively of New Yorkers, staffed by New Yorkers, drawing upon New York academics, and examining only New York alternative models. Is New York prepared to learn from other parts of the country? If its political establishment listens to citizen groups such as Rochester's Metropolitan Forum, it may.

Foundations: Key Regionalism Supporters

One other set of partners in regional coalition building deserves special mention: local philanthropic foundations. In general, I have been critical of the focus of most philanthropic giving: helping poor people try to run up the down escalator (see chapter 3). However, local foundations are becoming more and more supportive of the regional agenda. In my own case, for example, Baltimore's Abell Foundation commissioned *Baltimore Unbound.* It provided a follow-up grant to the Citizens Planning and Housing Association for Myron Orfield's mapping studies of the Baltimore region and helped finance the Greater Baltimore Committee's initiatives for regional reform. The foundation's president, Robert Embry, is one of the nation's most knowledgeable experts on housing and metropolitan development. For many years he was housing chief for Baltimore City and later assistant secretary for community development during the Carter administration.[40]

One could not have a better local sponsor in Baltimore than Bob Embry and the Abell Foundation. They combine all the desirable qualities of the perfect sponsor—deep knowledge, deep commitment, deep pockets—with one crucial exception. As a charitable, tax-exempt organization, the founda-

---

ference on Regional Governance in June 1997. Organized by Buffalo attorney-activist Kevin Gaughn, the conference brought more than 200 concerned citizens from western New York, plus a substantial attendance from around the country, for three days of lectures and discussions at the famed Chautauqua Institution. The faculty was an all-star cast of noted speakers and practitioners of regionalism, including Neal Peirce and Curt Johnson, Ted Hirshfield of the University of Pennsylvania, Richard Nathan of the Rockefeller Institute, Myron Orfield, and myself.

40. We first met in 1980 when I was mayor of Albuquerque, pursuing a "pocket of poverty" urban development action grant for a new factory in Albuquerque's South Valley; see chapter 9.

tion cannot lobby actively for legislation. A foundation cannot publicly lead the reform movement. A foundation's activities must be undertaken with a view to providing the public with information about the issues.

The same institutional limitation applies to other foundations that are beginning to support the regional agenda, such as the MacArthur Foundation in Chicago, the Gund Foundation in Cleveland, the Heinz Endowments in Pittsburgh, or the Kellogg Foundation in Battle Creek. They can support, but they cannot lead. Foundations cannot fill the leadership gap.

Mayors: Missing in (In)Action

That leadership gap is not being filled by big city mayors either. There are exceptions, such as Rochester's William Johnson, Grand Rapids's John Logie, or Richmond's Larry Chavis. (The latter two are both part-time mayors who chair their city councils under council-manager governments. For them, being mayor is not a career.)

To my knowledge, only one of the mayors of America's fifty largest central cities has taken a vigorous stand, for example, in favor of formal city-county consolidation. In 1991 W. W. Herenton, former city school superintendent, became the first black mayor of Memphis. Through about 1980 Memphis had always annexed most new development in Shelby County. Then the process stopped abruptly.[41] Despite the creation of prestigious new downtown neighborhoods such as Harbor Town (on Mud Island in the middle of the Mississippi) and the Bluffs, Memphis was unable to capture most new high-end growth without annexations. With the city stagnating and new suburbs such as Germantown and Collierville soaring, Memphis's average income plummeted precipitously, from 97 percent of suburban levels in 1979 to just 76 percent in 1989.[42]

Annexations were always hotly contested (even though Memphis, like Charlotte, has formally defined future "annexation reserves" with five of six

41. By about 1980 a majority-black Memphis City Council may have consciously put the brakes on annexations, which kept adding overwhelmingly white subdivisions to the city electorate. By 1990, 55 percent of Memphis's residents were black. Herenton won the mayor's chair by a bare handful of votes in an election sharply split along racial lines. Very popular throughout his first term, Mayor Herenton won reelection with almost 80 percent of all votes cast in 1995.

42. The twenty-one-point drop was the largest experienced by any central city during the 1980s, a fact I highlighted in comparing Memphis with Baltimore, Saint Louis, Jacksonville, and Charlotte (my client) in a report to the National Football League's Expansion Committee in October 1993.

suburban municipalities). After a year in office, Herenton had a different suggestion: dissolve the city of Memphis—turn in its municipal charter—and make Shelby County the government for the area. Shelby County as a whole—755 square miles, 826,000 residents, and growing—would loom larger on the national scene than the city of Memphis itself. Future politics? "I'll just run for mayor of Shelby County," Herenton suggested.[43]

The new mayor's proposal was assailed from all sides. Many white residents of unincorporated Shelby County, believing they had successfully fled the city's problems, violently rejected possible unification with Memphis. Many black residents were equally critical. "We've just captured control of City Hall," they said. "What are you *doing* suggesting that Memphis be dissolved? Let's enjoy our victory a while!" After a face-saving exploration of whether Memphis could simply "turn in its charter" (a citizens' committee cited many legal complications), Mayor Herenton put his proposal on the back burner.

He continues to see city-county consolidation in Memphis's future, however. "It just makes too much sense. City-county consolidation is inevitable," he told a Leadership Memphis workshop in November 1996. "Besides, within a decade black residents will be in the majority in Shelby County."[44]

And therein lies the issue. Herenton, his city's first black mayor, can embrace city-county consolidation, in part, because he believes African Americans will still be very electable in the consolidated entity. To many black political leaders, regionalism—whether formal (consolidation) or functional (power sharing)—looks like twofold dilution, both of the black community's voting power and of a mayor's political influence.

I know the latter feeling. As mayor of Albuquerque I was a sporadic and generally reluctant participant in the activities of the Middle Rio Grande Council of Governments (COG). Composed of elected officials from a four-county area, COG's principal activity was recommending the annual allocation of federal transportation assistance. In part, my lack of enthusiasm for

43. Shelby County is governed by a thirteen-member county council and an elected county executive, who is formally styled mayor of Shelby County. Thus Memphis advertises itself as "the city with two mayors."

44. A decade may be nine years too late. In July 1997, in an eleventh-hour, almost secret maneuver, the Tennessee legislature suspended the state's ban on new incorporations outside major cities' boundaries for a year. Instantly, local movements sprang up to incorporate seven new, independent municipalities in Shelby County outside Memphis ("toy towns," the newspapers dubbed them). Mayor Herenton and allies fought hard against the separatist movement and managed to get the state Supreme Court to overturn the hastily enacted law.

COG's activities was based on my belief that a strong city of Albuquerque was the best guarantor of a strong Middle Rio Grande region. (That was virtually a truism; Albuquerque accounted for more than two-thirds of the four-county region's population when I was mayor.) In part, also, my discomfort was based on internal city government politics. In Albuquerque's strong mayor-council system, the mayor headed the executive branch, and the city council was the legislative branch. In effect, the mayor had one vote, the council one vote.[45] But within the voluntary council of governments the mayor was just another vote in a five-member Albuquerque delegation. Under the COG structure, a mayor had less leverage on any issue that fell within its purview. It was a scene that I generally avoided.

So it is easy for me to understand why many mayors approach regionalism skeptically and reluctantly. Mayoral resistance is doubly understandable when some "national expert" like myself blows into town, citing census statistics that show, for instance, a dramatic increase in poverty since 1970, despite a city government's best efforts. ("Old data" is the rejoinder. "We've turned things around since then.") Or even worse, that outsider may state that the mayor's city has passed a statistical point of no return. (Such a judgment is often dismissed as "an unproven *theory*," despite the fact that the point of no return is a set of statistical observations whose downward trend is thus far unreversed in at least two dozen instances. "My city will prove that Rusk is wrong," some mayors respond.)

Actually, I would like nothing better than to be proven wrong about the point of no return. Yet I am reminded of an experience in June 1996, when I was conducting a workshop in Gary for the Northwest Indiana Federation of Interfaith Organizations mentioned earlier in the chapter. Toward the end of an invigorating day, a familiar face dropped by. It was Richard Hatcher, former mayor of Gary. Hatcher had been the first African American mayor of a major American city. His long mayoralty (1968–88) and my short one (1977–81) had overlapped, and we had come to know each other in meetings of the U.S. Conference of Mayors.

We reminisced about old times, in particular, the joint appearance we had made on *Meet the Press* (I believe) in 1978 during a mayors' conference

---

45. The Albuquerque City Council could always have the last word whenever it could cast six votes (out of nine) to override the mayor's veto. The veto power was rarely used, however. Under New Mexico law, the city of Albuquerque is a municipal corporation whose governing body is the city council. I constantly deferred publicly to the council's status and independence, while succeeding in gaining its approval for virtually all of my administration's agenda.

in Atlanta. In my mind's eye I recalled the youthful mayor, exuding optimism, energy, and confidence. Now that the black community has gained control of city hall, the mayor had said, we are going to turn Gary around. We are going to make a difference. Twenty years later, neither Mayor Hatcher nor his successors had really made a difference. All their efforts had not turned back the various waves of change eroding Gary: abandoned factories, vacant stores and offices, empty houses, the handiwork of sprawl and race.

Yet how can new mayors anywhere *not* believe that their administrations will make a difference? Optimism and self-confidence are prerequisites for the job. With energy (and some luck) most mayors can point to tangible achievements when they leave office: a new sports stadium, a renovated historic hotel, a new downtown office complex, a riverfront park, a festival marketplace, a tourist-attracting aquarium. It is the Tale of the Tracts that tells the other story, a story of the city's steady strangulation by poverty-stricken neighborhoods.

It is as if a mayor of Gary (or Cleveland or Hartford or Detroit) is invited to play poker, deuces wild. Around the table are his suburban counterparts: township supervisors, county commissioners, village administrators. Every time the cards are dealt, the mayor must fill an inside straight to win. His suburban competitors are always dealt a wild card. Once in a while, the mayor will successfully draw to fill the inside straight (a downtown ballpark, for example) and win a hand. But the odds are overwhelming that the mayor will lose many, many more hands than he wins. He is playing against a stacked deck.

Each new mayor thinks he or she can beat the odds. The record shows that it cannot be done. It is a game that cannot be won. What can be done is to change the rules of the game, to get a chance to play with a fair deck. That is what the regional strategies advanced in this book are all about. The political rules will not change until a few more players at the table—usually inner suburbanites and their state legislators—come to recognize that they are no longer being automatically dealt the wild cards either.

14

Changing Attitudes, Changing Laws

I HAVE ARGUED that two major factors have shaped America's urban areas today: sprawl and race. My analysis has revolved around racial poles. In the preceding chapters the terms "race" and "racial" have appeared numerous times. There have been constant references to "colored," "Negro," "black," and "African American" (depending on the era about which I am writing). I have used "Hispanic" as a general term covering "Latino," "Puerto Rican," "Mexican American" and other terms defining Hispanic origin many times. "Whites" and "Anglos" have been mentioned constantly. Of the thirty tables and figures that appear in the previous chapters or the appendix, almost half document racially based social and economic trends.

In all of this book's discussion of racial issues, however, there are two words that I have not used: *racist* and *racism*. Nor, to my recollection, have I ever used these two words in the hundreds of speeches, talks, and work- shops that I have given over the past six years.

Some readers—in particular, some African American readers—may dis- miss my practice as an example of just another white man who refuses to acknowledge what they see as the fundamental and unchanging reality of American society. Others may discern in my approach the propensity of a politician (even a defrocked one like myself) to avoid alienating potential supporters.

I myself am naturally reluctant to brand the attitudes of persons or audiences that I do not know well, and, for me, the words "racist" and "racism" are terms inextricably linked to personal attitudes, feelings, and values. Yet, the best explanation for my practice is that, as America stands on the threshold of the twenty-first century, I doubt that the precipitous deterioration of urban ghettos and barrios is based primarily on continued racism in American society.

I recall an incident from the mid-1950's when I was a teenager. President Eisenhower had been criticized heavily in liberal circles for his hands-off attitude toward enforcing the Supreme Court's rulings desegregating public schools and for his failure to submit a civil rights bill to the Congress. "You can't legislate morality," Ike proclaimed.

You may not be able to legislate morality, I reflect now, thinking back to that time, but you can legislate conduct, particularly, public conduct. Changing society's formal rules may not eliminate prejudice (what individuals *feel*), but changing the rules can greatly diminish discrimination (what individuals and institutions *do*). In time, new social circumstances—integrated offices, integrated factories, integrated restaurants, integrated theaters, integrated schools, and integrated neighborhoods—change private attitudes. Less discrimination leads to less prejudice. Racism wanes.

That is just what has happened, I believe. Four decades after Ike's dismissive remark, America's most popular public figure (Colin Powell), America's most popular entertainer (Oprah Winfrey, by income, or Bill Cosby, by sentiment), and America's most idolized athlete (Michael Jordan) are all African American.

Is it naïve to attach importance to that simple list of "mosts"? I do not think so. Granted, Colin Powell is a victorious general (albeit on a lesser scale than Ike was) with a Horatio Alger life story, but is it conceivable that any Negro could have become America's most respected public figure thirty or forty years ago? Outside of the readership of *Ebony* and *Jet*, who knew back then of General Benjamin O. Davis Sr.? For that matter, almost thirty years ago, Martin Luther King Jr. was assassinated, probably more reviled than revered at the time by white Americans.

Of course, there were popular colored and Negro entertainers in earlier eras, but they were invariably cast in race roles. Some performers—such as Stepin Fetchit or Butterfly McQueen, who perpetuated minstrel show stereotypes—would make most white moviegoers squirm in embarrassment today (as I suspect they made many in black audiences cringe at the time). Many other entertainers, such as Harry Belafonte and Lena Horne, were popular not just because they were highly talented but because they were, well, so *white*. What strikes me as remarkable about Bill Cosby or, in particular, about Oprah Winfrey, is that their appeal transcends—no, obliterates—race with most of their vast audiences.

And Michael Jordan? And the stratospheric success of the National Basketball Association (NBA), the world's most popular professional sports league, with more than 80 percent of its rosters now African American? When I first began to follow the NBA in 1952–53 as a New York Knicks fan, Nate "Sweetwater" Clifton was the Knicks' only Negro player (and just the second in the entire league).

In fact, looking back, the most remarkable sports-linked racial controversy of my youth might have revolved around a college football game. The University of Pittsburgh was invited to play Georgia Tech in the Sugar Bowl in New Orleans on New Year's Day, 1956. The Georgia legislature was thrown into a frenzy when legislators realized that Pitt had a Negro second-string fullback who was likely to play. Defile the sacred fields of Southern manhood by allowing a colored boy to step on the same gridiron with our young white men? Outrageous! The aroused, all-white legislature almost succeeded in pulling Georgia Tech out of the Sugar Bowl.

In retrospect, what was so truly remarkable about that episode was not the race-baiting demagoguery of Dixiecrat politicians or Georgia Tech's lily-white football team but that as late as 1956 Pitt had only two Negro players on the roster.[1]

By contrast, for the 1998 season, 43 percent of the Pitt Panthers' football squad was African American, a figure exceeded by Georgia Tech's 49 percent. And the Georgia legislature has thirty-three black state representatives and eleven black senators—about one-fifth of the legislative seats. (As a reminder of the distance still to be traveled in contemporary America, however, all but two of the black Georgia legislators represent majority-black districts.)

Integrating Neighborhoods

Recently, a feature writer in the *Washington Post* dug back through the files of the long-defunct Roper poll.[2] The writer found a 1939 report on attitudes

---

1. For that matter, as a college freshman, I cheered the Golden Bears of the University of California at Berkeley on to the 1958–59 NCAA national basketball championship, and Cal did not have a single Negro player on the team.

2. Richard Morin, "The Ugly Way We Were," *Washington Post*, April 6, 1997, p. C-5.

of 5,146 randomly selected Americans toward racially integrated neighborhoods. Some 41 percent believed that "there should be laws compelling Negroes to live in certain districts." While not advocating formal laws, another 42 percent polled believed that "there should be no laws, but there should be an unwritten understanding, backed by social pressure, to keep Negroes out of the neighborhoods where white people live." Only 13 percent of those polled (including, presumably, most Negroes whose opinions were sampled, if any) held that "Negroes should be allowed to live wherever they want to live."

Almost sixty years later, a 1997 Gallup poll reported that, if a black family moved in next door, only 1 percent of whites stated that they would move out. Undoubtedly, that 1 percent is an understatement. Probably it is a more accurate measure of how socially unacceptable it is today to utter outright racist sentiments.[3] Despite integration of factories and offices, theaters and restaurants, city halls and county courthouses, for example, many white Americans are still uncomfortable with living in biracial communities.

A compelling reminder was provided by a thoughtful *Dateline* television special, hosted by NBC's Tom Brokaw, in June 1997. Titled "Why Can't We Live Together?" *Dateline* noted that, despite progress in other fields, housing remains the most racially segregated aspect of American life. The one-hour special report examined Matteson, Illinois, a solidly middle-class suburb of Chicago. A village of 12,000 residents, Matteson has been undergoing steady racial change. Virtually an all-white community in the 1970s, by the mid-1990s Matteson had become about 50 percent African American. The Board of Realtors reported black home seekers outnumbered white home seekers by about 25 to 1. Spurred by that report, the Matteson village council began advertising actively for white homebuyers to try to stabilize and maintain a racially balanced community. "Yet after more than a year of the village's advertising campaign," Brokaw reported, "only a few whites have moved in, and a few dozen more have left."

Why were whites steadily moving out? NBC reporters asked scores of current and former white residents. Rising crime, declining schools, falling

---

3. Fifty years ago Jackie Robinson was bombarded with racist abuse from opposing baseball fans and dugouts alike. Compare that with the incident involving golf pro Fuzzy Zoeller at the 1997 Master's Tournament when the forty-something veteran referred to the twenty-one-year-old winner, Tiger Woods, as a "little boy" and flippantly cracked that Woods should not select fried chicken as the menu for the champions' banquet on the eve of the next year's tournament. Engulfed by an avalanche of criticism, Zoeller issued an immediate public apology, withdrew voluntarily from further tournament competition until he could apologize face to face to the young, multiracial phenomenon, and, to boot, lost a $2 million endorsement contract from a longtime sponsor.

home values were the most frequent answers. NBC checked the facts behind white perceptions. The village police chief reported that the "crime rate has been pretty stable over the last 22 years."[4] The principal at Rich Central High School (now 80 percent black) reported no actual change in student achievement levels (a statement seconded by NBC). Finally, "there was no evidence," the network's own researchers concluded, "that the price of houses in Matteson had fluctuated any more than in most other Chicago suburbs." NBC cited a 32 percent increase in housing prices in Matteson from 1990 to 1995.

One particular interview, perhaps, reached the heart of the issue. Brokaw was questioning a former white resident, by all appearances a well-educated, upper-middle-class woman named Sallie, about why she had recently moved from Matteson. She conceded that she and her husband had never encountered any problems. She professed not to be surprised by Brokaw's statement that Matteson's crime rate, school performance, and housing values had all been stable. Coming any more to Lincoln Mall, where the majority of shoppers were black, she observed, just made her "uncomfortable."

"How do we get beyond that, Sallie, you know, that you don't feel 'comfortable'?" Brokaw asked.

"I don't know . . . I think . . . I don't know how you do that?" she confessed. "I mean, it's just a fact of life, and unfortunately, I think, a lot of people just move, and they keep moving away from it. They know it's here, and they don't want to live around it. So they move away, move somewhere else where it's not going to happen for a few more years."

Watching the show that evening, I realized that I had probably never heard a more compelling, man-on-the-street connection between the issues of race and sprawl. Quoting an unidentified black resident of Matteson, Brokaw suggested that "whites don't like the idea of becoming a minority in their school, their community, or anywhere else."

Yet what was really the "it" to which Sallie referred? Was "it" just having black neighbors today? That did not quite seem to be the case. Many current and former white residents interviewed, instead, were concerned with what might happen tomorrow. Rising crime, declining schools, falling home values—these might not be happening in Matteson *yet*, many white residents moving out conceded. However, as *Dateline* itself depicted, that was the current reality in many black neighborhoods in Chicago itself or suburbs closer

4. The opening of the Lincoln Mall in 1975 had boosted petty crimes such as shoplifting and bad check writing ever since, the police chief noted.

in. Many were the places—once all-white neighborhoods—where a large number of white Matteson residents or their parents had once lived. In earlier decades, realtors' block-busting tactics, playing on white fears, caused panic selling, tumbling home values and accelerating white flight, first from Chicago, then from many inner suburbs. "Get out of Matteson while the getting's still good" seemed to be the common, if unspoken, motivation of many white movers today.

"Matteson is known as a town that is changing color in a country where color counts," Brokaw noted. Then, introducing a more upbeat note, he concluded that "yet it is important to remember that half of the whites are still here. It's safe to say that a large portion of them are here because they want to be. Other towns are watching to see if these folks can live together—black and white—in the same neighborhoods. There still may be time before the last door closes on the last white to leave Matteson." The Matteson story illustrates how deeply embedded in white consciousness are past racial attitudes and reactions. As William Faulkner wrote, "The past is never dead. It isn't even past."

Racial Segregation, Economic Segregation

I have presented many statistics in this book. The most significant, I believe, appear in appendix table A-5, which reports my calculations of the percentages of poor persons who in 1990 lived in poverty neighborhoods (that is, in census tracts with more than a 20 percent poverty rate). For the fifty-eight metro areas I studied (preparing for local speeches and workshops), one out of four poor whites lived in a poverty neighborhood. By contrast, one-half of poor Hispanics and three-quarters of poor blacks lived in poverty neighborhoods.

The contrast by race was even greater for high-poverty neighborhoods (that is, tracts with more than a 40 percent poverty rate in 1990). Only 5 percent of all poor whites lived in high-poverty neighborhoods compared with 22 percent of poor Hispanics and 33 percent of poor African Americans.

With such a clear racial bias in the geography of poverty, how can I argue that the accelerating collapse of high-poverty ghettos and barrios is not based primarily on continued racism? One reason is aptly summarized by john powell, former national director of the American Civil Liberties Union and currently director of the University of Minnesota's Institute on Race and Poverty: "So many middle-class African Americans have moved out of high-poverty neighborhoods that it's hard to label whites as racists when they do the same."

I would not totally absolve whites from the charge of racism just because black middle-class families are now making the same choices white middle-class families made two or three decades earlier. Because of the civil rights revolution, middle-class blacks now have choices they were denied before. They have every right to seize those opportunities.

A racist act, to me, must be based on more than a racially warped worldview. A racist act must also be an *irrational* act. It might be argued, for instance, that racism is at work in the resegregation of Matteson.[5] Many former white residents of Matteson irrationally rejected all objective evidence that contradicted their fears.

But is it irrational to want to get out of high-poverty neighborhoods? No. It is neither irrational nor racist to want to move out of a high-crime neighborhood. It is neither irrational nor racist to seek a safer, better school environment for your child. It is neither irrational nor racist to want a better house that may well appreciate in value, will have better nearby shopping, and may be closer to your job. In this book I have documented the destructive impact of high-poverty neighborhoods.

All parents—white or black—have the right and responsibility to do what is best for their families. That often compels the decision to leave such literally deadly neighborhoods. The sad irony, of course, is that each such individual decision to move out deprives the remaining residents of the local buying power, the social stability, and often the community leadership that the now-departed family represented. The neighborhood's downward spiral continues. The constant outward flight of people and investment, the abandonment of poverty-stricken neighborhoods, the growing concentration of poverty, and the associated decline of many central cities are, at the level of the *individual*, neither racist nor irrational acts. But from the perspective of *society* as a whole, these trends are immensely wasteful and tragically unnecessary.

Throughout this book I have sought to illustrate how wasteful the conjunction of sprawl and race is. We are wasting our natural heritage of wilderness lands, clear skies, and clean rivers and lakes; productive farm and forestlands; nonrenewable energy resources, in particular through our pro-

5. Albeit a very polite form of racism. Commenting on the same *Dateline* show, the *Washington Post*'s William Raspberry, nationally syndicated columnist, wrote that the whites interviewed were so *likable*.

digious consumption of gasoline made necessary by sprawling development patterns; tax dollars through the duplication of costly infrastructure; older housing in older neighborhoods; and tax dollars for greater social welfare programs and the criminal justice systems. Most of all, we are wasting the potential talents and productive capabilities of millions of children trapped in high-poverty ghettos, barrios, and slums.

Some may argue that these are just the necessary costs of the American way. It is not, however, Stuttgart's way, or Lyons's way, or Osaka's way, the way of major international competitors of our own regions. By the mid-1990s, the American economy is once again outpacing those of our international competitors. I would argue, however, that our current achievements are in spite of—not because of—our wasteful systems.

More to the point of this book, the core of our nation's urban problem—the concentration of poor minorities—is just plain unnecessary. America is not a third world county in which the poor are many and the middle classes are few. On the contrary, the middle classes are many and the poor are relatively few. The growing segregation of America's urban areas by income reflects the same convergence of public policy reinforcing private prejudice that was the structure of officially sanctioned racial segregation in an earlier era.

I do not claim, however, that classism has replaced racism in American society either. Race still shapes the concentration of poverty. The overall poverty rate in America's metropolitan areas in 1990 was 12 percent. Out of every hundred residents of the typical metro area only six were poor and white, yet only about one of those six poor whites lived in poverty neighborhoods. Roughly five out of six poor whites lived in nonpoor communities. Most poor whites are "mainstreamed." Few lived in slums, ghettos, and barrios.

By contrast, out of every hundred residents of the typical metro area only six were poor and black or poor and Hispanic. Yet four or five out of those six poor minorities lived in poverty neighborhoods, and two probably lived in high-poverty neighborhoods. Most poor minorities are segregated away from mainstream communities in poverty-stricken ghettos and barrios.

If American society simply functioned for poor minorities the way it functions for poor whites, the opportunities—and odds—for many minorities to escape poverty would be substantially improved. The growing isolation of poor blacks and Hispanics resists civil rights–type legislation. The forces shaping the growth of high-poverty ghettos and barrios are embedded in metropolitan development and housing patterns that promote greater and greater economic segregation even as purely racial isolation slowly recedes.

New housing developments only for above-average-income households, new shopping centers and regional malls, new office and industrial parks—all constantly mushrooming on the urban periphery—have been a part of the metropolitan scene for so long that these development patterns are viewed as if, as Myron Orfield has quipped, "they were ordained by God and Adam Smith."

In fact, as I illustrated in chapter 5 ("The Sprawl Machine"), a complex system of laws was created to shape and foster the suburbanization of America. While America was officially dismantling Jim Crow by race, it was substituting Jim Crow by income. Throughout the nation (North and South), suburban zoning boards, usually filled with earnest, likable citizen volunteers, assumed the functional role of the stereotypical Southern rural sheriff.

Across the country, from the federal government down to the most modest township, transportation, land development, and housing policies are at work that divide our society more and more by income, with tragic consequences for poor black and Hispanic households in a still racialized society.

Changing the Regional Rules

By the mid-1960s the civil rights movement had succeeded in changing the rules in order to advance the cause of racial opportunity. By the mid-1970s the environmental movement had succeeded in changing the rules in order to advance the cause of clean air and water and to protect endangered animals and plant life from extinction.

It is time to change the rules again if our country is to slow the voracious consumption of our countryside, the steady decline of cities and older suburbs, and the rapid growth of "deadly neighborhoods" that destroy good people (mostly blacks and Hispanics).

In part 2 of this book, I offered models of what I consider to be the essential components of changing the rules: regional land use planning and growth management, regional fair-share low- and moderate-income housing requirements for all new construction, and regional tax base or revenue sharing. Other issues could be added to the mix. These three, however, are the key ones.

The federal government certainly has had a major influence in shaping national land use and housing patterns. However, the 1997 agreement to balance the federal budget by the year 2002 cravenly sidestepped once again the long-term crisis in social security and medicare. Without major cutbacks in these almost sacrosanct middle-class entitlements, federal expenditures for all other discretionary domestic programs will shrink year by year.

In *Cities without Suburbs* I proposed a four-part agenda for federal action. It was based on two principles. "First, echoing the old Hippocratic oath, 'do no more harm.' Second, echoing the apparent message of the 1994 congressional elections, 'spend no more money.' " Those recommendations called for incentives for metropolitan reorganization, conditions on federal infrastructure grants in order to slow rather than accelerate urban sprawl, changes in other federal anticity policies (including tax policies), and an end to traditional high-density public housing projects.

Since 1993 there has been modest progress on that agenda. The Intermodal Surface Transportation Efficiency Act (ISTEA) was reauthorized in 1998 despite the campaign of traditional highway lobbies to roll back the regional planning process. Congress and President Clinton embraced the research of the Ohio Housing Research Network (if not its "urban policy" motivation) and repealed capital gains taxation on home sales in 1997 (see chapter 13). The country's worst high-density public housing ghettos are literally being dynamited and replaced by (somewhat) mixed-income, more human-scale townhouse and garden apartment complexes. However, appropriations for HUD's most effective tool for deconcentrating poor households—rent vouchers used regionwide—always face an uncertain future.

In the face of the devastating baby boomer impact on social security and medicare, the federal government's traditional leverage—the strings attached to federal grants to state and local government—will grow weaker and weaker. Unlike activists' principal target during the civil rights movement of the 1960s or the environmental movement of the 1970s, Washington is not "where it's at."

"Where it's at" is state legislatures. State legislatures set the rules for local governments' land use planning power (that is, potential antisprawl controls), zoning powers (potential mixed-income housing mandates), and intergovernmental agreements (potential revenue or tax base–sharing agreements). The next decade's battle must be fought in the statehouses.

Among the three basic policies I have recommended (regional growth management, fair-share affordable housing, and revenue sharing), which should be the priority? If I could wave a magic political wand across this country, I have no doubt which would be the most important policy: a mandatory mixed-income housing policy for all new residential construction.

Back to the Future: FHA's Rules

Albert Einstein conceived his general and special theories of relativity by playing mind games in his imagination. Let us play our own mind game. Imagine that the year is 1934, and the Federal Housing Administration is being established. Franklin Roosevelt and his advisers are considering the basic rules to govern the country's new federal mortgage insurance program. Alternative A bows to contemporary racism. The FHA will insure mortgages only in racially segregated communities and will favor new construction. Alternative B would be a bold departure. The FHA will insure mortgages only in racially *integrated* communities and will treat new construction and older housing equally.

Adopting Alternative B was, of course, politically impossible in the 1930s. A fundamental building block of FDR's New Deal coalition was the white, segregationist Solid South. A decade later, as commander in chief, FDR still fought World War II with a segregated army and navy.

But think what adopting Alternative B—limiting FHA insurance to racially integrated communities—would have meant. It would have shredded the practice of racial covenants in housing deeds that were not declared unconstitutional by the U.S. Supreme Court until 1948. It would have steadily promoted racially integrated neighborhoods in both cities and new suburbs. In fact, racial integration would probably have been the hallmark of postwar America's suburbanization. In turn, local schools would be much more racially integrated as a reflection of integrated housing patterns. Outside the South, still largely segregated neighborhoods are the structural basis for de facto segregation of schools and many local community institutions. Within the South, specifically integrated housing developments would probably have hastened the dismantling of the whole structure of Jim Crow.

Nationwide, a much more racially integrated society would probably be a less economically segregated society as well. We might anticipate that the economic isolation of poor minorities would be no greater than that of poor whites. I would argue that a major reason that overall white poverty rates (less than 8 percent) are so much lower than Hispanic and black poverty rates (24 percent and 28 percent, respectively) is the mainstreaming of most poorer white households in middle-class communities. Mainstreaming more poor minorities would lead to lower poverty rates among blacks and His- panics overall. High-poverty black ghettos and Hispanic barrios would be as rare as high-poverty white slums. The high crime rates bred by concen- trated poverty would be diminished. A vast array of social ills—and the higher taxes to counteract them—would be greatly reduced.

America would have no cities "past the point of no return." In effect, fiscal disparities between all central cities and their suburbs would be no greater than the modest gaps that exist between cities and suburbs in "white America."[6] Without high-poverty concentrations, many more city neigh- borhoods would have been able to attract and hold middle-class families.

In short, a different set of rules in just this one (though major) federal policy would have transformed social patterns in today's America. Adopting a Montgomery County–type policy even today would transform the social face of America over the first decades of the twenty-first century.

Regional Fair-Share Housing

Of course, a policy favoring racial integration could not politically have been adopted in the mid-1930s, and a housing policy favoring economic integra- tion will not be widely adopted in the late 1990s. I have identified only sev- eral dozen communities that require a certain percentage of affordable units in new housing developments. In many of these the goal of integrating lower- income families into middle-income communities is subtly subverted. Faced with statewide requirements, local governments in Massachusetts and New Jersey, for example, meet their targets largely by building senior citizen hous- ing. Other communities, such as Tallahassee, allow developers to make cash payments into an affordable housing fund in lieu of incorporating a per- centage of affordable units in new subdivisions. Almost all developers opt to make cash payments. As a result, the city builds more low-income housing in already low-income neighborhoods. Still other communities make clear that "affordable housing" really means housing for modest-income house- holds but not poor households. The Loudoun County, Virginia, program, for example, sets both maximum and *minimum* income eligibility standards.

By contrast, Montgomery County, Maryland, specifically requires that a percentage of all new housing constructed be acquired by its public hous-

---

6. In fifty-two metro areas that are at least 93 percent "Anglo," incomes of central-city resi- dents equaled suburban residents' incomes in 1990.

ing agency for poor households. That local policy was adopted in 1973. The policy is a time-tested, proven success, yet, as far as I can determine, no state and only one other local community (Fairfax County, Virginia) has adopted a similar policy. Part of the problem is that outside of a small circle of affordable housing advocates, Montgomery County's policy has not been widely known. Over the past six years, however, I personally have probably been its most constant publicist. I have talked about the policy of moderately priced dwelling units to hundreds of audiences, often showing pictures of mixed-income neighborhoods. Persons in many audiences have been intrigued, even excited by the possibilities. I have provided copies of evaluation reports and Montgomery County's ordinances to a dozen communities and legislators in several states.

But no one has acted yet. I am sure that widely held public fears cause good people to shrink from taking decisive action. It is a fear that seems to be justified by local television newscasts every night ("crime, weather, and sports"). Most middle-class white Americans cannot look past the color of the face of crime to see the impact of concentrated poverty.

And, frankly, I have no confidence that facts will dispel fear. All the careful academic studies will not put a dent in the political resistance. Fighting for widespread adoption of genuine mixed-income housing policies is tilting at windmills. What would best solve America's urban problems is also the hardest policy to achieve politically.

Regional Revenue Sharing

As an alternative, Myron Orfield argues that regional revenue sharing ought to be the first item on the regional reform agenda. It is essential to split the suburbs politically, Myron explains, and that can be most easily accomplished through regional revenue sharing. Revenue sharing is the foundation on which Myron and his allies cemented the coalition of the central cities and the inner suburbs in the Minnesota legislature.

Tax systems, of course, vary from state to state, but the politics of regional tax reform are straightforward. Question: What is the best revenue-sharing formula? Answer: Whatever can get a majority of the votes in the legislature. Whatever the formula, the analysis of underlying fiscal disparities is unambiguous and dramatic. A properly crafted bill can provide both a modicum of tax relief and additional money for better services. Regional revenue sharing can arm its proponents with a politically irresistible argument to make to legislators from potential net recipient districts: vote for this bill and your district will get lower taxes and better services. It is an argument that cuts effectively right across ideological, partisan, and, most important, racial lines.

Moreover, pushing for regional revenue sharing ought to work almost everywhere. Most larger metro areas have their "favored quarter," and, by implication, their "unfavored three quarters." Opponents may charge that revenue-sharing advocates are engaging in "Robin Hood politics," robbing the rich to pay the poor. Proponents have a ready rebuttal. The great bulk of tax-supported state and local investments have probably subsidized the favored quarter's growth; in effect, the poor have been taxed to subsidize the growing wealth of the rich. But casting the dispute as rich versus poor obscures the real political power of regional revenue sharing. It is blue-collar and pink-collar communities that will most benefit from revenue sharing. (Protecting the pocketbooks of the rich has rarely been a winning argument in American politics anyway.)

Standing alone, however, regional revenue sharing is merely a palliative. It has negligible impact on slowing suburban sprawl. It has no impact on dispersing the concentration of poverty. Regional revenue sharing merely shores up the fiscal health of communities that are already in social and economic decline.

Helping troubled communities provide a better level of services and perhaps reducing their high tax rates (made necessary by declining tax bases) are undeniably positive outcomes. But, standing alone, making regional revenue sharing the reform priority suggests that the region's problems would be solved by just giving the "inside game" more money. They would not. It is much more important to help the poor move to opportunity than to move more money to the poor.

Myron and I have discussed this many times. Our differences revolve around political strategy. "The key is to split the suburbs," Myron reminds me. "You can do that easiest around revenue sharing. Once you build that coalition, you can get your suburban allies to support anything that is in their self-interest: fair share affordable housing, urban growth boundaries, anything."

I have to respect Myron's experience as a successful politician. After all, he, not I, succeeded in building that coalition in Minnesota. Through his Metropolitan Area Program, he has mapped social, economic, and fiscal trends in almost two dozen major metropolitan areas. We share a common view of the core problems of metropolitan America. Yet I cannot bring myself to advocate regional revenue sharing as the cutting-edge issue. One reason is that I have read many times the dictum of the great turn-of-the-century urban planner Daniel Burnham. "Make no small plans," Burnham preached. "They have no power to move men's souls."

Regional Growth Management

I see fighting urban sprawl through regional growth management laws as the issue that can move men's souls. It is the lesson of my experience in more than sixty local communities in the past six years. You cannot win the inside game without controlling the outside game, and there is potentially a broader coalition of common interests that can be organized around growth management than around the other two strategies.

Regional growth management is the most politically achievable way to rewire that down escalator. How directly and quickly better growth management can be achieved will vary from state to state and region to region. "Big box" regions such as Tallahassee-Leon County (Florida), Charlotte-Mecklenburg County (North Carolina), Memphis-Shelby County (Tennessee), or Albuquerque-Bernalillo County (New Mexico) already have many tools available. Though suburbanization is now accelerating beyond the jurisdictional boundaries of their "big boxes," these core communities can still substantially call the development tune in their regions. The reformers' goal must be to develop greater political will to adopt more rigorous growth management policies within existing local government structures.

In "little box" regions, however, it is virtually impossible to achieve decisive action voluntarily among so many independent local governments. The regional reform priority must be to secure legislative passage of Oregon-type statewide growth management laws.

This is no easy task. After a quarter century of effort, largely by environmental advocates, only twelve states have any form of statewide growth management laws.[7] "My God, getting growth management laws through a legislature is really tough," one veteran state lawmaker once told me. "I put in a little bill last session. The Speaker and the majority leader called me into the Speaker's private office. They'd been supportive of some of my other legislation, but land use controls! They both shouted at me for an hour.

7. By 1998 states with growth management laws were Hawaii, Vermont, Florida, Oregon, Georgia, Washington, Maryland, Maine, Rhode Island, Delaware, New Jersey, and Tennessee.

'What do you think you're *doing?*' they screamed. They pulled out lists and showed me how much money affluent developers had contributed to our campaigns that helped us keep control of the House. You introduce a land use law, it gets really tough. They come after you with chain saws!"

Controlling sprawl is a cause that has the power to move souls in many, many communities. And the potential coalition is becoming much broader by the late 1990s. In earlier decades growth management laws were primarily the cause of the "greens"—the many-faceted environmental movement. Three new waves of recruits have now emerged in the 1990s, however, to lend their weight to the push for strong land use controls.

Declining Suburbs

First, the truth is that, with uncontrolled sprawl, "today's winners become tomorrow's losers." Central-city problems have moved out into the inner suburbs. The social, economic, and fiscal decline of many inner suburbs is becoming more and more evident. In scores of metro areas I have documented the decade-to-decade downward trends of inner suburbs: falling household incomes, rising poverty rates, declining tax bases, flagging home values, escalating percentages of poor children in suburban schools. For some suburban officials accustomed complacently to measuring their communities against their central cities, the statistical evidence comes as a shock. For more astute suburban leaders, the numbers confirm what they already know: their communities are in trouble.

For half a century the "suburbs" have faced off politically with the "cities" in state and national legislatures. I fell into that trap myself. That dual polarity shaped the approach of *Cities without Suburbs*, my first book. As I acknowledged in chapter 10, I myself first learned about "metropolitics" from Myron. Metropolitics can become a dominant political force in many state legislatures. The facts are there on which to build coalitions of common interest. A corps of advocates and publicists is at work. Citizen coalitions are forming. Missing from the action thus far are enough politicians.

Disenchantment in Paradise

The second new development is that more and more suburbanites are becoming disenchanted with the suburban dream. During my travels someone mentioned to me the so-called 20-70 rule. Under the 20-70 rule, when only 20 percent of a new suburban area is developed (let's call it Happy

Acres), it is paradise. Happy Acres' new homeowners look out over their back fences at rolling countryside. The kids can play kids' games in the still-vacant lots. There are not that many nearby stores, but the basics are all there—the supermarket, drugstore, dry cleaners, a few chain restaurants and fast food outlets—and they are easy to reach along uncluttered new roads. Happy Acres Elementary School has just opened and class sizes are small. The morning commute is quick, at least until you drive inside the beltway, where traffic slows down.

But the Good Life seems to melt away by the time 70 percent of Happy Acres has been built. Now that original Happy Acres homeowner looks over his back fence and sees somebody else's house, and then more and more of Happy Acres stretching off toward the horizon. The kids now have to be driven to soccer practice at Happy Acres Municipal Soccer and Tennis Complex several miles away. There are plenty of shopping choices, too many. Despite the best intentions of the planners, strip commercial centers line almost all the major arterial roads. Traffic (particularly, weekend traffic) is a nightmare, swelled by thousands of autos headed for the new Mid-America Mall four miles away. Happy Acres Elementary is overcrowded, and the Board of Education is purchasing temporary classrooms that will further shrink playground space. The morning rush-hour traffic jam begins just three blocks away as cars are lined up to turn into the first collector street (which is still a long way from the interstate). You can smell the smog on hot, muggy, windless summer days.

The Happy Acres Neighborhood Association rises up in arms at the planning commission meeting. Most of Happy Acres has single-family homes on half-acre lots. The original development plan envisioned several blocks of townhouses and an apartment complex, including some senior housing, on the still-vacant land. A thousand times no, screams the neighborhood association leadership. Won't maintain the "character" of the community. Will lower home prices. Too many new children for the already overcrowded school. Too much new traffic.

The planning commission bows. The original development plan is never completed. A few more single-family homes are built on the final lots, or the acreage may even be left vacant. (The neighborhood association will lobby for years to try to get a bond issue approved to build more sports fields.) And Happy Acres, built for a single type of household and age group, moves into a future unprepared for changes in family composition, age, and tastes.

Of course, a lot of the traffic that is jamming the arterial streets is not even coming from a more built-up Happy Acres. It is coming from Elysian

Fields, a thousand-home, even higher-income community three miles to the west whose development began ten years after Happy Acres. (In fact, the advent of Elysian Fields was a principal reason for the construction of the Mid-America Mall, and some higher-income Happy Acres residents have moved up to Elysian Fields.)

Under regional revenue sharing Happy Acres would probably be a net contributor into the regional pool. Elysian Fields would certainly be a net contributor, and the regional mall itself would be a crown jewel. Happy Acres (much less Elysian Fields) will not voluntarily embrace fair-share affordable housing. (Its residents will not even countenance market-rate town homes.)

But a considerable portion of those residents find that the suburban dream has soured on them. Something has gone wrong. *The plan was wrong.* What we need is better planning, not so much for Happy Acres, which is largely finished, but to control better what is happening out at Elysian Fields. In fact, there are likely to be some potential allies among new residents of Elysian Fields. And they will all be opposed to the plans for the 10,000-unit planned community called Paradise Valley (ten miles farther west), which is now being considered by the planning commission of the next county out.

So there are more potential recruits for regional growth management now than was the case in past decades: inner suburbs struggling to survive and some upper-crust new suburbanites worried about the erosion of their quality of life.

Faith Can Move (Political) Mountains

The third wave of new growth management advocates is perhaps the most politically potent of all: coalitions of central-city and suburban churches. In chapter 13, I profiled one such movement, the Northwest Indiana Federation of Interfaith Organizations. But there are many organizing, often under the auspices of the Chicago-based Gamaliel Foundation: Metropolitan Congregations United for Saint Louis, MOSES in Detroit, WECAN in Cleveland, and a dozen more.

Church-based coalitions bring three new strengths to the regional reform movement. First, they bring the potential for mobilizing thousands of parishioners and congregation members for political action. When city council members, county commissioners, and state legislators walk into a meeting with hundreds of aroused constituents, the politicians listen.

Second, the inner-city church activists open a political path to get around the turf protection of central-city politicians. However steep the decline of a

Saint Louis, a Detroit, a Gary may be, there is still power and prestige in being a mayor or city council member. Regional strategies raise the specter of the loss of power—as instinctively resisted by central-city politicians (whose communities would be clear beneficiaries) as by suburban politicians (for whose communities benefits may be less obvious). The people power of organized churches can either get established politicians to move or move them out of the way.

And third, the church coalitions bring an invaluable missing dimension to the debate. Building new roads, water lines, sewers, and schools versus maintaining older infrastructure, trends in real home values, the value of agricultural land versus new subdivisions, the social costs of high-poverty ghettos and barrios—the debates can get mired in dry, technical language. The churches raise the moral argument. Like Cleveland's Bishop Pilla, church leaders can speak to the issues of our moral responsibility, of responsible stewardship of our natural environment, of our stewardship toward our fellow human beings. The moral dimension is necessary to push the calculus of common political self-interest to the point of critical mass.

In *Cities without Suburbs,* I wrote:

> Redeeming inner cities and the urban underclass requires reintegration of city and suburb. . . . Sustained change will require a grass-roots movement like the civil rights movement or the environmental movement. This new movement will be tougher to begin. The civil rights movement in the 1960s mobilized moral outrage against Jim Crow laws. The environmental movement in the 1970s reflected compelling concern with human survival on a despoiled planet.[8]

I was wrong. What I have learned in the scores of communities that I have worked with over the past six years is that the civil rights movement and the environmental movement *can merge to become* the regionalism movement. The issues of social stewardship and environmental stewardship are inextricably interwoven. The connecting link is America's environmentally and socially destructive land development patterns. To win today's civil rights battles as well as today's environmental battles one needs to change the same set of rules.

In December 1996 I was in Milwaukee for a training workshop for field staff and church leaders from seventeen communities organized by the

---

8. Rusk (1995, pp. 128, 131).

Gamaliel Foundation. At the end of a long but energizing day, one of the participants offered a novel suggestion. "What our movement needs," he said, "are some new songs."

By the Second Metropolitan Summit in Saint Louis in June 1997, the church leaders of Metropolitan Communities United had the first new song. As the composer and lyricist, the Reverend Sylvester Laudermill, jokingly confessed, "You can't really sing 'control urban sprawl.'" Several hundred persons—black and white, Protestant, Catholic, Jewish, Muslim, city and suburb—joined in singing:

> This is God's world.
> We are God's people.
> We've been entrusted.
> This land is in our hands.
> "We must live together,"
> Our children are calling.
> Black, white, rich, or poor,
> For our future let's do more.

A new reform movement is beginning to move across the face of the land. "Our Song" was its first new anthem. It will not be the last. I believe that the chorus of voices will rise, region by region, across the nation until a new set of rules has been created, state by state, for most communities. These rules will emphasize our mutual responsibilities and the reality of our interdependence within America's urban regions. "E Pluribus Unum," "one nation, under God, indivisible, with liberty and justice for all"—these are the true definitions of the American dream. They still have the power to move our souls.

Appendix

Table A-1. *Population and Economic Trends in Communities Served by Twenty-Three Newer CDCs, 1980–90*

Percent unless otherwise noted

Community development corporation and year of incorporation	Poverty rate				Mean household income as percent of metro mean		Total number of households		Racial or ethnic composition						Change in total real income, 1980–90
	Family		Individual						Black		Hispanic		Asian		
	1980	1990	1980	1990	1980	1990	1980	1990	1980	1990	1980	1990	1980	1990	
East Boston Community Development Corporation (Boston, 1971)	15	17	17	20	61	56	11,977	12,432	0	3	3	18	0	4	26
Urban Edge Housing Corporation (Boston, 1974)	27	20	26	22	73	76	11,314	11,747	30	33	24	33	1	2	43
Bethel Housing, Inc. (Chicago, 1978)	35	37	36	40	57	48	16,192	11,852	98	99	1	1	0	0	–34
Greater South West Development Corporation (Chicago, 1974)	12	16	15	20	81	70	54,177	50,195	29	36	10	23	1	1	–12
Hispanic Housing, Inc. (Chicago, 1975)	21	27	24	28	67	59	142,136	126,143	19	26	47	53	1	2	–14
The Neighborhood Institute (Chicago, 1978)	17	21	18	23	75	63	38,748	32,504	86	92	7	6	0	0	–24
Walnut Hills Redevelopment Foundation (Cincinnati, 1977)	35	37	39	41	43	44	4,511	4,229	90	88	1	0	0	0	1

Organization															
Detroit Shoreway Community Development Corporation (Cleveland, 1973)	24	37	26	39	62	46	6,449	6,261	1	8	11	18	2	4	-25
Miles Ahead, Inc. (Cleveland, 1972)	10	11	12	16	89	73	1,740	1,755	98	98	1	1	0	0	-16
Denver Community Development Organization (Denver, 1971)	16	22	19	26	69	64	49,690	47,321	3	4	40	48	2	3	-12
Eastside Community Investments Inc. (Indianapolis, 1976)	19	26	22	28	62	56	14,161	13,051	5	13	3	3	3	3	-11
Blue Hills Home Corporation (Kansas City, 1974)	18	23	21	24	70	69	6,776	5,970	81	86	2	1	1	1	-19
Rehab Project Inc. (Lima, Ohio, 1977)	12	18	15	21	81	74	13,955	12,515	13	17	1	1	0	0	-19
Pacific Asian Community Development Corporation (Los Angeles, 1974)	26	30	28	32	53	47	73,076	65,147	8	6	60	72	14	18	-3
Vermont-Slausson Economic Development Corporation (Los Angeles, 1979)	29	31	31	33	53	50	83,050	81,062	68	45	26	52	2	2	15
Project for Pride in Living (Minneapolis, 1972)	15	25	18	26	63	58	66,037	63,487	14	23	2	3	1	6	-3

(table continues)

Table A-1 (*continued*)

Community development corporation and year of incorporation	Poverty rate Family 1980	Family 1990	Individual 1980	Individual 1990	Mean household income as percent of metro mean 1980	1990	Total number of households 1980	1990	Black 1980	Black 1990	Hispanic 1980	Hispanic 1990	Asian 1980	Asian 1990	Change in total real income, 1980–90
MBD Community Housing Corporation (Bronx, 1975)	45	43	47	45	43	41	5,850	6,279	47	41	51	57	0	0	37
Banana Kelly Community Development Corporation (Bronx, 1977)	49	51	46	53	46	37	9,897	11,698	21	18	76	83	0	0	28
La Casa de Don Pedro (Newark, 1972)	39	29	43	30	47	46	2,734	2,103	14	14	63	81	1	1	–3
Omaha Economic Development Corporation (Omaha, 1978)	21	28	24	31	68	58	18,582	18,394	55	62	2	2	0	0	–13
Mission Housing Development Corporation (San Francisco, 1971)	19	19	22	22	59	60	20,200	19,922	6	5	35	52	13	14	29
Chinese Community Housing Corporation (San Francisco, 1978)	13	15	19	18	88	80	9,671	10,566	2	2	3	3	60	61	28
Marshall Heights Community Development Corporation (Washington, 1979)	19	17	17	20	63	56	30,981	27,976	95	97	1	1	0	0	–4
Unweighted average	23	26	25	29	64	58	30,082	27,943	38	40	20	27	4	5	0

Table A-2. *Population and Economic Trends in Communities Served by Eleven Older CDCs, 1970–90*

Percent unless otherwise noted

Community development corporation and year of incorporation	Poverty rate				Mean household income as percent of metro mean		Total number of households		Racial or ethnic composition						Change in total real income, 1970–90
	Family		Individual						Black		Hispanic		Asian		
	1970	1990	1970	1990	1970	1990	1970	1990	1970	1990	1970[a]	1990	1970	1990	
Bickerdike Redevelopment Corporation (Chicago, 1967)	17	31	21	32	64	55	39,224	28,767	4	11	39	62	n.a.	1	–32
Community Development Corporation of Kansas City (Kansas City, 1970)	17	26	23	30	62	52	42,578	29,214	48	52	2	5	n.a.	1	–37
East Los Angeles Community Union (Los Angeles, 1968)	16	22	17	22	75	62	81,675	73,575	2	1	75	88	n.a.	5	17
New Community Corporation (Newark, 1968)	30	30	33	31	44	40	6,199	3,613	88	87	6	10	n.a.	0	–36
Bedford Stuyvesant Restoration Corporation (Brooklyn, 1967)	24	34	28	34	62	56	114,887	94,879	81	82	15	14	n.a.	1	–12
West Harlem Community Organization (New York, 1965)	25	40	30	42	48	43	14,415	7,891	98	88	2	13	n.a.	1	–42

(table continues)

Table A-2 (continued)

Community development corporation and year of incorporation	Poverty rate				Mean household income as percent of metro mean		Total number of households		Racial or ethnic composition						Change in total real income, 1970–90
	Family		Individual						Black		Hispanic		Asian		
	1970	1990	1970	1990	1970	1990	1970	1990	1970	1990	1970[a]	1990	1970	1990	
Harlem Community Council (New York, 1969)	18	29	23	33	59	56	98,531	78,828	75	68	8	25	n.a.	3	–18
Greater Jamaica Development Corporation (Queens, 1967)	9	11	12	14	91	85	30,826	30,345	43	52	10	26	n.a.	10	8
Spanish Speaking Unity Council (Oakland, 1964)	12	19	16	20	72	60	14,509	14,658	20	32	19	34	n.a.	21	11
Chicanos Por La Causa (Phoenix, 1969)	24	41	30	44	43	44	21,620	13,458	15	10	33	65	n.a.	1	–43
Realty House West (San Francisco, 1969)	14	26	22	26	46	31	15,668	13,979	4	11	5	11	n.a.	34	–17
Unweighted average	19	28	23	30	61	53	402,607	389,207	44	45	19	32	n.a.	7	–18

n.a. Not available.
a. Hispanics in 1970 may be double counted under other categories.

Table A-3. *Changes in Poverty Rates and Total Real Household Income in Seventeen Metropolitan Areas Served by Thirty-Four CDCs, 1970–90*

Percent

Metropolitan area	Poverty rate						Change in total real household income	
	Family			Individual				
	1970	1980	1990	1970	1980	1990	1980–90	1970–90
Boston	...	7.3	5.9	...	9.4	8.3	38	...
Chicago	6.8	8.8	9.5	9.3	11.3	12.4	13	26
Cincinnati	...	8.1	8.8	...	10.3	11.3	18	...
Cleveland	...	7.9	9.2	...	9.9	11.8	4	...
Denver	...	5.9	9.2	...	8.4	9.7	19	...
Indianapolis	...	7.1	7.2	...	9.3	9.6	22	...
Kansas City	6.8	6.6	6.7	9.1	9.0	8.9	6	32
Lima	...	6.8	8.8	...	8.6	10.8	2	...
Los Angeles	8.2	10.5	11.6	10.9	13.4	15.1	35	54
Minneapolis-St. Paul	...	4.9	5.7	...	6.8	8.1	33	...
Newark	6.8	8.8	6.7	9.1	10.8	8.9	24	36
New York	11.0	14.1	9.1	14.3	17.0	11.7	36	23
Oakland	7.5	...	6.2	9.9	...	9.0	...	85
Omaha	...	6.8	7.3	...	9.1	9.6	10	...
Phoenix	8.9	...	8.8	11.9	...	12.3	...	199
San Francisco	6.8	6.9	6.2	9.6	9.5	9.0	35	57
Washington	...	6.0	4.3	...	8.2	6.4	47	...
Unweighted average	7.9	7.9	7.7	10.5	10.3	10.2	22	64

Table A-4. *Measures of Urban Sprawl in Fifty-Eight Urbanized Areas, 1950–90*

Urbanized area	Growth in urbanized population (percent)	Growth in urbanized land (percent)	Land-to-population growth ratio	Density of new growth in 1980s (persons per square mile)	Density of central cities in 1950 (persons per square mile)
Akron OH	44	162	4 to 1	747	4,778
Albuquerque NM[a]	106	189	2 to 1	1,440[b]	3,580
Allentown-Bethlehem-Easton PA-NJ	82	188	2 to 1	1,879	5,017
Athens GA	n.a.	n.a.	n.a.	n.a.	n.a.
Atlanta GA	325	977	3 to 1	2,577	7,822
Baltimore MD	63	290	5 to 1	2,695	12,067
Battle Creek MI	n.a.	n.a.	n.a.	n.a.	n.a.
Buffalo NY	7	133	20 to 1	-429	12,879
Charlotte NC	223	601	3 to 1	2,029[b]	4,468
Chattanooga TN	77	410	5 to 1	871	4,680
Chicago IL	38	124	3 to 1	4,328	12,919
Cincinnati OH-KY-IN	49	250	5 to 1	1,198	6,711
Cleveland OH	21	112	5 to 1	-756	12,197
Columbus OH	116	435	4 to 1	2,797[b]	9,541
Dayton OH	77	337	4 to 1	2,160	9,755
Springfield OH[c]	8	170	22 to 1	561	6,488
Detroit MI	34	165	5 to 1	-144	12,066
Erie PA	17	94	6 to 1	1,453	6,958
Fort Wayne IN	77	365	5 to 1	1,496	7,107
Fort Worth TX[d]	274	451	2 to 1	4,587[b]	3,467
Gainesville FL[a]	82	111	1 to 1	2,440[b]	2,472

Gary-Hammond IN[e]	n.a.	n.a.	n.a.	n.a.	n.a.
Grand Rapids MI	92	378	4 to 1	920	7,543
Hartford CT	82	356	4 to 1	784	10,195
Indianapolis IN	82	418	5 to 1	1,823	7,739
Jamestown-Dunkirk NY	n.a.	n.a.	n.a.	n.a.	n.a.
Kalamazoo MI	97	300	3 to 1	1,251	6,557
Kansas City MO-KS	83	411	5 to 1	2,287	5,647
Lancaster PA	154	965	6 to 1	1,769	14,831
Lorain-Elyria OH[a]	50	78	2 to 1	1,488	3,490
Louisville KY-IN	60	324	5 to 1	1,400	9,251
Memphis TN-AR-MS	103	211	2 to 1	2,423	3,676
Minneapolis-St. Paul MN-WI	111	360	3 to 1	3,514	7,859
Mobile AL	64	458	7 to 1	260	5,079
Muskegon MI[a]	11	138	12 to 1	1,516	5,369
Nashville TN	121	800	7 to 1	673	7,923
New Haven-Meriden CT	84	301	4 to 1	2,152	9,187
New Orleans LA	58	148	3 to 1	535	6,633
Niagara Falls NY[f]	n.a.	n.a.	n.a.	n.a.	n.a.
Norfolk-Virginia Beach-Newport News VA[a]	85	162	2 to 1	4,648	3,217
Oklahoma City OK	185	865	5 to 1	557	4,927
Peoria IL	57	289	5 to 1	-1,522	6,857
Pittsburgh PA	10	207	22 to 1	-1,095	12,622
Portland OR-WA	129	242	2 to 1	3,744[b]	5,720
Reading PA	20	127	6 to 1	1,875	12,423
Richmond VA	129	525	4 to 1	2,219	6,208

(table continues)

Table A-4 (continued)

Urbanized area	Growth in urbanized population (percent)	Growth in urbanized land (percent)	Land-to-population growth ratio	Density of new growth in 1980s (persons per square mile)	Density of central cities in 1950 (persons per square mile)
Rochester NY	51	241	5 to 1	1,369	9,236
Saginaw MI	32	168	5 to 1	100	5,597
San Antonio TX	151	388	3 to 1	2,194[b]	5,877
Springfield MA	49	80	2 to 1	1,165	5,123
St. Louis MO-IL	39	220	6 to 1	1,351	10,968
Tallahassee FL[a]	31	29	1 to 1	1,827	2,755
Toledo OH	34	177	5 to 1	1,221	7,927
Utica-Rome NY	–14	51	–5 to 1	1,050	6,426
Washington DC	161	429	3 to 1	4,465	10,979
Worcester MA	44	218	5 to 1	1,495	5,500
York PA	81	529	7 to 1	1,752	14,275
Youngstown-Warren OH	–6	12	–2 to 1	214	5,132
Unweighted mean	80	305	4 to 1	1,573	7,504

n.a. Not available.
a. Data from 1960 to 1990, except for Gainesville and Tallahassee (1970–90).
b. Both suburban and elastic central-city growth.
c. I have consistently provided separate treatment for Springfield, Ohio (Clark County), which is otherwise a part of the Dayton metropolitan area.
d. Fort Worth and Dallas urbanized areas are combined.
e. Gary-Hammond urbanized area is included in Chicago urbanized area.
f. Niagara Falls urbanized area is included in Buffalo urbanized area.

346

Table A-5. *Segregation and Concentration of Poverty, by Race, in Poverty Tracts in Fifty-Eight Metropolitan Areas, 1990*
Percent unless otherwise noted

Metropolitan area	Metro poverty level	Black residential segregation index	Poor whites in poverty tracts[a]	Poor blacks in poverty tracts[a]	Poor Hispanics in poverty tracts[a]	Poor whites in high-poverty tracts[b]	Poor blacks in high-poverty tracts[b]	Poor Hispanics in high-poverty tracts[b]
Akron OH	12.1	69	34.1	75.0	61.7	15.9	28.0	27.7
Albuquerque NM	14.1	39	34.9	74.9	59.8	3.7	14.1	6.4
Allentown–Bethlehem–Easton PA-NJ	7.2	49	12.3	50.5	67.6	3.8	10.6	19.1
Athens GA[c]	12.0	45	7.5	50.3	n.a.	5.1	28.6	n.a.
Atlanta GA	10.0	68	10.4	64.9	25.8	2.1	30.3	8.2
Baltimore MD	10.1	71	23.7	72.3	39.6	4.9	33.4	14.0
Battle Creek MI	14.3	63	40.7	81.5	54.6	2.3	22.7	3.4
Buffalo NY	12.2	82	38.0	91.4	84.8	6.4	55.4	42.1
Charlotte NC-SC	9.6	53	9.9	54.1	29.3	0.8	21.3	12.8
Chattanooga TN-GA	13.6	72	37.3	91.0	28.0	9.5	41.9	5.5
Chicago IL	12.4	86	16.3	82.9	62.3	2.4	46.4	12.6
Cincinnati OH-KY-IN	11.4	76	33.7	77.2	43.4	9.7	51.9	21.8
Cleveland OH	11.8	85	37.3	91.0	79.4	9.5	41.9	33.4
Columbus OH	11.8	67	38.2	78.4	68.5	17.6	43.0	27.8
Dayton–Springfield OH	11.9	75	40.8	82.1	44.7	8.5	45.3	18.5
Springfield OH[d]	13.4	67	51.5	71.0	28.8	1.7	2.0	2.0
Detroit MI	12.9	88	30.2	89.8	82.9	12.7	54.2	32.1
Erie PA	12.9	65	40.1	90.1	47.3	9.8	50.7	25.7

(table continues)

Table A-5 (*continued*)

Metropolitan area	Metro poverty level	Black residential segregation index	Poor whites in poverty tracts[a]	Poor blacks in poverty tracts[a]	Poor Hispanics in poverty tracts[a]	Poor whites in high-poverty tracts[b]	Poor blacks in high-poverty tracts[b]	Poor Hispanics in high-poverty tracts[b]
Fort Wayne IN	7.6	73	14.0	60.2	54.4	1.3	24.5	13.6
Fort Worth TX	11.0	62	18.2	66.6	44.2	4.0	26.2	8.8
Gainesville FL[c]	14.2	38	24.6	47.9	n.a.	6.8	20.9	n.a.
Gary-Hammond IN	12.2	90	23.7	87.2	43.1	5.0	25.5	15.6
Grand Rapids MI	8.3	72	26.6	78.9	47.1	1.6	22.2	2.3
Hartford CT	7.1	70	11.8	78.6	87.2	2.9	62.4	47.2
Indianapolis IN	9.6	74	25.5	71.6	41.0	1.3	21.2	6.1
Jamestown-Dunkirk NY	13.8	52	32.8	46.9	59.4	14.1	32.3	8.4
Kalamazoo MI[c]	8.9	53	39.6	85.3	n.a.	7.5	44.5	n.a.
Kansas City MO-KS	9.8	73	17.5	80.1	60.8	3.9	19.7	23.6
Lancaster PA	8.0	64	4.7	76.2	73.0	1.2	31.0	23.6
Lorain-Elyria OH	11.5	56	34.3	73.5	66.2	3.2	2.8	1.7
Louisville KY-IN	12.7	69	31.0	81.0	42.4	6.3	22.5	12.4
Memphis TN-AR-MS	18.3	69	24.3	78.4	45.1	5.0	48.6	21.8
Minneapolis-St. Paul MN-WI	8.1	62	24.1	68.4	54.5	8.1	33.3	25.0
Mobile AL	19.9	66	31.2	83.3	48.6	4.2	54.7	16.0
Muskegon MI	15.3	77	27.4	89.6	52.9	10.1	48.7	17.3
Nashville TN	11.3	61	19.1	75.3	41.6	3.7	34.6	16.7
New Haven-Meriden CT	8.2	68	17.1	74.8	64.2	1.2	8.6	10.6
New Orleans LA	21.2	69	41.7	87.0	59.6	6.4	49.0	16.0

Niagara Falls NY	10.7	66	25.3	76.0	26.5	3.4	43.9	9.3
Norfolk-Virginia Beach-Newport News VA	11.5	50	13.1	59.5	22.5	4.3	29.3	7.9
Oklahoma City OK	13.9	60	34.2	66.1	62.0	7.8	21.6	20.6
Peoria IL	11.8	70	27.2	81.5	56.0	5.5	43.3	24.8
Pittsburgh PA	12.2	71	31.6	79.5	48.9	4.5	45.5	19.6
Portland OR-WA	10.0	66	19.8	56.1	15.4	3.2	25.5	4.0
Reading PA	8.0	63	25.2	82.3	79.8	2.6	21.1	34.1
Richmond VA	9.8	59	26.9	70.7	37.8	7.7	30.8	11.3
Rochester NY	9.8	67	28.1	79.4	69.8	3.0	27.1	31.8
Saginaw-Bay City-Midland MI	14.8	82	30.0	94.1	63.1	4.3	63.6	30.9
San Antonio TX	19.5	54	34.9	62.4	80.1	6.5	27.9	35.8
Springfield-Holyoke MA	12.3	68	20.8	80.2	79.1	9.0	41.4	60.3
St. Louis MO-IL	10.8	77	19.1	81.9	42.5	3.2	39.6	13.1
Tallahassee FL[c]	11.7	52	19.0	61.0	n.a.	3.0	22.0	n.a.
Toledo OH	13.9	74	39.7	84.6	66.5	11.7	36.9	26.9
Utica-Rome NY	12.2	68	31.7	74.5	45.7	2.8	17.4	3.5
Washington DC-MD-VA	6.4	66	7.1	43.5	13.2	0.5	6.6	1.1
Worcester MA	8.7	52	10.0	85.0	79.0	3.0	18.0	31.0
York PA	6.4	71	14.3	69.4	60.5	0.0	0.0	0.0
Youngstown-Warren OH	13.8	76	33.2	93.0	74.1	9.2	52.6	48.9
Unweighted mean	11.7	66	26.2	74.8	54.0	5.5	32.2	18.8

n.a. Not available.
a. More than 20 percent poverty.
b. More than 40 percent poverty.
c. Family poverty data rather than individual.
d. See table A-4.

349

Table A-6. Poverty and High-Poverty Census Tracts in Fifty-Eight Metropolitan Areas, 1970–90

Metropolitan area	Metro poverty level (percent)		Number of poverty tracts		Number of high-poverty tracts[a]	
	1970	1990	1970	1990	1970	1990
Akron OH	8.6	12.1	17	40	3	20
Albuquerque NM	16.3	14.1	25	30	6	5
Allentown-Bethlehem-Easton PA-NJ	7.5	7.2	7	14	0	2
Athens GA[b]	11.8	12.0	6	8	0	4
Atlanta GA	11.7	10.0	56	91	19	36
Baltimore MD	11.3	10.1	73	103	24	38
Battle Creek MI	10.6	14.3	4	11	1	1
Buffalo NY	9.3	12.2	24	60	1	23
Charlotte NC-SC	13.0	9.6	21	24	7	9
Chattanooga TN-GA	16.4	13.6	22	27	7	7
Chicago IL	9.3	12.4	234	440	47	182
Cincinnati OH-KY-IN	10.6	11.4	59	92	16	33
Cleveland OH	9.0	11.8	64	153	17	62
Columbus OH	10.7	11.8	45	88	6	24
Dayton-Springfield OH	8.3	11.9	29	52	4	17
Springfield OH[c]	9.6	13.4	5	13	0	1
Detroit MI	8.5	12.9	164	305	24	151
Erie PA	9.5	12.9	8	16	0	5
Fort Wayne IN	7.5	7.6	7	12	0	2
Fort Worth TX	10.3	11.0	23	65	6	16
Gainesville FL[b]	15.3	14.2	9	7	0	3

Gary-Hammond IN	8.8	12.2	12	44	1	11
Grand Rapids MI	8.2	8.3	12	22	0	4
Hartford CT	6.9	7.1	14	31	4	10
Indianapolis IN	8.8	9.6	38	54	5	10
Jamestown-Dunkirk NY	n.a.	13.8	n.a.	7	n.a.	2
Kalamazoo MI[b]	5.8	8.9	1	8	0	3
Kansas City MO-KS	9.6	9.8	65	98	9	25
Lancaster PA	9.2	8.0	5	7	0	2
Lorain-Elyria OH	7.5	11.5	3	15	1	2
Louisville KY-IN	11.3	12.7	43	57	15	8
Memphis TN-AR-MS	21.9	18.3	58	87	25	46
Minneapolis-St. Paul MN-WI	6.7	8.1	44	90	6	32
Mobile AL	23.3	19.9	64	57	21	26
Muskegon MI	10.0	15.3	5	12	0	5
Nashville TN	14.3	11.3	39	43	5	11
New Haven-Meriden CT	9.8	8.2	13	17	0	3
New Orleans LA	20.2	21.2	109	178	31	67
Niagara Falls NY	8.2	10.7	4	10	0	2
Norfolk-Virginia Beach-Newport News VA	15.6	11.5	71	61	23	23
Oklahoma City OK	12.5	13.9	46	72	10	20
Peoria IL	7.9	11.8	10	21	0	6
Pittsburgh PA	9.5	12.2	82	144	14	38
Portland OR-WA	9.7	10.0	23	35	3	9
Reading PA	7.8	8.0	6	14	0	2
Richmond VA	12.1	9.8	24	35	5	9

(table continues)

351

Table A-6 (continued)

Metropolitan area	Metro poverty level (percent) 1970	1990	Number of poverty tracts 1970	1990	Number of high-poverty tracts[a] 1970	1990
Rochester NY	7.4	9.8	23	54	0	16
Saginaw-Bay City-Midland MI	9.3	14.8	6	29	1	11
San Antonio TX	20.0	19.5	75	104	21	31
Springfield-Holyoke MA	9.0	12.3	17	23	2	11
St. Louis MO-IL	10.9	10.8	75	112	19	40
Tallahassee FL[b]	13.7	11.7	8	9	1	3
Toledo OH	9.2	13.9	18	48	5	16
Utica-Rome NY	9.8	12.2	10	20	1	4
Washington DC-MD-VA	8.3	6.4	60	72	8	10
Worcester MA	7.7	8.7	3	12	0	2
York PA	8.3	6.4	5	9	1	0
Youngstown-Warren OH	8.3	13.8	21	43	2	18
Unweighted mean	10.7	11.7	1,970	3,405	421	1,179

n.a. Not available.
a. More than 40 percent poverty.
b. Family poverty data rather than individual.
c. See table A-4.

Table A-7. *Average Home Value per Dollar of Income for Black and White Homeowners in Fifty-Eight Metropolitan Areas, 1990*

Metropolitan area	Residential segregation index	Home value per dollar of income (dollars)		Ratio of black home value per dollar of income to white (percent)	Segregation tax (percent)[a]
		Black	White		
Akron OH	69	1.36	1.79	76	−24
Albuquerque NM	39	2.36	2.25	105	5
Allentown–Bethlehem–Easton PA-NJ	49	2.30	2.62	88	−12
Athens GA	45	1.80	2.01	90	−10
Atlanta GA	68	1.84	2.08	89	−11
Baltimore MD	71	1.68	2.40	70	−30
Battle Creek MI	63	1.07	1.40	76	−24
Buffalo NY	82	1.51	1.99	76	−24
Charlotte NC-SC	53	1.70	2.09	81	−19
Chattanooga TN-GA	72	1.69	1.86	91	−9
Chicago IL	86	1.75	2.46	71	−29
Cincinnati OH-KY-IN	76	1.70	1.86	91	−9
Cleveland OH	85	1.51	1.98	76	−24
Columbus OH	67	1.62	1.90	85	−15
Dayton-Springfield OH	75	1.46	1.79	82	−18
Springfield OH[b]	75	1.28	1.64	78	−22
Detroit MI	88	1.02	1.78	57	−43
Erie PA	65	1.27	1.62	79	−21
Fort Wayne IN	73	1.21	1.59	76	−24
Fort Worth TX	62	1.71	1.82	94	−6

(table continues)

Table A-7 (continued)

Metropolitan area	Residential segregation index	Home value per dollar of income (dollars) Black	Home value per dollar of income (dollars) White	Ratio of black home value per dollar of income to white (percent)	Segregation tax (percent)[a]
Gainesville FL	38	1.88	1.90	99	–1
Gary-Hammond IN	90	1.18	1.69	70	–30
Grand Rapids MI	72	1.39	1.79	78	–22
Hartford CT	70	3.06	3.11	98	–2
Indianapolis IN	74	1.43	1.72	83	–17
Jamestown-Dunkirk NY	n.a.	1.29	1.63	79	–21
Kalamazoo MI	53	1.24	1.58	79	–21
Kansas City MO-KS	73	1.42	1.73	82	–18
Lancaster PA	64	1.75	2.26	77	–23
Lorain-Elyria OH	56	1.62	1.85	88	–12
Louisville KY-IN	69	1.32	1.70	78	–22
Memphis TN-AR-MS	69	1.73	1.87	92	–8
Minneapolis-St. Paul MN-WI	62	1.92	1.99	96	–4
Mobile AL	66	1.86	1.88	99	–1
Muskegon MI	77	1.29	1.56	83	–17
Nashville TN	61	1.93	2.08	93	–7
New Haven-Meriden CT	68	2.95	3.38	87	–13
New Orleans LA	69	2.17	2.07	105	5
Niagara Falls NY	66	1.21	1.82	66	–34
Norfolk-Virginia Beach-Newport News VA	50	2.03	2.32	87	–13

354

Oklahoma City OK	60	1.62	1.60	101	1
Peoria IL	70	1.17	1.41	83	-17
Pittsburgh PA	71	1.33	1.66	80	-20
Portland OR-WA	66	1.66	1.88	88	-12
Reading PA	63	1.26	2.17	58	-42
Richmond VA	59	1.74	1.99	87	-13
Rochester NY	67	1.64	2.04	80	-20
Saginaw-Bay City-Midland MI	82	1.09	1.46	74	-26
San Antonio TX	54	1.69	1.81	93	-7
Springfield-Holyoke MA	68	2.60	2.98	87	-13
St. Louis MO-IL	77	1.51	1.92	79	-21
Tallahassee FL	52	1.90	1.92	99	-1
Toledo OH	74	1.24	1.71	73	-27
Utica-Rome NY	68	1.50	2.07	72	-28
Washington DC-MD-VA	66	2.46	2.93	84	-16
Worcester MA	52	2.73	3.05	89	-11
York PA	71	1.42	2.12	67	-33
Youngstown-Warren OH	76	1.26	1.60	78	-22
Unweighted mean	66	1.66	1.99	83	-17

n.a. Not available.
a. Inverse of fourth column.
b. See table A-4.

Table A-8. *Nonpoor Married Couples with Children, by Race, in Fifty-Eight Metropolitan Areas, 1990*

Percent unless otherwise noted

Metropolitan area	Racial or ethnic group			Ranking by percentage of black married couples
	White	Black	Hispanic	
Akron OH	96	89	95	26
Albuquerque NM	96	90	84	15
Allentown-Bethlehem- Easton PA-NJ	98	90	78	15
Athens GA	93	89	88	26
Atlanta GA	97	92	88	13
Baltimore MD	98	94	95	5
Battle Creek MI	94	93	87	8
Buffalo NY	97	86	68	43
Charlotte NC-SC	97	93	94	8
Chattanooga TN-GA	93	90	79	15
Chicago IL	98	89	86	26
Cincinnati OH-KY-IN	96	90	94	15
Cleveland OH	96	89	82	26
Columbus OH	96	89	90	26
Dayton-Springfield OH	95	88	92	35
Springfield OH[a]	93	84	90	50
Detroit MI	96	89	90	26
Erie PA	96	83	62	53
Fort Wayne IN	97	93	97	8
Fort Worth TX	96	88	81	35
Gainesville FL	93	85	85	47
Gary-Hammond IN	97	90	92	15
Grand Rapids MI	97	90	87	15
Hartford CT	99	95	89	4
Indianapolis IN	96	90	96	15
Jamestown-Dunkirk NY	93	76	56	58
Kalamazoo MI	96	87	89	41
Kansas City MO-KS	96	90	93	15
Lancaster PA	96	94	87	5
Lorain-Elyria OH	96	84	83	50
Louisville KY-IN	95	89	94	26

Metropolitan area	Racial or ethnic group			Ranking by percentage of black married couples
	White	Black	Hispanic	
Memphis TN-AR-MS	96	85	83	47
Minneapolis-St. Paul MN-WI	98	88	94	35
Mobile AL	93	78	86	57
Muskegon MI	94	86	84	43
Nashville TN	96	93	94	8
New Haven-Meriden CT	99	97	95	1
New Orleans LA	93	82	87	56
Niagara Falls NY	95	87	96	41
Norfolk-Virginia Beach-Newport News VA	97	92	95	13
Oklahoma City OK	93	89	80	26
Peoria IL	95	83	89	53
Pittsburgh PA	94	86	85	43
Portland OR-WA	96	85	85	49
Reading PA	98	88	83	35
Richmond VA	98	94	100	5
Rochester NY	97	89	94	26
Saginaw-Bay City-Midland MI	94	83	85	53
San Antonio TX	95	90	78	15
Springfield-Holyoke MA	97	93	72	8
St. Louis MO-IL	97	88	94	35
Tallahassee FL	97	90	87	15
Toledo OH	95	86	81	43
Utica-Rome NY	94	88	87	35
Washington DC-MD-VA	99	97	93	1
Worcester MA	98	97	84	1
York PA	98	90	78	15
Youngstown-Warren OH	94	84	81	50
Unweighted mean	96	89	87	...

a. See table A-4.

Table A-9. *Poor Single Mothers with Children, by Race,*
in Fifty-Eight Metropolitan Areas, 1990
Percent unless otherwise noted

	Racial or ethnic group			Ranking by percentage of black single mothers
Metropolitan area	White	Black	Hispanic	
Akron OH	44	65	54	47
Albuquerque NM	27	51	49	16
Allentown-Bethlehem-Easton PA-NJ	25	51	81	16
Athens GA	35	59	89	38
Atlanta GA	20	43	36	5
Baltimore MD	24	47	30	9
Battle Creek MI	43	57	54	33
Buffalo NY	42	61	72	40
Charlotte NC-SC	24	46	17	6
Chattanooga TN-GA	24	46	17	6
Chicago IL	22	52	52	22
Cincinnati OH-KY-IN	37	61	58	40
Cleveland OH	32	55	70	29
Columbus OH	35	51	35	16
Dayton-Springfield OH	38	58	55	37
Springfield OH[a]	42	54	82	28
Detroit MI	37	57	60	33
Erie PA	48	69	85	53
Fort Wayne IN	25	36	25	2
Fort Worth TX	21	49	43	12
Gainesville FL	40	63	21	44
Gary-Hammond IN	37	62	60	43
Grand Rapids MI	32	52	60	22
Hartford CT	16	39	69	3
Indianapolis IN	28	48	74	11
Jamestown-Dunkirk NY	49	64	82	45
Kalamazoo MI	38	57	53	33
Kansas City MO-KS	27	49	41	12
Lancaster PA	24	49	70	12
Lorain-Elyria OH	41	66	78	48
Louisville KY-IN	35	60	62	39

Metropolitan area	Racial or ethnic group			Ranking by percentage of black married couples
	White	Black	Hispanic	
Memphis TN-AR-MS	26	57	45	33
Minneapolis-St. Paul MN-WI	32	66	52	48
Mobile AL	41	70	35	55
Muskegon MI	49	67	57	52
Nashville TN	28	52	31	22
New Haven-Meriden CT	22	46	65	6
New Orleans LA	39	66	43	48
Niagara Falls NY	45	61	70	40
Norfolk-Virginia Beach-Newport News VA	29	55	43	29
Oklahoma City OK	36	56	62	32
Peoria IL	44	70	52	55
Pittsburgh PA	43	64	54	45
Portland OR-WA	30	51	42	16
Reading PA	23	40	77	4
Richmond VA	22	47	28	9
Rochester NY	34	55	73	29
Saginaw-Bay City-Midland MI	50	73	65	57
San Antonio TX	28	53	58	25
Springfield-Holyoke MA	35	51	76	16
St. Louis MO-IL	31	53	41	25
Tallahassee FL	28	53	56	25
Toledo OH	37	66	62	48
Utica-Rome NY	42	75	83	58
Washington DC-MD-VA	13	25	24	1
Worcester MA	32	50	70	15
York PA	25	51	81	16
Youngstown-Warren OH	46	69	65	53
Unweighted mean	33	56	56	...

a. See table A-4.

Table A-10. *Ratio of All Married-Couple Families with Children to All Single-Mother Families, by Race, in Fifty-Eight Metropolitan Areas, 1990*

Percent unless otherwise noted

Metropolitan area	Number of married couples per 100 single mothers			Ranking by ratio of black married couples to black single mothers
	White	Black	Hispanic	
Akron OH	449	66	380	40
Albuquerque NM	425	227	275	1
Allentown-Bethlehem-Easton PA-NJ	678	100	173	10
Athens GA	517	79	473	22
Atlanta GA	602	103	565	8
Baltimore MD	520	74	411	28
Battle Creek MI	323	56	272	53
Buffalo NY	467	48	103	57
Charlotte NC-SC	564	102	393	9
Chattanooga TN-GA	500	74	424	28
Chicago IL	630	68	379	37
Cincinnati OH-KY-IN	471	62	270	46
Cleveland OH	518	69	190	35
Columbus OH	469	75	333	27
Dayton-Springfield OH	446	74	386	28
Springfield OH[a]	418	85	271	17
Detroit MI	473	60	219	48
Erie PA	413	55	161	54
Fort Wayne IN	565	72	403	32
Fort Worth TX	543	110	578	6
Gainesville FL	377	64	703	44
Gary-Hammond IN	561	77	313	24
Grand Rapids MI	586	64	320	44
Hartford CT	587	71	66	33
Indianapolis IN	477	84	369	18
Jamestown-Dunkirk NY	483	127	97	3
Kalamazoo MI	391	55	624	54
Kansas City MO-KS	475	84	394	18
Lancaster PA	776	88	136	15
Lorain-Elyria OH	492	88	260	15
Louisville KY-IN	419	67	560	38

Metropolitan area	Number of married couples per 100 single mothers			Ranking by ratio of black married couples to black single mothers
	White	Black	Hispanic	
Memphis TN-AR-MS	479	81	364	21
Minneapolis-St. Paul MN-WI	613	65	229	42
Mobile AL	484	79	551	22
Muskegon MI	455	45	172	58
Nashville TN	513	77	269	24
New Haven-Meriden CT	557	69	110	35
New Orleans LA	413	76	342	26
Niagara Falls NY	479	53	278	56
Norfolk-Virginia Beach-Newport News VA	553	122	590	4
Oklahoma City OK	439	100	500	10
Peoria IL	458	59	312	51
Pittsburgh PA	495	60	305	48
Portland OR-WA	456	93	327	13
Reading PA	655	82	81	20
Richmond VA	528	108	268	7
Rochester NY	486	67	204	38
Saginaw-Bay City-Midland MI	439	59	165	51
San Antonio TX	457	131	281	2
Springfield-Holyoke MA	418	65	53	42
St. Louis MO-IL	526	70	417	34
Tallahassee FL	366	89	394	14
Toledo OH	469	66	258	40
Utica-Rome NY	476	61	139	47
Washington DC-MD-VA	638	115	429	5
Worcester MA	475	73	72	31
York PA	678	100	173	10
Youngstown-Warren OH	443	60	196	48
Unweighted mean	501	80	310	...

a. See table A-4.

Table A-11. *Ratio of Married-Couple Families to Single-Mother Families in Poorest Census Tracts in Fifty-Eight Metropolitan Areas, 1990*

Metropolitan area	Married couples with children per 100 single mothers		Ranking by ratio of all married couples to all single mothers in poorest tracts
	Poorest tracts	*Rest of metro area*	
Akron OH	51	389	19
Albuquerque NM	174	345	3
Allentown-Bethlehem-Easton PA-NJ	62	575	13
Athens GA	49	375	20
Atlanta GA	26	370	49
Baltimore MD	24	322	52
Battle Creek MI	25	282	51
Buffalo NY	26	370	49
Charlotte NC-SC	30	402	43
Chattanooga TN-GA	17	414	56
Chicago IL	35	369	37
Cincinnati OH-KY-IN	31	405	42
Cleveland OH	37	348	35
Columbus OH	37	398	35
Dayton-Springfield OH	16	374	58
Springfield OH[a]	60	356	14
Detroit MI	41	347	27
Erie PA	56	416	16
Fort Wayne IN	47	475	22
Fort Worth TX	75	467	8
Gainesville FL	105	287	5
Gary-Hammond IN	27	424	48
Grand Rapids MI	32	492	41
Hartford CT	19	400	55
Indianapolis IN	46	375	24
Jamestown-Dunkirk NY	91	478	6
Kalamazoo MI	54	377	17
Kansas City MO-KS	48	383	21
Lancaster PA	66	667	11
Lorain-Elyria OH	219	410	2
Louisville KY-IN	33	338	39

Metropolitan area	Married couples with children per 100 single mothers		Ranking by ratio of all married couples to all single mothers in poorest tracts
	Poorest tracts	Rest of metro area	
Memphis TN-AR-MS	38	276	33
Minneapolis-St. Paul MN-WI	67	490	10
Mobile AL	45	383	25
Muskegon MI	42	343	26
Nashville TN	24	408	52
New Haven-Meriden CT	28	342	46
New Orleans LA	39	287	32
Niagara Falls NY	33	438	39
Norfolk-Virginia Beach- Newport News VA	29	386	45
Oklahoma City OK	80	391	7
Peoria IL	30	434	43
Pittsburgh PA	28	442	46
Portland OR-WA	72	427	9
Reading PA	59	543	15
Richmond VA	23	340	54
Rochester NY	41	402	27
Saginaw-Bay City- Midland MI	41	395	27
San Antonio TX	148	368	4
Springfield-Holyoke MA	47	256	22
St. Louis MO-IL	38	390	33
Tallahassee FL	34	260	38
Toledo OH	64	370	12
Utica-Rome NY	40	440	30
Washington DC-MD-VA	17	368	56
Worcester MA	40	416	30
York PA	0	0	1
Youngstown-Warren OH	54	408	17
Total	43	347	. . .

a. See table A-4.

References

All data presented are author's calculations from decennial reports of the U.S. Bureau of the Census, unless otherwise indicated.

Bureau of the Census. 1970. *Statistical Abstract of the United States, 1970.* Government Printing Office.

———. 1975. *Historical Statistics of the United States: Colonial Times to 1970.* Series Q 148–162.

———. 1994. *Statistical Abstract of the United States, 1994.* Government Printing Office.

———. 1996. *Statistical Abstract of the United States, 1996.* Government Printing Office.

———. 1997. *Statistical Abstract of the United States, 1997.* Government Printing Office.

Byrum, Oliver. 1992. *Old Problems in New Times: Urban Strategies for the 1990s.* Chicago, Ill.: American Planning Association.

Cisneros, Henry G. 1995. *Regionalism: The New Geography of Opportunity.* Department of Housing and Urban Development.

Clinton, Hillary. 1996. *It Takes a Village: And Other Lessons Children Teach Us.* Simon and Schuster.

Coleman, James S., and others. 1966. *Equality of Educational Opportunity.* U.S. Department of Health, Education and Welfare, Office of Education.

Committee for Economic Development. 1995. "Rebuilding Inner City Communities: A New Approach to the Nation's Urban Crisis."

Downs, Anthony. 1994. *New Visions for Metropolitan America.* Brookings.

Garreau, Joel. 1991. *Edge City: Life on the New Frontier.* Doubleday.

Hacker, Andrew. 1992. *Two Nations: Black and White, Separate, Hostile, Unequal.* Charles Scribner's Sons.

Harrington, Michael. 1962. *The Other America: Poverty in the United States.* Macmillan.

Innovative Housing Institute. 1998. "The House Next Door: A Study of the Impact of Subsidized Housing on Property Values of Private Market-Rate Housing in Mixed-Income Environments in Montgomery County, Maryland and Fairfax County, Virginia."

Jargowsky, Paul A. 1994. "Ghetto Poverty among Blacks in the 1980s." *Journal of Policy Analysis and Management* 13: 288–310.

———. 1996. "Take the Money and Run: Economic Segregation in U.S. Metropolitan Areas." *American Sociological Review* 61 (December): 984–98.

———. 1997. *Poverty and Place: Ghettos, Barrios, and the American City.* New York: Russell Sage.

Kasarda, John D., and Kwok-fai Ting. 1996. "Joblessness and Poverty in America's Central Cities: Causes and Policy Prescriptions." *Housing Policy Debate* 7 (2): 387–419.

Ladd, Helen F., and John Yinger. 1991. *America's Ailing Cities: Fiscal Health and the Design of Urban Policy.* Johns Hopkins University Press.

Leinberger, Christopher B. 1996. "Metropolitan Development Trends of the Late 1990s: Social and Environmental Implications." In *Land Use in America: The Report of the Sustainable Use of Land Project,* edited by Henry L. Diamond and Patrick F. Noonan, 203–22. Cambridge, Mass.: Lincoln Institute of Land Policy.

Lucy, William, and David Phillips. 1994. "The Urban Partnership: Energizing Virginia." Richmond: Cullen Management Services.

McDevitt, Suzanne. 1992. "Community Development Corporations: Antecedents, Influences, Results." Ph.D. dissertation, University of Northern Iowa.

Metropolitan Council. 1995. "Tax Base Sharing in the Twin Cities Metropolitan Area: Taxes Payable in 1995." February.

Metroscape. 1996. "The Revenge of the Baristas." Portland State University.

Montgomery County, Ohio. 1991. *The Economic Development and Government Equity Program: The Competitive ED/GE in Montgomery County: Municipal and Township Officials Handbook.* January.

Moore, Stephen, and Dean Stensel. 1993. "The Myth of America's Underfunded Cities." Washington: Cato Institute, February 22.

Moynihan, Daniel Patrick. 1965. "The Negro Family: The Case for National Action." U.S. Department of Labor.

Murray, Charles A. 1984. *Losing Ground. American Social Policy, 1950–80.* Basic Books.

Ohio Housing Research Network. 1994. *The IRS Homeseller Capital Gain Provision: Contributor to Urban Decline.* Ohio University.

Oliver, Melvin L., and Thomas M. Shapiro. 1995. *Black Wealth/White Wealth: A New Perspective on Racial Inequality.* London: Routledge.

1000 Friends of Oregon and HomeBuilders Association of Metropolitan Portland. 1991. "Managing Growth to Promote Affordable Housing: Revisiting Oregon's Goal 10: Executive Summary." September.

Orfield, Gary. 1996. "In Pursuit of a Dream Deferred: Linking Housing and Education; Metropolitan School Desegregation: Impacts on Metropolitan Society." *Minnesota Law Review* 80 (April): 834–85.

Orfield, Myron. 1997. *Metropolitics: A Regional Agenda for Community and Stability.* Brookings and Lincoln Institute of Land Policy.

Orlebeke, Charles J. 1997. *New Life at Ground Zero: New York, Home Ownership, and the Future of American Cities.* Albany, N.Y.: Rockefeller Institute Press.

Peirce, Neal R., and Curt Johnson. 1993. *Citistates: How Urban America Can Prosper in a Competitive World.* Washington: Seven Locks Press.

Pilla, Bishop Anthony M. 1996. "The Church in the City." Archdiocese of Cleveland and Akron.

Rusk, David. 1995. *Cities without Suburbs*. 2d. ed. Johns Hopkins University Press.

———. 1996. *Baltimore Unbound*. Johns Hopkins University Press.

Rusk, David, and Jeff Mosley. 1994. "The Academic Performance of Public Housing Children: Does Living in Middle Class Neighborhoods and Attending Middle Class Neighborhood Schools Make a Difference?" Urban Institute, May.

Stock, Richard D. 1996. "The Economic Impact of the Montgomery County Regional Arts and Cultural District." University of Dayton, School of Business Administration, October.

Thernstrom, Stephen, and Abigail Thernstrom. 1997. *America in Black and White: One Nation, Indivisible: Race in Modern America*. Simon and Schuster.

U.S. Department of Housing and Urban Development. 1996. "Public Housing That Works: The Transformation of America's Public Housing." Government Printing Office, May.

Vitullo-Martin, Julia. 1996. "Housing and Neighborhoods." In *Breaking Away: The Future of Cities: Essays in Memory of Robert F. Wagner, Jr.*, edited by Julia Vitullo-Martin, 105. New York: Twentieth Century Fund Press.

Welfeld, Irving. 1988. *Where We Live: A Social History of American Housing*. Simon and Schuster.

Wilson, William Julius. 1987. *The Truly Disadvantaged: The Inner City, the Underclass, and Public Policy*. University of Chicago Press.

———. 1996. *When Work Disappears: The World of the New Urban Poor*. Knopf.

Index

Abbott, Carl, 153, 159, 160
Abell Foundation (Baltimore), 311–12
ACLU. *See* American Civil Liberties Union
Adams, John, 247
Advanced Technological Solutions, 30
Advisory Commission on Metropolitan Governance (Minn.), 233, 234, 236, 238
Advisory Commission on Revitalization of Virginia's Urban Areas, 292
Affordable dwelling unit policy (Fairfax County, Va.), 198n
Affordable Housing Fund (Dayton), 214
African Americans: in Atlanta, 74–76; in Bedford Stuyvesant (N.Y.), 23, 32; in city neighborhoods, 7–8; educational issues, 112–13; employment, 113–18; family structure, 107–13; in ghetto areas, 78; housing, 93–95, 321; in Jamaica Plain (Mass.), 40; middle class, 80; in Mobile, 77; in Montgomery County (Md.), 191; in Ohio, 304–05; in Portland (Ore.), 164, 166–67; poverty of, 71, 72, 78, 80, 81, 105, 106, 117; public housing and, 119, 272; redlining, 86–87, 93–95; in suburbs, 78, 80; urban renewal and, 90; in Walnut Hills (Ohio), 39; in Washington (D.C.), 65–66; welfare effects, 116. *See also* Racial and minority issues

Agriculture. *See* Farmlands
Akron, 108–09, 137–38, 220, 297, 303
Albemarle County (Va.), 220
Albina (Portland, Ore.), 165–66, 167, 174
Albuquerque (N.Mex.): annexation, 132; City Council, 314n; costs of services, 141–42; Economic Development, 211; growth, 68, 130; housing, 95, 123–24, 170n; Housing Services, 261–62; political campaigns, 217; populations, 314; Rusk, David, and, 13; schools, 125; segregation, 164; services, 3–4, 142; taxes, 1–2; voter turnout, 218n
Alexandria (Va.), 63
Alinsky, Saul, 263, 279
Alliance for Metropolitan Stability (Minneapolis), 236, 242
Alliance of Midsized Cities (Penn.), 298, 299
American Civil Liberties Union (ACLU), 255n, 321
Anglos: in Albuquerque, 2; in Bedford Stuyvesant (N.Y.), 33. *See also* Racial and minority issues; Whites
Annexation and consolidation: in Charlotte (N.C.), 8, 312; in Dayton, 203, 204–05; in Detroit, 174n; effects of, 10, 67; elasticity and, 4–5, 132, 148; in Memphis, 312–13; in North Carolina, 293; in Ohio municipalities, 219; in Portland (Ore.), 158,

CPSIA information can be obtained
at www.ICGtesting.com
Printed in the USA
LVHW032108061222
734689LV00001B/69

9 780815 776512